Index
to
Loudoun County, Virginia
Land Deed Books
3W-4D
1831-1835

Patricia B. Duncan

WILLOW BEND BOOKS
2006

WILLOW BEND BOOKS

AN IMPRINT OF HERITAGE BOOKS, INC.

Books, CDs, and more—Worldwide

For our listing of thousands of titles see our website
at
www.HeritageBooks.com

Published 2006 by
HERITAGE BOOKS, INC.
Publishing Division
65 East Main Street
Westminster, Maryland 21157-5026

Copyright © 2006 Patricia B. Duncan

International Standard Book Number: 978-0-7884-4004-7

Introduction

The following is an extended index to Loudoun County, Virginia Deed Books 3W-4D. In addition to providing the basic information of book:page number, the date of the document and the date received in court, and parties involved, I have also included the type of document, and a brief description of the item, including adjoining neighbors, and witnesses.

Microfilms of these records are currently available from the Library of Virginia Interlibrary Loan Service. Copies of the documents may be obtained from the Office of Clerk of Circuit Court County of Loudoun, Box 550, Leesburg, VA 20178-0550.

Abbreviations:
ackn. - acknowledgment
Admr - Administrator
A/L – Assignment of lease
AlexDC – Alexandria, District of Columbia
B/S of – Bargain and sale
BaltMd – Baltimore, Maryland
beq. - bequeathed
BerkVa – Berkeley County, Virginia
BoS - Bill of sale
br/o – brother of
CamP – Cameron Parish in Loudoun
ChstrPa – Chester County, Pennsylvania
CoE - Certificate of examination [of wife]
CoI – certificate of importation [for slaves]
Commr - commissioner
cnvy/b – conveyed by (prior owner to person now selling the land)
cnvy/t – conveyed to
dau – daughter
DBk letter(s):numbers - deed book:page
delv. – examined and delivered to
dev. – devised to
div. – division (of estate of)
d/o - daughter of
DoE – Deed of Emancipation [for slaves]
Exor – Executor
Ffx – Fairfax County, Virginia
Fqr – Fauquier County, Virginia
FrdkMd – Frederick County, Maryland
FrdkVa – Frederick County, Virginia
Gent. – gentleman
h/o - husband of
HdnNJ – Hunterdon County, New Jersey

Hllb - Hillsborough
int. - interest
KingG – King George County, Virginia
L/L – Lease for life
L/R – Lease/release
Ldn – Loudoun County, Virginia
Lsbg - Leesburg
Mdbg – Middleburg
MontMd – Montgomery County, Maryland
[number]a = number of acres
PhilPa – Philadelphia County, Pa
PoA – Power of attorney
PrG – Prince George County, Maryland
PrWm – Prince William County, Virginia
prch/o – purchase(d) of
RichVa – Richmond County, Virginia
RtCt – returned to court and ordered to be recorded
S/L – Surrender of lease
s/o - son of
ShelP – Shelburne Parish in Loudoun
StafVa – Stafford County, Virginia
und. - undivided
w/o - wife of
WashDC – Washington, D. C.
WashMd – Washington County, Maryland
wd/o – widow of
WstmVa – Westmoreland County, Virginia

Loudoun Co Deed Books 3W-4D

3W:001   Date: 18 Apr 1831   RtCt: 23 Apr 1831
Abijah JANNEY (trustee of Ann HARPER late ELLICOTT w/o
Washington T. HARPER of AlexDC) to Nathan GREGG Sr. of Ldn.
B/S of 133a (from deed by Noble S. BRADEN Exor of Robert
BRADEN dec'd, Feb 1828, DBK PPP:400) adj Mary FOX, Lambert
MYERS, John BRADEN. Delv. to GREGG 10 Apr 1832.

3W:003   Date: 1 Oct 1829   RtCt: 13 Jun 1831
Lott BARR & wife Ann M. and Catharine M. CHINN of Ldn to
Townshend McVEIGH of Ldn. B/S of 91¼a Lot #1 in div. of Thomas
A. DENNIS adj Edwin C. BROWN, Silas BEATTY, Mrs. CHANNELL,
road from Handy's Mill to Mdbg. Wit: Burr POWELL, Abner GIBSON.
Gives plat. Delv. to McVEIGH 24 Jan 1832.

3W:007   Date: 23 Apr 1831   RtCt: 23 Apr 1831
Nathan GREGG Sr. of Ldn to John JANNEY of Ldn. Trust for debt to
Abijah JANNEY of AlexDC (trustee of Ann HARPER w/o
Washington T. HARPER) using 133a (see DBk 3W:001).

3W:008   Date: 21 Jan 1831   RtCt: 29 Apr 1831
George D. SMITH of Ldn to Richard H. HENDERSON of Ldn. Trust
for debt to George RUST Jr. of JeffVa using 318a prch/o Joseph
CALDWELL. Delv. to RUST 13 Dec 1831.

3W:010   Date: 1 Jun 1831   RtCt: 2 Jun 1831
Richard H. HENDERSON (Exor of Thomas R. MOTT dec'd) of Ldn
to James CROSS of Ldn. B/S of 147a 'Egypt' (late prop. of Thos. R.
MOTT) adj road to Francis' Mill, heirs of John WILDMAN, road to
Cochran's Mill.

3W:011   Date: 26 May 1831   RtCt: 2 Jun 1831
Thornton WALKER to Reuben TRIPLETT. Interest in debts due him
from Craven WALKER, George McGUIGUAN, Lewis FRENCH,
James BYRNE, Rozzell JACOBS, Seth SMITH, Benjamin
MITCHELL, Thomas J. BENNETT, Charles TRUSSELL, James B.
BISCOE, George E. LLOYD, William MILLER, Joseph A. LLOYD,
claims in hands of Thomas L. HUMPHREY and Peyton SILCOTT,
John PAYNE, Eve GIBSON, John B. MILLER, Benjamin STUMP,
Jonah PUGH, Enoch BIRK in trust to pay balances due to Boothe &
Brooks, post office, Josiah GREGG, John D. SHANK, H. B.
POWELL, TRIPLETT.

3W:012   Date: 22 Sep 1830   RtCt: 4 Jun 1831
Samuel MASSIE & wife Catharine of Ldn to Stephen T. CONARD
and Ellwood B. JAMES of Ldn. B/S of 74a (from land dev. by William
BERKLEY to son Thomas) adj Joseph THOMAS, Richard
THATCHER, James NICHOLS. Wit: Craven OSBURN, Thomas
NICHOLS. Delv. to CUNNARD 12 Mar 1833.

3W:014 Date: 22 Sep 1830 RtCt: 4 Jun 1831
Samuel MASSIE & wife Catharine of Ldn to Stephen T. CONARD
and Ellwood B. JAMES of Ldn. B/S of 100a on top of Blue Ridge adj
survey made for Edward SNICKERS for 352a, William BERKLEY,
Thomas KIRKPATRICK's survey. Delv. to S. T. CUNNARD 12 Mar
1833.

3W:017 Date: 28 Apr 1821 RtCt: 4 Jun 1831
James WARFORD & wife Elizabeth of Livingston Co Ky to Samuel
MARKS of Ldn. B/S of 35a Lot #3 (allotted Elizabeth from div. of
father Abel MARKS dec'd) adj Morris OSBURNE.

3W:019 Date: 4 Jun 1831 RtCt: 4 Jun 1831
David LOVETT of Ldn to Timothy TAYLOR Jr. of Ldn. Trust for debt
to Swithin NICHOLS and Edith HATCHER of Ldn using 76a cnvy/b
by Mortimore McILHANY; __a cnvy/b Charles J. KILGORE & wife
Louisa that was her share from estate of her sister Elizabeth
McILHANY; and 86a (formerly of James BRADFIELD now dec'd).
Delv. to NICHOLS 15 May 1832.

3W:022 Date: 14 Feb 1831 RtCt: 5 Jun 1831
Narcissa GHEEN, Thomas GHEEN and William GHEEN of Ldn to
John PANCOAST Jr. of Ldn. Trust for debt to David YOUNG of Ldn
using 164a bequeathed by William SUDDITH dec'd to heirs of
William GHEEN & wife Narcissa. Delv. pr order 9 Oct 1835.

3W:024 Date: 9 Jun 1828 RtCt: 5 Jun 1831
George W. SEEVERS Marshall of Sup. Ct. Winchester (case of
George THOMAS agst Henry ASHTON, Apr 1827) to David LEWIS
of Ldn. B/S of 442¾a on Broad Run adj Mrs. BERKLEY, __
CLEVELAND, __ BUCKNER.

3W:027 Date: 7 May 1831 RtCt: 5 Jun 1831
Michael SOUDER & wife Susan of Ldn to Henry SPRING of Ldn.
B/S of 1a adj __ STOUTSENBERGER, __ STONEBURNER, Levi
COLLINS. Wit: Samuel DAWSON, Geo. W. SHAWEN. Delv. to
grantee 30 Mar 1857.

3W:030 Date: 5 Jun 1831 RtCt: 6 Jun 1831
Joseph MERCER of Ldn to Samuel SUFFRON of Ldn. B/S of house
& 2a lot where SUFFRON now lives adj Miriam HOLE, Josiah HALL,
heirs of JANNEY (see will of Major HUNT dec'd).

3W:031 Date: 21 May 1831 RtCt: 6 Jun 1831
Sally Ann RUSSELL, Eliza RUSSELL and Charley A. E. Jane
RUSSELL of Ldn to Gabriel VANDEVENTER of Ldn. Trust for debt
to John CARR and David CARR of Ldn using house and lot on
Market St in Lsbg adj Presbyterian Church yard. Wit: John MARTIN,
Wm. CLINE, Joseph HILLARD. Delv. to David CARR 14 Jan 1831.

3W:033 Date: 21 May 1831 RtCt: 28 May 1831
John CARR and David CARR & wife Susannah of Ldn to Sally Ann
RUSSELL, Eliza RUSSELL and C. A. E. Jane RUSSELL of Ldn. B/S

of house and lot as above. Wit: Tasker C. QUINLAN, Presley CORDELL. Delv. to Sally Ann RUSSELL 8 Mar 1832.

3W:036 Date: 16 May 1831 RtCt: 28 May 1831
Thomas MOSS to Albert WATERMAN. Trust for debt to Isaiah CHAPPELL using168a where MOSS lives adj James ALLEN. Delv. to CHAPPELL 1 May 1832.

3W:038 Date: 7 Jun 1831 RtCt: 8 Jun 1831
Nathaniel TYLER & wife Caroline G. to Robert BENTLEY. B/S of house and lot on S side of Cornwall St in Lsbg (prch/o James McILHANY). Wit in Fqr: Thos. INGRAM, Richard THOMPSON.

3W:040 Date: 8 Jun 1831 RtCt: 8 Jun 1831
William DODD of Ldn to son James DODD and daus. Elizabeth TIPPETT late DODD and Sarah DODD of Ldn. Gift to James of Negro girl Maria abt 4y old dau. of Harriet; to Elizabeth Negro girl Delila abt 10y old dau. of Barbara; Negro girl Harriet abt 19y to Sally (paying up a note given by me to James BEST).

3W:041 Date: 8 Jun 1831 RtCt: 8 Jun 1831
William DODD of Ldn to Samuel DODD of Ldn. BoS for Negro girl Amelia abt 8y old and boy Nathan abt 6y old.

3W:042 Date: 4 May 1831 RtCt: 4 May/8 Jun 1831
John CRIDLER of Ldn to John A. BINNS and Josiah L. DREAN of Ldn. Trust for debt to James BRADY of Ldn using leased lot on Loudoun St in Lsbg (cnvy/b Richard Henry LEE as trustee of St. James Church).

3W:043 Date: 7 Jun 1831 RtCt: 8 Jun 1831
John CRIDLER & wife Elizabeth of Ldn to Samuel M. BOSS of Ldn. Trust for debt to John MARTIN using lot on W end of Lsbg adj __ FRENCH, __ CARR, __ SOWWICK, __ BRADY.

3W:045 Date: 18 May 1831 RtCt: 10 Jun 1831
William CLINE of Ldn to John A. McCORMICK of Ldn. LS of 20y of lot on S side of Cornwall St in Lsbg adj William D. DRISH.

3W:046 Date: 3 Jun 1831 RtCt: 11 Jun 1831
Samuel G. HAMILTON & wife Ann H. of Licking Co Ohio to Samuel M. BOSS of Ldn. B/S of lot in Lsbg adj John McCORMICK, C. DOWLING heirs, Geo. K. FOX (See DBk, YY:281 and CCC:258). Wit: E. A. WHIPPLE, M. DARLENTON. Delv. to BOSS 2 Mar 1832.

3W:049 Date: 20 Nov 1830 RtCt: 11 Jun 1831
James THOMAS of Ldn to Charles G. ESKRIDGE of Lsbg. B/S of 2a lot (part of prch/o Israel WILKINSON) and 5a (prch/o John BURTON). Delv. to ESKRIDGE 7 Sep 1836.

3W:050 Date: 13 Jun 1831 RtCt: 13 Jun 1831
Charles BINNS, R'd. H. HENDERSON, John ROSE and John GRAY. Bond on BINNS as Clerk of the County Court.

3W:051   Date: 28 Mar 1831   RtCt: 13 Jun 1831
Richard Chichester McCARTY, Dennis McCARTY and Margaret McCARTY wd/o Dennis McCARTY dec'd of Ldn to George W. McCARTY of Ldn. B/S of 43¾a on Goose Creek, Snickers Gap Turnpike road and 6¼a from estate of Dennis McCARTY dec'd. Wit: C. N. GALLEHER, Stephen W. McCARTY, William T. McCARTY. Delv. to his son 11 Jun 1836.

3W:053   Date: 29 Oct 1830   RtCt: 13 Jun 1831
Levi JOHNSON, Charles JOHNSON, Elizabeth CLAYCOMB late JOHNSON and Granville JOHNSON of Ky and Jacob HUFF & wife Melinda late JOHNSON of Ohio (heirs of Charles JOHNSON dec'd late of Ldn) and William K. ESKRIDGE & wife Henrietta late JOHNSON (wd/o Charles dec'd) of Ohio to Timothy TAYLOR Jr. and Charles TAYLOR of Ldn. B/S of 66a adj TAYLOR, Abraham SILCOTT, Thomas NICHOLS in trust for benefit of John WEST & wife Hannah of Ldn (Oct 1830 John WEST sold 171a to Morris OSBURNE which Hannah has dower claim she does not want to relinquish without equivalent land). Delv. to TAYLOR 9 Oct 1843.

3W:057   Date: 20 Sep 1830   RtCt: 13 Jun 1831
William K. ESKRIDGE & wife Henrietta late JOHNSON wd/o Charles JOHNSON late of Ldn, Jacob HUFF & wife Melinda late JOHNSON d/o Charles dec'd of Brown Co Ohio to Levi JOHNSON of Mercer Co Ohio. PoA for sale from estate of Charles JOHNSON dec'd. Wit: G. W. KING Jr., James TRIBY.

3W:059   Date: 2 Sep 1830   RtCt: 13 Jun 1831
Elizabeth CLAYCOMB late JOHNSON of Brackenridge Co Ky (ch/o Charles JOHNSON dec'd late of Ldn) to Levi JOHNSON of Mercer Co Ky. PoA for sale from estate of Charles JOHNSON dec'd.

3W:061   Date: 11 Sep 1830   RtCt: 13 Jun 1831
Charles JOHNSON now of Jessamine Co Ky (heir of Charles JOHNSON dec'd late of Ldn) to brother Levi JOHNSON of Mercer Co Ky. PoA for sale from estate of Charles JOHNSON dec'd.

3W:063   Date: 18 Jan 1831   RtCt: 13 Jun 1831
Granville JOHNSON of Jefferson Co Ky (s/o Charles JOHNSON dec'd) to brother Levi JOHNSTON of Mercer Co Ky. PoA for interest in sale of 65¾a of Charles JOHNSON dec'd in Ldn.

3W:065   Date: 5 Mar 1831   RtCt: 13 Jun 1831
George WINCEL of Ldn to George SMITH of Ldn. B/S of ½ of 1a lot (from trust of Jun 1830 from John G. HILL for debt to John WINE).

3W:067   Date: 29 Jan 1831   RtCt: 11 Apr/13 Jun 1831
Thomas GORE, Joseph GORE and Joshua OSBURN (Exors of Joseph GORE dec'd) of Ldn to William HATCHER of Ldn. B/S of 60a on Goose Creek adj George FAIRHURST, Aquilla MEAD, Israel JANNEY, Blackstone JANNEY. Wit: Abram YOUNG, Manley MEAD, Craven POPKINS. Delv. to HATCHER 1 Mar 1834.

3W:069 Date: 2 Apr 1831 RtCt: 13 Jun 1831
Archibald VICKERS & wife Pleasant to Nathaniel NICHOLS. Trust
for debt to Sarah NICHOLS using 40a (prch/o William CHAMBLIN)
adj Abel MARKS dec'd, __ HUMPHREY. Wit: Craven OSBURN,
John WHITE.

3W:071 Date: 30 Apr 1831 RtCt: 13 Jun 1831
John BEVERIDGE Sr. of Ldn, but moving. DoE for mulatto girl Mary
abt 11y old after John and wife are dead and she has reached 21y
old. Wit: Alfred McFARLAND, Asa ROGERS, Jas. ROGERS.

3W:072 Date: 13 Jun 1831 RtCt: 13 Jun 1831
William CLENDENING, James McILHANY and William RUSSELL.
Bond on CLENDENING as constable.

3W:073 Date: 13 Jun 1831 RtCt: 13 Jun 1831
William ELLZEY of Ldn to Amos JANNEY of Ldn. B/S of 27a on E
side of Short Hill (cnvy/b Ferdinando FAIRFAX Jan 1805, DBk
FF:318) adj __ EVERHARD. Delv. to JANNEY 29 Jun 1833.

3W:075 Date: 16 May 1831 RtCt: 16 May 1831
John RICHARDS & wife Margaret of Ldn to George W. HUNTER of
Ffx. Trust for debt to Erastus TODD of Ffx using 11¾a (allotted to
Margaret from div. of Adam CORDELL dec'd). [not signed by
Margaret]

3W:077 Date: 8 Apr 1829 RtCt: 27 Jun 1831
William KING & wife Susan of Lsbg to Jesse TIMMS and Richard H.
HENDERSON. Trust for debt to Eliza A. BARRY of Ldn using lot on
W side of King St in Lsbg (cnvy/b John MONROE). Wit: Tasker C.
QUINLAN, Presley CORDELL. Delv. to TIMMS 5 May 1834.

3W:081 Date: 8 Feb 1831 RtCt: 11 Jul 1831
Burr W. HARRISON and Jesse TIMMS) to Joseph HAWKINS. B/S
of 219a (from trust of Nov 1828 from insolvent debtor Tasker C.
QUINLAN) on S side of Goose Creek adj __ TILLETT, __
SHERARD, __ MERCER. Delv. to HAWKINS 14 Feb 1837.

3W:083 Date: 11 Jul 1831 RtCt: 11 Jul 1831
Joshua LEE & wife Theodocia of Ldn to son Matthew LEE of Ldn.
Gift of 150a on road from Lsbg to Gumspring or Springfield adj A.
LEE. Wit: Walter POWER, Thomas DARNES, Presley CORDELL.
Delv. to M. LEE 15 May 1834

3W:085 Date: 23 Jun 1831 RtCt: 11 Jul 1831
William GRAHAM & wife Tamer of Ldn to Joshua OSBURN of Ldn.
Trust for debt to Laurence MINK of Ldn using lots cnvy/b MINK Jun
1831). Wit: Mortimer McILHANY, John WHITE.

3W:089 Date: 6 Oct 1830 RtCt: 11 Jul 1831
Benjamin GRAYSON & wife Nancy of Ldn to Richard O. GRAYSON
of Ldn. B/S of 200a (cnvy/b carpenter Thomas DRAKE to William
GRAYSON) adj Bloomfield, Thomas HUMPHREY s/o Abner,
Dempsey CARTER, John W. GRAYSON; and 37a on road from

Bloomfield to Gibson's old mill now Jesse RICHARDS adj George M. GRAYSON, Mary D. GRAYSON. Wit: Edward HALL, John W. GRAYSON.

3W:093   Date: 23 May 1831   RtCt: 11 Jul 1831
Thomas G. HUMPHREY & wife Phebe of Ldn to Richard O. GRAYSON of Ldn. B/S of right to change bed and convey by mill race (GRAYSON abt to erect a grist and a saw mill on his 'Greenway' estate adj HUMPHREY and both would benefit by a change in course of north fork of Beaverdam passing thru land of HUMPHREY adj Joshua FREDD, Joseph FREDD, Benj. GRAYSON, John G. HUMPHREY to land of Richard O. GRAYSON). Wit: Benjamin GRAYSON, John W. GRAYSON.

3W:095   Date: 10 Mar 1831   RtCt: 29 Jun 1831
Henry BELL & wife Ruth of Nelson Co Ky to Thomas RODGERS of Ldn. B/S of 9a Lot #8 in div. of George NIXON dec'd on Goose Creek. Delv. to ROGERS 6 Sep 1831.

3W:097   Date: 27 Jun 1831   RtCt: 29 Jun 1831
Richard H. HENDERSON & wife Orra D. and John J. HARDING & wife __ of Lsbg to William D. DRISH of Lsbg. B/S of und, 2/5th of lot on Market St in Lsbg (held jointly by HENDERSON and HARDING, DRISH, Presley CORDELL and heirs of Thomas MORRALLEE. [not signed by wives].

3W:099   Date: 15 Apr 1830   RtCt: 7 Jul 1831
Elizabeth Taliaferro BRYERLY w/o Samuel BRYERLY of FredVa to Ann Sarah ARMISTEAD of Fqr and dau. Frances Barnes TALIAFERRO. B/S of 2/3rd of 200a adj Wm. C. FITZHUGH, Vincent MORSE, Sydnor BAILEY, Laurence BATTAILE, J. HICKS, __ COLESON; with provisions for remaining 1/3rd. Wit: Robt. L. ARMISTEAD, John CARTER. Delv. pr order 20 Mar 1834.

3W:102   Date: 1 Jan 1831   RtCt: 7 Jul 1831
John C. ARMISTEAD & wife Ann S. of Fqr to William Thomas Warren TALIAFERRO of Fqr. B/S of 100a (und. int. in 'Fernew' in Ldn, cnvy/b Elizabeth T. BRYERLY to her daus. Ann S. ARMISTEAD & Frances Barnes TALIAFERRO).

3W:104   Date: 28 Jun 1831   RtCt: 28 Jun 1831
Noble S. BRADEN (Exor of Robert BRADEN dec'd) to John LESLIE of Ldn. B/S of 10a in German Settlement on Big Dutchman Creek. Delv. to LESLIE 24 Apr 1832.

3W:105   Date: 26 Mar 1831   RtCt: 9 Jul 1831
Mortimer McILHANY & wife Mary Ann of Ldn to Daniel HINES of Ldn. B/S of 7a. Wit: John WHITE, Geo. W. SHAWEN.

3W:108   Date: 30 Apr 1831   RtCt: 15 Jun 1831
Nathan NEER & wife Eliza of Ldn to Samuel ZIMMERMAN of Ldn. B/S of 3a adj Thomas HOUGH now dec'd, Hugh THOMPSON dec'd,

James THOMPSON. Wit: Craven OSBURN, John WHITE. Delv. to ZIMMERMAN 19 Jan 1838.

3W:110   Date: 24 Jun 1830   RtCt: 17 Jun 1831
David HESSER & wife Alcinda of Ldn to John HESSER of Ldn. B/S of interest in 94a (formerly held by Andrew HESSER dec'd, over what was already cnvy/b John HESSER & wife Lydia). Wit: Notley C. WILLIAMS, Thomas NICHOLS. Delv. to Jno. HESSER 23 Jun 1837.

3W:112   Date: 16 Apr 1831   RtCt: 15 Jun 1831
Noble S. BRADEN (Exor of Robert BRADEN dec'd) of Ldn to Asa BROWN of Ldn. B/S of lot in Hllb cnvy/b John B. STEVENS & John BRADEN (Exors of Thomas D. STEVENS dec'd in Mar 1817) on S side of Turnpike road adj Richard COPELAND. Wit: Jos. L. POTTS, J. G. PAXSON, Fleming HIXON, Jos. A. BRADEN. Delv. to BROWN 9 May 1833.

3W:113   Date: 2 Mar 1831   RtCt: 14 Jun 1831
Samuel HAMMONTREE of Ldn to Craven VANHORN of Ldn. Trust for debt to Edward PRIESTLY of BaltMd using horse.

3W:115   Date: 4 Jan 1831   RtCt: 13 Jun 1831
Joseph LAYCOCK to Isaac E. STEER. Trust for debt to Rebecca KENWORTHY using interest in 100a (sold by John BENEDUM to John CUMMINS except 1a cnvy/t Thomas HALL). Wit: Beulah JANNEY, Sarah G. JANNEY.

3W:116   Date: 14 Jun 1831   RtCt: 14 Jun 1831
Robert MOFFETT & wife Ellen and Benjamin SHREVE of Ldn to John J. HARDING of Ldn. B/S of lot on E side of King St. in Lsbg adj William JOHNSON (cnvy/b Charles DRISH Jan 1820, DBk ZZ:412). Wit: William B. HARRISON, Tasker C. QUINLAN.

3W:119   Date: 30 May 1831   RtCt: 14 Jun 1831
David CARR & wife Susannah of Ldn to Harmon BITZER of Ldn. B/S of 4a adj Nathan GREGG Sr., David CARR, Poplar Spring (cnvy/b Nathan GREGG Sr. Apr 1831). Wit: Presley CORDELL, Tasker C. QUINLAN. Delv. to G. L. BITZER Exor 13 Mar 1835.

3W:122   Date: 4 Jun 1831   RtCt: 14 Jun 1831
John MORAN of Ldn to Edward WILLSON of Ldn. B/S of 2 small lots detached part of tract where MORAN lives adj where WILLSON lives.

3W:123   Date: 21 Aug 1830   RtCt: 25 Jun 1831
George BAYLY & wife Mary Anne of Shanandoah Co Va to Marcus C. BUCK of Culpeper Co Va. B/S of 40a, 200a and 20a (cnvy/b Strother M. HELM Mar 1819).

3W:127   Date: 22 Jun 1831   RtCt: 27 Jun 1831
Lawrence MINK & wife Elizabeth of Ldn to William GRAHAM of Ldn. B/S of 125a (cnvy/b Joseph LEWIS Sept 1803), 79a (cnvy/b Michael BALLMER May 1801), 17a on E side of Short Hill (cnvy/b

Christopher BURNHOUSE Sep 1816), and 50a (cnvy/b Ferdinando FAIRFAX Apr 1803). Wit: George W. SHAWEN, John WHITE. Delv. to GRAHAM 10 Apr 1834.

3W:130   Date: 6 Jun 1831   RtCt: 13 Jun 1831
Joseph EVERHART of Ldn to John WENNER of Ldn. B/S of 14a on E side of Short Hill (from Emanuel WALTMAN dec'd). Delv. to WENNER 12 Aug 1837.

3W:132   Date: 4 Jun 1831   RtCt: 14 Jun 1831
Edward WILSON & wife Mary of Ldn to John MORAN of Ldn. B/S of 1a on W side of line dividing the two parties. Wit: A. GIBSON, Francis W. LUCKETT. Delv. to MORAN 20 Nov 1832.

3W:134   Date: 19 Feb 1829   RtCt: 27 Jun 1831
Charles SHEPHARD of Ldn. DoE for Negro man Admiral.

3W:135   Date: 13 May 1831   RtCt: 12 Jul 1831
John LEVERTY to Michael MORRALLEE of Lsbg. Owes debt, sold him a horse, which MORRALLE agrees to let LEVERTY keep until 1 Aug next.

3W:136   Date: 10 Feb 1831   RtCt: 22 Jul 1831
John BOYD of Mdbg to Albert G. WATERMAN of Mdbg. Trust for William K. ISH and Edward SUMMERS as securities on bond for BOYD to carry mail from Ffx courthouse thru Ldn to Winchester using Lot #53 & part of #54 with tavern in Mdbg.

3W:139   Date: 9 May 1831   RtCt: 8 Jul 1831
Elizabeth MARKS wd/o Isaiah MARKS dec'd and Thomas F. THOMPSON & wife Lucinda D. late MARKS dau. of Isaiah dec'd of Daviess Co Ky to Elisha S. MARKS of Daviess Co Ky. PoA for dealing with Joshua PANCOAST Admr of Isaiah dec'd.

3W:141   Date: 13 Apr 1831   RtCt: 20 Jul 1831
Lewis JUREY of Marion Co Ohio to James ALDER of Ldn. PoA for transactions with estate of David JUREY dec'd of Ldn, including leased farm

3W:143   Date: __ Jul 1831   RtCt: 22 Jul 1831
Jonah HATCHER of Ldn to Levi & Obediah COOKSEY of Ldn. B/S of 1/5th of 1/3rd interest in 11a adj Bernard TAYLOR, Samuel IDEN (sold by Walter KERRICK to William PIGGOTT, Samuel HATCHER & Thomas HUGHS).

3W:144   Date: 22 Jul 1831   RtCt: 22 Jul 1831
Jonah HATCHER of Ldn to William HATCHER of Ldn. B/S of 1/5th of ½ interest in 134a farm of Rebecca HATCHER dec'd adj Goose Creek Meeting House, George FAIRHURST, Yardley TAYLOR, Jesse HIRST. Delv. to Wm. HATCHER 1 Mar 1834.

3W:145   Date: 22 Jul 1831   RtCt: 22 Jul 1831
Jonah HATCHER of Ldn to Thomas HATCHER of Ldn. B/S of 1/5th interest in 113a farm of Samuel HATCHER dec'd adj William

NICHOLS, William PIGGOTT, Swithen NICHOLS. Delv. to Thos. HATCHER 1 Mar 1834.

3W:146   Date: 22 Jul 1831   RtCt: 22 Jul 1831
Jonah HATCHER of Ldn to Isaac PIGGOTT of Ldn. B/S of 1/5th interest in 80a 'Greenway Farm' as heir of Samuel HATCHER dec'd in div. of Samuel & Joseph HATCHER partnership.

3W:148   Date: 9 Apr 1831   RtCt: 25 Jul 1831
George WARNER & wife Sarah of Ldn to John JANNEY of Ldn. Trust for debt to Abijah JANNEY of AlexDC using 146a cnvy/b Abijah Apr 1831.

3W:150   Date: 17 Aug 1830   RtCt: 23 Jul 1831
Solomon HOUSEHOLDER of Ldn to Daniel HOUSEHOLDER of Ldn. B/S of 38a (from Adam HOUSEHOLDER dec'd) adj Amos JANNEY, __ FRYE.

3W:152   Date: 28 Jul 1830   RtCt: 30 Jul 1831
William S. EACHES & wife Ann B. and John & Thompson BENNETT of Ldn to William HOLMES of Ldn. B/S of 203a (belonged to Charles BENNETT & wife Mary). Wit: John H. McCABE, Presley CORDELL.

3W:154   Date: 10 Jun 1831   RtCt: 29 Jul 1831
Horace LUCKETT & wife Louisa A. of Ldn to John ISH of Ldn. B/S of house & lot in Aldie (formerly of insolvent Abraham M. FULTON, cnvy/t Sheriff then to LUCKETT). Wit: Hamilton ROGERS, A. GIBSON. Delv. to ISH 1 May 1833.

3W:156   Date: 25 Jul 1831   RtCt: 25 Jul 1831
Commr. Nathaniel SEEVERS of Chancery Ct. Winchester to William SMITH of Ldn. B/S of 22a adj Goose Creek Meeting house lot (from case of Lydia PANCOAST agst Lydia NICHOLS, see DBk TTT:64).

3W:159   Date: 14 May 1831   RtCt: 13 Jun 1831
Ellen F(O)ULTON (wd/o Abraham FOULTON dec'd) of Ldn to John ISH of Ldn. B/S of right of dower in two ½a lots with log house in Aldie. Wit: George BRISCOE, Peter SKINNER, Florence McCARTY. Delv. to ISH 1 May 1833.

3W:160   Date: 24 Jun 1831   RtCt: 29 Jul 1831
John HESSER & wife Lydia of Ldn to David HESSER of Ldn. B/S of 61a (division of jointly held 156a former prop. of father Andrew HESSER dec'd, John entitled to 2/3rd and David to 1/3rd). Wit: Notley C. WILLIAMS, Thomas NICHOLS. Delv. to David HESSER 20 Jun 1840.

3W:162   Date: 2 Apr 1831   RtCt: 25 Jul 1831
William CHAMBLIN & wife Asenath of Ldn to Archibald VICKERS of Ldn. B/S of interest in 40a where CHAMBLIN now lives (allotted to Lydia MARKS now HESSER in div. of Abel MARKS dec'd and sold to CHAMBLIN). Wit: John WHITE, Craven OSBURN.

3W:164 Date: 6 Nov 1830 RtCt: 30 Jul 1831
John GEORGE of Ldn (Commr. in Chancery Ct of Ldn Apr 1830) to John SORBAUGH of Ldn. B/S of 4a (former prop. of Jacob FILLER Sr. dec'd). Wit: John GRUBB, Adam KARN, Thos. J. MARLOW, John CONARD. Delv. to SARBAUGH 10 Nov 1834.

3W:166 Date: 16 May 1831 RtCt: 13 Jun 1831
Ellen F(O)ULTON (wd/o Abraham FOULTON dec'd) of Ldn to Horace LUCKETT of Ldn. B/S of right of dower in two ½a lots with brick house in Aldie. Wit: Florence McCARTY, Peter SKINNER, George BRISCOE.

3W:168 Date: 30 Jul 1831 RtCt: 30 Jul 1831
Philip HEATER and John GEORGE to Adam KARN Sr. (Exor of Magdalena SHOVER dec'd). Bond on HEATER and GEORGE to refund a portion of balance paid for __ SYPHERD & wife to cover future debts of the estate. Wit: James L. HAMILTON, Saml. S. WHITING.

3W:169 Date: 20 Oct 1830 RtCt: 8 Nov 1830
Sarah BROWN, Hiram BROWN and Sarah BROWN Jr. of Ldn to James COCHRAN Sr. of Ldn. B/S of 62a adj maple tree with a hickory growing out of the root under which repose the ashes of John BROWN dec'd at the corner of land of late Mahlon GREGG dec'd, adj Joel OSBURN Jr., Elizabeth RUSSELL, COCHRAN. Wit: S. B. T. CALDWELL, Enos NICHOLS, Tholemiah COCHRAN. Delv. to COCHRAN 23 Sep 1834.

3W:170 Date: 1 Aug 1831 RtCt: 1 Aug 1831
Loveless CONWELL & wife Elizabeth to Isaac CONWELL and Jonathan CONWELL. B/S of und. 1/4th of estate of Josiah HALL dec'd - Loveless entitled to und. 1/4th of estate of Josiah HALL dec'd and wish to convey it to children Sarah CARNICLE, Ellen BOLEN, Mary CONWELL, Isaac CONWELL, Josiah CONWELL, Jonathan CONWELL and Elizabeth CONWELL at death of Elizabeth the elder; in trust for benefit of Elizabeth during her lifetime. Wit: Tasker C. QUINLAN, Presley CORDELL.

3W:174 Date: 14 Jul 1831 RtCt: 3 Aug 1831
Mortimer MCILHANY & wife Mary A. of Ldn to Joseph & Edward MORRISON of Ldn. B/S of 70a (prch/o John LESLIE in 1830) adj Thomas WHITE, John DAVIS, Frederick A. DAVISON, John STATLER. Wit: Ebenezer GRUBB, John WHITE. Delv. to Jos. MORRISON 27 Sep 1832.

3W:176 Date: 4 Mar 1831 RtCt: 3 Aug 1831
John LESLIE & wife Rachel of Ldn to Jane MORRISON Jr. of Ldn. B/S of 1/11th share of 206a farm where widow of Archibald MORRISON dec'd now lives called 'the parish of Shelver' [Shelburne]. Wit: Mortimer McILHANY, John WHITE.

3W:179 Date: 9 Jun 1831 RtCt: 1 Aug 1831
Caldwell CARR Esqr of Upperville Fqr to Dr. Thomas W. SMITH of Upperville Fqr. Release of trust - Elizabeth GIBSON wd/o John GIBSON dec'd as Guardian for his children made trust in Jun 1820 using 14½a and trust of Mar 1821 using 80a dower land, DBk BBB:37 and CCC:186. All children now of age. SMITH purchased lots.

3W:180 Date: 3 Aug 1831 RtCt: 4 Aug 1831
Edward HA(Y)NES & wife Sarah of Ldn to James GARRISON of Ldn. B/S of lot on N side of Market St in Lsbg (prch/o Peter FITCHTER as lease and of Rebecca SHAW as fee simple). Wit: John ROSE, Samuel M. EDWARDS. Delv. to GARRISON 17 Mar 1837.

3W:183 Date: 4 Aug 1831 RtCt: 14 Aug 1831
Diadema PAXSON of Ldn to William HOLMES of Ldn. B/S of interest in land (from div. of Thomazin ELLZEY dec'd cnvy/t HOLMES Nov 1829) adj Joshua PUSEY, Sally L. MANNING.

3W:184 Date: 4 Aug 1831 RtCt: 4 Aug 1831
William HOLMES & wife Eliza T. of Ldn to Diadema PAXSON of Ldn. B/S of 110a adj Joshua PUSEY, Sarah MANNING (cnvy/b Commrs. of Thomazin ELLEZEY dec'd and lying to S side of above land.) Wit: Tasker C. QUINLAN, Presley CORDELL.

3W:188 Date: 3 Aug 1831 RtCt: 3 Aug 1831
James L. MARTIN of Ldn to Robert ROBERTS of Ldn. Release of trust of Jul 1830 for debt to Christopher FRYE using 27a.

3W:190 Date: 23 Jul 1831 RtCt: 8 Aug 1831
Hamilton ROGERS. Commission as Lt. Colonel of 57th Reg of Infantry, 6th Brig, 2nd Div of Va Militia from 24 May 1831.

3W:190 Date: 3 Aug 1831 RtCt: 8 Aug 1831
William W. KITZMILLER. Commission as Lt. of Light Infantry in 2nd Batt., 57th Reg, 6th Brig, 2nd Div of Va Militia

3W:191 Date: 9 Aug 1831 RtCt: 10 Aug 1831
William DOVE. Commission as Ensign in 57th Reg, 6th Brig, 2nd Div of Va Militia.

3W:191 Date: 8 Aug 1831 RtCt: 10 Aug 1831
Joseph A. WILLIAMSON. Oath as commissioner to take depositions and state accounts from the Honorable John SCOTT Judge of Circuit Superior Ct of Law & Chancery from Ldn.

3W:192 Date: 9 Aug 1831 RtCt: 10 Aug 1831
Alex'r D. LEE. Commission as Lt. in 57th Reg, 6th Brig, 2nd Div of Va Militia.

3W:192 Date: 9 Aug 1831 RtCt: 10 Aug 1831
Gunnell DARNE. Commission as Lt. in 57th Reg, 6th Brig, 2nd Div of Va Militia.

3W:192   Date: 9 Aug 1831   RtCt: 9 Aug 1831
Nelson H. HAWLEY. Commission as Ensign of Infantry in 57th Reg, 6th Brig, 2nd Div of Va Militia.

3W:193   Date: 9 Aug 1831   RtCt: 9 Aug 1831
John BARRETT. Qualified as Ensign in Va Militia.

3W:193   Date: 9 Aug 1831   RtCt: 10 Aug 1831
John M. EDWARDS. Commissioned 28 May 1831 as Ensign in Va Militia.

3W:193   Date: 9 Aug 1831   RtCt: 10 Aug 1831
Newton KEENE. Commission as Captain in 57th Reg, 6th Brig, 2nd Div of Va Militia.

3W:194   Date: 4 Mar 1829   RtCt: 10 Aug 1831
John H. MONROE. Commission. [entry does not state rank but notation on side states as Captain]

3W:194   Date: 14 Mar 1831   RtCt: 5 Sep 1831
Charles Turner to William WILKINSON. B/S of 1/6th interest from will of William SUDDITH dec'd (from trust of Oct 1823 from William GHEEN since dec'd & wife Narcissa & son James GHEEN, land dev. Narcissa from father William SUDDITH) adj North Fork Meeting House, Abraham SKILMAN, Jesse ATWELL. Delv. pr order of WILKINSON 20 Oct 1843.

3W:197   Date: 5 Sep 1831   RtCt: 6 Sep 1831
Lucy D. CARR late of Ldn now of Culpeper Co Va to Burr W. HARRISON of Ldn. B/S of Lot #9 on Market & Church St in Lsbg adj HARRISON.

3W:199   Date: 3 Sep 1831   RtCt: 13 Sep 1831
Elizabeth HILL wd/o William WOODFORD Jr. dec'd . Allotment of dower from 334a, including 114a dower of Susanna CARTER dec'd from her former husband William WOODFORD Sr. dec'd. Court order dated 10 Jan 1831 in case of John CROZIER & wife Eleanor late BRADFIELD, etc. agst James HILL & wife, etc. – 79a dower to Mrs. HILL, 114a dower to Mrs. CARTER. Gives plat. Divisors: James STEPHENSON, Joshua OSBURN, James COCKRAN.

3W:202   Date: 13 Sep 1831   RtCt: 13 Sep 1831
Jesse McVEIGH and John HUMPHREY. Bond on McVEIGH as Commissioner of Revenue in 2nd District.

3W:202   Date: 12 Sep 1831   RtCt: 12 Sep 1831
Jesse TIMMS and Gustavus ELGIN. Bond on TIMMS as Commissioner of Revenue in 1st District.

3W:203   Date: 22 Aug 1831   RtCt: 24 Aug 1831
Lydia COLEMAN wd/o William dec'd of Ldn and Edmund W. COLEMAN of Ldn. Partition of 315a estate of William COLEMAN dec'd – all to Lydia, with 120a to dau. Julia E. COLEMAN and balance to son Edmund W. Agree Lydia to have 75a with mansion

house with remainder to Edmund. Wit: Sanford J. RAMEY, John THOMAS, Wm. SEEDERS.

3W:207 Date: 24 Aug 1831 RtCt: 24 Aug 1831
Jacob G. PAXSON & wife Mahala of Ldn to Samuel McPHERSON of Ldn. Trust for debt to Ebenezer GRUBB Jr. using 108a (prch/b William PAXON of Exor of John HOUGH dec'd Apr 1806). Wit: M. McILHANY, Samuel HOUGH. Delv. to E. GRUBB 22 Sep 1832.

3W:210 Date: 15 Apr 1831 RtCt: 19 Aug 1831
Edward A. GIBBS & wife Elizabeth of Berkley Co Va and Stephenson HIXON & wife Alice of Ldn to Samuel HOUGH of Ldn. B/S of 76a (91a less 5a and 9a already sold) on Kittocton Creek adj __ BENNETT. Wit: Johnston MAGOWAN, John S. HAMSON. Delv. to HOUGH 2 Sep 1833.

3W:215 Date: 19 Aug 1831 RtCt: 19 Aug 1831
David REECE (Exor of Matthew BEANS dec'd) of Ldn to Aaron MILLER of Ldn. B/S of 13a on road from Hllb to Lsbg adj Thomas WHITE, __ THOMPSON, __ McCARTOR, __ HOLMES (see DBk WW:219).

3W:217 Date: 19 Aug 1831 RtCt: 19 Aug 1831
Aaron MILLER of Ldn to Gabriel VANDEVANTER of Ldn. Trust for debt to David REECE using 13a as above. Delv. to VANDEVANTER 8 Jan 1835.

3W:219 Date: 5 Sep 1831 RtCt: 5 Sep 1831
Samuel HOUGH of Ldn to Charles G. ESKRIDGE of Ldn. Trust for debt to Charles BINNS Sr. using 4a mill lot, mill & saw mill (sold by John A. BINNS to Jacob AXLINE) adj Henry RUSSELL, Jacob MOCK, estate of John A. BINNS. Delv. to BINNS 8 Sep 1836.

3W:222 Date: 3 Sep 1831 RtCt: 5 Sep 1831
Thomas HALL of Ldn to John SAUNDERS of Ldn. Trust for debt to George RHODES of Ldn using und. 1/6th of 1/4th interest in real estate of uncle Josiah HALL dec'd. Delv. to RHODES 9 Sep 1836.

3W:224 Date: 21 Dec 1830 RtCt: 8 Aug 1831
Charlotte Eliza MASON of Ldn, John T. MASON (br/o Armistead dec'd) of Mt. Stirling, Montgomery Co Ky, William Temple T. MASON of Ldn and Thomson MASON of St. Augustine Florida (Exors of Armstead T. MASON dec'd of Ldn) to George HOFFMAN, John HOFFMAN, Peter HOFFMAN and Samuel HOFFMAN of BaltMd. B/S of 200a and 49a mountain land (parts of 'Raspberry Plain'). Wit: Jno. ROSE, James RUST, Henry CLAGETT Jr., Jno. CHALMERS, B. K. MORSELL, Joseph HUNTER, Garret BRUISTER.

3W:230 Date: 20 Mar 1824 RtCt: 11 Apr/12 Sep 1831
Jacob EVERHEART, John EVERHEART, and Joseph EVERHEART of Ldn to John PEACHER of JeffVa. B/S of 10a on N end of Short Hill on Potomac, with privilege of erecting a mill. Wit: Jno. J.

MATHIAS, Saml. HAMMATT, Alfred A. ESKRIDGE. Delv. to P. C. McCABE pr order 12 Jun 1832.

3W:232 Date: 5 Sep 1831 RtCt: 5 Sep 1831
Aaron COOPER & wife Susannah of Ldn to William STOCKS of Ldn. B/S of 12¾a (prch/o Jonathan POTTERFIELD) adj __ WILLIAMS. Wit: S. HOUGH, Wilson C. SELDEN Jr. Delv. to STOCKS 27 Sep 1832.

3W:235 Date: 23 Jul 1831 RtCt: 5 Sep 1831
Stephen McPHERSON & wife Cecelia of Ldn to Jonathan EWERS of Ldn. Trust for debt to Elisha S. MARKS of Daviess Co Ky using 135a (from suit of Joshua PANCOAST Admr of Isaiah MARKS dec'd agst McPHERSON) adj Benjamin STRINGFELLOW, heirs of Abijah SANDERS. Wit: Notley C. WILLIAMS, Thomas NICKOLS. Delv. to McPHERSON pr order of EWERS 20 Mar 1835.

3W:238 Date: 12 Jul 1831 RtCt: 12 Jul/8 Sep 1831
Garrett WALKER & wife Ruth of Ldn to David CARR and John H. MONROE of Ldn. Trust for debt to William CARR of Ldn using 36a adj B. WALKER, Samuel BEAVERS, James BROWN, Ann VANHORN; 17a adj James BROWN, __ SWICK, widow VANHORN; and 10a. Wit: Josiah L. DREAN, Presley CORDELL, Tasker C. QUINLAN. Delv. to CARR 10 Sep 1834.

3W:242 Date: 11 Aug 1831 RtCt: 9 Sep 1831
John THAYER & wife Sarah of Ldn to James B. WILSON of Ldn. B/S of interest in farm where Sarah E. RUSSELL now lives (will of Thaddeus McCARTY of Aug 1812 beq. to Sarah E. RUSSELL & children, dau. Sarah RUSSELL m. John THAYER) adj Mary McCARTY on road from Mdbg, WILSON on road from Little River. Wit: John WHITE, Mortimer McILHANY. Delv. to WILSON 28 Dec 1832.

3W:246 Date: 11 Aug 1831 RtCt: 9 Sep 1831
Jane RUSSELL of Ldn to James B. WILSON of Ldn. B/S of B/S of interest in farm where Sarah E. RUSSELL now lives (will of Thaddeus McCARTY of Aug 1812 beq. to Sarah E. RUSSELL & children, Jane is a dau.) adj Mary McCARTY on road from Mdbg, WILSON on road from Little River. Delv. to WILSON 28 Dec 1832.

3W:248 Date: 6 Aug 1831 RtCt: 9 Sep 1831
Casper SPRING & wife Elizabeth, David WIRE & wife Catharine Elizabeth and Jacob FRY & wife Elizabeth of Ldn to Henry FAWLEY of Ldn. B/S of und. 3/12th int. in 102½a in German Settlement (cnvy/t Andrew SPRING Apr 1796, DBk W:459) and 14a (cnvy/t Andrew SPRING Mar 1812, DBk PP:126). Wit: Saml. DAWSON, Geo. W. SHAWEN. Delv. to FAWLEY 31 May 1831.

3W:251 Date: 1 Apr 1831 RtCt: 10 Sep 1831
John DODD (Exor of Jane DODD dec'd) of Ldn to Richard BROWN of Ldn. B/S of 201a above Catocton Mt. adj heirs of

VANDEVANDER, John CARR, __ PEARPOINT, __ WARNER, __ BROWN. Delv. to BROWN 27 Jul 1832.

3W:254 Date: 1 Apr 1831 RtCt: 10 Sep 1831
Richard BROWN & wife Elizabeth of Ldn to Erasmus G. HAMILTON of Ldn. Trust for debt to John DODD Exor of Jane DODD dec'd using 98a of above land. Wit: Saml. M. EDWARDS, W. C. SELDEN Jr.

3W:257 Date: 1 Apr 1831 RtCt: 10 Sep 1831
Richard BROWN & wife Elizabeth of Ldn to John DODD of Ldn. B/S of 103a (part of land in DBk 3W:251 above). Wit: W. C. SELDEN Jr., S. M. EDWARDS. Delv. to DODD 27 Apr 1832.

3W:260 Date: 18 Aug 1831 RtCt: 18 Aug 1831
Samuel HOUGH of Ldn to Charles G. ESKRIDGE of Ldn. Trust for debt to Joshua OSBURN of Ldn using 76a (cnvy/b Edward A. GIBBS Apr 1831).

3W:263 Date: 9 Aug 1828 RtCt: 13 Apr/20 Aug 1831
Mary E. FORREST of Ffx to Edward HALL of Ldn. B/S of 250a given to Julia CLAGGETT by Benjamin DULANEY adj HALL, John P. DULANEY, Gourley REEDER, John G. HUMPHREY, Samuel DUNKIN, heirs of Samuel SMITH. Wit: John C. GREEN, Thos. S. HALL, Chas. GILL, James RUST.

3W:265 Date: 6 Jun 1831 RtCt: 8 Aug 1831
H. B. POWELL to Noble BEVERIDGE. B/S of Lot #29 in Mdbg (from trust of Feb 1820 from John HARRIS for debt to Noble BEVERIDGE). Delv. to BEVERIDGE Jun 1833.

3W:267 Date: 25 Jun 1831 RtCt: 9 Aug 1831
John NICHOLS of Belmont Co Ohio to Thomas JAMES of Ldn. B/S of 1a (from div. of George NICHOLS dec'd conveyed in part to James NICHOLS since dec'd) adj John BAZIL, heirs of James NICHOLS, JAMES. Wit: George ALBAN, Joseph CALDWELL. Delv. to JAMES 22 Nov 1832.

3W:270 Date: 20 Jul 1831 RtCt: 9 Aug 1831
Daniel BROWN of Ldn to Mahlon CRAVEN of Ldn. Trust for debt to Bernard WATKINS of Ldn using farm and household items. Delv. pr order 25 Mar 1835.

3W:272 Date: 9 Aug 1831 RtCt: 9 Aug 1831
John BOYD & wife Elizabeth of Mdbg to A. G. WATERMAN of Lsbg. Trust for William K. ISH, Horace LUCKETT and James WEEKS as endorsers on bond using Lot #53 with house in Mdbg where BOYD resides. Wit: Wm. CHILTON, Fielding LITTLETON, Saml. C. CLARK.

3W:275 Date: 1 Jul 1831 RtCt: 9 Aug 1831
John M. WILSON of Ldn to Enoch FRANCIS of Ldn. B/S of leasehold interest in 236a (cnvy/b Silas & Daniel O. REESE Nov 1818 to FRANCIS).

3W:276   Date: 13 Jun 1831   RtCt: 9 Aug 1831
Harrison FITZHUGH & wife Ann Carr of Ffx to Nathaniel Harrison
FITZHUGH of Ffx. B/S of undivided ½ interest in 160a 'Rattlesnake
Den' (dev. by William LANE Sr. to dau. Lydia LANE {will at
Centerville, Queen Anne Co Md} who beq. to her sister Ann Carr
FITZHUGH) adj Robert DARNE, Robert HUNTER. Delv. pr order 22
Sep 1840.

3W:278   Date: 1 Jul 1831   RtCt: 10 Aug 1831
James W. F. MACRAE & wife Amanda M. of Ldn to Joseph LEWIS
of Ldn. B/S of 226a nr Turnpike road and Clifton Mill adj __
BOWLES, LEWIS, heirs of John GIBSON. Wit: Benjamin
GRAYSON, Cuthbert POWELL.

3W:281   Date: 1 Jun 1831   RtCt: 9 Aug 1831
Nathan GREGG of Ldn to Coonrad BITZER of Ldn. B/S of 1a adj
BITZER, David CARR, __ BROWN.

3W:282   Date: 5 Aug 1831   RtCt: 10 Aug 1831
William W. KITZMILLER & wife Elizabeth of Lsbg to Richard H.
HENDERSON, Burr W. HARRISON and Charles G. ESKRIDGE.
Trust for debt to George CARTER of Oatlands using interest from
estate of Martin KITZMILLER dec'd. Delv. to Jesse FINN? pr
direction G. CARTER.

3W:286   Date: 20 Jul 1831   RtCt: 15 Aug 1831
Fielder BURCH & wife Sarah of WashDC to William CLINE of Ldn.
B/S of lot in Snickersville now in possession of Timothy CONNER
(cnvy/b Robert BREDEN [BRADEN] but no deed executed so
Richard H. HENDERSON Admr of William CLAYTON dec'd in Apr
1830 deeded to BURCH, DBk TTT:383). Wit: Henry WERTZ, B. K.
MORSELL. Delv. to CLINE 31 Aug 1832.

3W:290   Date: 17 Dec 1830   RtCt: 16 Aug 1831
Price JACOBS & wife Catharine of Ldn to Isaac PIGGOTT of Ldn.
B/S of 296a on S fork of Beaverdam adj Benjamin MITCHEL, __
GALLAHER, Mrs. DRAKE, John WHITACRE, Ann BROWN, Michael
PLASTER, Henry HUTCHISON. Wit: Francis W. LUCKETT, Edward
HALL. Delv. 27 Feb 1873.

3W:293   Date: 10 Mar 1830   RtCt: 17 Aug 1831
John BITZER & wife Polly late BEATY of Ldn to William
BEVERIDGE of Ldn. B/S of ¼ interest in 38a (where BITZER
resides, dev. by Elizabeth BEATY dec'd m/o Polly) adj Burr
POWELL. Wit: Burr POWELL, John ISH, Abner GIBSON.

3W:296   Date: 1 Jul 1831   RtCt: 31 Aug 1831
James BROWN atty in fact of John BROWN of Ldn to Joseph C.
BROWN of Ldn. B/S of 10a adj Union, Mahlon BALDWIN, Isaac
BROWN.

3W:298 Date: 16 Nov 1830 RtCt: 19 Aug 1831
Edward A. GIBBS of Berkley Co Va to Benjamin ORRICK of Berkley
Co Va. PoA for transactions involving 76a now unlawfully in
possession of Stephenson HIXON, sold under trust given by HIXON
to Mr. HENDERSON of Lsbg for debt to GIBBS who became the
purchaser.

3W:300 Date: 12 Sep 1831 RtCt: 12 Sep 1831
Garrison B. FRENCH, Jno. HOLMES and Timothy TAYLOR Sr.
Bond on FRENCH as constable.

3W:301 Date: 8 Sep 1831 RtCt: 12 Sep 1831
William T. HOUGH (s/o John HOUGH and grands/o William HOUGH
dec'd) of Ldn to John SCHOOLEY of Ldn. B/S of 1/7th of 1/10th
interest in land in Ohio from estate of William HOUGH dec'd. Delv.
pr order 27 Jan 1852.

3W:303 Date: 2 Sep 1831 RtCt: 12 Sep 1831
Mary JACKSON (wd/o John JACKSON and granddau. of William
HOUGH dec'd) of Ldn to John SCHOOLEY of Ldn. B/S of int. in land
in Ohio from estate of William HOUGH dec'd. Delv. pr order 27 Jan
1852.

3W:305 Date: 8 Sep 1831 RtCt: 12 Sep 1831
William T. HOUGH (s/o John HOUGH dec'd and grands/o William
HOUGH dec'd) of Ldn to William H. HOUGH of Ldn. B/S of interest
in lot in AlexVa from estate of William HOUGH dec'd. Delv. W. H.
HOUGH 21 Apr 1834.

3W:308 Date: 4 Dec 1829 RtCt: 12 Sep 1831
Edward PAINTER & wife Guliema of Ldn to Ebenezer Grubb of Ldn.
B/S of interest (for life of Guliema) in land where they lately resided,
adj George JACOBS, Elizabeth JACOBS, Saml. NEER, Ebenezer
GRUBB, Valentine JACOBS. Wit: Craven OSBURN, John WHITE.

3W:310 Date: 19 Mar 1831 RtCt: 12 Sep 1831
Dec 1830 petition of Hamilton ROGERS for a new road from corner
of Chas. BINNS & Wm. MEAD [later given as Joseph] on Carolina
road to the Avon Mills on Goose Creek. Mathew ELGIN, James
WILDMAN, Robt. ELGIN and Joseph NEWTON to view area, done
in May 1831. Recommend road to pass lands of BINNS, Joseph
MEAD, John HALLING Jr., Isaac HALLING, John HAWLING Sr.,
Henry CLAGETT, road leading to Thomas LITTLETON's old saw
mill, James WILDMAN, Charles SHREVE, Gustavus ELGIN Sr.,
reps. of Charles THRIFT, Edward E. COOKE to Avon Mill. Panel
hearing objections of damages from Henry CLAGGETT: James
CROSS, John MOSS, John M. WILSON, Amos BEALES, Horatio
BALL, Gustavus ELGIN, John CARR, Levi G. EWERS, John
LITTLETON, James GARRISON, Joseph HILLIARD, John A.
McCORMICK. They agree with original viewers on road location.

3W:314   Date: 23 Dec 1830   RtCt: 12 Sep 1831
Edward DOWLING of Ldn to Ebenezer GRUBB Sr. of Ldn. B/S of 187a on W side of Short Hill adj Christian MILLER, John POTTS dec'd, David POTTS. Delv. to John SMITH 18 Oct 1853.

3W:317   Date: 3 Sep 1831   RtCt: 6 Sep 1831
Jacob WALTMAN & wife Mary of Ldn to Ishmael VANHORN of Ldn. B/S of 115a adj John COMPHER, Frederick COOPER, Geo. BAKER, __ WILLIAMS, Catocton Creek. Wit: Samuel DAWSON, George W. SHAWEN. Delv. pr order 4 Jul 1832.

3W:320   Date: __ 1828   RtCt: 21 Sep 1831
Sarah ELLZEY of Ldn to Eliza D. PEYTON of Ldn. B/S of 83a (within lines of 1000a Ashton patent in case of Henry A. ASHTON agst Lewis ELLZEY & Sarah ELLZEY etc). Wit: L. ELLZEY, V. PEYTON, Isaiah CHAPPEL, Wm. W. ELLZEY.

3W:322   Date: 28 Jul 1831   RtCt: 23 Sep 1831
Levin M. POWELL & wife Virginia Augusta to Cuthbert POWELL. B/S of 201a (dev. by grandfather Levin POWELL dec'd) adj Joseph LEWIS, James RUST, Ann & Sarah FAIRFAX, __ SEATON. Wit: Jno. M. BROWE?, Daniel TAGGERT, Jno. ROBERTS. Ackn. in FredVa. Delv. to C. POWELL __.

3W:326   Date: 22 Mar 1831   RtCt: Sep 1831
Isaiah B. BEANS & wife Elizabeth d/o Thomas MOSS dec'd of Ldn to Samuel BEANS of Ldn. B/S of 104a Lot #3 in div. of estate of Thomas MOSS dec'd. Wit: Presley CORDELL, Craven OSBURN.

3W:329   Date: 2 Apr 1831   RtCt: 23 Sep 1831
Robert SINGLETON & wife Jane of Fqr to William FLETCHER of Fqr. B/S of und. share (prch share from Joshua SINGLETON and also 1/4th of 1/7th of share of Allen SINGLETON, and 2/6th of 1/7th purchased from shares of Agness SINGLETON and Ellen MILLER late SINGLETON of Ky, and his own 1/6th of 17th share totaling 72a) of 290a of Samuel SINGLETON dec'd on Ashby's Gap turnpike road below Goose Creek Bridge (mansion house in Fqr, most of land in Ldn).

3W:332   Date: 29 Aug 1831   RtCt: 27 Sep 1831
Samuel BEANS & wife Pleasant of Ldn to Isaiah B. BEANS of Ldn. B/S of 104a (dev. to Elizabeth BEANS w/o Isaiah from father Thomas MOSS dec'd and cnvy/b Isaiah to Samuel Mar 1831). Wit: Craven OSBURN, Mortimer McILHANY.

3W:335   Date: 14 May 1831   RtCt: 28 Sep 1831
Mary SCOTT of Ldn to John CONARD Sr. of Ldn. B/S of 1a adj CONARD. Delv. pr order filed DBk 3X:167, 16 May 1833.

3W:337   Date: 6 Sep 1831   RtCt: 5 Oct 1831
Samuel DUNKIN & wife Ann(a) of Ldn to Moses BROWN of Ldn. B/S of 124a on S fork of Beaverdam adj SW side of Union, Gurley REEDER, Jacob SILCOTT, __ COWGILL, __ KEENE, __ BROWN.

Wit: Benjamin GRAYSON, Edward HALL. Delv. to Jno. L. GILL pr order 2 Oct 1838.

3W:340   Date: 15 Sep 1831   RtCt: 7 Oct 1831
Yeoman John G. HUMPHREY & wife Mary of Ldn to Edward HALL Esqr of Ldn. B/S of 95a (from trust of William VICKERS to Gourley REEDER) adj Joshua B. DUNKIN, William RICHARDS, __ SEATON, __ WORNALL, HALL. Wit: Notley C. WILLIAMS, Benjamin GRAYSON. Delv. to HALL 22 Sep 1840.

3W:342   Date: 19 Jul 1831   RtCt: 27 Sep 1831
Yeoman William RICHARDS (of John) & wife Margaret of Ldn to Edward HALL Esqr. of Ldn. B/S of 80a (from trust of William VICKERS to Francis W. LUCKETT) on S fork of Beaverdam adj Joshua DUNCAN, Hiram SEATON, Isaac PIGGOTT. Wit: A. GIBSON, Francis W. LUCKETT.

3W:345   Date: 28 Sep 1831   RtCt: 28 Sep 1831
Adam SPRING & wife Elizabeth of Ldn to John ROBINSON of Ldn. B/S of 1a (prch/o Samuel CLAPHAM) adj Jacob SMITH, Henry GOODHEART, Henry STONEBURNER, Peter FRY, George BEAMER. Wit: William ELLZEY, John H. McCABE. Delv. to ROBINSON 13 Aug 1832.

3W:347   Date: 19 Feb 1831   RtCt: 12 Sep 1831
Jacob STOUSBERGER to Henson MARLOW. B/S of 98a (from trust of Apr 1822 by Edward MARLOW, DBk EEE:187 for debt to John STOUSBERGER Exor of Conrod SHAFFER dec'd, trust paid in full, land sold to Henson).

3W:349   Date: 9 Jan 1827   RtCt: 24 Sep 1831
Wilson C. SELDEN & wife Mary B. of Ldn to Evelyn Bird DOUGLAS (wd/o Patrick H. DOUGLAS dec'd), Patrick H. DOUGLAS, William Byrd DOUGLAS and Evelyn DOUGLAS (ch/o Patrick H. dec'd) and George LEE of Ldn. B/S of 217a (cnvy/b Richard H. HENDERSON trustee of Richard H. LOVE Apr 1817, DBk VV:186, and now part of suit of George LEE agst Evelyn B. DOUGLAS). Wit: W. C. SELDEN Jr., Samuel M. EDWARDS.

3W:351   Date: 10 May 1831   RtCt: 28 Sep 1831
Israel PARSONS & wife Anne and Margaret COXE of Ldn to Robert COCKRELL of Ldn. B/S of 1/11th interest in real estate (cnvy/b John BLAIR) of Ebenezer WILSON dec'd to dau. Nancy COX m/o Anne PARSONS; adj heirs of Thomas HOUGH, Jacob SHUTT, Jesse EVANS, COCKRELL. Wit: Ebenezer GRUBB, John WHITE. Delv. to COCKERELL 7 Apr 1836.

3W:354   Date: 14 Sep 1831   RtCt: 29 Sep 1831
Elizabeth HUNSERLING/HINSERLING wd/o yeoman Harman HUNSERLING dec'd late of Ldn and her heirs George & wife Hester, William, Mary HINSLING and Henry CLAYCOME & wife Dolly/Dorothy all of St. Clair township, Bedford Co Pa to George

SMITH of Ldn. B/S of 1a adj Isaac BALL. Wit: John HARDMAN, Phil. BROLLIER. Delv. to Henry SNOOTS pr order 1 Jan 1849.

3W:357 Date: 13 Sep 1831 RtCt: 29 Sep 1831
Elizabeth HINSERLING wd/o Harman HINSERLING dec'd late of Ldn and her heirs George, William & Mary HINSERLING and Dolly CLAYCOME late HINSERLING of St. Clair township, Bedford Co Pa to William WIRE of Ldn. B/S of 60 sq. pole lot (cnvy/b David LOVETT Jun 1820) adj WIRE. Wit: Jos. B. AKE, John HARDMAN. Delv. to WIRE 11 Jun 1833.

3W:360 Date: 6 May 1831 RtCt: 1 Oct 1831
John F. COMBS of Ldn to John JONES of Ldn. B/S of 26 pole lot in Hllb adj heirs of Elisha JANNEY dec'd, __ HAMILTON, John JONES. Wit: John WHITE, Saml. D. LESLIE, Joseph LESLIE.

3W:362 Date: 1 Sep 1831 RtCt: 12 Sep 1831
Elizabeth JANNEY, John JANNEY and Amos JANNEY of Ldn to Michael FRY of Ldn. B/S of 40a adj FRY, Philip FRY, Amos JANNEY. Wit: Mortimer McILHANY, Geo. W. SHAWEN.

3W:365 Date: 9 May 1831 RtCt: 27 Sep 1831
Philip HUNT & wife Mary of Belmont Co Ohio, John GRIGBSY & wife Sarah of Muskingum Co Ohio, Amos WHITACRE & wife Lydia of Ldn, Daniel COCKERELL & wife Esther of Ldn and John HANDLEY & wife Hannah of Licking Co Ohio (heirs of Giles CRAVEN dec'd) to Charles TAYLOR and Timothy TAYLOR Jr. of Ldn. B/S of 79a adj Stephen WILLSON, Joel CRAVEN, Thomas NICHOLS, Isaac HOGUE, __ EVANS. Wit: Daniel HARVEY, John CAMPBELL. Thomas NICHOLS, John WHITE.

3W:369 Date: 8 Jun 1831 RtCt: 12 Sep 1831
Valentine JACOBS & wife Harriet of Ldn to Jonathan PAINTER of Ldn. B/S of 6a (former land of Peter JACOBS dec'd) adj Ebenezer GRUBB, PAINTER. Wit: Ebenezer GRUBB, John WHITE.

3W:372 Date: 19 Aug 1831 RtCt: 12 Sep 1831
John McKINLEY & wife Elizabeth M. and Willis POPE & wife Mary L. of Lauderdale Co Alabama and Sarah ELLZEY of Ldn to John BAILEY. B/S of 257 1/10tha (dev. by William ELLZEY dec'd to daus. Sarah and Lucy M. who m. Robert ARMISTEAD and died leaving daus. Elizabeth M. & Mary L. who m. John McKINLEY and Willis POPE) Delv. to BAILEY 20 Jul 1832. Wit: D. McNEIL, G. S. HOUSTON, H. A. BRAGG, Jas. BALEY Jr., Margaret BAILEY, Isaiah CHAPPEL.

3W:375 Date: 10 Oct 1831 RtCt: 10 Oct 1831
Thomas POULTON, Thomas MORRIS and Jesse ATWELL. Bond on POULTON as constable.

3W:376 Date: 10 Oct 1831 RtCt: 10 Oct 1831
Edward THOMPSON, Geo. W. HENRY and Jacob WALTMAN. Bond on THOMPSON as constable.

3W:376   Date: 9 Aug 1831   RtCt: 10 Oct 1831
David WEATHERLY. Oath as 1st Lt. of artillery in 2nd Reg, 6th Brig, 2nd Div of Va Militia.

3W:377   Date: __   RtCt: 11 Oct 1831
Elizabeth OVERFIELD dec'd wd/o Martin OVERFIELD. Division –
court order dated 20 Dec 1822; 27a Lot #1 to Stephen JANNEY;
27a Lot #2 to William BRONAUGH Guardian for Hudson
OVERFIELD; 57a Lot #3 to Joshua B. OVERFIELD. Divisors:
Jonathan EWERS, Edward B. GRADY.

3W:377   Date: 16 Sep 1831   RtCt: 10 Oct 1831
Commr. John M. HARRISON (court case for heirs of Israel LACEY
dec'd) to John P. SMART. B/S of interest of heirs of Israel LACEY
dec'd in 4100a Big Spring Mill (prch/o Charles B. BALL by LACEY &
William COOKE dec'd).

3W:378   Date: 30 Sep 1831   RtCt: 10 Oct 1831
John TAYLOR & wife Susannah of Ldn to Jacob MOCK of Ldn. B/S
of 64a (allotted from land of Jesse TAYLOR dec'd) adj William
RUSSELL. Delv. to MOCK 1 Aug 1832. Wit: John ROSE, Saml. M.
EDWARDS.

3W:379   Date: 22 Sep 1831   RtCt: 10 Oct 1831
John TOWPERMAN & wife Sarah of Ldn to Mariah HAINES of Ldn.
B/S of 15½a on S side of Goose Creek where TOWPERMAN now
lives adj Edward WILLSON, John MORAN, Peter TOWPERMAN,
Samuel DISHMAN. Wit: Abner GIBSON, Francis W. LUCKETT.
Delv. pr order 11 Apr 1836.

3W:380   Date: 29 Sep 1831   RtCt: 29 Sep 1831
William WIRE & wife Catharine of Ldn to Casper SPRING of Ldn.
B/S of 3a (prch/o Peter STUCK Jan 1813) adj Michael SOUDER,
school house lot. Wit: Wm. SLATER, Wm. SPRING. Delv. to
SPRING 5 Aug 1832.

3W:381   Date: 1 Apr 1831   RtCt: 8 Oct 1831
William MILLER & wife Maria and Joseph A. LLOYD of Ldn to
Richard H. HENDERSON of Ldn. Trust for debt to Thornton
WALKER using house & lot in Union. Wit: Edward HALL, Notley C.
WILLIAMS.

3W:382   Date: 6 Jun 1811   RtCt: 12 Aug 1811/12 Sep 1831
Isaac BROWN & wife Hester of Ldn to Elizabeth RUSSELL of Ldn.
B/S of 1½a adj Abel MARKS, John BROWN. Wit: Edward CUNARD
Jr., Mason CHAMBLIN, Humphrey WHITE, Nicholas OSBURN.

3W:383   Date: 9 Aug 1831   RtCt: 12 Sep 1831
Philip FRY of Ldn to Amos JANNEY of Ldn. Release of mortgage of
Apr 1822. Wit: James GRUBB, George RICKARD, Daniel FRY.

3W:384   Date: 4 Oct 1831   RtCt: 5 Oct 1831
Saddler Abner CARTER & wife Martha E. of Union to Henry
PLASTER Jr. of Ldn. Trust for debt to Samuel DUNKIN of Ldn using

18a (from William GALLEHER dec'd), 12a on W end of previous lot; and 1a with brick house now occupied by CARTER. Wit: Francis W. LUCKETT, Benj. GRAYSON.

3W:386 Date: 28 Sep 1831 RtCt: 29 Sep 1831
Presley COMBS of Ldn to William J. HAULEY of Ldn. Trust for debt to John HOLMES using farm and household items.

3W:386 Date: 19 Feb 1829 RtCt: 23 Sep 1831
Agnes SINGLETON and Elon MILLER late SINGLETON of Todd Co Ky to Robert SINGLETON of Ldn. PoA for moneys from Hugh SMITH Admr. of Samuel SINGLETON dec'd.

3W:387 Date: 11 Jun 1831 RtCt: 12 Sep 1831
Robert PATTERSON of Ldn to Samuel RECTOR of Ldn. Trust for debt to Thomas SQUIRES using house & 1a lot in Millville (cnvy/b William VICKERS).

3W:389 Date: 27 Sep 1831 RtCt: 5 Oct 1831
Moses BROWN & wife Ann of Ldn to George KEENE of Ldn. Trust for debt to Samuel DUNKIN using 124a adj Union (cnvy/b DUNKIN). Wit: Edward HALL, Benj. GRAYSON.

3W:390 Date: 5 Oct 1831 RtCt: 5 Oct 1831
Richard H. HENDERSON of Ldn to Samuel DUNKIN of Ldn. Release of trust of __ 182_for debt to Joseph JANNEY of AlexDC) on 80-90a.

3W:391 Date: 3 Oct 1831 RtCt: 5 Oct 1831
Robert SANFORD & wife Sarah, Augustine M. SANFORD & wife Lydia and Stacey LACEY & wife Mahala of Ldn to Addison H. CLARKE of Ldn. B/S of 165a (cnvy/b James RATTAKIN May 1811, DBk NN:218) adj James NIXON, Benjamin STEER, __ SCHOOLEY. (also see DBk OOO:232 and OOO:331). Wit: Samuel HOUGH, George W. SHAWEN. Delv. to CLARKE 5 Mar 1835.

3W:394 Date: 20 Aug 1830 RtCt: 15 Oct 1831
Petition by Philip HEATER for road through lands of George Mason CHICHESTER and his infant dau. Sarah CHICHESTER from Awbrey's or Jenkins lands on the Potomac now prop. of Philip HEATER to road leading from Taylors Town to Heaters Ferry, affecting land of HEATER, Mason CHICHESTER, Edward MARLOW dec'd now Robert RUSSELL, __ BEAMER, __ HICKMAN, __ FAWLEY. Panel: Samuel DAWSON, J. G. PAXON, George COOPER, Sanford J. RAMEY, Michael SOWDER, Jacob KERN, Casper SPRING, Jacob ARNOLD, John SOWDER, John BOMCROTS, John COMPHER & Peter FRY. Road approved.

3W:395 Date: 17 May 1830 RtCt: 15 Oct 1831
Petition by Philip HEATER for road through lands of George BEAMER from Awbrey's or Jenkins lands on the Potomac now prop. of Philip HEATER to road leading from Taylors Town to Heaters Ferry, affecting land of HEATER, Mason CHICHESTER, Edward

MARLOW dec'd now Robert RUSSELL, __ BEAMER, __ HICKMAN, __ FAWLEY. Panel: Jonas P. SCHOOLEY, Daniel STONE, John SCHOOLEY, George COOPER, Jacob WALTMAN, John HAMILTON Jr., Peter FRY, Casper SPRING, Henry RUCE, Elijah JAMES, William H. HOUGH & John BROWN. Road approved.

3W:397 Date: 17 May 1830 RtCt: 15 Oct 1831
Petition by Philip HEATER for road through lands of Robert RUSSELL from Awbrey's or Jenkins lands on the Potomac now prop. of Philip HEATER to road leading from Taylors Town to Heaters Ferry, affecting land of HEATER, Mason CHICHESTER, Edward MARLOW dec'd now Robert RUSSELL, __ BEAMER, __ HICKMAN, __ FAWLEY. Panel: Jonas P. SCHOOLEY, William H. HOUGH, John BROWN, George COOPER, Jacob WALTMAN, Elijah JAMES, John SCHOOLEY, John HAMILTON Jr., Peter FRY, Casper SPRING, Daniel STONE, Henry RUSE. Road approved.

3W:399 Date: 17 May 1830 RtCt: 15 Oct 1831
Petition by Philip HEATER for road through lands of John HICKMAN from Awbrey's or Jenkins lands on the Potomac now prop. of Philip HEATER to road leading from Taylors Town to Heaters Ferry, affecting land of HEATER, Mason CHICHESTER, Edward MARLOW dec'd now Robert RUSSELL, __ BEAMER, __ HICKMAN, __ FAWLEY. Panel: Jonas P. SCHOOLEY, Daniel STONE, John SCHOOLEY, John HAMILTON Jr., William H. HOUGH, John BROWN, George COOPER, Jacob WALTMAN, Henry RUCE, Elijah JAMES, Casper SPRING, Peter FRY. Road approved.

3W:400 Date: 17 May 1830 RtCt: 15 Oct 1831
Petition by Philip HEATER for road through lands of Jacob FAWLEY from Awbrey's or Jenkins lands on the Potomac now prop. of Philip HEATER to road leading from Taylors Town to Heaters Ferry, affecting land of HEATER, Mason CHICHESTER, Edward MARLOW dec'd now Robert RUSSELL, __ BEAMER, __ HICKMAN, __ FAWLEY. Panel: Jonas P. SCHOOLEY, William H. HOUGH, John HAMILTON Jr., Daniel STONE, Jacob WALTMAN, George COOPER, Peter FRY, Henry RUSE, John BROWN, Casper SPRING, John SCHOOLEY, Elijah JAMES. Road approved.

3W:402 Date: 12 Apr 1831 RtCt: 19 Oct 1831
Richard H. HENDERSON & wife Orra Moore of Ldn to Jesse MILLAN of Ldn. B/S of 81a (prop. of Stephen W. ROZELL dec'd which desc. from his brother Stephen C. ROZELL dec'd and exchanged between heirs Sep 1827) adj road from North fork meeting house, Philip VANSICKLE (already sold lots to Philip VANSICKLE and Pompey a man of colour). Delv. pr order 26 Oct 1836.

3W:403 Date: 11 Oct 1831 RtCt: 12 Oct 1831
Philip THOMAS & wife Sarah of Ldn to Mahlon THOMAS of Ldn. B/S of undivided ½ interest in 12a on main road from Snicker's Gap

to Lsbg (part of land prch/o James NICHOLS by Adonijah FARNSWORTH) adj Owen THOMAS; and undivided ½ interest in 12a (cnvy/b John FARNSWORTH to Joseph & Philip THOMAS) on S side of Blue Ridge adj W. L. LEE, __ WARNER, THOMAS. Wit: Notley C. WILLIAMS, Thomas NICHOLS. Delv. pr order 15 May 1838.

3W:405   Date: 7 May 1831   RtCt: 14 Nov 1831
Henry GREENWOOD & wife Margaret of Ldn to Jacob SMITH of Ldn. B/S of 13a (to Margaret as heir of Daniel STONEBURNER dec'd) and 1/9th interest in dower. Wit: Samuel DAWSON, George W. SHAWEN. Delv. to SMITH 22 Aug 1834.

3W:407   Date: 8 Oct 1831   RtCt: 27 Oct 1831
Joseph POSTON & wife Elizabeth of Ldn to Elijah PEACOCK of Ldn. B/S of 103½a now occupied by Poston adj William HOUGH, Nicholas FRANCE (cnvy/b John HOUGH to Leonard POSTON). Wit: John H. McCABE, Saml. M. EDWARDS.

3W:408   Date: 15 Oct 1831   RtCt: 15 Oct 1831
Frederick A. DAVISSON of Ldn to Joseph MORRISON of Ldn. B/S of 134a (cnvy/b Daniel COOPER Mar 1827) adj Mortimer McILHANY, James MERCHANT, John STATLER, Edward MORRISON, Joseph MORRISON. Delv. to MORRISON 27 Sep 1832.

3W:409   Date: 11 Oct 1831   RtCt: 11 Oct 1831
William ELLZEY of Ldn to Jesse NEAR of Ldn. B/S of 140a adj Philip EVERHARD, heirs of Conrod ROLLER (leased to John HACKLEROAD Mar 1806, DBk P:151). Delv. to NEAR 10 Jun 1833.

3W:410   Date: 24 Sep 1831   RtCt: 10 Oct 1831
Calvin THATCHER of Ldn to Mason CHAMBLIN of Ldn. B/S of 98a (prch/o James BRADFIELD May 1823). Delv. to CHAMBLIN 29 Jun 1838.

3W:411   Date: 6 Sep 1831   RtCt: 15 Oct 1831
Elijah PEACOCK & wife Nancy of Ldn to Joseph MORRISON and Edward MORRISON of Ldn. B/S of 3½a (part of tract of Frances McKIMIE sold to MORRISON under decree of ct). Wit: Samuel HOUGH, Mortimer McILHANY. Delv. to Jos. MORRISON 27 Sep 1832.

3W:413   Date: 14 Jul 1831   RtCt: 15 Oct 1831
Margaret McILHANY of Ldn to Mortimore McILHANY of Ldn. Gift of 29¼a Lot #18 on Blue Ridge (part of mountain land of Elizabeth McILHANY dec'd allotted to Margaret).

3W:414   Date: 10 Nov 1831   RtCt: 10 Nov 1831
John SOUDER of Ldn to Michael SOUDER of Ldn. B/S of 28a Lot #8 and 4a Catocton Mt. Lot #2 & 28a Lot #9. Wit: Michael SOUDER 1 Jul 1835.

3W:415   Date: 3 Nov 1831   RtCt: 11 Nov 1831
George RICHARDS & wife Anne B. of Ldn to Samuel M. BOSS of Ldn. B/S of interest in lot in Lsbg on NE part of King St (of Thomas JACOBS dec'd, cnvy/b Samuel C. B. McCLELLAN Sep 1823, DBk GGG:112, to BOSS and then to RICHARDS, QQQ:17). Delv. to BOSS 9 Sep 1836.

3W:416   Date: 23 Jul 1831   RtCt: 10 Nov 1831
Stephen McPHERSON & wife Cecelia of Ldn to Benjamin JACKSON of Ldn. B/S of 24a (prch/o George MARKS) on road from Drake's Mill to Bloomfield adj JACKSON, John JENKINS, Benjamin STRINGFELLOW, Thomas DRAKE. Wit: Notley C. WILLIAMS, Thomas NICHOLS. Delv. to JACKSON 22 Apr 1840.

3W:418   Date: 3 Nov 1831   RtCt: 10 Nov 1831
George MARKS & wife Mahala of Ldn to Benjamin JACKSON of Ldn. B/S of 53¼a (cnvy/b Thomas TRAYHORN Oct 1827, DBk PPP:171). Wit: Notley C. WILLIAMS, Thomas NICHOLS. Delv. to JACKSON 22 Apr 1840.

3W:419   Date: 6 Oct 1831   RtCt: 7 Nov 1831
William GIBSON & wife Sarah S. of Fqr to James BOWLES of Ldn. B/S of interest in estate of Isaac GIBSON Sr. dec'd, now in occupation of BOWLES. Delv. to BOWLES 28 Jan 1836.

3W:420   Date: 7 Apr 1831   RtCt: 7 Nov 1831
Joseph GIBSON of Ldn to James BOWLES of Ldn. B/S of interest in 12-13a from estate of Isaac GIBSON Sr. dec'd.

3W:421   Date: 5 Sep 1831   RtCt: 7 Nov 1831
Moses GIBSON & wife Betsey W. of Culpepper Co Va to James BOWLES of Ldn. B/S of interest in estate of Isaac GIBSON Sr. dec'd now occupied by BOWLES. Delv. to BOWLES 28 Jan 1836.

3W:422   Date: 27 Jul 1831   RtCt: 7 Nov 1831
Horace LUCKETT & wife Louisa A. of Ldn to Caleb N. GALLEHER of Ldn. B/S of 3a adj GALLEHER, heirs of Dennis McCARTY (part of tract cnvy/b Alfred LUCKETT Feb 1830). Wit: Robert BAILEY, Abner GIBSON. Delv. to GALLEHER 1 Aug 1836.

3W:424   Date: 24 Sep 1831   RtCt: 13 Oct 1831
Esther DANIEL, James DANIEL, Mary DANIEL and Hannah L. DANIEL (heirs of Benjamin DANIEL dec'd & wife Jane dec'd, d/o James LOVE Sr.) of Ldn to Eli PIERPOINT of Ldn. B/S of interest in estate of parents including 1/3 part of tract James LOVE Sr. prch/o James McILHANY May 1796; interest in L/L on 2 lives on 160a on N Kittocton Creek adj Thomas LOVE, James COPELAND, William RUSSELL.

3W:426   Date: 5 Nov 1831   RtCt: 5 Nov 1831
James THOMAS & wife Ann of Ldn to Edward FRANCIS of Ldn. B/S of lot in Lsbg on S side of Royal St. (prch/o Samuel M. EDWARDS

Dec 1822, DBk FFF:228). Wit: Tasker C. QUINLAN, Presley CORDELL.

3W:427   Date: 13 Oct 1831   RtCt: 14 Nov 1831
Joseph A. LLOYD of Ldn to William MILLER of Ldn. B/S of house & lot in Union (cnvy/b Thor[n]ton WALKER Apr 1831 to LLOYD & MILLER).

3W:428   Date: 27 Apr 1827   RtCt: 11 Nov 1831
Zachariah DULANEY and Noble S. BRADEN of Ldn to Samuel HOUGH of Ldn. B/S of 7a (from trust of Jan 1823 from Thomas DONALDSON) adj __ JENNERS, Nicholas MONEY. Wit: Isaac WALKER, Daniel STONE, Reed THOMPSON.

3W:429   Date: 20 Sep 1830   RtCt: 11 Nov 1831
Lydia HOUGH of Ldn to daus. Mary HOUGH & Sarah HOUGH. Gift of house & lot in Wtfd adj William NETTLE, Mary TAYLOR; and adj lot which adj R. H. HENDERSON. Wit: M. McILHANY, John WHITE. Delv. to G. W. HOUGH pr order S. HOUGH 6 Jun 1833.

3W:430   Date: 14 Oct 1831   RtCt: 28 Oct 1831
Henry Jr. PLAISTER Jr. & wife Fanny of Union and Benedict PADGET & wife Eleanor. Exchange of 31 poles of land. Wit: N. C. WILLIAMS, Francis W. LUCKETT.

3W:432   Date: 16 Apr 1830   RtCt: 14 Dec 1830
Samuel DUNKIN Sr. of Ldn to Charles L. CLOWES of Ldn. B/S of 2 brick houses & lots in Union – ½a cnvy/b George LLOYED near center of town adj. Joseph A. LOYD, Seth SMITH, John ANDERSON now occupied by Thornton WALKER and Ann TORREYSON and ¼a formerly owned by Lewis HUNT adj other lot and Samuel HAMMONTREE, Mahlon BALDWIN, Seth SMITH now occupied by William C. FULKERSON. Wit: Joseph A. LLOYD, Reuben TRIPLETT, James B. DUNKIN.

3W:433   Date: 8 Oct 1831   RtCt: 11 Oct 1831
Jesse NEER & wife Matilda and Joseph NEER of Ldn to Jacob SHRIVER, Samuel BAKER and David SHRIVER of Ldn. B/S of 135a (cnvy/b Ann NEER wd/o Conard NEER and others to Jesse & Joseph) on E side of Blue Ridge adj __ CLENDENING, __ GRUBB. Wit: John WHITE, Ebenezer GRUBB. Delv. to BAKER 7 Sep 1836.

3W:435   Date: 20 Jul 1831   RtCt: 12 Nov 1831
Sally L. MANNING of Ldn to Euphemia MANNING of Ldn. B/S of land on road from Lsbg to Hllb (from div. of Thomazin ELLZEY dec'd, Nov 1829).

3W:436   Date: 1 Apr 1831   RtCt: 14 Nov 1831
Thornton WALKER & wife Fanny of Ldn to William MILLER and Joseph A. LLOYD of Ldn. B/S of house & lot in Union (cnvy/b Craven WALKER Apr 1824). Wit: Notley C. WILLIAMS, Edward HALL.

3W:438 Date: 2 Oct 1830 RtCt: 2 Nov 1831
Thomas B. BEATTY, Polly BEATTY, Sally BEATTY & William
BEATTY all formerly of Montgomery Co Ky now of Beatholomew Co
Indianna (4 of the 5 ch/o Sarah BEATTY dec'd late TURNER a ch/o
Sarah TURNER dec'd sister of the whole blood of Thomazin
ELLZEY dec'd) to Burr W. HARRISON and Henry T. HARRISON.
B/S of interest in estate of Thomazin ELLZEY dec'd formerly of Ffx.

3W:439 Date: 19 Oct 1831 RtCt: 19 Oct 1831
Peter OATYER of Ldn to Elijah KENT of Ldn. LS of house & lot in
Lsbg at Loudoun & Air St. Wit: Saml. M. EDWARDS.

3W:440 Date: 3 Sep 1831 RtCt: 14 Oct 1831
Philip THOMAS & wife Sarah of Ldn to heirs of Joseph THOMAS
dec'd of Ldn. B/S of interest in land of Owen THOMAS dec'd on
Goose Creek nr blue [ridge] mt. adj Sarah NIXON, now in
possession of Martha THOMAS. Wit: Craven OSBURN, Thomas
NICHOLS.

3W:442 Date: 9 May 1831 RtCt: 12 Oct 1831
Charles P. JOHNSTON (s/o Dennis McCarty JOHNSTON) of BaltMd
late of AlexDC to Charles LEWIS. B/S of 111a of Dennis M.
JOHNSTON dec'd nr Gumsprings (died intestate leaving children
Charles P. JOHNSTON, John D. JOHNSTON, Sarah M.
JOHNSTON, & Alexander M. JOHNSTON and Sarah departed
interstate without children, then Alexander died leaving no children
and willed his land to Elizabeth McKENZIE w/o Alex'r. who later
cnvy/t Charles P. & John D. JOHNSTON and John D. cnvy/t Charles
P.) Wit: Newton KEENE, Jon'a SHILLABER.

3W:444 Date: 2 May 1831 RtCt: 12 Oct 1831
John D. JOHNSTON of AlexDC to Charles P. JOHNSTON late of
AlexDC now of BaltMd. B/S of interest in 111a of Dennis M.
JOHNSTON (see above deed). Wit: Robert FULTON, Thos. M.
DAVIS, Thos. BUTTS.

3W:445 Date: 15 Aug 1827 RtCt: 17 Aug 1831
Ct. Commrs. Humphrey PEAKE and George WISE to James
NEWTON of Ldn. B/S of 56a Lot #11 (part of lands of late Ricketts &
Newton) on Goose Creek. Wit: Jas. HANSBOROUGH Sr., Rich. H.
LOVE, David RICKETTS.

3W:446 Date: 16 Jun 1831 RtCt: 15 Oct 1831
Sup. Ct. of Winchester Marshall John S. MAGILL to U. S. Bank. B/S
of 464a (originally from father of BRONAUGH's wife in case of John
W. BRONAUGH agst William S. MOORE Admr of Samuel G.
GRIFFITH dec'd; deed from BRONAUGH to GRIFFETH Jan 1814)
on Potomac River & Sugar Land Run. Delv. to Bank 22 Aug 1835.

3W:447 Date: 8 Sep 1831 RtCt: 15 Nov 1831
Sup. Ct. of Winchester Marshall John S. MAGILL to Wilson C.
SELDON Jr., James L. McKENNA, Johnston CLEVELAND and

William MERSHON. B/S of 1344 (case of Thomas GRIGGS Admr of Elizabeth LEE dec'd agst Ludwell LEE) below Goose Creek.

3W:450   Date: 10 Oct 1831   RtCt: 11 Nov 1831
George RICHARDS and John ROSE. Bond on RICHARDS as Treasurer of Literary Fund.

3W:450   Date: 5 Nov 1831   RtCt: 5 Nov 1831
Peter BENEDUM of Ldn to Samuel M. EDWARDS of Ldn. Trust for debt to Sarah YANTES of Ldn using farm animals, farm and household items. Wit: Erasmus G. HAMILTON. Delv. to EDWARDS 19 Feb 1835.

3W:451   Date: 7 Oct 1831   RtCt: 8 Oct 1831
James L. HAMILTON of Ldn to John H. BENNETT of Ldn. Release of trust for debt to Charles B. HAMILTON using interest in estate of father. Wit: Saml. C. CLARK, Jas. SINCLAIR, H. R. MATHIAS.

3W:452   Date: 26 Sep 1831   RtCt: 31 Oct 1831
Ann CROSBY, Martha MERVINE late WALKER and John SNYDER & wife Elizabeth late SNYDER to Johns HOPKINS of PhilPa. PoA for legacies from John G. HUMPHREY Exor of widow Jane HUMPHREY dec'd.

3W:454   Date: 14 Oct 1831   RtCt: 15 Oct 1831
Eleanor PEERS of Ldn to John JANNEY of Ldn. Trust for debt to Elizabeth WILSON of Charles Co Md using house & lot in Lsbg occupied as tavern by PEERS. Delv. 24 Aug 1834.

3W:455   Date: 15 Oct 1831   RtCt: 15 Oct 1831
Joseph MORRISON of Ldn to John WRIGHT of Ldn. Trust for debt to Frederick A. DAVISON using 134a cnvy/b DAVISON. Delv. to Jos. LESLIE pr order 11 Mary 1840.

3W:456   Date: 10 Oct 1831   RtCt: 11 Oct 1831
John G. HUMPHREY & wife Mary of Ldn to Silas GARRETT of Ldn. Trust for debt to Joshua GREGG using 117a and 80a (dev. from father Abner HUMPHREY dec'd) adj Bloomfield. Wit: Notley C. WILLIAMS, Thomas NICHOLS. Delv. to GARRETT 5 Apr 1837.

3W:458   Date: 10 Oct 1831   RtCt: 12 Oct 1831
Yeoman Silas GARRETT & wife Jemima of Ldn to Thomas HATCHER of Ldn. Trust for debt to yeoman Joshua GREGG using 48¾a. Wit: Notley C. WILLIAMS, Thomas NICHOLS. Delv. to GREGG 13 Feb 1840.

3W:460   Date: 24 Sep 1831   RtCt: 24 Sep 1831
Samuel HOUGH to James McILHANY. Trust for debt to Andrew GRAHAM using 184a on Beaverdam Creek adj William H. HOUGH, Elijah PEACOCK, heirs of Michael COOPER; and 60a nr Wtfd adj Dr. John H. McCABE, Quaker meeting house, heirs of Asa MOORE. Delv. to GRAHAM ___.

3W:462 Date: 20 Apr 1829 RtCt: 15 Oct 1831
William ELLZEY of Ldn to Burr W. HARRISON and John T. M.
HARRISON. ELLZEY soon to marry Rebecca PAGE wd/o Carter B.
PAGE late of RichVa – Rebecca's property put in trust. Delv. to
ELLZEY 29 Sep 1832.

3W:465 Date: 11 Oct 1831 RtCt: 11 Oct 1831
Jacob SHRYVER, David SHRYVER and Samuel BAKER & wife
Sarah of Ldn to Burr W. HARRISON and Thos. ROGERS of Ldn.
Trust for debt to William ELLZEY using 135a cnvy/b Jesse NEAR,
etc. Oct 1831. Delv. to ELLZEY 1 Oct 1832.

3W:467 Date: 25 Oct 1831 RtCt: 29 Oct 1831
Joseph POSTON of Ldn to John HAMILTON of Ldn. PoA for debts
on eastern side of the Alleghany Mt.

3W:468 Date: 11 Jun 1830 RtCt: 14 Nov 1831
Sheriff William B. HARRISON to Thornton WALKER. B/S of house &
lot in Union (from insolvent debtor). Wit: Wm. WILKENSON,
Stephen McPHERSON, Jas. ROGERS.

3W:469 Date: 13 Oct 1831 RtCt: 17 Oct 1831
Perrin WASHINGTON to Thornton F. OFFUTT. Trust for debt to
Thomas DRAKE using ¼a in Snickersville and slaves Jenny,
Charity, Cynthia, Jane, Fanny, William & infant.

3W:471 Date: 30 Sep 1831 RtCt: 25 Oct 1831
George LEE & wife Sarah M. of Ldn to Samuel M. BOSS of Ldn.
Trust for debt to John C. LYON of Ldn using 300a (derived from
father George LEE dec'd) now occupied by William MILLS & James
SOLOMON; and 72a adj James L. McKENNA, __ DOUGLAS, __
CLEVELAND, Church Road. Wit: John H. McCABE, Saml. M.
EDWARDS.

3W:474 Date: __ 1831 RtCt: 15 Sep 1831
William KING to Tacey DANIEL wd/o Joseph DANIEL dec'd.
Marriage contract – Tacey's rights to estate of father Thomas
HUMPHREY dec'd put in trust with John M. YOUNG.

3W:475 Date: 31 Oct 1831 RtCt: 14 Nov 1831
William HOGE (Exor of Isaac NICHOLS dec'd) to Thomas M.
JONES or Henry PLASTER Jr. Release of trust of Apr 1828 for debt
to Isaac NICHOLS Sr.

3W:476 Date: 3 Sep 1811 RtCt: 17 Nov 1831
Andrew TORBERT & wife Jane of Upper Merion township,
Montgomery Co Pa (heir of Samuel TORBERT dec'd of Ldn) to John
TORBERT. B/S of undivided 1/9th interest in 100a adj Ebenezer
Meeting House; and undivided 1/9th of 14a adj Thomas
HEREFORD. Wit: George SHANNON, Bird WILSON. Delv. to Jno.
TORBERT 29 Oct 1883.

3W:478 Date: 17 Oct 1831 RtCt: 18 Oct 1831
William H. GLASGOW & wife Ann of AlexDC to James GILMORE of Ldn. B/S of undivided interest in 2 houses & lots on King St (from father Henry GLASGOW dec'd). Wit: Tasker C. QUINLAN, Presley CORDELL.

3W:479 Date: 11 Oct 1831 RtCt: 11 Nov 1831
Jacob SHRIVER. Oath as 1st Lt. in 56th Reg Va Militia.

3W:480 Date: __ Sep 1831 RtCt: __
Josiah HALL dec'd. Division – 76a Lot #1 to Elizabeth BATEY; 90a Lot #2 to heirs of Wm. HALL dec'd; 70a Lot #3 to Saml. HALL; 101¼a Lot #4 to Elizabeth CONWELL ;100a to Mrs. BATEY. Divisors: William HOLMES, George RHODES, Joel NIXON. Gives plat.

3W:483 Date: 3 Sep 1831 RtCt: 7 Sep 1831
John W. WILLIAMS & wife Eliza of Ldn to Jonas P. SCHOOLEY of Ldn. B/S of 183a (prch/o William PAXSON by Enos WILLIAMS and divided between John W. and brother Sidnor) adj Adam HOUSHOLDER, __ BAKER, __ RAMEY. Wit: Samuel DAWSON, George W. SHAWEN.

3W:485 Date: 12 Dec 1831 RtCt: 12 Dec 1831
Peter OBRIEN. Report of alien property to his becoming a citizen: b. Cavan Co, Ireland, age 27y, nation – Great Britain and Ireland, allegiance to King of Great Britain and Ireland, migrated from Belfast Ireland, intends to settle in Ldn.

3X:001 Date: 18 Oct 1831 RtCt: 14 Nov 1831
Elijah PEACOCK & wife Ann of Ldn to Conrad BITZER. Trust for debt to Joseph POSTON using 103½a (part of tract cnvy/b John HOUGH to Leonard POSTON) adj William HOUGH, Beaverdam branch. Wit: Samuel HOUGH, George W. SHAWEN.

3X:003 Date: 28 Mar 1831 RtCt: 10 Dec 1831
Andrew BEVERIDGE to William MERSHON. Trust for debt to Nathan SKINNER using Negro boy Benjamin.

3X:005 Date: 31 Mar 1831 RtCt: 10 Dec 1831
Evan EVANS of Ldn to Presley CORDELL of Ldn. Trust for debt to William STEER of Ldn using land prch/o Noble S. BRADEN Exor. of Robert BRADEN dec'd. Wit: Nicholas OSBURN, M. PURSELL, Jno. WOLFORD.

3X:006 Date: 3 Oct 1831 RtCt: 10 Dec 1831
Archibald CARR of Ldn to Richard H. HENDERSON of Ldn. Trust for debt to John FRANCIS of Ldn using undivided 1/6th interest in 221a from father Thomas CARR dec'd. Delv. pr order 20 Oct 1833.

3X:008 Date: 12 Oct 1831 RtCt: 14 Nov 1831
Samuel DUNKIN Jr. of Ldn to Mahlon BALDWIN of Ldn. Trust for John LOVETT as security to Isaac PIGGOTT using farm animals, farm and household items. Delv. to John LOVETT 28 Jul 1832.

3X:009   Date: 27 Jul 1827   RtCt: 27 Jul 1827/17 Nov 1831
Amos BEALES & wife Elizabeth of Ldn to David LOVETT of Ldn.
Trust for debt to John TEMPLER of Ldn using 105a (cnvy/b David
BEALES) adj James GREE[N]LEASE, Benjamin WHITE. Wit: Wm.
J. JONES, Roberdeau ANNIN, Alfred A. ESKRIDGE, John
McCORMICK, John SIMPSON.

3X:012   Date: 28 Nov 1831   RtCt: 28 Nov 1831
Jonathan MILBURN & wife Sarah of Ldn to Thomas ROGERS of
Ldn. Trust for debt to Elijah HOLMES of Ldn using 15a (dev. by
Benjamin SAUNDERS to dau. Sarah). Wit: Presley CORDELL, John
H. McCABE. Delv. to ROGERS 1 Sep 1836.

3X:014   Date: 14 Apr 1831   RtCt: 12 Dec 1831
George W. SHAWEN of Ldn to Charles B. HAMILTON Jr. of Ldn.
Trust for benefit of his wife Jane SHAWEN using interest in estate of
John HAMILTON dec'd f/o Jane. Wit: John GRUBB, G. W.
BROUNAKER.

3X:015   Date: 12 Nov 1831   RtCt: 17 Nov 1831
Caroline Grayson McCARTY of Ldn to John SMARR of Ldn. B/S of
part of 8a (undivided from father Dennis McCARTY dec'd) adj
Snickers Gap turnpike rd. Wit: Archibald CARR, Thomas JOICE,
Lewis FRANCIS.

3X:016   Date: 16 Nov 1831   RtCt: 18 Nov 1831
Caroline G. McCARTY of Ldn to Richard C. McCARTY & Dennis
McCARTY of Ldn. B/S of interest in real and personal estate of
father Dennis McCARTY dec'd. Wit: Gabriel SKINNER, C. N.
GALLIHER, Jno. BAZILL.

3X:017   Date: 12 Nov 1831   RtCt: 17 Nov 1831
Caroline Grayson McCARTY to John SMARR. BoS for Negro,
horse, furniture and other items under will of father Dennis
McCARTY dec'd. Wit: Archibald CARR, Thomas JOICE, Lewis
FRANCIS.

3X:018   Date: 16 Sep 1831   RtCt: 12 Dec 1831
William HATCHER of Ldn to Aquila MEAD of Ldn. B/S of 1/10th of 1a
(from Joseph GORE Sr. dec'd) adj MEAD.

3X:020   Date: 12 Apr 1831   RtCt: 14 Nov 1831
Jesse MELLON & wife Elizabeth of Ldn to Charles WRIGHT of Ldn.
B/S of 1½a on road from north fork meeting house to Jesse
ATWELL (prch/o Abraham SKILLMAN, DBk KKK:178). Wit: Saml.
M. EDWARDS, Hamilton ROGERS.

3X:022   Date: 1 Aug 1831   RtCt: 6 Dec 1831
George MARKS & wife Mahala of Ldn to Thomas FRED of Ldn. B/S
of 198a adj Benjamin JACKSON, road to Drake's Mill, Mathias HAN.
Wit: Notley C. WILLIAMS, Edward HALL. Delv. to FRED 18 Oct
1832.

3X:025 Date: 10 Oct 1831 RtCt: 15 Nov 1831
Joshua GREGG & wife Lydia of Ldn to Silas GARRETT of Ldn. B/S of 48¾a adj Stephen McPHERSON, Barton EWERS, Notley C. WILLIAMS. Wit: Notley C. WILLIAMS, Thomas NICHOLS. Delv. 28 Mar 1837.

3X:027 Date: 29 Aug 1831 RtCt: 16 Nov 1831
Sarah DONOHOE of Ldn to Phebe ROSZEL of Ldn. B/S of undivided 1/5th of 100a (from mother Mrs. Sarah ROSZEL held under will of husband Stephen ROSZELL; at Sarah's death to go to son Stephen Wesley ROSZELL who sold to brother Stephen Chilton ROSZEL who died intestate and goes to Sarah DONOHOE, Stephen George ROSZEL, Phebe ROSZEL, Nancy ROSZEL & Stephen Wesley ROSZEL). Wit: Notley C. WILLIAMS, Samuel M. EDWARDS.

3X:029 Date: 23 Jul 1831 RtCt: 1 Dec 1831
Stephen McPHERSON & wife Cecilia of Ldn to Benjamin STRINGFELLOW of Ldn. B/S of 50a adj Thomas DRAKE, McPHERSON, heirs of Abijah SANDS, STRINGFELLOW. Wit: Notley C. WILLIAMS, Thomas NICHOLS. Delv. to F. FURR Admr wwa 14 Aug 1866.

3X:032 Date: 5 Sep 1831 RtCt: 21 Nov 1831
George SLATER & wife Sarah of Ldn to John COMPHER of Ldn. B/S of 26a (Lot #7 & #8 in div. of John SLATER dec'd, Lot #8 cnvy/b to George by Anthony SLATER). Wit: Mortimer McILHANEY, George W. SHAWEN. Delv. to Wm. SLATER 24 Jul 1847.

3X:034 Date: 9 Apr 1831 RtCt: 12 Dec 1831
Robert WHITE & wife Jane of Georgetown DC to Aquilla MEAD of Ldn. B/S of 46¼a (part of land cnvy/b Thomas WHITE, 10 Nov 1827) on both sides of Blue Ridge (part in Ldn, part in FredVa) adj __ JANNEY. Wit: James GETTYS, J. HOLTZMAY.

3X:036 Date: 3 Dec 1831 RtCt: 8 Dec 1831
John J. COLEMAN to Elizabeth TIPPETT. Trust for benefit of Mary A. BURR w/o Charles BURR and after her death for Elizabeth C., John R. & Sarah B. BURR their children using 300a (prch/o Nathaniel TYLER & John FITZHUGH).

3X:038 Date: 3 Dec 1831 RtCt: 12 Dec 1831
George W. SHAWEN & wife Jane W., George W. HENRY & wife Dewanner B. and Mary B. HAMILTON of Ldn to Charles B. HAMILTON Jr. of Ldn. B/S of 200a (residue of land of home estate of John HAMILTON dec'd) on Catocton Creek adj __ MEAD. Wit: Samuel DAWSON, Saml. HOUGH. Delv. to C. B. HAMILTON 19 Nov 1833.

3X:040 Date: 9 Dec 1826 RtCt: 16 Nov 1831
Samuel NEER & wife Sarah of Ldn to Presley WIGGINGTON of Ldn. B/S of 5¾a on W side of Short Hill (part of land of heirs of

Connard NEER dec'd) adj George MILLER. Wit: Ebenezer GRUBB, John WHITE.

3X:042 Date: 16 May 1831 RtCt: 15 Nov 1831
Gerard L. W. HUNT & wife Jane of Ffx to Caleb N. GALLAHER of Ldn. B/S of 41 1/8a on N side of Snickers Gap Turnpike road (assigned Jane JOHNSON in div. of father's estate and small lot prch/o William RANDALL in 1824). Wit: Rob. RATCLIFFE, Jas. L. TRIPLETT, Edw'd. W. SIMPSON. Delv. to GALLEHER 1 Aug 1836.

3X:044 Date: 21 Nov 1831 RtCt: 28 Nov 1831
John WHITE & wife Nancy of Ldn to Mortimer McILHANY of Ldn. B/S of "Garlic Level" (Nancy's share from father James McILHANEY dec'd) adj James & Thomas WHITE, heirs of James NIXON dec'd, James ROACH, Mary RUSE, John FRYE. Wit: Ebenezer GRUBB, Samuel HOUGH.

3X:045 Date: 11 Dec 1830 RtCt: 14 Nov 1831
Noble S. BRADEN of Ldn to John MOORE of Ldn. B/S of 13½a (from trust of Feb 1825 from George SHOVER to BRADEN, sold to Robert BRADEN who died before conveyance made). Wit: J. G. PAXSON, Fleming HIXSON, Jos. A. BRADEN.

3X:047 Date: 14 Nov 1831 RtCt: 14 Nov 1831
Andrew BAUGHMAN & PETER DERRY of Ldn to Adam KARN surviving Exor of Magdalena SHOVER dec'd. Bond that BAUGHMAN (an heir) will refund to KARN to pay any debts still due. Wit: J. J. HAMILTON, Saml. S. WHITING.

3X:048 Date: 25 Nov 1831 RtCt: 29 Nov 1831
John H. BEATTY to Robert SINGLETON. Agreement to pay $10 to rent household items for 12 months.

3X:049 Date: 31 May 1831 RtCt: 12 Dec 1831
Joseph LEWIS & wife Elizabeth O. of Ldn to John GEORGE of Ldn. B/S of 101a (now in poss. of Susanna SMITH under will of her husband Jacob SMITH dec'd under assignment of L/L from George Wm. FAIRFAX to Daniel SHOEMAKER) in Piedmont adj GEORGE, Christian EVERHEART. Wit: Benjamin GRAYSON, John W. GRAYSON. Delv. to GEORGE 28 Apr 1838.

3X:051 Date: 12 Dec 1831 RtCt: 12 Dec 1831
William ELLZEY of Ldn to Horatio BALL & John B. BALL of Ldn. B/S of __a between lines of Michael SHRYOCK, Horatio BALL, TEBBS' heirs and line of George CARTER's prch/o VANPELT now occupied by William BEAVERS and Jacob MINTINGER (cnvy/b Thomas PRITCHARD Mar 1794, DBk Y:099). Delv. to Horatio & John B. BALL 25 Sep 1835.

3X:053 Date: 21 Oct 1831 RtCt: 12 Dec 1831
Gourley R. HATCHER of Fqr to William HATCHER of Ldn. B/S of 137a adj Jesse HIRST, George FAIRHURST, Yardly TAYLOR, Goose Creek meeting house (dev. by Thomas HATCHER dec'd to

Rebecca HATCHER then to heirs of Samuel HATCHER and Gourley). Delv. to Wm. 1 Mar 1834.

3X:054   Date: 29 Oct 1831   RtCt: 12 Dec 1831
David CARR & wife Susan of Ldn to John SURGHNOR of Ldn. B/S of lot on W side of King St in Lsbg adj William TAYLOR, Joseph BEARD, Thomas SAUNDERS. Wit: Wilson C. SELDEN Jr., Tasker C. QUINLAN. Delv. to SURGHNOR 27 Oct 1832.

3X:056   Date: 29 Oct 1831   RtCt: 12 Dec 1831
John SURGHNOR of Ldn to William CARR Jr. & Josiah L. DREAN of Ldn. Trust for debt to David CARR using above lot.

3X:058   Date: 12 Dec 1831   RtCt: 12 Dec 1831
Horatio BALL and John B. BALL & wife Sarah Ann of Ldn to Wm. Alexander POWELL & Henry T. HARRISON of Ldn. Trust for debt to William ELLZEY using lot cnvy/b ELLZEY 12 Dec 1831. Wit: Francis W. LUCKETT, Thomas SAUNDERS. Delv. to ELLZEY 29 Sep 1832.

3X:061   Date: 31 May 1831   RtCt: 12 Dec 1831
John GEORGE of Ldn to Joseph LEWIS of Ldn. Mortgage on 101a in Piedmont Manor now in possession of Susanna SMITH. Wit: J. GRUBB, R'd. O. GRAYSON.

3X:063   Date: 17 Dec 1831   RtCt: 20 Dec 1831
Foushee ASHBY of JeffVa to Franklin A. SWEARINGEN of Ldn. B/S of 350a (prch/b father Martin ASHBY formerly of PrWm from Edward SNIGGERS of FredVa) adj Benjamin GRAYSON, __ RUST, __ POWELL. Wit: Thos. COCKERILL, Jno. G. COCKRILL, Jno. McDONALD.

3X:065   Date: 27 Jan 1826   RtCt: 21 Dec 1831
Thomas SWANN Esqr. now of WashDC to Richard H. HENDERSON, Robert J. TAYLOR & Jesse TIMMS of Ldn. Trust for debt to George CARTER of Oatlands using 1400a nr Lsbg and slaves John commonly called John FITZHUGH a carpenter, John a carpenter, Phil, Davy a blacksmith, Sam a stone mason, Oliver, Bill, Moses, Adam, Billy, Jim SHEPPARD, Jim GARDNER, Tom OWENS, Robert, Sina, Molly, Milly, Betsey MARSHALL, Betty Patty, & Maria. Delv. to TIMMS __.

3X:069   Date: 1 Oct 1831   RtCt: 24 Dec 1831
John BAYLY of Ldn to Jonathan BEARD of Ldn. B/S of 257 1/10tha (cnvy/b John McKINLY, Willis POPE & Sarah ELLZEY Aug 1831). Delv. pr order 14 Dec 1838.

3X:072   Date: 24 Dec 1831   RtCt: 24 Dec 1831
B. HOUGH to Richard H. HENDERSON and Asa PECK. Bond for note using his house & lot in Lsbg occupied by Dr. T. MATHIAS & Hamilton R. MATHIAS.

3X:072 Date: 20 Dec 1831 RtCt: 26 Dec 1831
Richard H. HENDERSON (as Commr. in Spencer BROWN Admr. of
John BROWN dec'd agst Enos POTTS) of Ldn to Philip
VANSICKLER of Ldn. B/S of 65a. Wit: Mahlon CRAVEN, John
VANSICKLER, Hiln [Hiland] CRAVEN. Delv. to VANSICKLER 16
Jan 1838.

3X:074 Date: 3 Oct 1828 RtCt: 26 Dec 1831
Giles HAMMAT & wife Alice of Ldn to James MILLS of Ldn. B/S of
lot in Lsbg (cnvy/b Thomas R. MOTT) adj Everett SAUNDERS, Wm.
HAWKES' heirs, Wilson C. SELDEN. Wit: Presley CORDELL, John
J. MATHIAS.

3X:076 Date: 12 Dec 1831 RtCt: 30 Dec 1831
James RUST & wife Sarah of Ldn to James GARNER of Ldn. B/S of
21a adj Robert J. TAYLOR, Carolina road, GARNER. Wit: William
ELLZEY, Francis W. LUCKETT. Delv. to GARNER 20 Nov 1832.

3X:078 Date: 3 Oct 1831 RtCt: 28 Dec 1831
Samuel PALMER Jr. & wife Sarah H. of Ldn to Timothy TAYLOR Jr.
of Ldn. Trust for debt to Solomon VANVACTER of Ldn using 50a on
S side of round hill adj Joseph LODGE, Samuel PALMER Sr., Jonah
PURCEL, Joseph RICHARDSON, Joshua B. OVERFIELD. Wit:
Notley C. WILLIAMS, Thomas NICHOLS.

3X:081 Date: 28 Dec 1831 RtCt: 2 Jan 1832
Thomas J. MARLOW & wife Mary of Ldn to Benjamin JACKSON of
Ldn. B/S of 394a "Woolards tract" (beq. to Mary from grandfather
William DULIN after death of his wife) adj Jacob TODHUNTER, __
MASON, __ CLAPHAM, road to Nolands Ferry. Wit: Mortimer
McILHANEY, George W. SHAWEN. Delv. to JACKSON 31 Oct
1832.

3X:083 Date: 3 Jan 1832 RtCt: 3 Jan 1832
John INSOR & wife Mary Jane of Ldn to Josiah L. DREAN of Ldn.
Trust for Michael MORALLEE as security on bond to Samuel M.
BOSS using interest in estate of Elizabeth WOODDY dec'd.

3X:085 Date: 22 Jul 1831 RtCt: 2 Jan 1832
John WORSLEY (Exor of Charles BENNETT Jr. dec'd) of Ldn and
William HOLMES of Ldn. Articles of covenant – David LACEY dec'd
sold BENNETT 160a under decree of chancery ct. but unable to
make good title. HOLMES had purchased reversionary rights to land
from reps. of ELLZEY. WORSLEY feels impelled to bring suit agst
reps of ELLZEY for loss of interest of children James BENNETT,
Elizabeth McCOWETT or her reps. and Sydney and M. Winefred
BENNETT infants. HOLMES agrees to pay children for any loss of
land.

3X:086 Date: 1 Jan 1832 RtCt: 6 Jan 1832
Benjamin R. LACY of Ldn to Ludwell LAKE of Ldn. B/S of 250a
(cnvy/b Ann C., Mary A. B., Margaret A. & John B. HEREFORD) adj

Maj. POWELL, __ SKINNER, __ SWART. Delv. pr order 28 Jun 1833.

3X:088   Date: 10 Dec 1831   RtCt: 10 Jan 1832
Benjamin C. BROWN & wife Catharine E. late LACY (d/o Israel LACY dec'd) now of Henry Co Tn to brother Robert A. LACY now of Washington City. PoA for sale of interest in father's "Big Spring Mill" property. Delv. to Robt. A. LACY 2 Oct 1832.

3X:091   Date: 13 Dec 1825   RtCt: 9 Jan 1832
Saml. M. EDWARDS, Everett SAUNDERS & James RUST to Ldn justices. Bond on EDWARDS as committee of estate of Susanna ANSELL.

3X:092   Date: 5 Sep 1831   RtCt: 9 Jan 1832
Levi GULICK. Oath as Lt. of Infantry in 132nd Reg 6th Brig 2nd Div of Va Militia.

3X:092   Date: 19 Sep 1831   RtCt: 23 Sep 1831/10 Feb 1832
T. D. PEYTON to Richard H. HENDERSON and Charles G. ESKRIDGE of Lsbg. Trust for debt to George CARTER of Oatlands using land dev. by father Francis PEYTON dec'd adj Horace LUCKETT, James HIXSON. Wit: Jordon B. LUCK, Asa JACKSON, Jesse TIMMS. Delv. to TIMMS as directed by CARTER __.

3X:096   Date: 23 Dec 1831   RtCt: 27 Dec 1831/12 Jan 1832
Richard H. HENDERSON, Burr W. HARRISON, Jesse TIMMS & Charles G. ESKRIDGE of Ldn to James RUST of Ldn. Release of trust of 26 Dec 1831 for debt to George CARTER using 21a.

3X:097   Date: 21 Jan 1832   RtCt: 21 Jan/23 Jan 1832
John H. MCCABE & wife Margaret H. D. of Lsbg to Saml. M. EDWARDS of Lsbg. Trust for debt to Samuel M. BOSS of Lsbg using 5a adj Academy lot, Charles BINNS, road from Lsbg to Wtfd, Wm. WRIGHT's reps, 29a (prch/o Catharine DOWLING Jan 1827), 8a on King St in Lsbg adj James STEADMAN, Thomas R. SAUNDERS, Wm. HAMERLY, W. C. SELDEN, heirs of Charles B. BALL, and 20a adj Wtfd (DBk SSS:482). Wit: Wilson C. SELDEN Jr., Tasker C. QUINLAN. Delv. to BOSS 17 Jan 1833.

3X:102   Date: 25 Aug 1831   RtCt: 9 Jan 1832
Elizabeth QUEEN of Ldn to Maaziah THOMAS of Ldn. B/S of 20a (part of tanyard lot Benjamin GRAYSON prch/o Jonathan McCARTER) adj Enoch FURR Sr., Joshua FRED.

3X:104   Date: 26 Dec 1831   RtCt: 9 Jan 1832
Isaac NICHOLS (James HOGUE now dec'd, Henry S. TAYLOR as Guardian of James' children) to James RUST. Release of trust for Isaac & Samuel NICHOLS using 21a.

3X:105   Date: 6 Jun 1831   RtCt: 9 Jan 1832
Thomas W. SMITH MD of Upperville Fqr (from trust of Feb 1826 for use of Elizabeth GIBSON wd/o of John GIBSON dec'd of Ldn as

Guardian of children) to yeoman Mahlon GIBSON (s/o John dec'd) of Ldn. B/S of

3X:107   Date: 31 Dec 1831   RtCt: 9 Jan 1832
James SANDERFORD of Ldn to James McFARLAND of Ldn. BoS for household furniture. Wit: J. CAYLOR, Jno. MILLS.

3X:108   Date: 1 Jan 1832   RtCt: 14 Jan 1832
William THRIFT & wife Maria of Ldn to M. C. SHUMATE of Ldn. B/S of 140a on Secolin Run on road from Lsbg to Gumspring abt 4m S of Lsbg (cnvy/b John T. BROOKE May 1825). Wit: Hamilton ROGERS, John SIMPSON. Delv. to SHUMATE 7 Jun 1834.

3X:110   Date: 1 Jan 1832   RtCt: 14 Jan 1832
Murphey C. SHUMATE & wife Margaret to Burr W. HARRISON. Trust for debt to William THRIFT using above land. Wit: John SIMPSON, Hamilton ROGERS.

3X:114   Date: 16 Jan 1832   RtCt: 16 Jan 1832
John WILLIAMS & wife Jane of Ldn to Curtis GRUBB of Ldn. Trust for debt to Ebenezer GRUBB using 50a with fulling mill. Wit: Tasker C. QUINLAN, Saml. M. EDWARDS. Delv. to CURTIS 22 Sep 1832.

3X:116   Date: 20 Jun 1831   RtCt: 16 Jan 1832
Yeoman Gourley REEDER & wife Catharine of Ldn to yeoman Abraham VICKERS (of William) of Ldn. B/S of lots cnvy/b Richard H. HENDERSON Aug 1826 (DBk MMM:407). Wit: Francis W. LUCKETT, Edward HALL.

3X:118   Date: 16 Jan 1832   RtCt: 17 Jan 1832
Benjamin MITCHELL & wife Martha C. of Ldn to Samuel BEAVERS of Ldn. B/S of 76¾a (Lot #4 in div. of Col. Joseph LANE dec'd) subject to trust given to Christopher FRYE. Wit: Benjamin GRAYSON, Notley C. WILLIAMS. Delv. to Thomas BEAVERS Exor. of S'l. BEAVERS 16 Mar 1839.

3X:121   Date: 3 Jan 1832   RtCt: 17 Jan 1832
John LOGAN & wife Alice/Ailsey and Alfred LOGAN of Ldn to James BOWLES of Ldn. B/S of undivided interest of Alice as heir of Isaac GIBSON Jr. Wit: Cuthbert POWELL, Edward HALL. Delv. to BOWLES 28 Jan 1836.

3X:123   Date: 16 Jan 1832   RtCt: 17 Jan 1832
Benjamin MITCHELL & wife Martha C. of Ldn to Peter GREGG of Ldn. B/S of 4a wood lot adj GREGG (allotted Martha in div. of Catharine LANE dec'd). Wit: Benjamin GRAYSON, Notley C. WILLIAMS.

3X:125   Date: 4 Sep 1822   RtCt: 18 Jan 1832
Samuel SINCLAIR of Ldn to nephew Robert SINGLETON of Ldn. Gift of 130a on Goose Creek adj __CHILTON, James MONTEITH, __ TRIPLETT. At Sup. Ct. of Chancery in FredVa 9 Dec 1831, case of Robert SINGLETON vs. Joshua SINGLETON & John SINGLETON. Supoenas could not be served. Deed from Samuel

SINGLETON dec'd to Robert of Sep 1822 for 130a. Sydnor BAILEY, Uriel GLASCOCK, James RUST & John J. MATHIAS to div. land between Defts. Joshua SINGLETON, John SINGLETON, Agnes GRAY, Elizabeth YOUNG, heirs of William SINGLETON dec'd, heirs of Sally YOUNG dec'd, heirs of John SINGLETON dec'd.

3X:127   Date: 18 Mar 1830   RtCt: 19 Jan 1832
Andrew S. ANDERSON of Ldn to Gabriel VANDEVANTER of Ldn. Trust for debt to Archibald MAINS of Ldn using 86a and interest of Samuel HIXSON & wife in dower of widow of Timothy HIXSON dec'd and interest of Samuel & wife in lands of Timothy HIXSON dec'd not allotted (see DBk SSS:458). Wit: D. CONRAD.

3X:129   Date: 26 Dec 1831   RtCt: 19 Jan 1832
Albert G. WATERMAN of Ldn to James SWART of Ldn. B/S of Lot #15 in Mdbg now occupied by Thomas J. NOLAND.

3X:131   Date: 26 Feb 1830   RtCt: 19 Jan 1832
Rich'd H. HENDERSON to Mr. A. S. ANDERSON. HENDERSON sold 2½a "Meadow Lot" (not house or attached lot) formerly prop. of John MORROW now WINE for note of Js. T. GRIFFITH. Giving ANDERSON deed with general warranty.

3X:132   Date: 20 Jan 1832   RtCt: 21 Jan 1832
Samuel M. EDWARDS and Conrad BITZER to John H. McCABE and Samuel HOUGH. Release of trust of Mar 1821 (DBk CCC:367) on 80a.

3X:133   Date: 21 Jan 1832   RtCt: 21 Jan 1832
John H. McCABE & wife Margaret H. D. of Ldn to James STEADMAN of Ldn. B/S of ¼a in Lsbg. Wit: Wilson C. SELDEN Jr., Tasker C. QUINLAN. Delv. to STEADMAN 8 Apr 1834.

3X:135   Date: 6 Jan 1832   RtCt: 23 Jan 1832
Mary STOVEN (Admx of Charles J. STOVEN) of Fqr to Alexander D. LEE of Ldn. Trust for benefit of Mary and Charles James STOVEN using 215a and Henry SETTLE.

3X:137   Date: 23 Jan 1827   RtCt: 23 Jan 1832
Catherine DOWLING late McCABE of Ldn to John H. McCABE of Ldn. B/S of 29a adj Lsbg (allotted in div. Henry McCABE dec'd) adj main road from Lsbg to Wtfd, Charles BINNS.

3X:139   Date: 21 Jan 1832   RtCt: 23 Jan 1832
Richard H. HENDERSON & wife Orra Moore of Ldn to Andrew S. ANDERSON of Ldn. B/S of 2½a "Meadow Lot" former prop. of John MORROW. Wit: Wilson C. SELDEN, Francis W. LUCKETT. Delv. to F. HIXSON Admr. of A. S. ANDERSON 15 Oct 1836.

3X:141   Date: 17 Jan 1832   RtCt: 24 Jan 1832
William KING & wife Susan of Lsbg to William D. DRISH of Lsbg. B/S of lot occupied as a store by Anthoney ADDISON on King St. between John GRAY and Albert G. WATERMAN (Robert J.

TAYLOR of AlexVa has lien on lot). Wit: Samuel M. EDWARDS, Wilson C. SELDEN Jr. Delv. to DRISH 2 Oct 1832.

3X:142 Date: 24 Jan 1832 RtCt: 26 Jan 1832
Amasa HOUGH & wife Ann E. of Ldn to John SCHOOLEY of Ldn. B/S of interest in land in Ohio and interest in ground rent of lot in AlexVa from will of William HOUGH dec'd. Wit: Samuel HOUGH, Mortimer McILHANEY.

3X:145 Date: 24 Jan 1832 RtCt: 26 Jan 1832
Curtis GRUBB & wife Harriet of Ldn to William H. HOUGH of Ldn. B/S of Harriet's interest in ground rent of lot in AlexVa and land in Ohio from will of William HOUGH dec'd. Wit: Samuel HOUGH, Mortimer McILHANEY. Delv. to Wm. H. HOUGH 21 Apr 1834.

3X:147 Date: 24 Jan 1832 RtCt: 26 Jan 1832
Benjamin HOUGH & wife Elizabeth of Ldn to John SCHOOLEY of Ldn. B/S of 1/10th interest in ground rent of lot in AlexVa and land in Ohio from will of William HOUGH dec'd. Wit: Samuel HOUGH, Mortimer McILHANEY.

3X:149 Date: 24 Jan 1832 RtCt: 26 Jan 1832
Elizabeth HOUGH (d/o John HOUGH and grandd/o William HOUGH dec'd) to William H. HOUGH of Ldn. B/S of interest in ground rent of lot in AlexVa and land in Ohio from will of William HOUGH dec'd. Delv. to W. H. HOUGH 21 Apr 1834.

3X:151 Date: 28 Jul 1831 RtCt: 27 Jan 1832
Harvey HAMILTON & wife Lucina of Ldn to Stephen WILSON of Ldn. B/S of 37a on NW fork of Goose Creek adj Isaac HOGE, __ BEALL, John HOLMES. Wit: Notley C. WILLIAMS, Thomas NICHOLS.

3X:154 Date: 20 Jan 1832 RtCt: 13 Feb 1832
Thomas R. SAUNDERS of Ldn to Jesse GOVER of Ldn. B/S of lot in Wtfd on N side of Main St and E of tavern formerly occupied by Joseph TALBOTT now by John PAXSON (see DBk LLL:236). Wit: John H. McCABE, Samuel M. EDWARDS.

3X:156 Date: 25 Jan 1832 RtCt: 27 Jan 1832
Stephen WILSON & wife Hannah P. of Ldn to Thomas P. MATHEWS of BaltMd. B/S of 37a on NW fork of Goose Creek adj David F. BEALL, Isaac HOGE, John HOLMES. Wit: Notley C. WILLIAMS, Thomas NICHOLS. Delv. to MATTHEWS 11 Mar 1843.

3X:158 Date: 20 Jan 1832 RtCt: 27 Jan 1832
Thomas P. MATHEWS of BaltMd to John SMITH of Ldn. Trust for debt to Stephen WILSON of Ldn using 37a as above.

3X:160 Date: 3 Dec 1831 RtCt: 1 Feb 1832
Amos JANNEY & wife Mary Ann of Ldn to James GRUBB of Ldn. B/S of 3a on E side of Short Hill. Wit: George W. SHAWEN, S. HOUGH.

3X:163   Date: 19 Jan 1832   RtCt: 1 Feb 1832
Daniel CRIM & wife Mary of Ldn to Jacob CRIM of Ldn. B/S of 1/12th interest in dower land of Catherine CRIM wd/o Charles CRIM Sr. dec'd. Wit: Ebenezer GRUBB, Mortimer McILHANEY. Delv. pr order 7 Mar 1834.

3X:165   Date: 30 Apr 1831   RtCt: 2 Feb 1832
Craven OSBURN to Joseph LESLIE. B/S of 14a (from defaulted trusts of Oct 1829 from Samuel WILLIAMS, DBk SSS:369 and SSS:426). Wit: Jas. C. JANNEY, Joseph LYONS, Saml. D. LESLIE. Delv. to Jos. LEWIS 9 Dec 1837.

3X:167   Date: 20 Jan 1832   RtCt: 2 Feb 1832
James McILHANEY of Ldn to John H. MCCABE of Lsbg. Release of trust of Jul 1828 for debt to Robert BENTLEY using 9a nr Lsbg. Ackn. by McILHANEY from Henrico Co.

3X:169   Date: 1 Feb 1832   RtCt: 3 Feb 1832
John A. BINNS of Ldn to Aaron DAILEY of Ldn. Release of trust of May 1820 (DBk BBB:385) for debt to Isaac WRIGHT of Ldn.

3X:170   Date: 4 Feb 1832   RtCt: 4 Feb 1832
Abraham SKILLMAN of Ldn to Jesse ATWELL of Ldn. Trust for debt to Abraham SKILLMAN Sr. of Ldn using farm animals, household items.

3X:171   Date: 10 May 1828   RtCt: 6 Feb 1832
Saml. M. EDWARDS of Ldn to Saml. DAILEY of Ldn. B/S (from defaulted trust of Jan 1824 of Aaron DAILEY, DBk GGG:307) of [20a] less ½a on N side of Lsbg Turnpike Rd (cnvy/b Isaac WRIGHT to Aaron, May 1820, DBk AAA:366).

3X:173   Date: 22 Apr 1831   RtCt: 6 Feb 1832
Amos JANNEY & wife Sarah of Stark Co Ohio, Stephen JANNEY & wife Letitia, Aaron JANNEY & wife Elizabeth, John PURSELL & wife Mary, Jacob JANNEY and Rachel JANNEY of Ldn, Joseph JANNEY & wife Elizabeth of Highland Co Ohio, Amos LUPTON & wife Hannah and Elisha FAWCETT & wife Rebecca of FredVa to William LODGE of Ldn. B/S of 163a (where Joseph JANNEY dec'd formerly resided) adj Stephen JANNEY, Joseph LODGE, Laben LODGE, __ THOMAS. Wit: James DOWNING, John ROSS, John SHACKLEY, Nathaniel WALTON, Notley C. WILLIAMS, Thomas NICHOLS.

3X:180   Date: 4 Feb 1832   RtCt: 7 Feb 1832
John R. COOKE & wife Maria P. of FredVa to Alexander S. TIDBALL. Trust for debt to Farmers Bank of Va using 438a on Goose Creek. Delv. pr order 28 Sep 1833.

3X:183   Date: 15 Mar 1831   RtCt: 7 Feb 1832
Joseph T. NEWTON of Ldn to Westley S. McPHERSON of Ldn. B/S of 56a (Lot #11, prch/o Commrs. Humphrey PEAKE & Geo. WISE in 1827) on Goose Creek and Tuscarora. Delv. to grantee 16 Feb 1870.

3X:186   Date: 15 Oct 1831   RtCt: 9 Feb 1832
Samuel KENNERLY & wife Ann A. of Augusta Co Va to William L. POWELL of Lsbg. B/S of Lot #10 in Lsbg adj heirs of Enos WILDMAN dec'd, __ McCABE, __ POWELL.

3X:188   Date: 25 Mar 1829   RtCt: 9 Feb 1832
Adam JACOBS & wife Rachel of Ldn to John JACOBS of Ldn. B/S of 10a (Lot #8 in div. of Peter JACOBS dec'd) between Short Hill and Blue Ridge adj Mrs. JACOBS. Wit: Ebenezer GRUBB, John J. MATHIAS. Delv. to Jno. JACOBS 10 Mar 1835.

3X:191   Date: 14 Jan 1832   RtCt: 10 Feb 1832
Joab OSBURN & wife Martha of Ldn to Balaam OSBURN of Ldn. B/S of 127a on Goose Creek adj Leven LUCKETT. Wit: John WHITE, Mortimer McILHANEY.

3X:193   Date: 10 Feb 1832   RtCt: 10 Feb 1832
James GRUBB of Ldn to Benjamin GRUBB of Ldn. B/S of 3a (cnvy/b Amos JANNEY) on Short Hill.

3X:195   Date: 10 Feb 1832   RtCt: 10 Feb 1832
Commr. Richard H. HENDERSON of Ldn to Benjamin SHREVE Jr. of Ldn. B/S of 30a "Tuscarora Lot" (from estate of Thomas R. MOTT dec'd in ct. case) adj heirs of __ SUTHERLAND, SHREVE, James L. MARTIN. Delv. to SHREVE 9 Jun 1838.

3X:196   Date: 21 Nov 1831   RtCt: 11 Feb 1832
John WHITE & wife Nancy of Ldn to Frederick A. DAVISSON of Ldn. B/S (in trust for benefit of Margaret R. MILTON w/o Richard MILTON (formerly DAVISSON a d/o Nancy WHITE) of land on Blue Ridge mt. allotted Nancy in div. of Elizabeth McILHANEY dec'd. Wit: Ebenezer GRUBB, Saml. HOUGH. Delv. to DAVISSON 24 Nov 1837

3X:199   Date: 21 Nov 1831   RtCt: 11 Feb 1832
Taliafarro Milton McILHANY & wife Anne and John WHITE & wife Nancy of Ldn to Frederick A. DAVISSON of Ldn. B/S of (in trust as above) land adj. above land, heirs of Francis STRIBLING, Jonathan TAYLOR (from estate of Elizabeth McILHANEY that was assigned as dower to her mother Margaret McILHANEY). Wit: Ebenezer GRUBB, Samuel HOUGH. Delv. to DAVISSON 24 Nov 1837.

3X:202   Date: 9 Feb 1832   RtCt: 11 Feb 1832
Jacob SHUTT & wife Caroline, Hamilton & Lewright and Samuel D. LESLIE of Ldn to Frederick A. DAVISSON of Ldn. B/S of interests in ¾a in Hllb adj heirs of Elisha JANNEY on main road (cnvy/b Jesse EVANS Mar 1817 to Samuel D. LESLIE, then to Thomas LESLIE Jan 1820, dev. by will of Thomas dec'd to Saml.) Wit: Mortimer McILHANEY, John WHITE.

3X:206   Date: 18 Mar 1831   RtCt: 13 Feb 1832
Peter H. BAUGUS/BOGGESS to Joseph WOOD. Trust for debt to
Jesse GOVER using house & lot in Wtfd (prch/o Sandford
EDMONDS) and household items. Delv. to GOVER 23 Apr 1835.

3X:209   Date: 7 Aug 1829   RtCt: 13 Feb 1832
George MILLER & wife Mary of Ldn to Christian MILLER Sr. B/S of
6a adj swamp, William POTTS, Ebenezer GRUBB, George ABLE.
Wit: Ebenezer GRUBB, M. McILHANEY. Delv. to C. MILLER 19 Mar
1833.

3X:211   Date: 17 Sep 1831   RtCt: 13 Feb 1832
Ann BROWN of Ldn to Michael PLAISTER of Ldn. B/S of 23a adj
Henry PLAISTER, Isaac PIGGOTT, John WHITACRE. Delv. to
PLAISTER 21 Aug 1833.

3X:213   Date: 3 Dec 1831   RtCt: 13 Feb 1832
Elizabeth JACOBS of Ldn to Zedekiah KIDWELL of Ldn. B/S of 27a
adj Ebenezer GRUBB, John JACOBS, Samuel NEER, __
COCKERILL. Delv. to KIDWELL 9 Feb 1835.

3X:215   Date: 29 Dec 1831   RtCt: 13 Feb 1832
Valentine MILLER & wife Sarah of Champaign Co. Ohio to Christian
MILLER Jr. of Ldn. B/S of 8a on W side of Short Hill adj David
POTTS, __ GRUBB, __ DOWLING. Wit: Benjamin S. TAYLOR,
Anthony CONRAD. Delv. to Christian MILLER 19 Mar 1833.

3X:217   Date: 23 Jan 1832   RtCt: 13 Feb 1832
Daniel JANNEY of Ldn to William HOGUE. B/S of 109¼a (from
defaulted trust of Jun 1822 from John WINN & wife Susanna) on
Beaverdam adj Benjamin BIRDSALL, Enoch FRANCIS, __
WILKINSON.

3X:219   Date: 13 Feb 1832   RtCt: 13 Feb 1832
Thomas L. HUMPHREY, John G. HUMPHREY, Josias W. BEATTY
& Archibald CARR. Bond on Thomas L. as constable.

3X:220   Date: 8 Feb 1832   RtCt: 13 Feb 1832
James GREENLEASE of Ldn. DoE for Negro girl Emily aged abt
16y the 1st of May last, of dark or black complexion. Wit: Saml. M.
EDWARDS, Chs. G. ESKRIDGE, Chas. W. D. BINNS.

3X:221   Date: 27 Aug 1831   RtCt: 15 Feb 1832
Ruth JANNEY of Ldn to Daniel HOUSHOLDER of Ldn. B/S of 18¾a
(part of land of Amos JANNEY Sr. dec'd) adj Amos JANNEY,
HOUSHOLDER, __ FRYE.

3X:223   Date: 4 Nov 1831   RtCt: 10 Dec 1831
Edmund TYLER of Ldn to George RICHARDS of Ldn. Trust for
Daniel P. CONRAD of FredVa, William GULICK & Stephen
GARRETT of Ldn as endorsers on notes using 59a (see DBk
SS:302) and undivided interest in adj tract where his mother &
sisters now reside, and Negro man Henry a blacksmith by trade and
Negro woman Barbara. Delv. to RICHARDS 10 Jan 1843.

3X:225 Date: 13 Jan 1832 RtCt: 16 Jan/13 Feb 1832
John G. HUMPHREY, Abraham VICKERS & William RICHARDS Jr.
to Thomas HATCHER. Trust for debt to Jonah HATCHER using
107a adj Edward HALL, James WORNELL, Elizabeth MURRY
(where VICKERS now lives formerly William VICKERS' home farm).

3X:226 Date: 6 Feb 1832 RtCt: 13 Feb 1832
Burr Washington McKIM & wife Catharine to William STEER. Trust
for debt to John WINE using 2a adj William HOUGH, John HOUGH
dec'd. Wit: Daniel BOLAND, Jacob WATERS, Geo. WHITMORE.

3X:229 Date: 8 Feb 1832 RtCt: 13 Feb 1832
Jacob CARNICKLE/CARNICLE & wife Sarah of Ldn to James
HIGDON of Ldn. B/S of lot prch/o Peter BENEDUM Dec 1822 (DBk
FFF:171). Wit: Saml. M. EDWARDS, Thos. SAUNDERS.

3X:230 Date: 15 Jul 1831 RtCt: 17 Feb 1832
John BROWN of Kalamazoo Co Michigan to Isaac BROWN Sr. of
Ldn. PoA. Wit: Bazil HARRISON, Aaron BURSON.

3X:231 Date: 23 Feb 1832 RtCt: 23 Feb 1832
James GILMORE of Ldn to Robert McINTYRE of Ldn. B/S of
undivided interest of William H. GLASGOW & wife Ann in 2 houses
& lots former prop. of Henry GLASGOW f/o William on King St Lsbg
(cnvy/b GLASGOW to GILMORE Oct 1831). Delv. to McINTYRE 1
Sep 1834.

3X:233 Date: 24 Feb 1832 RtCt: 25 Feb 1832
John SURGHNOR of Ldn to Samuel M. EDWARDS of Ldn. Trust for
William W. KITZMILLER, Caleb C. SUTHERLAND, Samuel M.
BOSS, John MARTIN & Daniel G. SMITH of Ldn as endorsers using
lot in Lsbg cnvy/b Samuel RICHARDSON Nov 1822 (DBk FFF:115).
Delv. to EDWARDS 16 Dec 1836.

3X:235 Date: 1 Mar 1832 RtCt: 1 Mar 1832
Samuel DAILEY & wife Fanny to S. M. EDWARDS. Trust for debt to
Samuel M. BOSS using lot on N side of Lsbg turnpike road NW of
road from Turnpike rd to Edwards Ferry adj Dr. W. C. SELDEN, B.
SHREVE, heirs of Geo. HAMMAT. Wit: Wilson C. SELDEN Jr., John
H. McCABE. Delv. to BOSS 9 Aug 1836.

3X:238 Date: 1 Mar 1832 RtCt: 1 Mar 1832
William CARR of Ldn to Christopher FRYE of Ldn. A/L of 63 perches
(DBk FFF:362) and ½a (DBk VVV:046) (original LS from James
HEREFORD to Patrick CAVAN in Aug 1798).

3X:239 Date: 11 Feb 1831 RtCt: 2 Mar 1832
William CARR of Ldn to John FICHTER (father & trustee of Harriet
T. LYLES w/o Archibald M. LYLES of Ldn). A/L of 1a (Lot #5 which
fell to Elizabeth McKINNEY late THOMAS w/o George McKINNEY
and cnvy/t CARR). Delv. to FICHTER 26 Dec 1832.

3X:240   Date: 3 Mar 1832   RtCt: 3 Mar 1832
Evan WILKINSON & wife Sally of Ldn to William FULTON & David CARR of Ldn. Trust for debt to David P. FULTON of Ldn using ½ of tract adj CARTER & RUST (prch/o William CARR Mar 1832). Wit: Samuel M. EDWARDS, John H. McCABE.

3X:244   Date: 11 Jun 1831   RtCt: 3 Mar 1832
John G. HUMPHREY & wife Mary, Wm. RICHARDS Jr. & wife Margaret, Abraham VICKERS & wife Maria of Ldn to Elijah ANDERSON of Ldn. B/S of 31a adj Elisha POWELL, __ CARTER. Wit: Edward HALL, Francis W. LUCKETT.

3X:246   Date: [25 Feb 1832?]   RtCt: 3 Mar 1832
Former slaves Daniel COATS & Peter ALEXANDER to George W. GUNNELL. PoA to collect funds to transport. Robert GUNNELL of Ldn died 18__ and will stated slaves to be freed with expenses paid to a free state. Geo. HUNTER Jr. withdrew funds but did not pay former slaves.

3X:247   Date: 25 Feb 1832   RtCt: 5 Mar 1832
William KING & wife Susan to Samuel M. EDWARDS. Trust for Joseph HILLIARD, John THOMAS, Samuel M. BOSS & C. C. SUTHERLAND as endorsers using lot at King and Cornwell Sts Lsbg adj Robert BENTLEY and household items. Delv. to EDWARDS 1 Sep 1832.

3X:251   Date: 29 Apr 1830   RtCt: 5 Mar 1832
Jane D. WILDMAN (Admx wwa of John WILDMAN dec'd) of Ldn to Henry CLAGETT of Ldn. B/S of 144a (derived by John dec'd from father Jacob WILDMAN dec'd and deed from bros. Joseph & James WILDMAN) and 7a adj other lot (see DBk AAA:301), and 178a adj S. DONOHOE (see DBk FF:066).

3X:254   Date: 5 Mar 1832   RtCt: 5 Mar 1832
William BRADFIELD (as Commr in John CROZIER agst William PENQUITE) of Ldn to Samuel LODGE of Ldn. B/S of 254a (less 79a dower of Elizabeth HILL formerly wd/o William WOODFORD dec'd) adj Nathaniel NICHOLS, Thomas JAMES, Samuel PALMER, Joseph LODGE, Laben LODGE.

3X:255   Date: 5 Mar 1832   RtCt: 5 Mar 1832
Samuel LODGE to William BRADFIELD. Trust for debt to Commr. William BRADFIELD using above land. Delv. to BRADFIELD 11 Aug 1834.

3X:257   Date: 1 Mar 1832   RtCt: 5 Mar 1832
George W. TAYLOR & wife Ann Eliza of FredVa to James B. WHITE of Ldn. Trust for benefit of Ann Eliza using her interest in estate of father Josiah WHITE Sr. dec'd. Wit: Mortimer McILHANEY, John WHITE. Delv. to John STONE pr order 7 Feb 1838.

3X:259 Date: 19 May 1823 RtCt: 8 Mar 1832
Bernard HOUGH (Admr dbn of Patrick CAVANS dec'd) of Ldn to
Samuel M. EDWARDS of Ldn. A/L of lot LS to Wm. BLINSTON
(commonly called Wm. McCABE) Mar 1801 DBk LL:425 then sold to
EDWARDS by BLINSTON's wife Elizabeth now SPATES and son
John Thomas BLINSTON alias McCABE Feb 1821. Wit: Thomas
BIRKBY, Jno. NEWTON, Patrick McMANUS.

3X:260 Date: 6 Feb 1832 RtCt: 10 Mar 1832
John McKINLY & wife Elizabeth and Willis POPE & wife Mary L. of
Lauderdale Co Alabama to Sarah ELLZEY of Ldn. B/S of undivided
½ of 70a, 94a and 334a now in possession of Charles ELLMORE &
Andrew S. HOSKINSON (William ELLZEY Sr. dev. to daus. Lucy
Margaret ELLZEY & Saray ELLZEY as tenants in common.
Margaret m. Robert ARMSTEAD and they had Elizabeth M. now the
w/of John McKINLEY and Mary L. now w/o Willis POPE, all of
Florence Alabama, Lucy ARMSTEAD now dec'd). Wit: Danl.
McNEILE, Alex. H. WOOD, Jno. POPE. Delv. to Wm. ELLZEY 16
Sep 1833.

3X:264 Date: 20 Jun 1830 RtCt: 12 Mar 1832
Joel NICHOLS & wife Sarah of Belmont Co Ohio, Samuel PRIOR &
wife Emily of Pekaway Co Ohio, Archibald VICKERS & wife
Pleasant and Harman NICHOLS of Ldn to Craven OSBURN of Ldn.
B/S of 46a on E side of Blue Ridge (formerly of James NICHOLS
dec'd) adj __ LODGE, __ JAMES, __ MASSEY. Wit: William LONG,
Dolphin NICHOLS, Geo. NICHOLS, John BARTON, Robert WHIT,
Mic[h]ael FUNK, Levi FODDUS, Mortimer MCILHANY, John WHITE.
Delv. to Craven OSBURN 29 Nov 1836.

3X:269 Date: 10 Mar 1832 RtCt: 12 Mar 1832
Jacob STOUTSEBERGER, Samuel STOUTSEBERGER & wife
Mary of Ldn to John COMPHER of Ldn. B/S of 8a adj __
STONEBURNER and 4½a (from div. of John SLATER dec'd to son
Michael SLATER, DBk LLL:034). Wit: Samuel DAWSON, Geo. W.
SHAWEN. Delv. to Wm. SLATER coms. 24 Jul 1847.

3X:271 Date: 10 Mar 1832 RtCt: 12 Mar 1832
John COMPHER & wife Elizabeth of Ldn to William SLATER of Ldn.
Trust for debt to Jacob STOUTSENBERGER (as Commr. for sale in
case of 8 Nov Samuel STOUTSEBERGER & wife Mary late
SLATER Guardian of infant John M. SLATER ch/o Michael SLATER
dec'd agst John M. SLATER and reps. of John SLATER dec'd) using
above lots. Wit: Samuel DAWSON, George W. SHAWEN.

3X:276 Date: __ 1832 RtCt: 12 Mar 1832
Simon SHOEMAKER of Ldn to James MERCHANT of Ldn. Release
of trust of May 1827 for debt to John COOPER using 31a. Delv. to
MERCHANT 6 Jan 1834.

3X:278   Date: 1 Feb 1832   RtCt: 12 Mar 1832
Joseph LEWIS & wife Elizabeth O. of Ldn to Nathan LUFBOROUGH of DC. Trust for debt to Hamilton LUFBOROUGH of Fqr using 310a formerly occupied by Jonathan McCARTY as tenant, 80a where Andrew THOMPSON formerly lived, and 50a wood lot adj previous other lots, all which adj. Mahlon JANNEY, Michael SHAFFER, Jonathan McCARTY. Wit: Benjamin GRAYSON, Edward HALL. Delv. to Chas. LEWIS pr order 10 Dec 1832.

3X:280   Date: 17 Oct 1831   RtCt: 12 Mar 1832
Abner LODGE & wife Tamson of Belmont Co Ohio and Sarah NICHOLS of Ldn to Craven OSBURN of Ldn. B/S of 11½a Lot #12 & #13 in div. of James NICHOLS dec'd mt. land adj. Thomas JAMES, Nathaniel NICHOLS, OSBURN. Wit: Henry AMICH, Wm. LONG, Alfred YOUNG, George ALBAN, Jno. INSKEEP. Delv. to OSBURN 15 Jun 1838.

3X:283   Date: 21 Jun 1830   RtCt: 12 Mar 1832
Joseph RUSSELL & wife Nancy of Champaign Co Ohio to Aaron RUSSELL & Mahlon RUSSELL of Ldn. B/S of undivided 1/9th interest in 130a (dev. by Wm. RUSSELL dec'd f/o Joseph to Edith RUSSELL and at her death to her 9 children). Wit: John ARROWSMITH, John DAGGER.

3X:285   Date: 29 Jul 1831   RtCt: 12 Mar 1832
John SHRIVER & wife Nancy of Champaign Co Ohio to Aaron RUSSELL of Ldn. B/S of 1/9th interest in land (dev. as above to ch/o Wm.'s wife Edith) adj Hannah PARKER, Margaret McILHANY, Peter COMPHER, John JANNEY. Wit: John ARROWSMITH, Judy? B. ARROWSMITH.

3X:288   Date: 21 Feb 1832   RtCt: 12 Mar 1832
Archibald VICKERS & wife Pleasant of Ldn to Craven OSBURN of Ldn. B/S of interest in farm where Craven now resides. Wit: Mortimer McILHANEY, John WHITE.

3X:289   Date: 9 Sep 1830   RtCt: 12 Mar 1832
Mahlon RUSSELL & wife Mary Ann of Ldn to Aaron RUSSELL of Ldn. B/S of interest in land dev. by Wm. RUSSELL dec'd f/o Joseph to Edith RUSSELL and at her death to her 9 children. Wit: Mortimer McILHANEY, John WHITE.

3X:291   Date: 26 Dec 1831   RtCt: 12 Mar 1832
John INGRAM & wife Thamer of Ldn to Calvin THATCHER of Ldn. B/S of 68a where INGRAM now resides adj Henry ORAM, Jesse HOWELL, __ McILHANEY. Wit: Craven OSBURN, Joseph WORTHINGTON, Henry AMICK, Mahlon RUSSELL, Abram YOUNG, Alfred YOUNG.

3X:293   Date: __ Dec 1831   RtCt: 13 Mar 1832
Frederick COOPER dec'd. Division – Court order dated 15 Nov 1831, 10a Lot #1 to John COOPER; 22a Lot #2 to William

COOPER; 30a Lot #3 to Jacob COOPER; 30a Lot #4 to George COOPER; 47½a Lot #5 to George COOPER in his own right and from his prch/o Jacob COOPER; 32a Lot #6 to John COOPER; 28a Lot #7 & 4a wooded Lot #8 to William COOPER. Gives plats. Divisors: George VINSEL, Peter COMPHER.

3X:298 Date: 12 Mar 1832 RtCt: 12 Mar 1832
Johnston CLEVELAND, Wilson C. SELDEN Jr., Aris BUCKNER, Robert M. NEWMAN, Wm. MERSHON, Hugh SMITH, Abner GIBSON, Thomas ROGERS, Arthur ROGERS, Hamilton ROGERS, James ROGERS, Samuel ROGERS & Asa ROGERS. Bond on CLEVELAND as Sheriff to collect levies and poor rates.

3X:299 Date: 12 Mar 1832 RtCt: 12 Mar 1832
Johnston CLEVELAND, Wilson C. SELDEN Jr., Aris BUCKNER, Robert M. NEWMAN, Wm. MERSHON, Hugh SMITH, Abner GIBSON, Thomas ROGERS, Arthur ROGERS, Hamilton ROGERS, James ROGERS, Samuel ROGERS & Asa ROGERS. Bond on CLEVELAND as Sheriff to collect officers fees.

3X:301 Date: 12 Mar 1832 RtCt: 12 Mar 1832
Johnston CLEVELAND, Wilson C. SELDEN Jr., Aris BUCKNER, Robert M. NEWMAN, Wm. MERSHON, Hugh SMITH, Abner GIBSON, Thomas ROGERS, Arthur ROGERS, Hamilton ROGERS, James ROGERS, Samuel ROGERS & Asa ROGERS. Bond on CLEVELAND as Sheriff to collect taxes.

3X:302 Date: 12 Mar 1832 RtCt: 15 Mar 1832
Jonah TAVENER dec'd. Division – 113a Lot #1 to Jonathan TAVENER (3/8th share); 41a Lot #2 and 18a Lot #3 to Lott TAVENER; 51a Lot #4 to Jesse TAVENER; 56a Lot #5 with ¼a belonging to school house to Mahlon TAVENER; 53a Lot #6 to Jonah TAVENER; 50a Lot #7 to Feilding & Hannah TAVENER. Gives plat. Divisors: Thomas NICHOLS, Timothy TAYLOR Jr., Stephen McPHERSON.

3X:305 Date: 12 Mar 1832 RtCt: 12 Mar 1832
John D. SHANK, Henry PLAISTER & Joseph P. McGEATH. Bond on SHANK as constable.

3X:306 Date: 12 Mar 1832 RtCt: 12 Mar 1832
William ROSE Jr., William ROSE Sr. & James SWART. Bond on William Jr. as constable.

3X:306 Date: 12 Mar 1832 RtCt: 12 Mar 1832
Jacob WATERS, Michael EVERHEART & Emanuel WALTMAN. Bond on WATERS as constable.

3X:307 Date: 12 Mar 1832 RtCt: 12 Mar 1832
Joseph HAWKINS, Jesse TIMMS & John SIMPSON. Bond on HAWKINS as constable.

3X:307   Date: 27 Feb 1832   RtCt: 14 Mar 1832
On 12 Jul 1830 on motion of George W. HENRY, ordered that Robert RUSSELL, James McCLAIN, Samuel DAWSON & Thomas RUSSELL view way to open road from Taylor Town to Wtfd on lines between HENRY and Joshua RATCLIFFE and HENRY and Robert MOFFETT. Maj. HENRY states he would pay RATCLIFFE for his ¾a that would be inconvenienced. Panel found road should be opened. RATCLIFFE to give est. on cost of required fencing.

3X:310   Date: 6 Mar 1832   RtCt: 14 Mar 1832
Same motion as above but as related to Robert MOFFETT's costs.

3X:313   Date: 15 Mar 1832   RtCt: 15 Mar 1832
John J. MATHIAS, James L. MARTIN & Edward HAMMATT. Bond on MATHIAS as surveyor of the county.

3X:314   Date: 24 Sep 1831   RtCt: 12 Mar 1832
Samuel O'BANION & wife Frances of Ldn to Thomas B. MERSHON of Ldn. B/S of 93a adj Charles B. O'BANION, old Lsbg road. Wit: Charles LEWIS, John BAYLY.

3X:316   Date: 12 Mar 1832   RtCt: 12 Mar 1832
John H. MONROE & wife Catharine E. of Ldn to John MARTIN of Ldn. Trust for debt to Samuel M. BOSS using house & lot where MONROE now resides adj Jno. A. BINNS on S side of Loudoun St in Lsbg, and lot adj above at Back & Royal Sts now occupied by John's mother, and undivided ½ of lot on S side of Loudoun St. now occupied by Charles T. MAGILL adj. reps. of Charles B. BALL dec'd. Wit: Thomas SAUNDERS, John H. McCABE. Delv. to BOSS 25 Mar 1833.

3X:319   Date: 12 Mar 1832   RtCt: 12 Mar 1832
Hector PIERCE/PEARCE & wife Maria of Ldn to John B. YOUNG of Ldn. B/S of lot in Snickersville on W side of road from Snickersville to Lsbg N of reps. of Amos CLAYTON. Wit: Francis W. LUCKETT, John SIMPSON.

3X:320   Date: 31 Mar 1831   RtCt: 12 Mar 1832
John CARR of Ldn to William GILMORE of Ldn. B/S of 21a below Lsbg on SW side of turnpike road lately the prop. of Samuel CARR dec'd adj __ SHREVE, GILMORE.

3X:322   Date: 27 Feb 1832   RtCt: 12 Mar 1832
George C. POWELL of Ldn to George LOVE of Fqr. Trust for debt to John L. DAGG of PhilPa using Lot #26 & #32 in Mdbg. Delv. pr order 25 Jun 1834.

3X:323   Date: 13 Mar 1832   RtCt: 13 Mar 1832
Abraham SKILLMAN of Ldn to Richard H. HENDERSON, Jesse TIMMS & Burr W. HARRISON of Ldn. Trust for debt to George CARTER of Oatlands using 150a adj James CARTER, __ CAMPBELL, __ McINTYRE, Jesse MELLON, __ BROWN. Delv. to Jesse TIMMS by dir. of CARTER __.

3X:326 Date: 29 Jan 1832 RtCt: 13 Mar 1832
Notley C. WILLIAMS of Ldn to Silas GARRETT of Ldn. B/S of ¾a on old Alexandria road adj WILLIAMS, GARRETT. Wit: John GULICK, John WRIGHT, Francis A. WILLIAMS. Delv. pr order 1 Feb 1834.

3X:328 Date: 13 Mar 1832 RtCt: 13 Mar 1832
Bricklayer Henry H. HUTCHISON of Ldn to Seth SMITH of Union. Trust for Isaac PIGGOT as security for note to Michael PLAISTER using land given in trust before to SMITH to secure William HOGUE. Delv. to SMITH 16 Feb 1835.

3X:329 Date: 13 Mar 1832 RtCt: 13 Mar 1832
Daniel JANNEY & Henry S. TAYLOR of Ldn to Abraham SKILLMAN of Ldn. Release of trust for debt to George GRIMES and his assignee John IREY on 150a.

3X:340 Date: 12 Mar 1822 [32?] RtCt: 13 Mar 1832
John WADE of Ldn and John F. BARRETT of Ldn. Articles of agreement – loan of household items for use of Caroline M. E. BARRETT w/o John F. and d/o WADE.

3X:341 Date: 13 Mar 1832 RtCt: 13 Mar 1832
Joshua PANCOAST to Michael PLAISTER. Release of trust of Spring 1830 for debt to Joshua GREGG.

3X:342 Date: 6 Feb 1822 [32?] RtCt: 14 Mar 1832
Benjamin HAGERMAN & wife Violinda of Ldn to Elias LACY of Ldn. B/S of two ½a Lots #6 & #7 on Mercer St. in Aldie. Wit: Samuel SIMPSON, Elizabeth SIMPSON, Jas. SIMPSON, Danl. P. CONRAD, Robert ARMISTEAD, William NOLAND.

3X:343 Date: 1 Jan 1832 RtCt: 14 Mar 1832
Ludwell LAKE & wife Agnes of Ldn to Elias LACY of Ldn. Trust for debt to Benjamin R. LACY using 250a where LAKE now resides cnvy/b by Benj. LACY. Wit: Charles Lewis, Robert BAYLY. Delv. pr order 22 Feb 1833.

3X:346 Date: 13 Mar 1832 RtCt: 14 Mar 1832
Humphrey B. POWELL to heirs of Matthew ADAM dec'd (William F. ADAM, Martha L. DRISH late ADAM & John M. ADAM). Release of trust of Jun 1823 for debt to Samuel & Joseph HATCHER using undivided ½ of 253a (paid by Notley C. WILLIAMS who m. Susan L. ADAM wd/o of Matthew).

3X:347 Date: 1 Jan 1832 RtCt: 14 Mar 1832
Elias LACY of Ldn to Benjamin R. LACY of Ldn. B/S of Lots #6 & #7 on Mercer St. in Aldie.

3X:349 Date: 14 Mar 1832 RtCt: 15 Mar 1832
John LAMPHIER of Mdbg to Townshend McVEIGH of Ldn. Trust for debt to H. & J. H. McVEIGH using household items. Delv. pr order to F. LITTLETON 1 Feb 1834.

3X:350   Date: 10 Dec 1831   RtCt: 16 Mar 1832
Noble S. BRADEN (Exor of Robert BRADEN dec'd) of Ldn to John
CONARD of Ldn. B/S of 33a in German Settlement adj David
AXLINE, __ MARLOW, __ GRUBB. Wit: Henry WARD, John
CONARD Jr., Abner CONARD.

3X:352   Date: 31 Dec 1830   RtCt: 16 Mar 1832
Noble S. BRADEN (Exor of Robert BRADEN dec'd) of Ldn to James
TEMPLER of Ldn. B/S of 2a adj Joshua PUSEY, Archibald MAINS.
Wit: Joseph A. BRADEN, A. S. ANDERSON, Thomas PHILLIPS,
Isaac WALKER. Delv. to TEMPLER 28 Aug 1837.

3X:353   Date: 19 Jul 1831   RtCt: 16 Mar 1832
Isaac PIGGOTT & wife Rebecca of Ldn to Price JACOBS of Ldn.
B/S of 80a (see DBk TTT:252) and 61a (see DBk TTT:253). Wit:
Benjamin GRAYSON, Edward HALL. Delv. to JACOBS 21 Feb
1834.

3X:354   Date: 19 Aug 1828   RtCt: 16 Mar 1832
John WHITE, Ebenezer GRUBB & John WRIGHT of Ldn to Isaac
HOLMES of Ldn. B/S of 44a (from defaulted trust of Mar 1827 from
Nathaniel MANNING) adj bank of mill race, John WRIGHT, __
BRADEN, __ McCARTOR. Delv. to HOLMES 13 May 1833.

3X:356   Date: 11 Feb 1832   RtCt: 24 Mar 1832
William C. LUCKETT & wife Matilda of Ldn to Peter O'BRIAN of Ldn.
B/S of 11a (Lot #4 allotted Elizabeth JACOBS in div. of Hugh
FULTON dec'd, except 1½a deeded by Elizabeth now dec'd to John
VARNS). Wit: Samuel DAWSON, George W. SHAWEN. Delv. to
O'BRIEN 4 Sep 1834.

3X:358   Date: 8 Mar 1832   RtCt: 24 Mar 1832
George B. SULLIVAN (now 21y old, heir of Owen SULLIVAN dec'd
of Fqr) to Mary Francis, Nancy, Pamelia, Margaret and John J.
CURRELL (heirs of John J. CURRELL dec'd). B/S of 230a (as
cnvy/b Owen dec'd in 1829 to John J. dec'd) adj Sandford ROGERS.

3X:360   Date: 24 Mar 1832   RtCt: 24 Mar 1832
Simon SHOEMAKER (as Commr. to sell estate of George SMITH
dec'd) of Ldn to Peter COMPHER of Ldn. B/S of 1a adj __ SHAFER,
__ DAVIS. Delv. to COMPHER 28 Jan 1836.

3X:361   Date: 27 [26?] Mar 1832   RtCt: 26 Mar 1832
James GARRISON of Ldn to Thomas S. DORRELL (as trustee for
benefit of Julia Ann DORRELL w/o John M. DORRELL & her
children). B/S of household items (purchased at sale under distress
for rent made by Edith SAUNDERS).

3X:362   Date: 10 Mar 1832   RtCt: 27 Mar 1832
David REESE (as Commr. Jan 1832 in Anna GOODIN, Maria
GOODIN, John GOODIN, Susanna PIERCE, Thomas TRIBBY &
wife Deborah, Susanna POULSON, Mary POULSON, Rachel
GOODIN, Martha GOODIN, David GOODIN, Elizabeth GOODIN,

Catharine Ann GOODIN & Jonathan C. GOODIN heirs of David GOODING dec'd agst Margaret SPENCER, John TRIBBY & wife Lydia, William POULSON & Robert WHITE & wife Mary heirs of Jasper POULSON dec'd) to Anna GOODING. B/S of 40a (dower of Agnes POULSON now dec'd wd/o Jasper) abt 8m W of Lsbg & 1m N of new road called Lsbg & Snickers Gap turnpike adj GOODING, Absolom BEANS, Isabella POULSON, __ JAMES. Delv. to GOODIN 12 Sep 1844.

3X:366 Date: 12 Mar 1830 RtCt: 14 Jun 1830
Robert WYNN (f/o Elisha WYNN dec'd) to Notley C. WILLIAMS. B/S of 160a of bounty land in NE quarter of section 8 of township 9 N in range 1 W in Illinois. Wit: Geo. H. ALDER, Thomas ROGERS, James C. WILLIAMS. Delv. to WILLIAMS 10 Dec 1833.

3X:367 Date: 21 Dec 1831 RtCt: 28 Mar 1832
William WIRTS & wife Elizabeth of Botetout Co Va to John CONNARD of Va. B/S of 19a (cnvy/b Lewis P. W. BALCH) adj John ROLLER, __ BELTZ, __ RHORBACK. Delv. pr order 16 May 1833.

3X:369 Date: 23 Mar 1832 RtCt: 29 Mar 1832
Richard F. PEYTON & wife Verlinda of Ldn to Townshend McVEIGH of Ldn. B/S of 128¼a on Little River adj Hugh ROGERS, Capt. SUMMERS. Wit: Abner GIBSON, Hamilton ROGERS. Delv. to McVEIGH 24 Sep 1833.

3X:371 Date: 15 Dec 1831 RtCt: 29 Mar 1832
Price JACOBS & wife Catharine of Ldn to Catherine HEREFORD & Mary A. B. HEREFORD of Ldn. B/S of 52a (prch/o Palmer & Chamblin) adj __ HATCHER, __ KEENE, Mrs. HUMPHREY, __ BALDWIN. Wit: Benjamin GRAYSON, Francis W. LUCKETT, Edward HALL.

3X:373 Date: 28 Mar 1832 RtCt: 29 Mar 1832
Jacob VOGDES of Ldn to Daniel T. MATHIAS of Ldn. Trust for debt to Thomas LITTLETON using farm tools. Delv. to VOGDES pr order of LITTLETON 5 Dec 1832.

3X:375 Date: 2 Apr 1832 RtCt: 2 Apr 1832
Edward FRANCIS & wife Anne E. of Ldn to John HAMILTON of Ldn. B/S of 60a adj heirs of Francis McKEMMY, Charles B. HAMILTON, George SAUNDERS; and 12½a in short hill adj James McILHANEY, James NIXON (lots assigned Ann E. in div. of father James HAMILTON dec'd). Wit: John J. MATHIAS, Presley CORDELL.

3X:377 Date: 31 Mar 1832 RtCt: 2 Apr 1832
Hester DANIEL, Joseph P. GRUBB & wife Mary, James DANIEL and Hannah DANIEL of Ldn to Richard ADAMS of Ldn. B/S of 26a, 6a & 3a (lots from estate of John LOVE dec'd). Wit: Mortimer McILHANEY, John WHITE. Delv. to ADAMS 9 Feb 1835.

3X:380   Date: 3 Apr 1832   RtCt: 4 Apr 1832
William JACKSON of Ldn to Barbara DRISH of Ldn. Trust for support of wife Margaret JACKSON and son Thomas JACKSON now in his 2nd year using house & 9a (allotted to Margaret STONEBURNER from her father before her m. to JACKSON) and farm and household items.

3X:381   Date: 19 Sep 1831   RtCt: 7 Apr 1832
James William STEWART (one of 2 ch/o Rebecca STEWART who was d/o William WRIGHT dec'd formerly of Ldn) & wife Paulina of Louisville Ky to Hamilton STEWART of Pittsburg Pa. B/S of interest in real estate of William WRIGHT dec'd – lot on Market St. in Lsbg, 3a on western end of Market St., and 1½a on King & Back Sts. (from case of 1828 of Ann WRIGHT agst Isaac WRIGHT Admr. of William dec'd). Wit: J. FURGUSON, Robert H. GRAYSON. Delv. to STEWART 30 Oct 1832.

3X:384   Date: 12 Mar 1832   RtCt: 5 Apr 1832
Samuel SINCLAIR of Ldn to George SINCLAIR of Ldn. B/S of interest in 100a from father George SINCLAIR dec'd (including 10a prch/o Amos SINCLAIR dec'd).

3X:386   Date: 23 Sep 1831   RtCt: 29 Mar 1832
George RICKARD of Ldn to John J. MATHIAS of Ldn. Trust for Gideon HOUSHOLDER and Michael RICKARD as security (for George as Guardian to Mary, William, Duanah, John & Emeline Jane RICKARD his <21y children by first wife) using 140a where he now lives. Wit: H. B. POWELL, Jas. H. CHAMBLIN, B. PURSELL. Delv. to MATHIAS 28 Aug 1835.

3X:388   Date: 28 Mar 1832   RtCt: 6 Apr 1832
Henson ELLIOTT to Calvin THATCHER. Trust for debt to Joseph RICHARDSON using Negro girl Martha abt 6-7y old, Va born.

3X:389   Date: 21 Sep 1831   RtCt: 12 Nov 1831/7 Apr 1832
Mary BEVERIDGE of Ldn to Mahala BEAVERS. Gift of Negro boy George abt 9y old, and silver teaspoons. Wit: Richard VANPELT, Charles RETTICER. Delv. to BEAVERS 23 Sep 1835.

3X:390   Date: 8 Mar 1832   RtCt: 9 Apr 1832
Thomas R. SAUNDERS. Qualified as Major of 57th Reg Va Militia.

3X:390   Date: 12 Mar 1832   RtCt: 22 Mar/7 Apr 1832
John T. BARRETT of Ldn to Charles G. ESKRIDGE of Ldn. Trust for debt to John WADE of Ldn using farm animals, household items.

3X:392   Date: 27 Mar 1832   RtCt: 14 May 1832
David BEATTY the elder dec'd. Division – (ct. ordered Feb 1830 in case of William McCLURE & wife Mary Ann &c agst Mary Elizabeth BEATTY & S. Catharine BEATTY infant ch/o John BEATTY dec'd) 93a Lot #1 to heirs of John BEATTY dec'd; 33a Lot #2 & 21a Lot #4 to heirs of William BEATTY dec'd; 35a Lot #3 to Robert BEATTY.

Divisors: John J. MATHIAS, Benj. JACKSON, Alfred BELT. Gives plat.

3X:395   Date: 5 Dec 1831   RtCt: 28 Apr 1832
Charles B. HAMILTON Jr. & wife Sally C. of Ldn to Charles G. ESKRIDGE of Ldn. Trust for debt to George W. HENRY, George W. SHAWEN & Mary B. HAMILTON of Ldn using 200a with merchant and saw mill late prop. of John HAMILTON Esq. (prch/o SHAWEN & HAMILTON). Wit: Saml. DAWSON, Saml. HOUGH.

3X:398   Date: 28 Apr 1832   RtCt: 3 May 1832
Daniel T. MATHIAS & Hamilton R. MATHIAS to Samuel M. EDWARDS. Trust for debt to Daniel T. MATHIAS, Jane D. WILDMAN, Samuel STERRETT, Henry M. DOWLING, Saml. M. BOSS, Edward STONE, Enos B. CORDELL & Henry T. HARRISON using Negro woman Cintha & her child Andrew, horse, household items, bond of William FLETCHER of Culpeper.

3X:401   Date: 24 Aug 1831   RtCt: 14 Aug 1831/19 Apr 1832
John J. and Hamilton R. MATHIAS of Ldn to Wilson C. SELDEN Jr. of Ldn. Trust for debt to Henry ALLISON (rep. of Jonathan SWIFT dec'd of Madison Co Va) using 214a below Goose Creek on Rocky branch adj Ludwell LEE.

3X:403   Date: 9 May 1832   RtCt: 9 May 1832
Philip REED & wife Amanda of Ldn to Saml. E. EDWARDS of Ldn. Trust for John TOWNER as security on rent bond of Ldn using lot in Wftd from Amanda's father Levin SMALLWOOD dec'd and household items. Wit: Thomas SAUNDERS, John H. McCABE.

3X:406   Date: 18 Jun 1830   RtCt: 18 Apr 1832
Michael ARNOLD & wife Christiana to Aaron RUSSELL, Taliafarro M. McILHANEY, James WHITE (s/o Thomas), Absolam CULP & Thomas J. MARLOW (trustees of Methodist Episcopal Church). B/S of 1a (part of where ARNOLD now lives) adj John JANNEY, Peter COMPHER, to erect house of worship. Wit: Mortimer McILHANEY, John WHITE. Delv. to C. C. GAVER 21 Jul 1834.

3X:409   Date: 4 May 1832   RtCt: 4 May 1832
Archibald CARR (in jail at suit of James D. KERR & Norman R. FITZHUGH merchants) of Ldn to Thomas ROGERS of Ldn. Trust for debt to Joseph CARR of Ldn using undivided reversionary int. in 221a of Thomas CARR dec'd (f/o Arch. and Joseph) where widow Pricilla CARR resides; and 1/6th int. in pers. estate of father at death of Pricilla; int. in ½a nr Lsbg.

3X:412   Date: 10 Apr 1832   RtCt: 7 May 1832
Thomas GORE & wife Sarah of Ldn and brother Joseph GORE & wife Jane of Ldn. Partition of 274a from father Joshua GORE dec'd, 137a to each. Wit: Thomas HUGHES, Samuel P. CANBY, John J. MATHIAS, Saml. M. EDWARDS.

3X:414 Date: 3 Mar 1832 RtCt: 17 Apr 1832
John M. SACKMAN & wife Mary Elizabeth of Ldn to James B. WIGGINTON of Ldn. B/S of 2a (cnvy/b Amos JANNEY Mar 1820) adj __ GRUBB, __ HICKMAN. Wit: Mortimer McILHANEY, Geo. W. SHAWEN.

3X:416 Date: 9 Apr 1832 RtCt: 17 Apr 1832
James B. WIGGINTON & wife Sarah Ann of Ldn to William GRAHAM of Ldn. Trust for debt to John Martin SACKMAN of Ldn using above land. Wit: Mortimer McILHANEY, Geo. W. SHAWEN. Delv. to GRAHAM 10 Apr 1834.

3X:419 Date: 10 Apr 1832 RtCt: 16 Apr 1832
John J. MATHIAS to Charles G. ESKRIDGE. Trust for debt to Wilson C. SELDON Jr., Wm. KING, Daniel T. MATHIAS, Everett SAUNDERS, James L. MARTIN, Edward HAMMAT, James SINCLAIR & John MARTIN of Ldn using 3a lot & house in Lsbg adj Fayette BALL between Markett & Lafayette Sts and 14a lot on N side of Lsbg turnpike adj John CAMPBELL, Edmond J. LEE.

3X:421 Date: 20 Apr 1832 RtCt: 20 Apr 1832
William H. JACOBS & wife Catherine to John A. CARTER. Trust for debt to John STEPHENSON using Lot #57 in Lsbg. Wit: Wilson C. SELDEN, John J. MATHIAS.

3X:424 Date: 13 Apr 1832 RtCt: 13 Apr 1832
Rebecca SHAW, Sydney H. A. W. SHAW and Mary B. SHAW to Saml. M. EDWARDS. Trust for debt to Samuel M. BOSS using lot & house in Lsbg (cnvy/b father John SHAW, Apr 1819, DBk YY:005). Delv. to BOSS 25 Jul 1837.

3X:426 Date: 5 Apr 1832 RtCt: 13 Apr 1832
Abner CARTER & wife Martha E. of Ldn to Edward CARTER of Ldn. B/S of 18a adj Henry PLAISTER, Seth SMITH, William GALIHERE, 12a wood lots #2-#5, and lot on N side of main road from Union adj Joseph GARDENER, John C. GREEN. Delv. pr order 30 Nov 1832.

3X:428 Date: 18 Apr 1832 RtCt: 18 Apr 1832
William H. JACOBS of Ldn to James GARNER of Ldn. Trust for debt to William W. KITZMILLER of Ldn using lot at Loudoun & Liberty Sts in Lsbg.

3X:430 Date: 24 Mar 1832 RtCt: 13 Apr 1832
Abraham VERNON & wife Mary and Elizabeth HARLAN of Chester Co Pa to Isaac NICHOLS and John GREGG of Ldn. PoA for legacies from Daniel VERNON dec'd late of Ldn (willed ½ of estate to his brother John VERNON f/o Abraham & Elizabeth, with legacies to nephew Aaron HARLAN & his sister Sarah EDWARDS and Esther VERNON, Daniel's widow is now dead). Wit: Daniel KENT, Jas. WALTON.

3X:432 Date: 9 Apr 1832 RtCt: 17 Apr 1832
William KEYES & wife Jane of Ldn to William GRAHAM of Ldn.
Trust for debt to Henry HICKMAN of Ldn using 3a cnvy/b HICKMAN.
Wit: Mortimer McILHANEY, Geo. W. SHAWEN.

3X:435 Date: 22 Mar 1832 RtCt: 15 May 1832
Motion of 15 Nov 1831 by George CARTER to open road from
house of John MORGAN on land of CARTER to public road from
Oatland Mills to Mdbg. Stephen GARRETT, Joseph HAWKINS,
William GULICK & John SIMPSON to view the way. Wm. L.
POWELL & Wm. THRIFT to come to court to air any objections to
road going through their land. Road ordered established.

3X:437 Date: 27 Feb 1826 RtCt: 15 May 1832
Elizabeth C. COE of PrWm to Lewis P. W. BALCH of Ldn. Trust for
debt to Conrad BITZER using 42¾a with stone mill on NW fork of
Goose Creek. Wit: C. W. D. BINNS, Roberdeau ANNIN, William J.
JONES. Delv. pr order of C. BITZER 27 Jul 1832.

3X:440 Date: 12 Apr 1832 RtCt: 23 Apr 1832
Daniel SCHOOLEY & wife Sarah of Ldn to Mary McSORELY &
Elizabeth BARROTT of Ldn. B/S of 1a adj __ MASON, __ SMITH,
__ MOFFETT. Wit: Samuel HOUGH, John J. MATHIAS. Delv. pr
order 16 Oct 1849.

3X:442 Date: 7 Apr 1832 RtCt: 9 Apr 1832
Jacob SHAFER & wife Charlotte of Ldn to John WENNER of Ldn.
B/S of 16½a Lot #3 allotted Charlotte in div. of William WENNER
dec'd. Wit: Mortimer McILHANEY, Geo. W. SHAWEN. Delv. pr order
1 Aug 1834.

3X:444 Date: 17 Apr 1832 RtCt: 17 Apr 1832
William H. JACOBS & wife Catharine of Ldn to Saml. M. EDWARDS
of Ldn. Trust for debt to Jane D. WILDMAN of Ldn using house & lot
at Loudoun & Liberty Sts. Lsbg. Wit: James RUST, Presley
CORDELL.

3X:446 Date: 19 Jan 1832 RtCt: 9 Apr 1832
Gourley HATCHER & wife Mary, Caleb RECTOR & wife Mary and
Nelson GIBSON & wife Emsey F. of Fqr to Gourley REEDER of Ldn.
B/S of 3/5th interest in 120a on S fork of Beaverdam adj Price
JACOBS, heirs of. Joseph LOVETT dec'd (part of "Greenway Mill"
estate of Joseph HATCHER dec'd). Delv. to REEDER 28 Aug 1833.

3X:449 Date: 3 Oct 1831 RtCt: 13 Apr 1832
Samuel DUNKIN & wife Ann and Joshua B. DUNKIN & wife Mary
now of Ldn to sadler Abner CARTER of Union. B/S of 18a Lot #3-#5
and 12a wood lots #2-#5 in div. of William GALLEHER dec'd, and lot
on main road thru Union adj Joseph GARDNER, Dr. John C.
GREEN. Wit: Francis W. LUCKETT, Benjamin GRAYSON.

3X:452 Date: 9 Apr 1832 RtCt: 14 Apr 1832
Samuel HALL & wife Mahala Ann of Ldn to Stephen FOUTY of Ldn. B/S of 1/6th interest in 90a Lot #2 from div. of Josiah HALL dec'd (allotted to William HALL dec'd). Wit: John J. MATHIAS, Saml. M. EDWARDS. Delv. to Stephen FOUTY 28 Jan 1833.

3X:454 Date: 10 Nov 1831 RtCt: 9 Apr 1832
Edward HALL of Ldn to George W. NORRIS of Ldn. Trust for debt to John P. DULANY of Ldn using 675a where HALL resides adj DULANY, Gourley REEDER, William CHAMBLIN, Price JACOBS, Hiram SEATON, Abraham VICKERS. Wit: Jos. W. BRONAUGH, Saml. W. DeBUTTS, Jno. C. ARMISTEAD. Delv. pr order 16 Aug 1838.

3X:456 Date: 16 Feb 1832 RtCt: 25 Apr 1832
William WILLIAMSON & wife Sarah of Fqr and Burr POWELL of Ldn. Exchange of 8 Apr 1830 has incorrect courses & distances. This deed makes corrections for land part in Ldn and part in Fqr. Wit: Cuthbert POWELL, Edward HALL.

3X:460 Date: 14 Apr 1832 RtCt: 23 Apr 1832
William ALLBRITTON & wife Mary of Ldn to Benjamin HIXSON of Ldn. B/S of 23a (Lot #7 in div. of Joseph DANIELS) adj James HIXSON. Wit: Tasker C. QUINLAN, Saml. M. EDWARDS. Delv. pr order 11 Jan 1833.

3X:462 Date: 10 Oct 1831 RtCt: 23 Apr 1832
James H. BENNETT & wife Mary Amelia of Ldn to John WORSLEY (Exor of Charles BENNETT dec'd). B/S of interest in 160a of father Charles BENNETT dec'd, 900a in Wood Co, 40a-50a assessed to widow Mary BENNETT, and any rents (to discharge judgment in DC ct on Apr 1830 agst BENNETT). Wit: Edward HALL, Benjamin GRAYSON. Delv. to Elizabeth WORSLEY 29 Apr 1833.

3X:464 Date: 28 Mar 1832 RtCt: 9 Apr 1832
Martin KIZER & wife Barbara of Ldn to Samuel DAWSON of Ldn. B/S of Barbara's share of land of George RAZOR dec'd, adj Richard H. HENDERSON, George M. CHICHESTER, George PRICE, Truman GORE. Wit: William B. HARRISON, Presley CORDELL. Delv. to Chs. GASSAWAY 29 Nov 1826.

3X:467 Date: 7 Apr 1832 RtCt: 2 May 1832
Ishmael VANHORN & wife Emeline of Ldn to Daniel POTTERFIELD of Ldn. B/S of 1a in Lovettsville (cnvy/b Harvey COGSILL). Wit: Mortimer McILHANEY, Geo. W. SHAWEN. Delv. to POTTERFIELD 12 Sep 1836.

3X:469 Date: 29 Mar 1832 RtCt: 10 Apr 1832
Merchant William ALLEN & wife Elizabeth of Union to Anna WILKINSON of Ldn. B/S of 15a on N fork of Goose Creek nr mill formerly owned by Isaac NICHOLS (cnvy/b Henry ELLIS Apr 1819)

adj Elizabeth BOLEN. Wit: Benjamin GRAYSON, Edward HALL. Delv. to Seth SMITH pr order 1 Apr 1833.

3X:471 Date: 3 Aug 1831 RtCt: 28 Apr 1832
Charles BINNS & wife Hannah of Ldn to Samuel HOUGH of Ldn. B/S of 4a with saw mill (John A. BINNS dec'd sold to Jacob AXLINE who failed to pay so sold again with Charles the buyer) adj Henry RUSSELL, Jacob MOCK. Wit: John H. McCABE, Saml. M. EDWARDS.

3X:474 Date: 28 Mar 1832 RtCt: 28 Apr 1832
Thomas WHITE to Andrew HILLMAN. Release of trust of Apr 1830 for debt to George SAUNDERS assigned to Saml. NIXON using 112a.

3X:476 Date: 28 Jul 1831 RtCt: 13 Apr 1832
Caleb N. GALLEHER & wife Lucinda of Ldn to Elizabeth GARRETT of Ldn. B/S of ½a (part of land cnvy/b David ALEXANDER). Wit: John SIMPSON, Notley C. WILLIAMS.

3X:478 Date: 1 May 1832 RtCt: 8 May 1832
Conrad BITZER & wife Catharine of Ldn to grandson Conrad R. DOWELL. Gift of 135a (prch/o Joshua LLOYD with a 5a reserve) adj William BROWN, William NICHOLS, __ WALTERS. Wit: Francis W. LUCKETT, John J. MATHIAS. Delv. to BITZER 17 Mar 1834.

3X:479 Date: 1 Mar 1832 RtCt: 1 May 1832
Conrad R. DOWELL & wife Malinda of Ldn to Conrad BITZER of Ldn. B/S of 2a adj BITZER, __ BROWN. Wit: Francis W. LUCKETT, John J. MATHIAS.

3X:481 Date: 1 Mar 1832 RtCt: 12 Mar 1832
Alice WHITACRE to Amos WHITACRE. B/S of 1/9th of estate of Benjamin WHITACRE dec'd (Benj. left estate to Alice and at her death to his children, son Amos already bought interest of brother Abner). Wit: John SILCOTT, Thomas NICHOLS, Thomas TEMPLER.

3X:483 Date: 20 Apr 1832 RtCt: 25 Apr 1832
H. B. POWELL to Joseph EIDSON. B/S of 6a (from defaulted trust of Mar 1824 from Hugh WILEY & wife Jane). Wit: Burr WEEKS, Rich'd F. SIMPSON.

3X:485 Date: 10 Aug 1831 RtCt: 18 Apr 1832
Joseph HOUGH & wife Lucy of Ldn to Henry CLAGETT of Ldn. B/S of 13a adj Bernard HOUGH. Wit: Erasmus G. HAMILTON, John J. HARDING, Wilson J. DRISH.

3X:487 Date: 5 Nov 1831 RtCt: 10 Apr 1832
John JANNEY & wife Elizabeth of Ldn to Amos JANNEY of Ldn. B/S of 8a & 10a (from div. of Amos JANNEY dec'd). Wit: George W. SHAWEN, Mortimer McILHANEY. Delv. to Amos 14 Aug 1833.

3X:489   Date: 7 Apr 1832   RtCt: 23 Apr 1832
Amos JANNEY & wife Mary Ann of Ldn to Benjamin GRUBB of Ldn.
B/S of 3a on E side of Short Hill. Wit: Mortimer McILHANEY, Geo.
W. SHAWEN.

3X:491   Date: 9 Apr 1832   RtCt: 9 Apr 1832
George HAMMOND & wife Mary of Ldn to Henry ADAMS of Ldn.
B/S of 1/6th interest in farm where Elizabeth McKEMIE wd/o Francis
McKEMIE dec'd now lives. Wit: John WHITE, Ebenezer GRUBB.
Delv. to ADAMS 16 Jun 1835.

3X:494   Date: 16 Nov 1831   RtCt: 12 Mar/9 Apr 1832
Richard C. McCARTY & Dennis McCARTY of Ldn to George
TURNER of Ldn. Trust for debt to James SWART using interest in
200a of father Dennis McCARTY dec'd.

3X:495   Date: 23 Apr 1832   RtCt: 24 Apr 1832
Leonard MYRES of Ldn to Alfred McFARLAND of Ldn. Trust for
debt to Asa ROGERS using household items, tools. Delv. to
ROGERS 8 Jul 1833.

3X:497   Date: 13 Feb 1832   RtCt: 13 Feb/5 May 1832
Valentine V. PURSELL & Henry S. TAYLOR (as trustees under will
of Henry GREGG dec'd of Ldn to Samuel PURSELL. B/S of 3a adj
Abdon DILLON, heirs of Henry SMITH, Samuel IDEN.

3X:498   Date: 1 Jul 1831   RtCt: 9 Aug 1831/1 May 1832
Nathaniel Harrison FITZHUGH of Ffx to Robert HUNTER of Ldn.
B/S of 160a "Rattle Snake Den" adj HUNTER, Robert DARN, Levi
HUMMER, Benjamin BRIDGES. Wit: George CHICHESTER, Robert
DARNE, Michael HILL, Sandford COCKERILL.

3X:500   Date: 7 Nov 1831   RtCt: 12 Mar/9 Apr 1832
Amos WHITACRE of Ldn to brother Abner WHITACRE of Ldn. B/S
of interest in land of mother Alice WHITACRE, adj Stephen
WILSON. Wit: G. B. FRENCH, John SILCOTT, Tho. NICHOLS.

3X:501   Date: 13 Apr 1832   RtCt: 13 Apr 1832
Rebecca SHAW, Sydney H. A. W. SHAW, Mary B. SHAW & Saml.
M. BOSS of Ldn to John SCHOOLEY of Ldn. Bond for $250 for
debts still owed in settlement of John SHAW dec'd by Admr. John
SCHOOLEY. Delv. to SCHOOLEY 31 Jan 1833.

3X:503   Date: 10 Jun 1831   RtCt: 1 May 1832
Benjamin C. BROWN & wife Catharine E. late LACY of Henry Co Tn
to Neomi, Huldah & Ruth LACEY of Ldn. B/S of interest in estate of
Tacy LACY dec'd.

3X:504   Date: 3 Apr 1832   RtCt: 12 Apr 1832
Richard D. EMERSON of Ldn to Geo. RICHARDS of Ldn. Trust for
debt to Samuel M. BOSS of Ldn using wagons and beds.

3X:506 Date: 13 Apr 1832 RtCt: 18 Apr 1832
John J. & Hamilton R. MATHIAS of Ldn to Daniel T. MATHIAS of Ldn. BoS of mill and household items, unexpired term of mill, crops. Wit: W. C. SELDEN Jr.

3X:507 Date: 2 Apr 1832 RtCt: 25 Apr 1832
J. A. WILLIAMSON (Commr. in ct. case for trust cnvy/b Zadock LANHAM to BAILEY and BOGGESS for benefit of J. CARR dec'd) of Ldn to Vincent MOSS of Ldn. Release of trust of Mar 1813 on 192 2/3a.

3X:509 Date: 13 Apr 1832 RtCt: 19 Apr 1832
Hamilton R. MATHIAS of Ldn to Daniel T. MATHIAS of Ldn. BoS for Negro slave Sinthy & her child Andrew, horse, household items. Wit: John J. MATHIAS.

3X:510 Date: 28 Apr 1832 RtCt: 28 Apr 1832
Charles G. ESKRIDGE & Charles BINNS Sr. of Ldn to Samuel HOUGH of Ldn. Release of trust of Sep 1831 for debt to Charles BINNS using 4a with mill.

3X:510 Date: 15 May 1832 RtCt: 15 May 1832
Alexander SKINNER. Oath at Lt. of grenadiers of 132nd Reg. of Infantry 6th Brig 2nd Div of Va Militia.

3X:511 Date: 14 May 1832 RtCt: 14 May 1832
Stephen DONOHOE, Lewis J. DONOHOE & Edward HAMMAT. Bond on Stephen as constable.

3Y:001 Date: 29 May 1832 RtCt: 29 May 1832
Rebecca DULIN wd/o John DULIN dec'd of Ldn to Elizabeth KEENE w/o Newton KEENE, Alfred DULIN, James DULIN and Lydia Ann DULIN of Ldn and Francis DULIN of Muskingum Co Ohio (ch/o Rebecca and John dec'd) of Ldn. B/S of interest in estate of father Thaddeus DULIN dec'd late of Fayette Co Ky where widow (m/o John) had life estate. Delv. to N. KEENE __.

3Y:002 Date: 14 Jun 1832 RtCt: 14 Jun 1832
James CAYLOR, William MERSHON, William CRAVEN & Johnston COLEMAN. Bond on CAYLOR as constable.

3Y:003 Date: 6 __ 1832 RtCt: 11 Jun 1832
Francis E. SHREVE. Oath as 2nd Lt. in 2nd Reg of Artillery 6th Brig 2nd Div of Va Militia.

3Y:003 Date: 8 Jun 1832 RtCt: 11 Jun 1832
George C. POWELL. Oath as Capt. of Grenadiers in 132 Reg of Infantry 6th Brig 2nd Div of Va Militia.

3Y:004 Date: 21 Apr 1832 RtCt: 11 Jun 1832
Margaret HARPER. Deposition from Warren Co Ohio, states that on William GREGG will be 21y of age the 13th of Apr 1832.

3Y:004   Date: 17 May 1832   RtCt: 11 Jun 1832
John A. CARTER. Oath as Ensign in 57th Reg of Infantry 6th Brig 2nd Div of Va Militia.

3Y:005   Date: 16 May 1832   RtCt: 11 Jun 1832
William WRIGHT. Oath as Capt. in 132nd Reg of Infantry 6th Brig 2nd Div of Va Militia.

3Y:005   Date: 25 Feb 1832   RtCt: 14 May 1832
Benjamin MOORE & wife Elizabeth of Lewis Co Va to Mary SCOTT of Ldn. B/S of interest in 2a lot & 3 rood lot (share of dower lots formerly of Levi PRINCE dec'd). Delv. to SCOTT 8 Jun 1835.

3Y:007   Date: 8 Apr 1832   RtCt: 14 May 1832
Burr POWELL & wife Catharine of Ldn to Albert G. WATERMAN of PhilPa. B/S of ½a Lot #15 in Mdbg (formerly James CHANNEL now dec'd) adj Oliver DENHAM, heirs of Nancy HARRISON. Wit: Abner GIBSON, Edward HALL.

3Y:009   Date: 12 May 1832   RtCt: 14 May 1832
Charles DOUGLAS of Ldn to John BRADEN (Exor of Abiel JENNERS dec'd) of Ldn. Release of trust of Jan 1824 for debt to John GRAY. Delv. to BRADEN 27 Apr 1833.

3Y:010   Date: 12 May 1832   RtCt: 14 May 1832
James L. MARTIN of Ldn to John BRADEN (Exor of Abel JENNERS dec'd). Release of trust of Jan 1822 for debt to John MILLER of Winchester using 260a. Delv. to BRADEN 27 Apr 1833.

3Y:012   Date: 20 Dec 1831   RtCt: 14 May 1832
Jane CASSADAY of Ldn to William HOLMES of Ldn. B/S of 200a (interest from father and mother's landed estate).

3Y:014   Date: 23 Apr 1831   RtCt: 14 May 1832
Amos JANNEY & wife Sarah of Stark Co Ohio, Stephen JANNEY & wife Letitia, Aaron JANNEY & wife Elizabeth, John PURSELL & wife Mary, Rachel JANNEY & Jacob JANNEY of Ldn, Joseph JANNEY & wife Elizabeth of Highland Co Ohio, Amos LUPTON & wife Hannah and Elisha FAWCETT & wife Rebecca of FredVa to Abel JANNEY of Ldn. B/S of 45a (formerly held by Joseph JANNEY dec'd & lot of Stephen JANNEY) adj William LODGE, Nancy THOMAS, Jonathan EWERS, Joshua B. OVERFIELD. Wit: John WOSS, James DOWNING, John SHACKLEY, Nathaniel WALTON, Notley C. WILLIAMS, Thomas NICHOLS.

3Y:019   Date: 7 Apr 1832   RtCt: 14 May 1832
John GEORGE to heirs of Samuel WRIGHT dec'd. Release of trust of Mar 1822 for debt to Joseph EVERHEART Admr of Jacob EVERHEART dec'd, Emanuel WALTMAN & Joseph WALTMAN Admrs. of Jacob WALTMAN 2nd dec'd, John WENNER & Jacob WALTMAN (of Samuel) of Ldn on 131a adj William & James THOMPSON.

3Y:021 Date: 15 May 1832 RtCt: 15 May 1832
Benjamin DAVIS & wife Sarah of Ldn to John WHITE and Daniel
WHITE of Ldn. B/S of 1/5th of 214a (undivided share of Sarah late
WHITE as rep. of William WHITE dec'd) adj Levi WHITE, Isaac
HUGHES, Howell DAVIS. Wit: John SIMPSON, Presley CORDELL.
Delv. to Daniel WHITE 1 Feb 1866.

3Y:023 Date: 15 May 1832 RtCt: 15 May 1832
Commr. Thomas ROGERS (Apr 1832 Thornton F. OFFUTT agst
Elizabeth CLAYTON wd/o Amos CLAYTON dec'd and children) to
Thornton F. OFFUTT. B/S of ½a on S side of Snickers Gap turnpike
in Snickersville. Delv. to OFFUT[T] 3 Jul 1834.

3Y:025 Date: 5 May 1832 RtCt: 16 May 1832
John JANNEY (Commr. in FredVa ct of Valentine V. PURCELL vs.
John T. STEWART) to John MARTIN of Lsbg. B/S of house & lot on
Loudoun & Back St. Lsbg.

3Y:025 Date: 28 Apr 1832 RtCt: 17 May 1832
Samuel HOUGH & wife Jane G. to Henry RUSSELL of Ldn. B/S of
4a with mills (John A. BINNS dec'd sold to Jacob AXLINE who failed
to pay, then Charles BINNS purchased who sold to HOUGH) adj
Henry RUSSELL, Jacob MOCK. Wit: Mortimer McILHANY, Geo. W.
SHAWEN. Delv. to RUSSELL 13 Feb 1838.

3Y:027 Date: 19 May 1832 RtCt: 26 May 1832
Henry M. DOWLING & wife Harriet J. of Ldn to George RUST Jr. of
Jeff Va. B/S of 28a nr Lsbg (N end of land allotted to Catharine
DOWLING dec'd as rep of Henry McCABE dec'd). Wit: F. A.
DAVISON, Presley CORDELL, Samuel M. EDWARDS.

3Y:029 Date: 9 Apr 1832 RtCt: 28 May 1832
Sarah NIXON of Ldn to Thomas OSBURN of Ldn. B/S of 155a on
SE side of Blue Ridge (prch/o Joshua OSBURN Exor of Sarah
NICHOLS Ex. of Nathan NICHOLS dec'd) adj Edward CUNARD's
heirs, Joseph heirs, heirs of Philip THOMAS. Delv. to OSBURN 15
Sep 1834.

3Y:030 Date: 26 May 1832 RtCt: 29 May 1832
Archibald VICKERS & wife Pleasant of Ldn to Richard OSBURN Sr.
of Ldn. B/S of 40a (allotted Lydia MARKS now HESSER from estate
of Abel MARKS dec'd) nr foot of Blue Ridge. Wit: Saml. M.
EDWARDS, Fayette BALL. Delv. to OSBURN 5 Jun 1851.

3Y:032 Date: 17 Apr 1832 RtCt: 29 May 1832
Elisha KITCHEN of Ldn to William D'BELL of Ldn. Trust for debt to
Sheriff Johnston CLEVELAND for execution by James CAYLOR as
security using 104a on old road from Lanesville to Alexandria.

3Y:034 Date: 23 May 1832 RtCt: 29 May 1832
Commr. of Edmund J. LEE Jr. (Sup. Ct. Winchester in suit of John
LLOYD & John H. LADD & Co agst William HERBERT, John A.
WASHINGTON & Bushrod C. WASHINGTON) to John A.

WASHINGTON & Bushrod C. WASHINGTON. B/S of 245a part of Shannondale tract adj E. GRUBB, Peter DERRY, R. GRUBB, __ WORKMAN, P. BURNS. Delv. to Bushrod C. WASHINGTON 18 Apr 1833. Gives plat.

3Y:037   Date: 21 May 1832   RtCt: 29 May 1832
Frederick A. DAVISON of Ldn to Joseph LESLIE of Ldn. B/S of lot in Hllb adj LESLIE on S side of main road (cnvy/b Joseph HOUGH) Oct 1829). Wit: Saml. CLENDENING, John McCABE, John JONES. Delv. to LESLIE 1 Oct 1836.

3Y:038   Date: 29 Feb 1832   RtCt: 30 May 1832
Charles L CLOWES of Columbiana Co Ohio and wife Edith P. of Ldn to Isaac BROWN Sr. of Ldn. B/S of 2 lots with houses in Union (½a formerly occupied by George E. LLOYD on S side of main street and ¼a formerly occupied by Lewis HUNT on S side of main street). Wit: J. G. WILLIARD, Notley C. WILLIAMS, John SIMPSON.

3Y:040   Date: 30 May 1832   RtCt: 30 May 1832
Samuel Craven SINCLAIR to James SINCLAIR. Trust for debt to Alfred BELT (Exor of Charles THORNTON dec'd) using slaves Sucky & her unnamed infant child, Amanda, Maria, Ann & Henry Joe. Wit: John LITTLEJOHN. Delv. to A. BELT 19 Jul 1834.

3Y:042   Date: 31 May 1832   RtCt: 31 May 1832
George W. McCARTY of Ldn to Richard C. McCARTY, Dennis W. McCARTY & Billington McCARTY (ch/o Dennis dec'd) of Ldn. B/S of land on Goose Creek (Dec 1819 Dennis McCARTY late of Ldn cnvy/t George W. McCARTY)

3Y:043   Date: 31 May 1832   RtCt: 31 May 1832
Thomas ODEN of Ldn and Barbara DRISH wd/o William DRISH dec'd. Marriage contract – puts household items and life estate on land where she resides being a dower from former husband Jacob STONEBURNER in trust to Samuel M. EDWARDS. Barbara not to have claim to ODEN's estate after his death nor he claim to hers. Delv. to Wm. ORANGE 29 Mar 1838.

3Y:045   Date: 1 Oct 1831   RtCt: 1 Jun 1831 [32]
Aaron RUSSELL & wife Tamson, Mary Anne RUSSELL, Emily Jane RUSSELL & Edith RUSSELL of Ldn to William CLENDENING of Ldn. B/S of 133a (dev. by William RUSSELL dec'd to Edith and at her death to her 9 children, Aaron owns 7/9ths shares) adj Hannah PARKER, __ LESLIE, __ JANNEY, __ McILHANY. Wit: Mortimer McILHANY, John WHITE. Delv. to John CLENDENING Admr. of grantee 19 Nov 1855.

3Y:047   Date: 9 Apr 1832   RtCt: 1 Jun 1832
Hugh HUGHES & wife Hannah (d/o John WILSON dec'd who was s/o Ebenezer dec'd, with Asa WILLSON dec'd also a son) of Green Co Pa to William CLENDENNING of Ldn. B/S of undivided 1/20th interest in land of Ebenezer WILLSON dec'd where Hannah

WILLSON now resides between Blue Ridge and Short Hill adj Thomas HOUGH, Jacob SHUTT, Jesse EVANS, Robert COCKERILL, John CAMPBELL. Wit: Daniel HOOK, Nicholas HAGER. Delv. to CLENDENING 12 Aug 1833.

3Y:049   Date: 21 Apr 1832   RtCt: 2 Jun 1832
Margaret HARPER & Ruth GREGG of Warren Co Ohio to William GREGG Jr. of Warren Co Ohio. PoA for funds from John SCHOOLEY & George GREGG (Exors. of Wm. GREGG dec'd). Wit: Jacob AUGKE Jr., John AUGKE.

3Y:050   Date: 19 Oct 1826   RtCt: __
Dower of Catharine LANE – Lavinia & her child to John CRAINE Jr. & wife Elizabeth, Mary Ann to Catharine JETT (with her father Peter JETT as Guardian), George to Benjamin MITCHELL & wife Martha C.. Negro woman Hannah does not appear belong to Mrs. C. LANE by dower but was from death of her son Joseph LANE. Divisors: William BENTON, Abriel GLASCOCK, Thornton WALKER.

3Y:051   Date: 2 Jun 1832   RtCt: 2 Jun 1832
William GREGG Jr. of Warren Co Ohio to Robert MOFFETT of Ldn. B/S of 1/4th int. in land in Ldn where his grandfather William GREGG lived at time of his death dev. to his widow which belonged to William Jr.'s brother Rezin GREGG who died intestate. Delv. to MOFFETT __.

3Y:052   Date: 27 Jul 1831   RtCt: 4 Jun 1832
John GOWER late of Ldn died leaving estate in part to ch/o Peter GOWER Sr. his father's brother of Somerset Co Pa. John GOWER of Randolph Co Va one of the children of PETER Sr. dec'd to Jacob J. SHOVER of Somerset Co Pa. PoA. Delv. to SHOVER __.

3Y:053   Date: 5 Sep 1831   RtCt: 4 Jun 1832
John GOWER late of Ldn died leaving estate in part to ch/o Peter GOWER Sr. his father's brother of Somerset Co Pa. Jacob GOWER, Adam GOWER & Henry GOWER [Stark Co Ohio] three children of Peter Sr. dec'd to Jacob J. SHOBER of Somerset Co Pa. PoA.

3Y:055   Date: 6 Jun 1831   RtCt: 4 Jun 1832
John GOWER late of Ldn died leaving estate in part to ch/o Peter GOWER Sr. his father's brother of Somerset Co Pa. Peter GOWER Jr., Mary BROOK (late GOWER) now wd/o William BROOK of Somerset Co Pa dec'd, John CROSSING & wife Elizabeth late GOWER heirs of Peter Sr. dec'd to Jacob J. SHOBER of Somerset Co Pa. PoA.

3Y:056   Date: 1 Aug 1831   RtCt: 4 Jun 1832
John GOWER late of Ldn died leaving estate in part to ch/o Peter GOWER Sr. his father's brother of Somerset Co Pa and ch/o Nicholas GOWER late of Alleghany Co Md dec'd. Adam GOWER, Jacob GOWER, John GOWER, Peter GOWER, Sarah GOWER who m. George HENRY, Augustus KUNTZ & Elizabeth GOWER now m.

to Lewis THOMPSON reps. of Nicholas dec'd to Jacob J. SHOBER of Somerset Co Pa. PoA.

3Y:058   Date: 26 Nov 1831   RtCt: 4 Jun 1832

Jacob J. SHOVER (attorney for heirs of John GOWER dec'd – Peter GOWER, Mary BROOKE, John CROSSIN, Elizabeth CROSSIN, John GOWER, George HENRY, Augustus KUNTS, Sarah KUNTS, Daniel GOWER, Jacob GOWER, John GOWER s/o Nicholas, Adam GOWER, Peter GOWER s/o Nicholas, Lewis THOMPSON, Elizabeth THOMPSON, Adam GOWER s/o Peter GOWER Sr. dec'd, Henry GOWER & Jacob GOWER s/o Peter dec'd) to John SHOVER. B/S of 10a (cnvy/b David LOVETT) adj John MOORE, David LOVETT, George MULL.

3Y:059   Date: 2 Jun 1832   RtCt: 6 Jun 1832

Philip EVERHART of Ldn to Joseph MILLER, Gideon HOUSEHOLDER, Michael FRY, Samuel KALB, Amos JANNEY, Jesse MILLER & John BOMCROTS (trustees of Axline's Schoolhouse). B/S of 20 sq. perch lot adj David AXLINE.

3Y:061   Date: 7 Dec 1831   RtCt: 9 Apr/7 Jun 1832

Sarah LACEY wd/o David LACEY dec'd of Ldn to Charles G. ESKRIDGE of Ldn. B/S of 2a allotted her in dower (formerly owned by James THOMAS). Wit: William HEATH, Daniel MAGINNIS, Diadema PAXON. Delv. to ESKRIDGE 6 Aug 1836.

3Y:062   Date: 21 May 1831   RtCt: 7 Jun 1832

Thomas SHEARMAN and Josiah MURRAY [ackn. in Fqr] to Lewis EDMUNDS. Trust for benefit of Juliet Ann ADAMS of Ldn w/o Henry ADAMS and her children using farm animals, black child named Lucy, farm and household items.

3Y:063   Date: 21 May 1831   RtCt: 8 Jun 1832

Amos GULICK of Ldn to Howell DAVIS of Ldn. Trust for debt to Benjamin DAVIS of Ldn using interest in tract belonging to heirs of Moses GULICK dec'd and in house and 1¼a on N side of turnpike road from Snickersville to Aldie formerly owned by Moses dec'd. Delv. to H. DAVIS 8 Jun 1833.

3Y:065   Date: 28 May 1832   RtCt: 8 Jun 1832

Charles GILL & wife Dolly of Hampshire Co Va to Edward HALL of Ldn. B/S of 5a (prch/o HALL some years ago) adj Abraham VICKERS, William VICKERS, HALL. Wit: Benjamin GRAYSON, N. C. WILLIAMS.

3Y:066   Date: 1 Aug 1831   RtCt: 8 Jun 1832

Stephen McPHERSON & wife Cecelia of Va to John N. MARKS of Ldn. Trust for debt to George MARKS of Ldn using 146a adj Thomas DRAKE, road from Drake's Mill to John WHITACRE, __ HAWS. Wit: Notley C. WILLIAMS, Edward HALL.

3Y:068 Date: 1 Aug 1831 RtCt: 8 Jun 1832
Thomas FRED & wife Rachel of Ldn to John N. MARKS of Ldn.
Trust for debt to George MARKS of Ldn using 198a adj Benjamin
JACKSON, road from Drake's mill to Matthias HAN. Wit: Edward
HALL, Notley C. WILLIAMS.

3Y:070 Date: 9 Apr 1832 RtCt: 11 Jun 1832
Colen AULD of AlexDC to Charles LEWIS of Ldn. B/S of 366a nr
Gum Spring (allotted to William LYLE Jr. s/o Robert by Charles
LEWIS & Johnston CLEVELAND as Commrs). Wit: C. BINNS, Chas.
G. ESKRIDGE, E. HAMMAT. Delv. to Amos LEWIS Exor. of Chs.
LEWIS dec'd __.

3Y:072 Date: __ 1832 RtCt: 11 Jun 1832
James CROSS of Ldn to dau. Fanny w/of Robert H. COCKRAN now
residing in Ldn. Trust for benefit and under control of Fanny (and at
her death div. amongst children) Negro woman Caty aged 45 & her
2 children Armistead abt 4y and Burr aged 1-2y.

3Y:072 Date: 18 Apr 1832 RtCt: 11 Jun 1832
Marilla BROOKS w/o Chancy BROOKS of BaltMd to Frederick
BROOKS. B/S of dower rights. Wit: David B. FERGUSON, Wm.
ASHMAN. See 3W:415 for deed from BROOKS to BROOKS now
delv. N. LODGE 8 Jul 1833.

3Y:074 Date: 18 Oct 1830 RtCt: 12 Jun 1832
Aaron S. GREGG & wife Elizabeth and Mahlon S. GREGG & wife
Emily to Barton EWERS. B/S of 13a (from estate of father Joseph
GREGG dec'd) adj EWERS, Joshua GREGG. Wit: Notley C.
WILLIAMS, David HANDLEY, Thomas EWERS, Thomas NICHOLS.

3Y:076 Date: 19 Jan 1832 RtCt: 29 Jun 1832
Henry F. LUCKETT & wife Maria A. of Ldn to Jacob SUMMERS of
Ldn. B/S of 200a on Ashbys Gap turnpike rd below Mdbg adj Jesse
McVEIGH, Hugh ROGERS, Lsbg road. Wit: Wm. B. HARRISON,
Abner GIBSON. Delv. pr order 28 May 1844.

3Y:080 Date: 24 Apr 1832 RtCt: 11 Jun 1832
Anna GOODIN of Ldn to Absalom BEANS of Ldn. B/S of 13a (prch/o
Thomas TRIBBY) adj late David GOODIN, James LOVE. Wit: David
REECE, Conard BITZER, John BROWN.

3Y:081 Date: 1 Mar 1832 RtCt: 11 Jun 1832
John KILE & wife Winefred and Mary KILE wd/o John KILE dec'd of
Ldn to Elijah ANDERSON of Ldn. B/S of 44a (cnvy/b Ralph LANE
Nov 1818 to John KILE dec'd). Wit: Francis W. LUCKETT, A.
GIBSON. Delv. pr order 26 Jan 1835.

3Y:082 Date: 30 Apr 1832 RtCt: 30 Jun 1832
Burr W. HARRISON (Commr. in case of John CAMPBELL agst
Samuel CARR & John Thomas CARR heirs of Samuel CARR dec'd,
Johnston CLEVELAND Admr. of Samuel dec'd & Burr W.
HARRISON trustee & John and James POGUE) to John

CAMPBELL. B/S of 4a on Lsbg Turnpike road abt 1m E of town (sold by Samuel CARR now dec'd Feb 1827 to CAMPBELL conveying int. of Samuel & John Thomas CARR & HARRISON) adj John J. MATHIAS, Mrs. HAINS, turnpike road opposite William GILMORE where CAMPBELL now resides. Delv. 1 Nov 1838 to J. CAMMELL.

3Y:084   Date: 14 Apr 1832   RtCt: 11 Jun 1832
Daniel POTTERFIELD & wife Mary of Ldn to Thomas J. MARLOW of Ldn. Trust for debt to Ishmael VANHORN of Ldn using 1a in Lovettsville German Settlement. Wit: Luther A. THRASHER, Daniel MILLER Jr., John A. McDONAUGH, Geo. W. SHAWEN, Samuel DAWSON.

3Y:086   Date: 1 Aug 1831   RtCt: 11 Jun 1832
George MARKS & wife Mahala of Ldn to Stephen McPHERSON of Ldn. B/S of 146a adj McPHERSON, Thomas DRAKE, John WHITACRE, Barton EWERS. Wit: Notley C. WILLIAMS, Edward HALL.

3Y:088   Date: 8 Feb 1830   RtCt: 11 Jun 1832
Thomas DRAKE of Ldn to Stephen McPHERSON of Ldn. B/S of 11a adj Thomas HEREFORD, John JINKINS. Wit: Thomas FRED, Charles CARPENTER, Lewis THOMPSON.

3Y:089   Date: 4 Jan 1832   RtCt: 12 Jun 1832
Rich'd H. HENDERSON of Ldn and Thompson F. MASON of AlexDC to Charles J. CATLETT of Ldn. B/S of 200a (from defaulted trust of Apr 1826 from Samuel CLAPHAM). Delv. to CATLETT 16 Jan 1833.

3Y:091   Date: 17 Apr 1832   RtCt: 11 Jun 1832
George THOMAS of WashDC to Nathaniel S. ODEN of Ldn. B/S of 284a adj Wm. LYONS. Wit: Chas. LEWIS, J. CLEVELAND, Lewis F. MANKIN. Delv. to ODEN 8 Jul 1833.

3Y:092   Date: 16 Apr 1832   RtCt: 15 May 1832
George THOMAS of WashDC to Michael VIRTS of Ldn. B/S of 215a adj Mrs. PEYTON, __ POWELL. Wit: Chas. LEWIS, J. CLEVELAND, Lewis F. MANKIN.

3Y:094   Date: 11 Jun 1822 [32?]   RtCt: 11 Jun 1832
Samuel PURSEL Jr. of Ldn to Valentine V. PURSEL of Ldn. B/S of 3a adj Abdon DILLON, Henry SMITH, Samuel IDEN. Delv. to V. V. PURCELL 9 Jul 1834.

3Y:095   Date: 10 Apr 1832   RtCt: 15 Jun 1832
Robert SINGLETON & wife Jane of Upperville Fqr to William FLETCHER of Robert of Fqr. B/S of 77a at edge of county (cnvy/b uncle Samuel SINGLETON, validity contested) on Goose Creek adj __ GLASSCOCK. Delv. to FLETCHER 29 Nov 1832.

3Y:097 Date: 27 Aug 1831 RtCt: 12 Sep 1831/11 Jun 8132
William CARR and Archibald MAINS of Ldn to David CARR of Ldn.
B/S of 207a (undivided share of 381½a - William MAINS Sr. dec'd &
William CARR purchased jointly of John C. HERBERT & Carlyle F.
WHITING, DBk BB:045 [041]) on Kittoctan Mt. Signed by William
CARR, Arch'd MAINS agent for Wm. MAINS, Elizabeth
VANDEVENTER, John CARR, William VANDEVENTER, Joseph L.
VANDEVENTER, John VANDEVENTER, Dewanner CHAMBLIN,
Leanner SINCLAIR, Mason CHAMBLIN, Jas. SINCLAIR. Wit:
Joseph L. VANDEVENTER, Lewis TORREYSON, Washington
VANDEVENTER. Delv. to D. CARR 31 Mar 1834.

3Y:101 Date: 12 Jun 1832 RtCt: 12 Jun 1832
George McPHERSON. DoE for son Joseph McPHERSON who he
purchased from John BRADEN of Ldn.

3Y:102 Date: 12 Jun 1832 RtCt: 12 Jun 1832
Matthew ELGIN to Murphey C. SHUMATE. Trust for debt to
Gustavius ELGIN as endorser on bank note, Wesley S.
McPHERSON, Hiram McVEIGH, Richard ADAMS, George
RHODES & Anna ROSZELL using Negro woman Nancy & her child
Sina, undivided 1/7th interest in 11 slaves former prop. of his father
Francis ELGIN dec'd and held by mother Jane ELGIN in dower,
undivided interest in right of wife Ann C. late BROADWATER in
estate Negroes from her father Charles G. BROADWATER dec'd
with 2 now in his possession, farm animals, farm and household
items, crops.

3Y:104 Date: 9 Aug 1830 RtCt: 13 Jun 1832
David RICKETTS & wife Elizabeth of Ffx to Samuel M. EDWARDS
of Ldn. B/S of 42a (cnvy/b Commrs. Humphrey PEAKE & George
WISE) on Lsbg turnpike rd & Goose Creek adj James F. NEWTON.

3Y:106 Date: 19 Jan 1832 RtCt: 2 Feb/11 Jun 1832
Sydnor B. RUST and mother Martha RUST of Ldn to William K. ISH
of Ldn. B/S of ½ of LS for 21y from late Mathew RUST to Sydnor B.
RUST on 435a (paid ½ of debts of estate of Matthew RUST dec'd
and portion of support for Martha & 2 old Negroes Peter & Sam).
Wit: Alfred GARRETT, Samuel SIMPSON, George SULLIVAN.

3Y:107 Date: __ 1832 RtCt: 15 Jun 1832
Sarah BINNS (wd/o Simon A. BINNS dec'd), Chas. BINNS Jr. (s/o
Simon A. dec'd & wife Mathy) and John A. BINNS Jr. (another son)
to Samuel M. EDWARDS. Trust for debt to Samuel M. BOSS using
1a lot with house and 30a (undivided int. dev. by John A. BINNS
dec'd to Mary Ann A. MURRAY late BINNS d/o Simon subject to life
estate of Dewanner WATT late BINNS, see DBk PPP:073 and
SSS:314). Wit: C. C. SUTHERLAND, D. G. SMITH, Jno.
SAUNDERS. Delv. to BOSS 23 Oct 1833.

3Y:110   Date: 19 Jun 1832   RtCt: 4 Jul 1832
Catharine HIXSON of Green Co Ohio to Daniel COOPER of Ldn.
B/S of 87a adj __ VIRTZ, __ JANNEY, __ RAMEY, __ COOPER.
Wit: Oliver F. HIXON, James C. JOHNSON. Delv. pr order 6 Jun 1834.

3Y:112   Date: 29 Jun 1832   RtCt: 9 Jul 1832
John WHITE, Mortimer McILHANY & Isaac WALKER freeholders appt'd to assess damages to Nathan NICKOLS & other heirs of James NICKOLS dec'd on land to be used for Lsbg & Snickers Gap turnpike rd. Assesses Turnpike Co. $75 in damages.

3Y:113   Date: 29 Jun 1832   RtCt: 9 Jul 1832
John WHITE, Mortimer McILHANY & Isaac WALKER freeholders appt'd to assess damages to Portia HODGSON & James HILL on land to be used for Lsbg & Snickers Gap turnpike rd. Assesses Turnpike Co. $50 in damages.

3Y:114   Date: 29 Jun 1832   RtCt: 9 Jul 1832
John WHITE, Mortimer McILHANY & Isaac WALKER freeholders appt'd to assess damages to Jas. BEST on land to be used for Lsbg & Snickers Gap turnpike rd. Assesses Turnpike Co. $245 in damages.

3Y:115   Date: 29 Jun 1832   RtCt: 9 Jul 1832
John WHITE, Mortimer McILHANY & Isaac WALKER freeholders appt'd to assess damages to Ruth THOMAS wd/o Joseph THOMAS and Mahlon THOMAS, Nancy THOMAS, Owen THOMAS, Hester THOMAS, Jonah THOMAS, Martha THOMAS & Jesse THOMAS on land to be used for Lsbg & Snickers Gap turnpike rd. No damages.

3Y:116   Date: 9 Jul 1832   RtCt: 9 Jul 1832
George ADIE, Richard H. HENDERSON and B. W. HARRISON. Bond on George ADIE Deacon of the Protestant Episcopal Church to celebrate rights of Matrimony.

3Y:116   Date: 5 Apr 1831   RtCt: 9 Jul 1832
Jacob EVERHEART dec'd. Division – court order of 9 Nov 1830 for land on Short Hill prch/b Jacob EVERHEART now dec'd, Joseph EVERHEART & John EVERHEART Exors. of Emanuel WALTMAN dec'd – 8a Lot #1 to John EVERHEART, 14a Lot #2 to Joseph EVERHEART, 20a Lot #3 to Sarah J. EVERHEART [plat indicates 4 lots]. Divisors: John GRUBB, John GEORGE, foreign name [John WENNER?].

3Y:118   Date: 13 Jun 1832   RtCt: 9 Jul 1832
Silas REESE dec'd. Division – court order of 14 Jun 1831 for land on Goose Creek; 102a Lot #1 & 25a Lot #2 to Alfred DULIN(G) & wife Sarah E.; 164a Lot #3 to John M. WILSON & wife Ann. WILSON and Betsey REESE are Admr. of estate. Divisors: Presley CORDELL, W. C. SELDEN Jr. Gives plat.

3Y:121 Date: 22 Jun 1832 RtCt: 9 Jul 1832
Commr. Wm. B. TYLER to Michael MORRALLEE. B/S of house and
& lot on Loudoun St. in Lsbg. Lot on King St. sold to John INSOR
who has failed to comply with terms of sale (from suit of 17 Nov
1831 James WOODY to John INSOR & wife Mary Jane and William
M. C. G.'GREEN). John A. BINNS was Guardian of Mary Jane
INSOR late WOODDY for interest in estate of Elizabeth WOODDY
dec'd. Delv. to Jno. A. BINNS 26 Mar 1836.

3Y:123 Date: 19 Jun 1832 RtCt: 4 Jul 1832
Daniel COOPER & wife Elizabeth of Ldn to Andrew S. ANDERSON
and Thomas WHITE of Ldn. Trust for debt to Catherine HIXON of
Green Co Ohio using land cnvy/b HIXON. Wit: John CARROLL,
Jacob CRUZEN, L. D. WORSLEY, Tasker C. QUINLAN, Presley
CORDELL.

3Y:124 Date: 31 Mar 1832 RtCt: 4 Jul 1832
Michael ARNOLD& wife Christina of Ldn to Richard GRUBB of Ldn.
B/S of land (see DBk III:114, less land cnvy/t Methodist Church
trustees in 1830) adj Peter COMPHER, James COPELAND, T. M.
McILHANY. Wit: John WHITE, Mortimer McILHANY. Delv. pr order
10 Mar 1835.

3Y:126 Date: 9 Apr 1832 RtCt: 2 Jul 1832
Aaron MILLER & wife Mary of Ldn to Sarah NIXON of Ldn. B/S of
16a (prch/o Hannah MILLER, etc) and 11a (prch/o Thomas WHITE).
Wit: John WHITE, Ebenezer GRUBB. Delv. to Jas. W. NIXON 17
Feb 1847.

3Y:128 Date: 9 Apr 1832 RtCt: 2 Jul 1832
Thomas OSBURN of Ldn to Thomas WHITE of Ldn. Trust for debt
to Sarah NIXON using 155a prch/o NIXON adj Joseph THOMAS
dec'd. Delv. to Sarah NIXON 22 Mar 1842.

3Y:130 Date: 30 May 1832 RtCt: 2 Jul 1832
John S. MAGILL (Sup. Ct. Marshall in suit of Mahlon COMBS &
Israel COMBS agst Joseph COMBS & Israel COMBS) to Amer
NICHOLS & wife Maria late BROWN, Sarah BROWN, Phebe
BROWN, John H. BROWN, Martha Ann BROWN, William H.
BROWN & Mary E. BROWN (heirs of Nathan BROWN dec'd). B/S of
undivided 1/6th interest of Andrew COMBS Jr. from 1773 will of
Andrew COMBS Sr. on N fork of Goose Creek; and interest of
William COMBS, Edward BROWN & wife Patty late COMBS,
Edward COMBS, Viena COMBS, Jonas LUCAS & wife Abigail late
COMBS, Mary COMBS & Lucinda COMBS (ch/o Andrew COMBS
Jr. dec'd) and Mary COMBS wd/o Andrew Jr. dec'd in that land.

3Y:132 Date: 2 Jul 1832 RtCt: 2 Jul 1832
Thomas ROGERS to Philip VANSICKLER. B/S of 80a (from trust of
Feb 1821 from Enos POTTS to Isaac NICHOLS Jr. & James
HOGUE, DBk CCC:172) adj John WARFORD, Jehu
HOLLINGSWORTH. Delv. to VANSICKLER 16 Jan 1838.

3Y:133 Date: 26 Jun 1832 RtCt: 26 Jun 1832
James MONROE of Ldn to John A. BINNS of Ldn. Trust for Michael MORALLEE as security on note to Joseph HILLIARD using crops. Delv. to BINNS 8 Aug 1833

3Y:135 Date: 19 Jan 1832 RtCt: 11 Jun 1832
William CLAYTON and Martha CLAYTON of Ldn to Hector PEARCE of Ldn. Relinquishes claim to lot (CLAYTON sold to Timothy CARRINGTON since dec'd lot in Snickersville on W side of road from Snickersville to Lsbg and N of prop. of Amos CLAYTON's reps. CARRINGTON sold lot to PEARCE who improved it and now occupies). Wit: James MURPHY, William BALL, Abraham NICHOLS.

3Y:135 Date: 25 Jun 1832 RtCt: 26 Jun 1832
Stacey TAYLOR & wife Ruth B. of Ldn to Maddison C. KLEIN of Ldn. B/S of 1a on S side of new turnpike road adj heirs of Henry SMITH. Wit: Francis W. LUCKETT, John H. McCABE. Delv. to KLEIN 11 Feb 1834.

3Y:137 Date: 26 Jun 1832 RtCt: 27 Jun 1832
James GARNER of Ldn to William H. JACOBS of Ldn. Release of trust of Apr 1832 for debt to William W. KITZMILLER on lot in Lsbg.

3Y:138 Date: 26 Jun 1832 RtCt: 26 Jun 1832
William H. JACOBS & wife Catharine of Ldn to Mrs. Thirza RICE of Ldn. B/S of part of Lot #57 in Lsbg on NE corner of Loudoun & Liberty Sts. Wit: John ROSE, John H. McCABE.

3Y:140 Date: 25 Jun 1832 RtCt: 26 Jun 1832
Joseph TAYLOR & wife Lydia of Ldn to Stacey TAYLOR of Ldn. B/S of 1a adj __ HEATON, __ BIRDSALL. Wit: Francis W. LUCKETT, John H. McCABE. Delv. to TAYLOR 23 Oct 1833.

3Y:142 Date: 18 Jun 1832 RtCt: 25 Jun 1832
Thomas FRED to Cyrus BURSON. Release of trust of Jun 1830 for debt to George KEENE using 134a. Delv. to BURSON 13 Apr 1833.

3Y:143 Date: 25 Jun 1832 RtCt: 25 Jun 1832
Thomas S. HAMERSLY of Ldn to George RICHARDS of Ldn. Trust for debt to Charles G. EDWARDS using crops nr Nolands Ferry and land in poss. of David JACKSON, Alexander DICKSON. Delv. to RICHARDS 17 Jun 1833.

3Y:145 Date: 2 Jun 1832 RtCt: 25 Jun 1832
Solomon RUSE & wife Tabitha, Eli TAVENER & wife Sarah, Amos WHITACRE & wife Nancy and Martha TAVENER of Ldn to Thomas ROGERS of Ldn. B/S of undivided 4/9th of 19a (Lot #6 in div. of George NIXON dec'd, DBk XX:202) on Goose Creek. Wit: Notley C. WILLIAMS, Benjamin GRAYSON.

3Y:146 Date: 18 Jun 1832 RtCt: 25 Jun 1832
Cyrus BURSON of Ldn to Michael PLAISTER of Ldn. Trust for debt to John BURSON using 134a cnvy/b John.

3Y:148 Date: 21 Jun 1832 RtCt: 22 Jun 1832
Jesse TRIPLETT of Ldn to John P. HALL of Ldn. Trust for debt to
Marcus D. BAKER of FredVa using interest in estate of father Enoch
TRIPLETT. Delv. to M. D. BAKER 9 Jan 1833.

3Y:149 Date: 2 Jan 1831 RtCt: 21 Jun 1832
William PAXON & wife Jane of Ldn to Samuel HOUGH of Ldn. B/S
of 4a Lot #1 and 4a Lot #2 (sold by Amos GIBSON) nr Wtfd adj Dr.
McCABE, Asa MOORE dec'd. Wit: Tasker C. QUINLAN, Presley
CORDELL. Delv. to HOUGH 11 Feb 1836.

3Y:151 Date: 28 Apr 1831 RtCt: 21 Jun 1832
Philip METTE & wife Elizabeth late BINNS of BaltMd to Samuel
HOUGH of Ldn. B/S of 19a (from div. of John A. BINNS dec'd). Wit:
T. SHEPPARD, J. L. MAGUIRE. Delv. pr order 6 Jun 1834.

3Y:153 Date: 23 Dec 1831 RtCt: 20 Jun 1832
John BUMCROTS & wife Christina of Ldn to Simon SHOEMAKER
Jr. of Ldn. B/S of interest in 15a dower of Catharine EMERY from
Jacob EMERY dec'd adj Benjamin SHREVE, George COOPER. Wit:
George W. SHAWEN, Mortimer McILHANY. Delv. to SHOEMAKER
26 Nov 1833.

3Y:155 Date: 15 Jun 1832 RtCt: 15 Jun 1832
William HARLE to Samuel J. WHITING. Trust for debt to Henry T.
HARRISON using farm animals, farm and household items.

3Y:155 Date: 19 Jun 1832 RtCt: 9 [19?] Jun 1832
William HEATH of Ldn to Jacob APSEY of Ldn. Trust for debt to
William APSEY of Ldn using slave for life Ann abt 18y old.

3Y:156 Date: 1 May 1832 RtCt: 18 Jun 1832
Joseph KNOX & wife Janet of Ldn to Isaac CONWELL of Ldn. B/S
of lot at Market & Liberty Sts. in Lsbg (part of lot dev. to Janet
PATTERSON now KNOX by Mathew CAMPBELL, remainder cnvy/t
John McCORMICK. Wit: John H. McCABE, Tasker C. QUINLAN.

3Y:158 Date: 15 Jun 1832 RtCt: 16 Jun 1832
William KEYES & wife Jane of Ldn to James MERCHANT of Ldn.
B/S of 3a nr stone church in German Settlement adj Benjamin
GRUBB and 4a on Short Hill (prch/o Amos JANNEY May 1832). Wit:
Presley CORDELL, Samuel M. EDWARDS. Delv. to Arch W.
MERCHANT an Exor. of grantee 8 Mar 1860 pr order filed 5R:049.

3Y:160 Date: 8 Jun 1832 RtCt: 16 Jun 1832
William DULANEY & wife Rachel of Ldn to William WRIGHT of Ldn.
B/S of undivided 1/8th interest of Rachel in land of Patterson
WRIGHT dec'd on Catoctin Creek held by widow Nancy WRIGHT.
Wit: Jos. H. WRIGHT, Samuel BAKER, David SHRIVER, John J.
MATHIAS, Presley CORDELL. Delv. to WRIGHT 24 Sep 1844.

3Y:162 Date: 6 May 1832 RtCt: 16 Jun 1832
Amos JANNEY & wife Mary Ann of Ldn to William KEYES of Ldn.
B/S of 4a (prch/o William ELLZEY) adj JANNEY, Phillip

EVERHEART. Wit: John WHITE, Mortimer McILHANY. Delv. to
KEYS 14 Nov 1833.

3Y:163   Date: 1 Jul 1824   RtCt: 14 Jun 1832
Christopher C. McINTYRE (Guardian at litem for Robert, Catharine,
Lucy, Laura F., Ellen, John, Alexander & Mary McINTYRE infant
ch/o Patrick McINTYRE dec'd) of Ldn to John McCORMICK of Ldn.
B/S of 10a (prch/o John SCHOOLEY Oct 1806).

3Y:165   Date: 4 Feb 1832   RtCt: 16 Jun 1832
Henry HICKMAN & wife Anna Mary of Ldn to William KEYS of Ldn.
B/S of 3a adj Mr. SACKMAN, Church lot, __ GRUBB, __ COOPER.
Wit: Mortimer MCILHANEY, George W. SHAWEN. Delv. to KEYS 14
Nov 1833.

3Y:167   Date: __ Jun 1832   RtCt: 27 Jun 1832
John A. Carter of Ldn to William H. JACOBS of Ldn. Release of trust
of Apr 1832 for debt to John STEPHENSON using lot in Lsbg

3Y:168   Date: 3 Jul 1832   RtCt: 9 Jul 1832
Richard H. HENDERSON of Lsbg to James GARRISON of Lsbg.
Release of trust of Mar 1828 for debt to Roberdeau ANNIN using
house & lot in Lsbg.

3Y:169   Date: 20 Jun 1832   RtCt: 9 Jul 1832
Herod THOMAS of Ldn to James ALEXANDER of Ldn. B/S of 3a nr
Blue Ridge adj Cuthbert POWELL, George RUST, __ MILEY. Delv.
to Chs. L. POWELL who filed the same for record.

3Y:170   Date: 13 Jul 1832   RtCt: 13 Jul 1832
John INSOR in right of his wife Mary Jane late WOODDY to Michael
MORRALLEE. Receipt for payment in full for house & lot on
Loudoun St. by William B. TYLER as Commr.

3Y:170   Date: 13 Jul 1832   RtCt: 13 Jul 1832
James WOODDY to Michael MORRALLEE. Receipt for payment in
full for house & lot on Loudoun St. by William B. TYLER as Commr.

3Y:170   Date: 8 Jul 1832   RtCt: 13 Jun 1832
Commr William B. TYLER (decree of Nov 1831 James WOODDY
agst John INSOR etc) to Michael MORRALLEE. B/S of house & lot
on Loudoun St.

3Y:172   Date: __ Jul 1832   RtCt: 13 Jul 1832
Michael MORALLEE to Commr. William B. TYLER. Trust for debt to
heirs of Elizabeth WOODDY using above house & lot.

3Y:173   Date: 11 Jul 1832   RtCt: 14 Jul 1832
Mandly T. RUST & wife Sally/Sarah of Ldn to William K. ISH of Ldn.
B/S of undivided int. in land of brother James T. RUST dec'd from
his father Mathew RUST, adj Lewis BERKLEY. Wit: Samuel
DAWSON, Tasker C. QUINLAN.

3Y:175   Date: 18 Jul 1831   RtCt: 16 Jul 1832
Elisha S. MARKS s/o Isaiah MARKS dec'd (formerly of Ldn but died in Daviess Co Ky), widow Elizabeth MARKS, Thomas F. THOMPSON & wife Lucinda D. late MARKS a d/o Isaiah dec'd and Elisha S. MARKS as Guardian of David D. & John D. MARKS infant children to Stephen McPHERSON. Release of trust for debt to heirs of Isaiah MARKS.

3Y:176   Date: 24 Sep 1831   RtCt: 16 Jul 1832
George KILE & wife Sally of Ldn to John KILE of Ldn. B/S of 35a adj John KILE, William BENTON (from will of father John KILE dec'd). Wit: Notley C. WILLIAMS, A. GIBSON. Delv. to ?? of PhilPa ?? 1842.

3Y:177   Date: 7 Apr 1830   RtCt: 14 Jul 1832
Colin AULD & William H. MILLER of AlexDC (trustees of Robert BRADEN, John MORGAN & Joseph EACHES late merchants under Braden, Morgan & Co) to Thomas PHILLIPS of Wtfd. B/S of 60a and 25½ sq poles (from trust of Mar 1825, DBk KKK:164). Delv. to Wm. H. MILLER Exor. of Thos. PHILIPS 20 Aug 1842.

3Y:180   Date: 19 Jul 1832   RtCt: 24 Jul 1832
Wilson C. SELDEN Jr. to Ramey G. SAUNDERS. Trust for benefit of Mrs. Matilda LOVE & children using household items purchased at sale of Richard H. LOVE dec'd.

3Y:180   Date: 14 Jun 1832   RtCt: 16 Jul 1832
Isaac M. BROWN & wife Christiana late KILE of Ldn to William BENTON of Ldn. Trust for John KILE & George KILE as security on note to John PANCOAST using int. in estate of father John KILE dec'd. Wit: Abner GIBSON, Edward HALL. Delv. pr order 9 Jun 1834.

3Y:183   Date: 18 Jul 1832   RtCt: 18 Jul 1832
David J. EATON of Ldn to Humphrey B. POWELL of Ldn. Trust for debt to Noble BEVERIDGE using household items.

3Y:184   Date: 14 Jul 1832   RtCt: 3 Aug 1832
Samuel McPHERSON & wife Mary of Ldn to Edward BOND of Ldn. Trust for debt to Thomas PHILLIPS of Ldn using lot with mill in Wtfd cnvy/b PHILLIPS. Wit: Samuel HOUGH, Mortimer McILHANY. Delv. pr order 30 Jul 1835.

3Y:186   Date: 14 Jul 1832   RtCt: 3 Aug 1832
Thomas PHILLIPS & wife Rachel of Ldn to Samuel McPHERSON & Edward BOND of Ldn. B/S of 3a with mill adj Amasa HOUGH (former prop. of Robert BRADEN dec'd). Wit: Mortimer McILHANY, Samuel HOUGH. Delv. pr order 30 Jul 1835.

3Y:189   Date: 2 Aug 1832   RtCt: 2 Aug 1832
Elias POOL & wife Margaret to George RICHARDS. Trust for Jno. A. BINNS, Michael MORRALLEE & George RICHARDS as security using wages in hands of John ROSE, int. of Margaret in trust deed

from POOL to Margaret TILLETT (now POOL), Honor TILLETT & Samuel CARR dated Jun 1827 (DBk OOO:170). Wit: Jno. J. MATHIAS, E. HAMMATT, Samuel M. EDWARDS.

3Y:190 Date: 9 Apr 1832 RtCt: 19 Jul 1832
John RUSE/RUCE & wife Sarah of Seneca Co Ohio to Ludwell Lee SANDS of Green Co Ohio. B/S of 15a on Kittocton Creek and 5a on NW side of Kittocton Mt. Wit: Reuben WILLIAMS, Jacob PLANE. Delv. to SANDS __.

3Y:193 Date: 20 Aug 1832 RtCt: 1 Sep 1832
Commr. Edmund CHRISTIAN to Benjamin BRIDGES. B/S of 1364a (from case of Thomas ASTLEY Exor of John PALMER dec'd who was Exor of Thomas PALMER dec'd agst John CAMPBELL, James GOVAN & Robert CAMPBELL). Delv. to BRIDGES 8 Apr 1833.

3Y:195 Date: 1 Sep 1832 RtCt: 1 Sep 1832
Benjamin BRIDGES & wife Keturah of Ldn to William CARTER of RichVa. Trust for debt to Commr. Edmund CHRISTIAN using above 1364a. Wit: Ludwell LEE, John J. MATHIAS. Delv. to CARTER 5 May 1833.

3Y:198 Date: 26 Mar 1831 RtCt: 2 Aug 1832
Daniel HINES & wife Sarah of Ldn to Wayne McKIMIE of Ldn. B/S of 1/6th int. in farm of Francis McKIMIE dec'd where Wayne now lives. Wit: John WHITE, George W. SHAWEN.

3Y:200 Date: 24 Jan 1829 RtCt: 2 Aug 1832
Mandly T. RUST & wife Sally of Ldn to William K. ISH of Ldn. B/S of undivided 1/6th of real estate of father Mathew RUST dec'd. Wit: Presley CORDELL, Samuel M. EDWARDS.

3Y:202 Date: 29 Jan 1832 RtCt: 1 Aug 1832
Moses BROWN & wife Ann of Ldn to his mother Ann BROWN of Ldn. B/S of 43a adj __ COGILL. Wit: Benjamin GRAYSON, Notley C. WILLIAMS. Delv. to Jno. L. GILL pr order of Mary BROWN Admr., see DBk 3W:337 pr order.

3Y:204 Date: 12 Jul 1832 RtCt: 31 Jul 1832
Robert J. TAYLOR & wife Molly Elizabeth of AlexDC to William CLINE of Ldn. B/S of lot on N side of Market St in Lsbg adj John GRAY, __ GARRISON. Delv. to CLINE 18 Oct 1833.

3Y:206 Date: __ Aug 1832 RtCt: 2 Aug 1832
Wilson C. SELDEN Sr. & wife Mary B. of Ldn to Charles A. ALEXANDER of Ldn. B/S of 16½a now occupied by William HAMMERLY as tenant nr turnpike road to Alexandria adj SELDEN. Wit: Carey SELDEN, Mary F. LIPPITT, Francis W. LUCKETT, Tasker C. QUINLAN.

3Y:207 Date: 5 Jun 1832 RtCt: 24 Jul 1832
Yeoman Enoch FURR & wife Sarah of Ldn to their son yeoman Jeremiah FURR of Ldn. B/S of 154a adj Mordecai THROCKMORTON, John BEAVERS, at foot of Blue Ridge on road

from Bloomfield to Snickersville. Delv. to Wm. J. COOK pr order of
Jeremiah FURR 17 Mar 1842.

3Y:209   Date: 31 Jul 1832   RtCt: 3 Aug 1832
William ISH & wife Sophonia to William L. POWELL and Asa
ROGERS. Trust for Hugh SMITH, Humphrey B. POWELL, William
BEVERIDGE & George SULLIVAN as endorsers on note to William
K. ISH using 435a adj Lewis BERKLEY (formerly of Mathew RUST
dec'd). Wit: Abner GIBSON, Jno. J. MATHIAS. Delv. to H. SMITH 26
Apr 1833.

3Y:211   Date: __ Oct 1826   RtCt: 4 Aug 1832
John JANNEY to Joseph HOUGH. Release of trust of Aug 1829 for
debt of Nathan NEAR (DBk SSS:258) on house & lot in Hllb.

3Y:213   Date: 5 Aug 1832   RtCt: 6 Aug 1832
Miriam HOLE wd/o Levi HOLE dec'd and Ann HOLE heir of Levi
dec'd of Ldn to John HUNT of Ldn. B/S of 15a (see DBk Y:033) adj
Major HUNT, Thomas CARR, Eli HUNT.

3Y:215   Date: 6 Aug 1832   RtCt: 6 Aug 1832
Richard H. HENDERSON Esqr of Lsbg to Jesse TIMMS and
Charles G. ESKRIDGE. Trust for debt to George CARTER of
Oatlands using 305a (prch/o reps. of Thomas CUMMINGS and part
from Burr POWELL now in occupation of Jacob STONEBURNER)
adj Charles BINNS, George RHODES, John CARR, Ellis WILLIAMS,
heirs of Jesse RICE, Charles G. ESKRIDGE. Delv. to TIMMS by
direct. of G. CARTER.

3Y:218   Date: 8 Aug 1832   RtCt: 8 Aug 1832
James CAYLOR Guardian for James H. MUSE infant ch/o Walker
MUSE dec'd who had interest in family of Negroes Peg & her 3
children now in possession of Elizabeth MOFFETT grandmother of
James H. MUSE. Peter OATYER desires of comfort of family of
Elizabeth MOFFETT to leave Negroes with her and gives bond of
indemnity. Wit: Rich'd. H. HENDERSON.

3Y:218   Date: 14 Nov 1831   RtCt: 8 Aug 1832
Henry SHAFFER of Ldn to Joseph P. GRUBB of Ldn. B/S of 6a on
S side of Kittocton Creek adj Samuel GREGG dec'd, Nathan
GREGG, Robert BRADEN. Delv. to GRUBB 16 Sep 1844.

3Y:220   Date: 29 Apr 1830   RtCt: 9 Aug 1832
Jane D. WILDMAN (Admr wwa of John WILDMAN dec'd) to James
WILDMAN of Ldn. B/S of 243a on Secolon adj __ SHREVE, __
CROSS, __ MOTT (prch/o DBk YY:377 less 14a sold in DBk
AAA:303).

3Y:222   Date: 8 Mar 1832   RtCt: 9 Aug 1832
James WILDMAN of Ldn to Jane D WILDMAN of Ldn. B/S of 166a
on Secolon adj Benjamin SHREVE, WILDMAN, James CROSS,
Saml. M. EDWARDS on W side of road from Lsbg to Cochran's Mill.

3Y:223 Date: 27 Feb 1832 RtCt: 9 Aug 1832
Henry CLAGETT of Ldn to Jane D. WILDMAN of Ldn. B/S of 144a, 7a and 178a (cnvy/b WILDMAN Apr 1830 under will of John WILDMAN dec'd).

3Y:225 Date: 24 Jul 1822 RtCt: 30 Oct 1824/14 Aug 1832
Cupid BLUE alias Cupid ROBERTSON of Ldn to Samuel M. EDWARDS of Ldn. Trust for Presley CORDELL & William CHILTON as bond on note to Henry RICHARDS to purchase slave Nancy his wife using lot adj Reuben SCHOOLEY, James WINTERS (prch/o Thomas HETHERLY). Wit: N. GREEN, Enos WILDMAN, Daniel LEWIS.

3Y:227 Date: 14 May 1832 RtCt: 14 Aug 1832
Report (on motion made 15 Nov 1831 by Thomas PHILLIPS & Samuel McPHERSON) by Isaac WALKER, Wm. B. STEER & Wm. H. HOUGH on route for a road from Wtfd to some point on Potomac opposite point of Rocks – from Wtfd with the Taylor town road as far as Andrew S. ANDERSON's farm then thru corner of that up to Cotocton Mt. and thru land of John ROBERTSON, Sydnor WILLIAMS, Israel WILLIAMS, Phineas WILLIAM & Phillip HEATER then down on E side of mt. thru land of Elizabeth PRICE (late CLAPHAM) thru Thomas JOHNSTON to end. Jury finds $120 damages to Andrew S. ANDERSON, $11 damages to Phillip HEATER, $6 to P. C. JONES.

3Y:235 Date: 12 Mar 1832 RtCt: 14 Aug 1832
Report (on motion made 11 Dec 1827 by Uriel Glascock) by William BENTON, Gabriel McGEATH & Gabriel SKINNER on route from Snickers Gap turnpike road nr Beaverdam Bridge to North fork meeting house & from bridge to Pot house – from Snickers Gap turnpike road on N side of Samuel BROWN's Mill down the N side of Beaverdam to old road then in line between William HOGE & Daniel McMULLEN turning to right on line between HOGE & McMULLEN to brow of a hill then turning right slanting down the hill to corner of William WILKINSON's fence in Uriel GLASCOCK's line formerly James MASH's line then in line of WILKINSON and GLASCOCK & Andrew CAMMEL & GLASCOCK into the old road on branch nr GLASCOCK & James CARTER's old mill race down S side of race crossing it at mill with old road thru Mrs. TUMBLESON's land to road from Benj. RUST's to North Fork Meeting house then commencing at bridge up hill on S side of old road intersecting line between POWELL & Stephen RAWLINGS to old road to William BRONAUGH's line then thru GLASCOCK's woods to road form Ezekiel MOUNT to the Pot House at foot of hill. Jury find $22.25 damages to David HIXON, $.19 damages to __ WILKINSON.

3Y:241 Date: 27 Apr 1832 RtCt: 13 Aug 1832
Isaac CONWELL & wife Margaret and Jonathan CONWELL of Ldn to John HALL of Ldn. B/S of 100½a Lot #4 from estate of Josiah

HALL dec'd to Elizabeth CONWELL (from trust of Aug 1831 from Lovelace CONWELL & wife Elizabeth). Wit: Presley CORDELL, Tasker C. QUINLAN.

3Y:244 Date: 28 Aug 1832 RtCt: 28 Aug 1832
Thomas ROGERS Depty Sheriff for Johnston CLEVELAND to George RHODES of Ldn. B/S of interest of John FICHTER in leased 14a adj RHODES, Charles BINNS, heirs of Robert CARR, and leased 6a adj Nancy THOMAS, Robert ROBERTS, heirs of Robert CAMPBELL. Delv. To RHODES 9 Sep 1836.

3Y:245 Date: 15 Apr 1831 RtCt: 5 Sep 1831
Abel JANNEY to Harvey HAMILTON. Release of trust Oct 1828 for debt to Bernard TAYLOR on 37a. Wit: Daniel COCKRILL, Jesse HIRST, Enos NICHOLS.

3Y:247 Date: 3 Dec 1822 RtCt: 12 Jun/13 Aug 1832
Deborah McKNIGHT of Ldn to Ely McKNIGHT of Ldn. B/S of 2a, adj John McKNIGHT. Wit: Charles CHAMBLIN, Thomas HART, Jeremiah GILL, Wm. McKNIGHT, H. ELLIOTT, Thomas NICHOLS.

3Y:248 Date: 19 Mar 1832 RtCt: 13 Aug 1832
Thomas MOSS & wife Sarah A. of Ldn to Samuel AYRES of Fqr. B/S of 168a adj James ALLEN, __ BEAVERS. Wit: Charles LEWIS, Robert BAYLY. Delv. to AYRES 6 Feb 1836.

3Y:250 Date: 21 Jul 1832 RtCt: 13 Aug 1832
Joseph HOUGH of Ldn to Enos NICHOLS of Ldn. Trust for debt to Samuel W. BROWN using 1½a (formerly owned by Washington WHITE) where HOUGH now lives adj Enos BEST, Mary LYDER, David LOVETT. Delv. to Enos NICHOLS trustee of Jno. A. BINNS 9 Jun 1835.

3Y:251 Date: 2 May 1832 RtCt: 13 Aug 1832
Elizabeth RUSSELL of Ldn to Joel OSBURN Jr. of Ldn B/S of 2a adj John GRAHAM, James COCKRAN. Wit: Morris OSBURN, Jonah OSBURN, Albert OSBURN.

3Y:252 Date: 16 Apr 1832 RtCt: 13 Aug 1832
Lewellyn POWELL & wife Sarah E. of Jefferson Co Ky to Reuben HUTCHISON of Ldn. B/S of lot on S side of Little River Turnpike Road adj Stephen BEARD (Sarah E.'s share from div. of Mathew HARRISON dec'd). Wit: Francis W. LUCKETT, Saml. M. EDWARDS. Delv. to HUTCHISON 8 Feb 1836.

3Y:254 Date: 17 Sep 1831 RtCt: 13 Aug 1832
Ann BROWN of Ldn to Isaac PIGGOTT of Ldn. B/S of 26a (cnvy/b Moses BROWN) adj John WHITACRE, Michael PLASTER. Delv. 27 Feb 1873.

3Y:256 Date: 6 Aug 1832 RtCt: 13 Aug 1832
George McPHERSON & wife Priscilla of Ldn to John WINE of Ldn. B/S of 3a (see DBk HHH:019) adj Andrew THOMPSON. Wit: Mortimer McILHANY, John WHITE. Delv. to WINE 10 Feb 1834.

3Y:258   Date: 6 Aug 1832   RtCt: __ [Aug 1832]
Jonathan McARTOR Sr. of Ldn to John WINE of Ldn. B/S of 3 roods (prch/o Lambert MYERS on title bond) adj __ LEWIS. Delv. to WINE 7 Feb 1834.

3Y:260   Date: 2 Jun 1832   RtCt: 13 Aug 1832
Anthony WRIGHT & wife Charlotte of Ldn to Conrad WIRTZ of Ldn. B/S of 2a on W side of Short Hill (prch/o John DEMORY) and 1a (prch/o William DERRY) adj other lot. Wit: Mortimer McILHANY, Geo. W. SHAWEN.

3Y:262   Date: 4 Aug 1832   RtCt: 13 Aug 1832
Alfred GULICK of Ldn to R. H. HENDERSON of Ldn. Trust for debt to John MOORE of Aldie using undivided int. in estate of father Moses GULICK dec'd

3Y:263   Date: 1 Jun 1832   RtCt: 13 Aug 1832
Nathan NEER & wife Eliza of Ldn to James THOMPSON of Ldn. B/S of undivided ½ int. of L/L where THOMPSON adj NEER (cnvy/b Craven OSBURN Sep 1829). Wit: John WHITE, Mortimer McILHANY. Delv. to THOMPSON 2 Jun 1834.

3Y:265   Date: 1 May 1832   RtCt: 13 Aug 1832
John HALL of Ldn to Thomas HUGHS of Ldn. B/S of 37a on NW fork of Goose Creek adj HUGHS, Samuel HALL's div. of Josiah HALL dec'd. Wit: James H. NICHOLS.

3Y:266   Date: 8 May 1830   RtCt: 13 Aug 1832
Gideon HOUSHOLDER & wife Julia Ann of Ldn to John H. BOGEN of Ldn. B/S of 3a adj David AXLINE, HOUSHOLDER. Wit: Mortimer McILHANY, George W. SHAWEN. Delv. to BOGEN 6 May 1833.

3Y:268   Date: 13 Aug 1832   RtCt: 13 Aug 1832
Thornton F. OFFUTT of Ldn to Perrin WASHINGTON of FredVa. B/S of ¼a on S side of Snickersville Gap Turnpike in Snickersville (prch/o Amos CLAYTON & cnvy/b Commr. Thomas ROGERS).

3Y:269   Date: 14 Aug 1832   RtCt: 14 Aug 1832
John RYAN to Henry T. HARRISON. Trust for debt to Edward E. COOKE using horse, cart, crops.

3Y:270   Date: 10 Aug 1832   RtCt: 15 Aug 1832
Samuel DAILEY & wife Fanny of Ldn to William HAMMERLY of Ldn. B/S of tract on N side of Leesburg Turnpike road & NW side of road from Turnpike road to Edward's Ferry adj Dr. W. C. SELDEN, heirs of HAMMAT (see DBk AAA:366, less ½a). Wit: Tasker C. QUINLAN, W. C. SELDEN Jr. Delv. to HAMMERLY 24 Sep 1833.

3Y:272   Date: 15 Aug 1832   RtCt: 15 Aug 1832
Thomas B. LOVE to Thomas NICHOLS & Presley CORDELL. Trust for debt to Jonah NICHOLS using undivided 3/7th int. in plantation of uncle John LOVE dec'd (descended to James LOVE, Elizabeth LOVE, Sarah LOVE, Eli PIERPOINT, the heirs of Thomas LOVE, heirs of Samuel LOVE & heirs of Benj. DANIEL with LOVE having

purchased int. of James LOVE and Eli PIERPOINT) adj Richard ADAMS.

3Y:274   Date: 10 Jun 1831   RtCt: 15 Aug 1832
Stephen McPHERSON of Ldn to Elisha S. MARKS of Daviess Co Ky. Benjamin STRINGFELLOW prch/o John MARKS late of Ldn now of Perry Co Ohio 50a – controversy with McPHERSON claiming under John MARKS or estate of his father Isaiah MARKS dec'd is entitle to remainder of purchase month. McPHERSON ackn. receiving ½ of money.

3Y:275   Date: 6 Aug 1832   RtCt: 17 Aug 1832
James H. BENNETT of Union to John B. HEREFORD of Ldn. Trust for debt to John HOOFF of AlexDC using claim on Isaac CANNELL of AlexDC upon George S. HOUGH & William L. HODGSON.

3Y:276   Date: 17 Aug 1832   RtCt: 17 Aug 1832
Ariss BUCKNER of Ldn to Samuel M. EDWARDS of Ldn. Trust for Richard B. BUCKNER of Fqr, Bernard H. BUCKNER & Charles LEWIS of Ldn as endorsers on bank loan using slaves Dick, Mary, Elizabeth Dilsa, William, Caty, Jacob, Jim, Jane, Anthony, Nelly, Lucinda, Ampsey?, Billy, Judy, John, Jinny, Dinah, Tom, Nancy, Tom, Betsy, John, Nancy, Willis, Sena? [Sam?], Ellias, Tom, Betsey, John, Cregar, Alfred, Charles, Moses, Cassius, Alice, Lucy, Martha Ann, Judy, Jesse on farm of Ariss in Ldn.

3Y:278   Date: 13 Aug 1832   RtCt: 18 Aug 1832
Richard H. HENDERSON & wife Orra Moore of Ldn to son Archibald HENDERSON Jr. of Ldn. Gift of 3a nr Lsbg adj Charles BINNS, reps. of Anthony LAMBAUGH dec'd, Col. Saml. M. EDWARDS. Wit: John ROSE, John J. MATHIAS.

3Y:279   Date: 15 Aug 1832   RtCt: 20 Aug 1832
Perrin WASHINGTON & wife Hannah F. of FredVa to William CLINE of Ldn. B/S of ¼a on S side of Snickers Gap Turnpike in Snickersville adj Dr. OFFUTT. Delv. to CLINE 18 Oct 1833.

3Y:281   Date: 20 Aug 1832   RtCt: 21 Aug 1832
William COOPER & wife Elizabeth of Ldn to Abraham BAKER of Ldn. B/S of 4a (allotted in div. of Frederick COOPER dec'd) adj Plum Run, __ COMPHER. Wit: Tasker C. QUINLAN, Jno. J. MATHIAS. Delv. pr order 20 Jan 1836.

3Y:283   Date: 29 Nov 1828   RtCt: 24 Aug 1832
Benjamin JACKSON of Ldn to George MARKS of Ldn. B/S of 142a adj __ McPHERSON, __ HAN, __ EWERS. Delv. to Stephen McPHERSON pr order 8 Dec 1834.

3Y:285   Date: 12 Mar 1832   RtCt: 25 Aug 1832
Thomas HALL & wife Elizabeth of Ldn to Joel NIXON of Ldn. B/S of undivided int. in real estate of Josiah HALL dec'd except house & lot in Lsbg adj Mrs. BLINCOE. Wit: Josiah L. DREAN, James RUST, Presley CORDELL. Delv. to NIXON 12 Aug 1833.

3Y:286 Date: 14 Jul 1832 RtCt: 21 Aug 1832
George EMERY of Franklin Co Ohio to Samuel M. BOSS of Lsbg.
B/S of lot on N side of Loudoun St in Lsbg adj Mrs. McCABE, BOSS.
Wit: Jno. W. EDMISTON, Wm. LONG. Delv. to BOSS 30 Jul 1834.

3Y:288 Date: 2 Jun 1832 RtCt: 27 Aug 1832
Thomas J. HARPER & wife Margaret (late GREGG wd/o Aaron
GREGG dec'd formerly of Ldn) of Warren Co Tn to Robert
MOFFETT of Ldn. B/S of 1/16th of 8a (from William GREGG the
elder dec'd subject to life estate of widow dev. to Aaron GREGG
who acquired by death of childless Rezin GREGG s/o Aaron dec'd
and from William GREGG the elder grandfather of William GREGG
who dev. to 4 ch/o his son Aaron). Wit: Lewis DAVIS, James
McEWEN, Thos. H. WILKINS.

3Y:290 Date: 25 Aug 1832 RtCt: 27 Aug 1832
John FICHTER of Ldn to Benjamin SHREVE Jr. of Ldn. B/S of lot on
N side of Loudoun St in Lsbg (prch/o John CRIDLER) adj John
SURGHNOR, S. M. EDWARDS. Wit: Chas. SHREVE, Presley
CORDELL, Jno. SANDERS.

3Y:291 Date: 25 Aug 1832 RtCt: 25 Aug 1832
Robert DARNE & wife Fanny/Frances to William H. CRAVEN. Trust
for debt to William MERSHON & James CAYLOR using 43a (part
prch/o David BRIDGES, part allotted Fanny from father William
HUMMER dec'd) adj Robert HUNTER, Washington HUMMER. Wit:
Charles LEWIS, Robert BAYLY.

3Y:294 Date: 28 Aug 1832 RtCt: 28 Aug 1832
Thomas ROGERS to Joseph CARR. B/S of 221a formerly of
Thomas CARR dec'd where widow Priscilla CARR now resides
(from defaulted trust of May 1832 for debt to Joseph CARR).

3Y:295 Date: 29 Aug 1832 RtCt: 29 Aug 1832
Abel JANNEY & wife Lydia of Ldn to Harvey HAMILTON of Ldn. B/S
of 45a on Rock[y] Run adj Stephen JANNEY, William LODGE,
Joshua B. OVERFIELD. Wit: John H. McCABE, Samuel M.
EDWARDS.

3Y:297 Date: 29 Aug 1832 RtCt: 29 Aug 1832
Harvey HAMILTON & wife Lucina of Ldn to Thomas NICHOLS Esqr.
of Ldn. Trust for debt to Abel JANNEY using 45a as above. Wit:
John H. McCABE, Saml. M. EDWARDS.

3Y:300 Date: 29 Aug 1832 RtCt: 29 Aug 1832
Abel JANNEY & wife Lydia M. of Ldn to David HANDLEY of Ldn.
B/S of 8a (part of land formerly of Mary OVERFIELD) adj Jehu
BURSON, Martin OVERFIELD. Delv. to HANDLEY 15 Sep 1834.

3Y:302 Date: 23 Aug 1832 RtCt: 29 Aug 1832
Bernard TAYLOR & wife Sarah of Ldn to Yardley TAYLOR of Ldn.
B/S of 105a (with 75a intended as gift) on NW fork of Goose Creek

(part of prch/o estate of William HATCHER dec'd). Delv. to Yardley 9 Feb 1835.

3Y:303 Date: __ Aug 1832 RtCt: 30 Aug 1832
Jonathan ROBERTS of Ldn to William CARR of Ldn. A/L of Lot #16 & #19 (see DBk PP:315).

3Y:304 Date: 14 Aug 1832 RtCt: 30 Aug 1832
Samuel B. HARRIS & wife Ann to Isaac WALKER. Trust for debt to David CUNARD using 308a (prch/o Exor. of Abiel JENNERS) nr Wtfd on W side of Cotocton Mt adj John A. BINNS' heirs, Jacob MOCK, William CASSADAY. Wit: Samuel HOUGH, Geo. W. SHAWEN. Delv. to Benj'n. HOUGH 5 Jan 1838 pr order.

3Y:307 Date: 19 Oct 1829 RtCt: 1 Sep 1832
William H. CRAVEN (Commr. for sale of estate of Amos SINCLAIR dec'd) of Ldn to Samuel C. SINCLAIR of Ldn. B/S of 92a adj heirs of John BEATTY, Hawlings ferry road, heirs of __ THORNTON, __ CLAPHAM. Delv. to SINCLAIR 23 Mar 1839.

3Y:308 Date: 1 Sep 1832 RtCt: 1 Sep 1832
Samuel C. SINCLAIR of Ldn to James H. CHAMBLIN. Trust for debt to William H. CRAVEN using above 92a. Delv. to CHAMBLIN 11 Sep 1833.

3Y:310 Date: 3 Sep 1832 RtCt: 5 Sep 1832
Bernard TAYLOR (only surv. trustee of Mahlon TAYLOR, Israel JANNEY, Jonathan TAYLOR, Samuel NICHOLS, James MOORE & Bernard TAYLOR) of Ldn to Yardley TAYLOR, John SMITH, Daniel JANNEY, Thomas NICHOLS, Henry S. TAYLOR, Bernard TAYLOR Jr., David BROWN & Joseph NICHOLS (trustees of Goose Creek Meeting House). B/S of 10a (in trust for Quakers) adj William HATCHER. Delv. to Yardley TAYLOR 30 Jun 1837.

3Y:313 Date: 24 May 1832 RtCt: 12 Jun/21 Sep 1832
Yeoman Henry H. HUTCHISON of Ldn to Seth SMITH. Trust for debt to John LOVETT as security on note to Jonah HATCHER using 106a. Delv. to SMITH 16 Feb 1835.

3Y:314 Date: 17 Sep 1832 RtCt: 17 Sep 1832
Caleb C. SUTHERLAND of Ldn to Richard H. HENDERSON of Ldn. Trust for debt to Kerr & Fitzhugh of AlexDC, Edward JENKINS & son of BaltMd and Anthony ADDISON of Ldn using undivided 1/4th int. in houses & lots at Loudoun & King Sts. in Lsbg, subject to dower of mother. Delv. to HENDERSON 20 May 1834.

3Y:316 Date: 9 Mar 1832 RtCt: 12 Sep 1832
Given HANDEY of Ldn to James MOUNT of Ldn. B/S of 142a (from heirs of Eli H. HANDEY dec'd who were heirs of John HANDEY dec'd) on N side of Goose Creek adj Enoch FRANCIS, James RUST. Delv. to MOUNT 3 Sep 1835.

3Y:318   Date: 15 Sep 1832   RtCt: 15 Sep 1832
Robert ROBERTS & wife Nancy of Ldn to Jacob FADELY of Ldn.
B/S of 28a (lots prch/o Benjamin TOMPKINS Apr 1815, John
LICKEY Oct 1817, James RUST Dec 1819) adj James RUST,
George RHODES, William CARR, and 1a exchanged from William
CARR (all lots adj). Wit: John McCABE, Presley CORDELL.

3Y:320   Date: 8 Sep 1830   RtCt: 14 Sep 1832
Robert J. TAYLOR & wife Molly Elizabeth of AlexDC to John J.
HARDING of Lsbg. B/S of stone tenement & lot on W side of King St
in Lsbg.

3Y:321   Date: 12 Sep 1832   RtCt: 12 Sep 1832
Presley CORDELL & wife Amelia of Ldn to Joshua PUSEY of Ldn.
B/S of 306a (prch/o Richard M. SCOTT Aug 1817) adj John
BRADEN, reps. of Sanford RAMEY dec'd, reps of Mary FOX dec'd,
PUSEY. Wit: Tasker C. QUINLAN, Saml. M. EDWARDS.

3Y:324   Date: 10 Sep 1832   RtCt: 13 Oct 1832
Samuel LUCKETT & Sarah C. LUCKETT dec'd. Division – 34½a
held jointly, 18a allotted William C. LUCKETT as heir of Sarah C.
LUCKETT, and 16½a held jointly allotted to heirs of Samuel
LUCKETT dec'd. 41a Lot #1 to William C. LUCKETT from joint land
and 1/6th interest in residue & 1/6th prch/o Charles B. HAMILTON;
11a Lot #2 [16a on plat] to Robert C. LUCKETT; 40a Lot #3 to
Josiah C. LUCKETT; 24a Lot #4 to Luther C. LUCKETT. Divisors:
Britton SANDERS, Geo. MARLOW, Charles WILLIAMS. Gives plat.

3Y:327   Date: 15 Aug 1832   RtCt: 24 Sep 1832
Samuel M. EDWARDS (Commr. in case of Ruth STONE agst
Thomas STONE) to Edmund J. LEE of AlexVa. B/S of 87a adj
Stacey HAINS, __ SELDEN, __ LEE, __ SAUNDERS (cnvy/b
Stacey HAINS to James STONE now dec'd Aug 1822, DBk
EEE:450). Delv. pr order __.

3Y:329   Date: 8 Sep 1832   RtCt: 11 Sep 1832
Philip KIST & wife Ann of Ldn to John WENNER of Ldn. B/S of 2a
adj Catharine MULL (cnvy/b John BOOTH Feb 1826, DBk LLL:398).
Wit: Ebenezer GRUBB, George W. SHAWEN. Delv. to W. W.
WENNER Admr 12 Aug 1837.

3Y:331   Date: 6 Nov 1829   RtCt: 10 Sep 1832
Ludwell LEE of Ldn to John WATERS of Ldn. B/S of 1a adj gravel
road intersecting Mdbg line.

3Y:332   Date: 26 Dec 1831   RtCt: 12 Mar/10 Sep 1832
John INGRAM & wife Thamer/Tamer of Ldn to Calvin THATCHER of
Ldn. B/S of 68a where INGRAM now resides adj Henry ORAM,
Jesse HOWELL, top of Blue Ridge, __ McILHANY. Wit: Craven
OSBURN, Joseph WORTHINGTON, Henry AMICK, Mahlon
RUSSELL, Abraram [Abraham] YOUNG, Alfred YOUNG. CoE for
Tamer in FredVa.

3Y:334 Date: 23 May 1832 RtCt: 13 Aug/1 Oct 1832
Perrin WASHINGTON of Ldn to Thornton WALKER of Ldn. Trust for Thornton F. OFFUTT & Stephen CONROD as security on bonds to William CLEVELAND using merchandise and household items, and int. in land where Stephen CONROD now resides. Wit: Samuel SHIPMAN, Samuel NIXON, Alfred CLINE.

3Y:337 Date: 22 Jun 1832 RtCt: 10 Sep 1832
Andrew BEVERIDGE to William MERSHON. Trust for debt to Nathan SKINNER using slaves Simon & Charles.

3Y:338 Date: 5 Sep 1832 RtCt: 11 Sep 1832
G. W. MALONE of Tuscumbia Alabama. DoE for grandson Rudolph. MALONE purchased Negro women Dinah & her son Rudolph b. 22 Nov 1830 from Isaac SETTLE of Fqr; on 20 Jun 1831 MALONE gave Rudolph as gift to his grandfather George RIVERS (a free man of colour) of Ldn.

3Y:339 Date: 18 Sep 1832 RtCt: 27 Sep 1832
Amos JANNEY & wife Mary Ann of Ldn to Joseph MORRISON. Trust for debt to Ruth JANNEY using 38a adj B. GRUBB, George RICKARD, Adam HOUSEHOLDER's heirs. Wit: Mortimer McILHANY, George W. SHAWEN. Delv. pr order 6 Sep 1833.

3Y:342 Date: 11 May 1832 RtCt: 23 Sep 1832
James BROWN & wife Ruth of Ldn to James MEGEATH of Ldn. B/S of 45a on NW fork of Beaverdam adj Samuel PEUGH, Stacey J. TAVENER, __ WALKER. Wit: Notley C. WILLIAMS, John SIMPSON. Delv. to McGEATH 27 Feb 1834.

3Y:344 Date: 2 Apr 1830 RtCt: 14 Sep 1832
Thompson F. MASON & wife Betsey C. and Matilda R. PRICE of AlexDC to John J. HARDING of Ldn. B/S of undivided 1/4th int. in house & lot in Lsbg (Betsey & Matilda as reps of Mrs. Sarah PRICE dec'd, will of Mrs. Rebecca GRIFFITH). Delv. to HARDING 10 Mar 1835.

3Y:346 Date: 17 Aug 1832 RtCt: 21 Sep 1832
Charles BINNS of Ldn to daus. Ann Alexander BINNS and Elizabeth D. BINNS of Ldn. Gift of Lot #51 & Lot #52 in Lsbg. Delv. to A. A. & E. D. BINNS 7 Aug 1833.

3Y:347 Date: 10 Aug 1832 RtCt: 20 Aug 1832
George DAY of Ldn to Samuel M. EDWARDS of Ldn. Trust for debt to Asa PECK using household items.

3Y:349 Date: 15 Aug 1832 RtCt: 19 Sep 1832
Edmund J. LEE & wife Sally of AlexDC to Samuel M. EDWARDS of Ldn. Trust for debt to heirs of James STONE dec'd using 80a. Wit: R. JOHNSTON Jr., Geo. DRINKER, Adam LYNN. Delv. pr order 8 Apr 1835.

3Y:351   Date: 16 Feb 1832   RtCt: 7 Sep 1832
David GIBSON, Eli GIBSON, Rebecca HIXON, Abner GIBSON &
wife Susanna, Hamilton ROGERS & wife Nancy late HIXSON, Burr
POWELL & wife Catharine (representing the int. of Levi GIBSON) to
Isaac BOWLES. B/S of int. as heirs of late Rebecca VERNON wd/o
Daniel VERNON dec'd and 1 undivided moiety in mill lot. Wit:
Cuthbert POWELL, Edward HALL, A. GIBSON, Notley C.
WILLIAMS. Delv. to Jas. BOWLES pr order 26 May 1836.

3Y:354   Date: 4 Sep 1832   RtCt: 4 Sep 1832
John ROSE (Exor of Susan CHILTON dec'd and Commr. in decree
of Apr 1830) to Benjamin SHREVE Jr. & Stephen N. C. WHITE
(Admrs of David TRUNDLE dec'd late of MontMd). Release of trust
of Aug 1830, DBk UUU:186 [187].

3Y:355   Date: 4 Sep 1832   RtCt: 6 Sep 1832
Enoch G. DAY of Ldn to Charles W. D. BINNS of Ldn. Trust for debt
to Parkinson L. LOTT of Ldn using household items.

3Y:356   Date: 24 Aug 1832   RtCt: 5 Sep 1832
Sydnor B. RUST of Ldn to H. B. POWELL of Ldn. Trust for George
SULLIVAN as security on debt to Tiffany & Co using farm animals,
household items, Negro man George. Wit: Francis HAMPTON,
Arthur SULLIVAN, George KINSEL.

3Y:358   Date: 13 Aug 1832   RtCt: 11 Sep 1832
Gabriel VANDEVENTER. Qualified as Capt. in 56th Reg of Infantry
6th Brig 2nd Div of Va Militia.

3Y:358   Date: 28 Aug 1832   RtCt: 10 Sep 1832
Wm. F. CLARKE. Oath as Lt. in 132nd Reg of infantry 6th Brig 2nd Div
of Va Militia.

3Y:358   Date: 10 Sep 1832   RtCt: 10 Sep 1832
Jesse TIMMS & Henry CLAGETT. Bond on TIMMS as
Commissioner of Revenue in First District.

3Y:359   Date: 10 Sep 1832   RtCt: 10 Sep 1832
Jesse McVEIGH & Hugh SMITH. Bond on McVEIGH as
Commissioner of Revenue in Second District.

3Y:359   Date: 1 Sep 1832   RtCt: 10 Sep 1832
Division of James NICHOLS dec'd. 1/4th part of 25a to Nathan
NICHOLS & Isaiah NICHOLS sons of James NICHOLS the 1st or
elder, adj Thomas OSBURN, heirs of Edward CONARD, __ LODGE.
Divisors: Thomas JAMES, John GRAHAM.

3Y:360   Date: 7 Sep 1832   RtCt: 7 Sep 1832
Edward HAYNES to Samuel M. EDWARDS. Trust for John
CAMPBELL as security on bond to Henry W. TALBOTT Guardian of
heirs of J. STONE dec'd using farm animals, household items.

3Y:362   Date: 22 Aug 1832   RtCt: 10 Sep 1832
Eve WATERS dec'd. Court order of 12 Jun 1832 in suit of Jacob
WATERS &c vs Jacob WALTMAN – 1/8th part (13½a on plat) to

heirs of Eve WATERS dec'd. Did not lay off share of Nicholas ROPP. Divisors: Geo. W. SHAWEN, Thos. J. MARLOW, foreign name

3Y:363 Date: 17 Apr 1832 RtCt: 11 Jun/10 Sep 1832
George THOMAS of Washington to Charles LEWIS of Ldn. B/S of 137a adj Broad Run, William AMBLER, __ BUCKNER, LEWIS. Wit: J. CLEVELAND, Saml. O'BANION, Lewis F. MANKIN. Delv. to LEWIS 10 Nov 1834.

3Y:364 Date: 17 Apr 1832 RtCt: 13 Aug/10 Sep 1832
George THOMAS of Washington to Jonathan BEARD of Ldn. B/S of 270a adj Mrs. PEYTON, Miss ELLZEY. Wit: Chas. LEWIS, J. CLEVELAND, Saml. O'BANION. Delv. pr order 14 Dec 1838.

3Y:366 Date: 1 Sep 1832 RtCt: 10 Sep 1832
George W. WASHINGTON to Thomas WHITE & John HAMILTON. Trust for debt to John DAVIS using 179a prch/o DAVIS.

3Y:368 Date: 11 Sep 1832 RtCt: 11 Sep 1832
Charles BINNS & Charles G. ESKRIDGE. Bond on BINNS as clerk of the court.

3Y:368 Date: 23 Aug 1832 RtCt: 10 Sep 1832
Charles B. HAMILTON Jr. & wife Sarah C. and Samuel C. LUCKETT of Ldn to William C. LUCKETT of Ldn. B/S of interest in "Cross Roads Farm" former prop. of Samuel LUCKETT Sr. dec'd adj __ BROWN, __ WILLIAMS, __ MARLOW, __JACKSON, __ ELGIN, __ SAUNDERS. Wit: George W. SHAWEN, John J. MATHIAS. Delv. to Wm. C. LUCKETT 16 May 1835.

3Y:370 Date: 10 Sep 1832 RtCt: [10 Sep 1832]
Edward COGHLIN a native of Ireland applied as Citizen of US. Certificate from clerk of Indiana Co Pa dated Dec 1827 with COGHLLIN then residing in Borough of Blairsville in Indiana Co Pa. Born in County of Tipperary 18 Mar 1800 and emigrated 8 May 1825 arriving in Baltimore 28 June. Proved by Daniel BOLAND that COGHLIN resided in US for 5 years and within Va for at least 1 year.

3Y:371 Date: 2 Aug 1832 RtCt: 3 Aug 1832
Isaac CANNELL of AlexDC to George S. HOUGH and William L. HODGSON of AlexDC. Trust for debt to Wm. M. JONES &c using 500a nr Chester Town in Kent Co Md and stock at his store in Union under management of James H. BENNETT, and household items.

3Z:001 Date: 19 Sep 1832 RtCt: 21 Sep 1832
Ludwell GULICK & wife Elizabeth of Ldn to George RICHARDS of Ldn. Trust for debt to Edmund TYLER Guardian of Angelina K. BOYLE of Ldn using undivided int. in estate of father Moses GULICK dec'd. Wit: Abner GIBSON, John SIMPSON. Delv. to RICHARDS 13 Jul 1836.

3Z:003 Date: 13 Sep 1832 RtCt: 3 Oct 1832
Samuel HOUGH & wife Jane Gray of Ldn to Andrew GRAHAM of Ldn. B/S of 169a "Beaverdam tract" adj __ WIRTS, __ COOPER, __ HAMILTON, __ PEACOCK, Wm. A. HOUGH. Wit: Presley CORDELL, Saml. M. EDWARDS. Delv. to GRAHAM 7 Sep 1838.

3Z:005 Date: 14 Sep 1832 RtCt: 25 Sep 1832
Jonathan BEARD of Ldn to Lewis BEARD of Ldn. B/S of 50a adj Mrs. PEYTON, Miss ELLZEY. Wit: John L. RINIKER, Thos. M. WRENN, John MOORE. Delv. to BEARD 28 Dec 1838.

3Z:007 Date: 18 Sep 1832 RtCt: 25 Sep /29 Sep 1832
Alfred GULICK of Ldn to Robert A. ISH of Ldn. Trust for debt to John ISH of Ldn using undivided int. in real estate of father Moses GULICK dec'd nr Aldie. Wit: John MOORE, William E. SPINDLE, John M. SPENCER. Delv. to Jno. ISH 14 Jun 1832.

3Z:009 Date: 11 Jan 1832 RtCt: 23 Sep 1832
Yeoman Mahlon GIBSON & wife Elenora of Ldn to Jesse RICHARDS of Ldn. B/S of 80a dower land of Elizabeth GIBSON from John GIBSON dec'd (except 4a where Elizabeth now lives) and int. of David E. BROWN & Mahlon GIBSON in land by virtue of LS of Jun 1819 (DBk BBB:169). Wit: Edward HALL, Cuthbert POWELL. Delv. to C. L. POWELL pr order __.

3Z:011 Date: 6 Apr 1831 RtCt: 26 Sep 1832
Patrick Curran MCCABE & wife Maria C. L. of Harpers ferry JeffVa to Otis DUDLEY of Harpers ferry JeffVa. B/S of 1000a (from will of George LEE dec'd to Maria Carter LEE at marriage of her mother or at age 16y) adj Ludwell LEE, Thomas L. LEE (br/o George dec'd).

3Z:013 Date: 12 Sep 1832 RtCt: 27 Sep 1832
Ishmael VANHORNE & wife Emiline of Ldn to Jacob SMITH of Ldn. B/S of 115a adj John COMPHER, Frederick COOPER, Samuel BAKER, __ WILLIAMS, Catoctin Creek. Wit: Mortimer McILHANEY, Geo. W. SHAWEN. Delv. to SMITH 22 Aug 1834.

3Z:015 Date: 7 Apr 1832 RtCt: 27 Sep 1832
Joseph WALTMAN of FredMd to Jacob SMITH of Ldn. B/S of 15a and 6a (from Jacob WALTMAN dec'd). Delv. to SMITH 6 Sep 1837.

3Z:017 Date: 1 Feb 1831 RtCt: 31 Mar 1831
Adah CONARD, Stephen CONARD, Luther CONARD, Thomas STONE & wife Sarah and George S. MARKS & wife Nancy of Ldn to Jefferson C. THOMAS of Ldn. B/S of 20a (formerly of Edward CONARD Jr. dec'd) on SE side of Blue Ridge adj great road, THOMAS, Elizabeth U. THOMAS, Sarah NIXON. Wit: Joshua OSBURN, Charles McKNIGHT, A. G. CHAMBLIN. Delv. to Hanson ELLIOTT pr order 12 Aug 1839.

3Z:019 Date: 10 Aug 1832 RtCt: 24 Sep 1832
Calvin THATCHER of Ldn to Jesse HOWELL of Ldn. B/S of 68a on E side of Blue Ridge (granted John INGRAM by patent Jan 1828

and cnvy/t THATCHER) adj Henry OREM, HOWELL, __ McILHANEY. Delv. to HOWELL 14 Oct 1851.

3Z:021   Date: 25 Sep 1832   RtCt: 27 Sep 1832
George WINCEL of Ldn to Elizabeth EMORY of Ldn. B/S of 51a at Peter WIRTS, George COOPER. Delv. to John TIMMS 24 Dec 1833.

3Z:022   Date: 7 Jun 1832   RtCt: 24 Sep 1832
William ROSE & wife Mary of PrWm to John JAMES of Ldn. B/S of 100a adj JAMES and 25a. Wit: Charles LEWIS, Rob't. BAYLY.

3Z:024   Date: 17 Sep 1832   RtCt: 25 Sep 1832
James L. McKENNA of Ffx to Ariss BUCKNER & wife Lucy of Ldn. Release of trust of Mar 1825 for debt to Alexandria Bank on 1400a.

3Z:026   Date: 1 Sep 1832   RtCt: 23 Sep 1832
James MONROE of NY City to William ELLZEY of Lsbg. PoA for case of A. G. MONROE &c agst James MONROE.

3Z:027   Date: 1 Oct 1832   RtCt: 1 Oct 1832
Richard H. HENDERSON of Ldn to Maria F. WHITING of Ldn. BoS for house & lot in Union now occupied by John HARDY prch/b Thomas N. JONES who directs HENDERSON to convey to WHITING. Delv. pr order 13 Feb 1838.

3Z:028   Date: 1 Oct 1832   RtCt: 1 Oct 1832
Michael MORALLEE. Surrender of real estate. Thomas MORALLEE dec'd late of Lsbg dev. to Michael MORRALLEE certain real estate except house occupied by THOMAS' widow at Markett & Back Sts and house opp. W. D. DRISH Tavern on King St. in trust for reps of John MORALLEE for purpose of being naturalized. Henry MORALLEE and William MORALLEE two ch/o John have become citizens.

3Z:029   Date: 9 Oct 1832   RtCt: 9 Oct 1832
George H. ALDER & Nathan NICHOLS. Bond on ALDER as constable.

3Z:030   Date: 8 Oct 1832   RtCt: 8 Oct 1832
William SAUNDERS. Qualified as Lt. of infantry in 56th Reg 6th Brig 2nd Div of Va Militia.

3Z:030   Date: 28 Jun 1832   RtCt: 4 Jul/28 Sep 1832
Margaret F. GHEEN of Ldn of Ldn to Henry EVANE. PoA for interest in Va. Wit: Thornton WALKER, Edmund ALLEN, Thos. FRED.

3Z:031   Date: 2 Mar 1832   RtCt: 12 Mar/27 Oct 1832
William CARR of Ldn to Evan WILKINSON of Ldn. B/S of 50a on S fork of Beaverdam (cnvy/b Samuel PROBASCO Sep 1801) and an adj. 84a (prch/o George NIXON dec'd Jun 1807) on road to Lsbg by Coe's Mill, and adj 51a (prch/o Abraham SKILLMAN Jul 1816) adj John VERNON. Delv. to WILKINSON 6 Dec 1834.

3Z:033   Date: 8 Jun 1832   RtCt: 8 Oct 1832
Benjamin R. LACY of Ldn to John ISH of Ldn. B/S of two ½a lots on main st. in Aldie with house and shop adj James SWART Sr. (formerly Mrs. JENKINS), Mrs. Jane LOVE, Charles F. MERCER. Delv. to ISH 21 Jun 1843.

3Z:035   Date: 12 Sep 1832   RtCt: 9 Oct 1832
John G. KOENER & wife Catharine of Ldn to William BROWN of Ldn. B/S of 70a (willed by Philip FRY to dau Catharine) on Catoctin Creek adj BROWN, Archibald McDANIEL, Amos JANNEY. Wit: Mortimer McILHANEY, John WHITE. Delv. to BROWN 6 Oct 1834.

3Z:038   Date: 23 Aug 1832   RtCt: 8 Oct 1832
Samuel SACKMAN & wife Susannah of Ldn to Peter FRYE Sr. of Ldn. one rood lot (cnvy/b Joshua PUSEY Nov 1826) adj George WINCEL, William GRAHAM. Wit: John J. MATHIAS, Geo. W. SHAWEN. Delv. to Peter FRY Sr. 8 Aug 1836.

3Z:040   Date: 1 Mar 1832   RtCt: 9 Oct 1832
Elijah ANDERSON & wife Eleanor/Elender of Ldn to Edward CARTER of Ldn. B/S of 31a adj CARTER, and 30a adj ANDERSON, James WORNAL, Robert MARTIN. Wit: Francis W. LUCKETT, A. GIBSON. Delv. to CARTER 26 Sep 1833.

3Z:042   Date: 19 Aug 1832   RtCt: 10 Oct 1832
William M. McCARTY & wife Emily of Ffx to Simon YEAKEY of Ldn. B/S of 140a in German Settlement (cnvy/b George M. CHICHESTER Apr 1827) with 20+ acres already cnvy/t YEAKEY.

3Z:044   Date: 10 Feb 1831   RtCt: 12 Oct 1832
James EAKIN of Washington Co to Richard H. HENDERSON. B/S of int. in land cnvy/b George W. SHAWEN in 1829 – EAKIN claims no responsibility for title.

3Z:045   Date: 12 Oct 1832   RtCt: 12 Oct 1832
Richard H. HENDERSON and Ebenezer GRUBB. Agreement – HENDERSON sold GRUBB 191a-193a farm where Thomas NICHOLS now lives with wood lots former prop. of George W. SHAWEN with GRUBB to give bonds for payment.

3Z:046   Date: 19 Oct 1832   RtCt: 19 Oct 1832
William T. T. MASON of Lsbg to George M. CHICHESTER of Lsbg. Release of trust of Apr 1827 for debt to Richard WILLIAMS (Admr. of Thomas CRAMPHIN dec'd of MontMd)

3Z:047   Date: 19 Oct 1832   RtCt: 19 Oct 1832
George M. CHICHESTER & wife Mary of Lsbg to William T. T. MASON of Lsbg. Trust for debt to Richard WILLIAMS of MontMd using 585a (cnvy/b William M. McCARTY Apr 1827).

3Z:050   Date: 27 Feb 1832   RtCt: 20 Oct 1832
Jonathan BUTCHER & wife Phebe of AlexDC to George RUST of JeffVa. B/S of 142a (from div. of Wm. RUST dec'd, DBk CC:150) adj __ EDMONDSON, __ GRAYSON. Charles McKNIGHT of AlexDC

also sells his interest in land. Wit: Adam LYNN, N. KEENE. Delv. to
RUST 4 Jan 1839.

3Z:052   Date: 17 Oct 1832   RtCt: 20 Oct 1832
George RUST Jr. & Maria C. of Harpers Ferry JeffVa to John
JANNEY of Lsbg. Trust for debt to Jonathan BUTCHER of AlexDC
using above land.

3Z:054   Date: 19 May 1831   RtCt: 20 Oct 1832
John FRYE & wife Elizabeth of Ldn to John RUSE of Ldn. B/S of 5a.
Wit: Mortimer McILHANEY, John WHITE.

3Z:056   Date: 19 Nov 1829   RtCt: 20 Oct 1832
Fleming W. P. HIXSON of Ldn abt to go to Florida to Noble S.
BRADEN. PoA.

3Z:058   Date: 30 Mar 1832   RtCt: 21 Oct 1832
Hiram McBRIDE & wife Harriet of JeffVa to Sarah THEYR
[THAYER] of Ldn. B/S of 22a adj Christian DERRY. Delv. pr order
17 Mar 1845.

3Z:060   Date: 18 Jul 1832   RtCt: 24 Oct 1832
James W. BRAWNER of Aldie to William NOLAND of Ldn. Trust for
debt to James LOVE of Ldn using house & ½a lot in Aldie. Wit:
Jonah HOOD, Edmund TYLER, Edgar EWELL.

3Z:062   Date: 6 Oct 1832   RtCt: 24 Oct 1832
James BOWLS & wife Elizabeth of Ldn to Joseph LEWIS of Ldn.
B/S of 4a where BOWLS now resides (formerly of Isaac GIBSON
dec'd) adj Clifton farm sold to James W. MACRAE, Rocky Hill,
Panther Skin. Wit: Cuthbert POWELL, Benjamin GRAYSON.

3Z:064   Date: 24 Oct 1832   RtCt: 24 Oct 1832
James NIXON & wife Susan Ann of Ldn to Peter COST of Ldn. B/S
of 21a (from div. of father George NIXON dec'd). Wit: Samuel M.
EDWARDS, Presley CORDELL.

3Z:066   Date: 27 Oct 1832   RtCt: 26 [27?] Oct 1832
Thomas LATIMORE of Ldn to John M. SPENCER of Ldn. BoS for
negro boy Henson abt 4y old (to be delivered after LATIMORE dies).

3Z:066   Date: 27 Oct 1832   RtCt: 27 Oct 1832
John S. HAWLING of Ldn to Hamilton ROGERS of Ldn. B/S of
undivided 1/5th int. in real estate of William HAWLING dec'd s/o
William HAWLING dec'd (see DBk QQQ:249).

3Z:067   Date: 1 Oct 1829   RtCt: 27 Oct 1832
Joshua PANCOAST & wife Sarah of Ldn to John PANCOAST Jr. of
Ldn. B/S of 59a adj John GREGG, David YOUNG, Edith HATCHER,
Jonah TAVENER, Abdon DILLON. Wit: Notley C. WILLIAMS, John
SIMPSON. Delv. to John PANCOAST Jr. 14 Oct 1833.

3Z:070   Date: 13 Oct 1832   RtCt: 30 Oct 1832
John SURGHNOR to Samuel M. EDWARDS. Trust for debt to
James SURGHNOR & wife Harriet P. formerly HARRISON of Ldn

using lot & house on Royal St in Lsbg (DBk FFF:115) and lot on Back & Royal St. (DBk HHH:062) and lot on Market St (DBk LLL:189) and lot on Loudoun St (DBk FFF:297) and residue (DBk FFF:303) (also see DBk LLL:244 for marriage contract and trust, which was revoked 19 Nov 1825 and SURGHNOR appt'd trustee). Delv. to EDWARDS 6 Jun 1833.

3Z:074   Date: 18 Sep 1832   RtCt: 1 Nov 1832
Ruth JANNEY of Ldn to Amos JANNEY of Ldn. B/S of 38a (allotted to Ruth from her father Amos JANNEY dec'd) adj George RICKARD, B. GRUBB, __ HOUSHOLDER. Delv. to Amos JANNY 18 Apr 1839.

3Z:076   Date: 4 Oct 1832   RtCt: 3 Nov 1832
Blacksmith Jesse JONES [signed as John] & wife Rachel of Ldn to Eleazer EVANS of Ldn. Trust for Rachel and children of land from father John EVANS dec'd of Ldn (his widow is also now dec'd) to keep out of control of Jesse JONES before all is sold. Wit: Saml. M. EDWARDS, Presley CORDELL.

3Z:078   Date: 11 May 1832   RtCt: 5 Nov 1832
Stacy J. TAVENER & wife Pleasant of Ldn to Jonathan TAVENER of Ldn. B/S of undivided 1/8th interest in 385a (from father Jonah TAVENER dec'd, subject to dower of widow Mariam TAVENER). Wit: Notley C. WILLIAMS, John SIMPSON. Delv. to Jonathan TAVENER 20 Feb 1835.

3Z:080   Date: 11 May 1832   RtCt: 5 Nov 1832
James BROWN & wife Ruth of Ldn to Stacy J. TAVENER of Ldn. B/S of 138a on Beaverdam adj Eli TAVENER, Jonah TAVENER, Sophia WALKER, Jas. MEGEATH, G. WALKER. Wit: Notley C. WILLIAMS, John SIMPSON. Delv. to S. J. TAVENER 15 Feb 1834.

3Z:083   Date: 11 May 1832   RtCt: 5 Nov 1832
Stacy J. TAVENER & wife Pleasant of Ldn to Naylor SHOEMAKER of Ldn. B/S of 46a on long branch of Beaverdam adj __ ROSZELL, __ GARRETT, __ TATE, __ YOUNG. Wit: Notley C. WILLIAMS, John SIMPSON. Delv. to SHOEMAKER 3 Feb 1834.

3Z:085   Date: 20 Feb 1832   RtCt: 5 Nov 1832
Benjamin W. GATCH & wife Marthey/Martha R. late CHINN of Ldn to Townshend McVEIGH of Ldn. B/S of any int. in 91¼a (sold by Lott BARR & wife Ann M. and Catharine M. CHINN to McVEIGH Oct 1829, DBk WWW:003). CoE for Martha from Norfolk Borough. Delv. to McVEIGH 24 Sep 1833.

3Z:087   Date: 7 Nov 1832   RtCt: 7 Nov 1832
Isaac M. BROWN (insolvent debtor) of Ldn to Sheriff Johnston CLEVELAND of Ldn. B/S of int. in real estate of John KILE dec'd.

3Z:088   Date: 2 Jun 1832   RtCt: 10 Nov 1832
George SHOVER of Ldn to Thomas J. MARLOW of Ldn. B/S of undivided int. in 33a (reverted to him by uncle Adam SHOVER dec'd allotted in div. of estate to Adam SHOVER, Catharine STETMAN

w/o John STETMAN, George SHOVER and Charlotte SHORTS w/o John SHORTS all ch/o George SHOVER br/o Adam SHOVER dec'd) and 9a timber lot allotted to ch/o George SHOVER dec'd.

3Z:090 Date: __ Oct 1813 RtCt: 12 Nov 1832
Dade P. NOLAND, Elizabeth NOLAND, Samuel NOLAND and Lloyd NOLAND ch/o Thomas NOLAND Esqr. dec'd of Ldn to Wilson C. SELDEN and Leven LUCKETT Esqrs. of Ldn. Trust for benefit of daughter Jane LOVE using slaves (will of Thomas NOLAND beq. to SELDEN and LUCKETT slaves Jane & Ann for Jane's use). Wit: Wm. NOLAND, Thos. NOLAND.

3Z:092 Date: 29 Aug 1832 RtCt: 12 Nov 1832
Edward FRANCIS & wife Ann E. B. late HAMILTON of Ldn to Samuel M. EDWARDS of Ldn. B/S of undivided 1/6th int. in house & Lot on N side of Market St. in Lsbg adj courthouse, John THOMAS, Wm. D. DRISH (cnvy/b Ann's grandfather Charles BENNETT, DBk TT:320). Wit: Wilson C. SELDEN Jr., Presley CORDELL. Delv. to S. M. EDWARDS 4 Jul 1836.

3Z:094 Date: 2 Mar 1831 RtCt: 12 Nov 1832
Joshua OSBURN of Ldn to Margaret CARRINGTON of Ldn. B/S of lot with house and store house in Snickersville lately occupied by Timothy and slaves Hannah abt 28y old, Emily abt 12y old, Frances abt 7y old, Sarah abt 5y old, Ellzey a boy abt 3y old, Clarissa a girl abt 8m old, and household items (from defaulted trust of Nov 1830 from Timothy CARRINGTON & wife Margaret). Wit: Herod OSBURN, James STEPHENSON, Roger CHEW. Delv. to Alfred GLASCOCK 8 Jan 1836.

3Z:096 Date: 6 Nov 1832 RtCt: 12 Nov 1832
Isaac M. BROWN & wife Christina of Ldn to Humphrey B. POWELL of Ldn. Trust for debt to Noble BEVERIDGE and Samuel TORRISON using prop. dev. by John KILE dec'd to his dau Christina BROWN w/o Isaac. Wit: H. H. HAMILTON, Jno. BROWN, Abner GIBSON, Cuthbert POWELL. Delv. to POWELL 12 Jun 1838.

3Z:098 Date: 6 Jun 1832 RtCt: 12 Nov 1832
Wesley HUTCHISON and John HUTCHISON of Ldn to Thomas SETTLE of Ldn. B/S of 53a on Elklick run adj Stephen DANIELS, old Alexandria road. Wit: Robert CUNNINGHAM, Nelson SETTLE, Thomas HUTCHISON. Delv. to SETTLE 14 Oct 1833

3Z:100 Date: 12 Nov 1832 RtCt: 12 Nov 1832
John L. GILL, John G. HUMPHREY & Thomas G. HUMPHREY. Bond on GILL as constable.

3Z:101 Date: 13 Mar 1832 RtCt: 16 Nov 1832
Benjamin JAMES dec'd. Division – 400a including mansion house allotted to David JAMES; 250a Lot #1 to Aaron JAMES; 238a Lot #2 to Bailes S. FOLEY in right of wife Icy; 188a Lot #3 and 51a wood lot

to Abigail JAMES. Divisors: Charles LEWIS, Sampson HUTCHISON & David KIMBLER. Gives plat.

3Z:105   Date: 12 Nov 1832   RtCt: 12 Nov 1832
James MONROE of Ldn to Michael MORRALLEE and William FULTON of Ldn. Trust for debt to William CARR using farm and household items.

3Z:106   Date: 17 Apr 1832   RtCt: 12 Nov 1832
George THOMAS of WashDC to Margaret FRENCH and Elizabeth FRENCH of Ldn. B/S of 160a adj broad run. Wit: J. CLEVELAND, Lewis F. MANKIN, Saml. O'BANION. Delv. pr order ___.

3Z:108   Date: 18 Apr 1832   RtCt: 12 Nov 1832
Benjamin MILES and Rachel MILES. No claim agst Henry HICKMAN as Guardian of Rachel HICKMAN now MILES w/o Benjamin and discharge him from Guardianship. Wit: George RICKARD, George BEAMER.

3Z:108   Date: 10 Nov 1832   RtCt: 13 Nov 1832
Isaac M. BROWN & wife Christina of Ldn to H. B. POWELL of Ldn. Trust for debt to Burr WEEKS using int. in estate of John KILE dec'd. CoE for Christina in Frederick Co. Delv. to POWELL 12 Jun 1838.

3Z:110   Date: 1 Nov 1832   RtCt: 13 Nov 1832
Eleazer EVANS & wife Mary, John EVANS & wife Sarah, John W. EVANS & wife Elizabeth, Jesse JONES & wife Rachel of Belmont Co Ohio, Joshua JORDON & wife Susanna of Guernsey Co Ohio, Asahel EVANS & wife Frances and John COLLINS & wife Nancy of Ldn (heirs of John EVANS Sr. dec'd) and Abel JANNEY & wife Lydia of Ldn to James HATCHER of Ldn. B/S of 151a on NW fork of Beaverdam adj __ TAYLOR, __ NICHOLS, Abel JANNEY. Wit: Benjamin G. WRIGHT, Hammond McBEE, Eli RYDER, John HUNTER, Notley C. WILLIAMS, John J. MATHIAS. Delv. to James HATCHER 22 Mar 1841.

3Z:115   Date: 13 Nov 1832   RtCt: 13 Nov 1832
Landon LYDER (heir of Lewis LYDER dec'd) of Ldn to Joseph LODGE of Ldn. B/S of int. in real estate of Lewis dec'd, being Lot #2 in div., DBk LLL:261). Delv. to LODGE 27 Aug 1836.

3Z:117   Date: 8 Sep 1832   RtCt: 16 Nov 1832
Isaac CARVER & wife Mary of Wilson Co Tn to Thomas AYRES of Ffx. B/S of 162a (Lot #7 in div. of William HUMMER dec'd f/o Mary). Delv. pr order 26 Sep 1835.

3Z:119   Date: 20 Apr 1832   RtCt: 16 Nov 1832
William BENTON & wife Sarah of Ldn to William LEITH of Ldn. B/S of 5a adj Sampson GUY, LEITH, Elijah ANDERSON. Wit: Francis W. LUCKETT, A. GIBSON. Delv. to H. H. LEITH 7 Aug 1873 [37?].

3Z:121   Date: 8 Aug 1832   RtCt: 19 Nov 1832
Samuel STATLER & wife Mary of Clinton Co Ohio to John STATLER of Ldn. B/S of 134¼a adj Capt. John ROSE, Charles

ELGIN dec'd, Philip HEATER dec'd (part dev. to Aaron OXLEY, Enoch OXLEY, Lewis OXLEY, Cynthia SMALLEY, Mary STEARNS & Frances BARCLEY by father Henry OXLEY dec'd and other part to them by their grandfather John OXLEY dec'd, then to STATLER, DEB TTT:025).

3Z:124   Date: 19 Nov 1832   RtCt: 19 Nov 1832
Sheriff Johnston CLEVELAND to Samuel HARPER of Ldn. B/S of 1a (from executions agst John FICHTER, where he now resides) adj Robert CAMPBELL now dec'd, Christopher FRYE. Delv. to HARPER 9 Nov 1839.

3Z:125   Date: 16 Nov 1832   RtCt: 20 Nov 1832
William Butler HARRISON & wife Penelope to John M. HARRISON. Trust for benefit of wife using house & lot in Mdbg exchanged with land in Ohio with Jacob MANN Oct 1828. Wit: J. J. MATHIAS, Hamilton ROGERS.

3Z:128   Date: 2 Oct 1832   RtCt: 24 Nov 1832
Julia A. WILSON wd/o John T. WILSON dec'd and Guardian of his infant children and William B. HARRISON to Burr W. HARRISON Admr. of John T. WILSON dec'd. Bond to receive estate funds. Wit: Jno. WILSON.

3Z:129   Date: 2 Feb 1832   RtCt: 26 Nov 1832
James WEST & wife Judith of Ldn to Samuel JACKSON of Ldn. B/S of 2a (cnvy/b Daniel BOLAND Mar 1831) adj __ MORRISON, __ SHOEMAKER. Wit: John H. McCABE, Presley CORDELL.

3Z:131   Date: 26 Oct 1832   RtCt: 26 Nov 1832
Elizabeth EMORY of Ldn to Simon SHOEMAKER Jr. of Ldn. B/S of int. in 15a where Simon resides (from Jacob EMORY dec'd) adj Benjamin SHREVE. Delv. to SHOEMAKER 26 Nov 1833.

3Z:133   Date: 27 Nov 1832   RtCt: 28 Nov 1832
John BRADEN of Ldn to Jesse HOGUE of Ldn. B/S of water rights as cnvy/b Noble S. BRADEN Exor of Robert BRADEN dec'd to HOGUE Jul 1831. Delv. to Josiah WOOD 31 Aug 1866.

3Z:134   Date: 29 Jul 1831   RtCt: 28 Nov 1832
Noble S. BRADEN (Exor of Robert BRADEN dec'd) to Joseph HOGUE. B/S of 1a with mill adj John BRADEN, George WARNER.

3Z:135   Date: 29 Jul 1831   RtCt: 28 Nov 1832
Jesse HOGUE of Ldn to David CONARD of Ldn. Trust for debt to Noble S. BRADEN (Exor of Robert BRADEN dec'd) using above land.

3Z:138   Date: 1 Oct 1832   RtCt: 6 Dec 1832
Jacob VOGDES to John Armstead CARTER. Trust for debt to John STEPHENSON using farm tools.

3Z:139   Date: 7 Dec 1832   RtCt: 7 Dec 1832
John J. MATHIAS of Ldn and Edmund J. LEE Jr. formerly of AlexDC now of Shepherdstown JeffVa to Edmund J. LEE Sr. of AlexDC. B/S

of 44a (from defaulted trust of Sep 1822 from Thomas KIDWELL) on W side of short hill adj __ SHRIVER, and 6a on W side of short hill adj __ DAVY, __ STUBBLEFIELD.

3Z:141   Date: 4 Dec 1832   RtCt: 7 Dec 1832
Joshua OSBURN (Commr. in Sep 1832 case of John NICHOLS &c agst Charity NICHOLS &c) to Thomas OSBURN of Ldn. B/S of 26a (from heirs of James NICHOLS the elder dec'd) adj Joseph THOMAS, John CHEW, __ HODSON, Samuel LODGE. Wit: Herod OSBURN, James C. JANNEY, William OSBURN. Delv. to Thomas OSBURN 31 May 1837.

3Z:143   Date: 5 Dec 1832   RtCt: 7 Dec 1832
Joshua OSBURN (Commr. in Sep 1832 case of John NICHOLS &c agst Charity NICHOLS &c) to Samuel LODGE of Ldn. B/S of 14a (from heirs of James NICHOLS the elder dec'd) adj __ HODSON, LODGE, Thomas OSBURN. Wit: Herod OSBURN, Enos NICHOLS, William OSBURN. Delv. to Saml. LODGE 26 Feb 1834.

3Z:144   Date: 3 Dec 1832   RtCt: 7 Dec 1832
Joshua OSBURN (Commr. in Sep 1832 case of John NICHOLS &c agst Charity NICHOLS &c) to Jefferson C. THOMAS of Ldn. B/S of 3a (from heirs of James NICHOLS the elder dec'd) on Goose Creek adj THOMAS, heirs of Edward CONARD. Wit: Herod OSBURN, Stephen T. CUNNARD, Thomas OSBURN.

3Z:145   Date: 3 Dec 1832   RtCt: 7 Dec 1832
Joshua OSBURN (Commr. in Sep 1832 case of John NICHOLS &c agst Charity NICHOLS &c) to Stephen T. CONARD of Ldn. B/S of 12a (from heirs of James NICHOLS the elder dec'd) adj above lots. Wit: Herod OSBURN, Thos. OSBURN, Jefferson C. THOMAS.

3Z:147   Date: 16 Nov 1832   RtCt: 11 Dec 1832
Dennis McCARTY dec'd. Division – Court order dated 10 Sep 1832; 76a with mansion house to widow Margaret McCARTY as dower; 8a to Caroline McCARTY; 8a to Margaret McCARTY; 27a Lot #1 and attached 18a wood Lot #1 to Billington McCARTY; Lot #2 and attached 12a wood Lot #2 to Dennis McCARTY; 42a Lot #3 to Richard C. McCARTY; undivided mill and 5a mill lott jointly to three males. Divisors: Geo. LOVE, Caleb N. GALLIHER, Horace LUCKETT. Give very detailed plat.

3Z:153   Date: 19 Nov 1832   RtCt: 19 Nov 1832
George RICHARDS & John ROSE to Literary Fund. Bond on RICHARDS as treasurer.

3Z:154   Date: 8 Jul 1830   RtCt: 11 Dec 1832
William MAINS dec'd in right of ch/o Anne dec'd w/o Isaac VANDEVANTER. Division – 50a Lot #1 to Fenton VANDEVANTER; 27a Lot #2 & 14a wood Lot #4 to Mason CHAMBLIN in right of wife Duanner; 42a Lot #3 to James SINCLAIR in right of wife Leanna; 14a Lot #4 & 19a wood Lot #4 to Joseph VANDEVANTER; 23a

wood Lot #5 to John VANDEVANTER; 43¼a Lot #6 to William VANDEVANTER. Divisors: Presley CORDELL, John BRADEN. Gives plat.

3Z:158 Date: 15 Dec 1830 RtCt: 11 Dec 1832
William HARDING dec'd and Henry HARDING. Division – Court order dated 12 Oct 1830; 65a Lot #1 (late residence of Elizabeth HARDING dec'd) to Henry HARDING; 63½a Lot #2 to heirs of Wm. HARDING. Divisors: Joseph HOCKINGS, William GULICK, Stephen GARRETT. Gives plat. From suit of Henry HARDEN agst Chs. G. ESKRIDGE, Guardian ad litem of Wm. HARDEN, Elizabeth HARDEN and Sarah HARDEN infants <21y.

3Z:160 Date: 9 Apr 1832 RtCt: 10 Dec 1832
Benjamin MITCHELL of Ldn, Guardian of DeWitt LANE to Peter GREGG of Ldn. PoA to receive rents of "the Pot house". Wit: Thomas A. H. EVANS, Thornton WALKER.

3Z:161 Date: 10 Dec 1832 RtCt: 10 Dec 1832
Daniel T. MATHIAS & wife Marthey of Ldn to John WAR and John J. MATHIAS of Ldn. Trust for debt to Samuel DAWSON using lot on Church St. in Lsbg (prch/o Henry M. DOWLING), and household items. Delv. to trustees herein named 26 Mar 1835.

3Z:164 Date: 1 Aug 1832 RtCt: 10 Dec 1832
Catharine MILLER (wd/o Peter MILLER dec'd) and Jesse MILLER & wife Rebecca of Ldn to Michael FRYE of Ldn. B/S of 209a adj George COOPER, __ MORRISON, Saml. BAKER, Daniel FRYE. Wit: John WHITE, Mortimer McILHANEY. Delv. to Exor. of M. FRY dec'd 7 Apr 1848.

3Z:167 Date: 18 Jun 1832 RtCt: 10 Dec 1832
Yeoman James BROWN & wife Ruth of Ldn and yeoman George KEENE & wife Nancy of Ldn. Exchange of 1a abt. 1m N of Union adj William CARTER, John WILKINSON, house formerly occ. by Joseph WILKINSON to KEENE and 17 sq poles adj late John WILLIAMS, Isaac BROWN, John WILKINSON to BROWN.

3Z:168 Date: 16 Feb 1832 RtCt: 11 Dec 1832
Asa ROGERS & wife Ellen L. of Ldn to William S. ELGIN of Ldn. B/S of house & 1a Lot #80 & #81 in Aldie adj Lewis BERKLEY (prch/o Townshend McVEIGH as trustee for James RUST). Wit: A. GIBSON, Hamilton ROGERS. Delv. to ELGIN 24 Aug 1833.

3Z:170 Date: 11 Dec 1832 RtCt: 11 Dec 1832
Edward HAINES to Manly HAINES. Trust for debt to John CAMPBELL using farm animals, household items.

3Z:171 Date: 29 Dec 1825 RtCt: 24 Oct 1832
Charles BINNS & wife Hannah of Ldn to Charles G. ESKRIDGE of Ldn. B/S of 20a (prch/o Peter BENEDUM) adj George RUST. Delv. to ESKRIDGE 4 Aug 1836.

3Z:173   Date: 12 Dec 1832   RtCt: 12 Dec 1832
James D. LOVE of Ldn to John MARTIN of Ldn. Trust for debt to Valentine V. PURCELL & Charles B. HAMILTON using horse, Negro woman Betty. Delv. to PURCEL 9 Jul 1834.

3Z:175   Date: 13 Nov 1832   RtCt: 14 Dec 1832
Joseph HILLIARD & wife Ann Eliza of Lsbg to Richard H. HENDERSON, Saml. M. EDWARDS, Jesse TIMMS & Burr W. HARRISON. Trust for debt to Eliza A. BARRY of Oatlands using lot on Back St in Lsbg (cnvy/b Samuel MURRY Dec 1817). Wit: Francis W. LUCKETT, Presley CORDELL. Delv. to Jesse TIMMS 29 Aug 1834.

3Z:178   Date: 15 Dec 1832   RtCt: 15 Dec 1832
David OGDEN & wife Eliza of Ldn to Thomas LITTLETON of Ldn. B/S of lot at King and Cornwall Sts in Lsbg. Wit: Tasker C. QUINLAN, Presley CORDELL.

3Z:181   Date: 1 Aug 1832   RtCt: 20 Dec 1832
Michael FRYE & wife Mary of Ldn to John HAMILTON & Samuel KALB of Ldn. Trust for debt to Jesse MILLER using 209a cnvy/b MILLER adj George COOPER, Samuel BAKER, Daniel FRYE. Wit: John WHITE, Mortimer McILHANEY.

3Z:184   Date: 21 May 1831   RtCt: 22 Dec 1832
Charles TYLER & wife Christian of WashDC to Robert ARMISTEAD of Ldn. B/S of 64a "Pullers lot" (allotted from John TYLER dec'd) adj __ DENNIS, Owsleys branch. Wit: James ORD, Charles H. W. WHARTEN.

3Z:186   Date: 10 Oct 1832   RtCt: 22 Dec 1832
Robert ARMISTEAD of Ldn to Thomas CAMRON of Ldn. B/S of 64a as above. Delv. to CAMERON 20 Dec 1833.

3Z:188   Date: 24 Dec 1832   RtCt: 24 Dec 1832
William FRY to William SLATES [SLATER?]. Trust for debt to Benjamin MILES using farm animals, household items.

3Z:189   Date: 13 Aug 1831   RtCt: 25 Dec 1832
Norman URTON & wife Bersheba of Hampshire Co Va to Mordecai THROCKMORTON of Ldn. B/S of 175a at Manner of Leeds adj reps. of William L. LEE. Delv. to John A. THROCKMORTON for Sarah M. THROCKMORTON 26 Jul 1838.

3Z:191   Date: 2 Sep 1832   RtCt: 27 Dec 1832
John DAVIS & wife Sarah of Ldn to George W. WASHINGTON of Ldn. B/S of 179a adj Mortimer McILHANEY, __ MORRISON, Thomas WHITE, heirs of James NIXON, Daniel HIND. Wit: Mortimer McILHANEY, John WHITE.

3Z:194   Date: 28 Dec 1832   RtCt: 28 Dec 1832
Bernard HOUGH of Lsbg to John A. BINNS of Lsbg. B/S of lot in Lsbg adj __ POTTER (formerly Joseph SMITH), Bernard HOUGH, Jacob FADELEY.

3Z:195   Date: 10 Aug 1832   RtCt: 28 Dec 1832
John HUNT Sr. of Ldn to Francis SIMPSON of Ldn. B/S of lot in Hllb (cnvy/b Isaac HOUGH of Cincinnati May 1820, DBk BBB:164). Delv. to SIMPSON 31 Dec 1834.

3Z:196   Date: 31 Dec 1832   RtCt: 31 Dec 1832
William HOUGH s/o Garret HOUGH of Ldn to Elijah JAMES of Ldn. Trust for debt to Joseph COX using household items.

3Z:198   Date: 13 Nov 1832   RtCt: 31 Dec 1832
Rachel HICKS of Ldn to James BOWLES of Ldn . B/S of 260a where BOWLES now lives (formerly of Isaac GIBSON Sr. dec'd) and her int. in estate of Isaac GIBSON Sr. dec'd). Delv. to BOWLES 28 Jan 1836.

3Z:199   Date: 13 Nov 1832   RtCt: 31 Dec 1832
James BOWLES & wife Elizabeth of Ldn to Kimble G. HICKS and Rachel HICKS of Ldn. Trust for debt to Rachel HICKS using above land. Wit: Cuthbert POWELL, Edw'd HALL.

3Z:201   Date: 5 Aug 1832   RtCt: 1 Jan 1833
Ann HOLE (heir of Levi HOLE dec'd) of Ldn to Eli HUNT of Ldn. B/S of 8a on Kittocton mt. adj Benjamin WHITE, Thomas CARR (part of land cnvy/b Israel & Blackstone JANNEY Sep 1797, DBk Y:033). Wit: Jno. H. McCABE, Tasker C. QUINLAN. Delv. to HUNT 12 Jan 1835.

3Z:203   Date: 1 Jan 1833   RtCt: 1 Jan 1833
Obed COOKSEY & wife Susan of Ldn to Levi COOKSEY of Ldn. B/S of undivided share from their 7a joint prch/o William PIGGOTT (DBk SSS:407) on NW fork of Goose Creek adj Samuel IDEN, and 3a adj Stephen WILSON, Bernard TAYLOR. Wit: Presley CORDELL, John H. McCABE. Delv. to Levi 8 Jul 1833.

3Z:206   Date: 3 Dec 1832   RtCt: 1 Jan 1833
James & William HOEY of Ldn to Daniel EVERHEART of Ldn. B/S of ¼a Lot #9 & ¼a Lot #10 in Lovettsville the German Settlement. Delv. to EVERHEART 18 Apr 1835.

3Z:207   Date: 2 Jan 1833   RtCt: 2 Jan 1833
Richard H. HENDERSON of Ldn to John ALLDER of Ldn. Release of trust of May 1828 for debt to Lewis WALKER. Delv. to ALDER 14 Jun 1838.

3Z:208   Date: 18 Jul 1826   RtCt: 3 Jan 1833
George FICHTER of Ldn to John FICHTER of Ldn. Trust for debt to Harriet T. FICHTER of Ldn using 1¼a (from div. of Leonard THOMAS dec'd allotted dau Sarah w/o FICHTER).

3Z:210   Date: 9 Jan 1833   RtCt: 9 Jan 1833
Thomas LITTLETON & wife Elizabeth of Ldn to Charles G. ESKRIDGE of Ldn. Trust for debt to John GRAY of Ldn using lot in Lsbg (cnvy/b David OGDEN Dec 1832). Wit: John J. MATHIAS, Presley CORDELL. Delv. to trustee __.

3Z:214 Date: 9 Jan 1833 RtCt: 9 Jan 1833
Richard H. HENDERSON of Ldn to Isaac BOWLES of Ldn. B/S of
int. in mill formerly of Daniel VERNON dec'd (from trust of David
GIBSON for wife Nancy now dec'd requested by Admr Hugh SMITH;
later says by David GIBSON for benefit of mother Nancy on estate
of Rebecca VERNON dec'd). Delv. to Jas. BOWLES per order filed
3Y?, 26 May 1836.

3Z:215 Date: 20 May 1832 RtCt: 10 Jan 1833
Francis W. LUCKETT (Exor of William BRONAUGH dec'd) and
widow Jane BRONAUGH of Ldn to Uriel GLASCOCK of Ldn. B/S of
189a adj Joseph LANE dec'd, William J. BRONAUGH, Mrs.
POWELL, and 6a (prch/o John IDEN, Aug 1816) adj __
GOCHNAUER.

3Z:218 Date: 7 Aug 1832 RtCt: 11 Jan 1833
James R. COLEMAN (insolvent debtor) of Ldn to Sheriff John
McNEALE of Culpeper Co & Sheriff Johnston CLEVELAND of Ldn.
B/S of int. in small "Cub Run tract" in Ldn and __a in Bourbon Co
Ky. Wit: William FOUSHEE.

3Z:220 Date: 31 Dec 1832 RtCt: 11 Jan 1833
Saddler Abner CARTER & wife Martha E. of Union yeoman Gourley
REEDER of Ldn. Trust for debt to yeoman John G. HUMPHREY in
own right and as agent for William RICHARDS & wife Margaret of
Illinois and Abraham VICKERS of William of Ldn using 115a on
Goose Creek now occ. by Abraham VICKERS. Wit: Edward HALL,
Benjamin GRAYSON.

3Z:223 Date: 1 Apr 1832 RtCt: 14 Jan 1833
Theodore N. DAVISSON & wife Sally of Ldn to Frederick A.
DAVISSON of Ldn. Trust for debt to John WHITE of Ldn using 103a
adj William STEER, __ EVANS. Wit: Mortimer McILHANEY,
Ebenezer GRUBB.

3Z:226 Date: 17 Sep 1832 RtCt: 11 Jan 1833
Isaac CONWELL & wife Margaret of Ldn to Lemuel WATSON of
Ldn. B/S of lot & house on Liberty St in Lsbg (cnvy/b Joseph KNOX
May 1832). Wit: John J. MATHIAS, Tasker C. QUINLAN. Delv. to
WATSON 19 Aug 1836.

3Z:228 Date: 17 Sep 1832 RtCt: 14 Jan 1833
Lemuel WATSON & wife Lucy H. of Ldn to Samuel M. BOSS of Ldn.
Trust for debt to Isaac CONWELL using lot on Liberty St. in Lsbg.
Wit: John J. MATHIAS, Tasker C. QUINLAN. Delv. to BOSS 1 Sep
1836.

3Z:230 Date: 14 Jan 1833 RtCt: 14 Jan 1833
Washington HUMMER & wife Martina to James CAYLOR. B/S of
86a (Lot #2 in div. of William HUMMER dec'd) nr Fairfax line. Wit:
Charles LEWIS, John BAYLY. Delv. to CAYLOR 7 Nov 1833.

3Z:232 Date: 1 Sep 1828 RtCt: 14 Jan 1833
John JANNEY of Lsbg to Benjamin LESLIE of Hllb. B/S of rights to use spring water for tanyard. Wit: J. A. MARMADUKE, Silas MARMADUKE, Saml. CLENDENING.

3Z:233 Date: 12 Jun 1832 RtCt: 14 Jan 1833
On motion of Jun 1832 of Thomas J. JOHNSON to esta. public landing on Potomack on his land opp. point of Rocks and esta. road. Benjamin P. SMITH, Joseph GORE, Benjamin JACKSON and George MARLOWE to view way for road nr land of heirs of Samuel LUCKETT dec'd to landing. Recommend continuing public road from Nolands Ferry rd to farm of Capt. Samuel DAWSON then to George PRICE then thru Mrs. PRICE's farm to James GRAHAM to landing. George PRICE & wife Elizabeth late CLAPHAM awarded $204.50 in damages on 3 Oct 1832.

3Z:238 Date: 12 Jun 1832 RtCt: 14 Jan 1833
Same motion and viewers as above. James GRAHAM awarded $200 in damages on 29 Jun 1832.

3Z:241 Date: 12 Jun 1832 RtCt: 14 Jan 1833
Same motion and viewers as above. Samuel DAWSON awarded $150 damages on 29 Jun 1832.

3Z:245 Date: 12 Jun 1832 RtCt: 14 Jan 1833
Same motion and viewers as above. Thomas J. JOHNSON awarded $150 damages on 29 Jun 1832.

3Z:249 Date: 31 Dec 1832 RtCt: 14 Jan 1833
Studley MIDDLETON dec'd. Division of Negroes – Negro man Moses & woman East[h]er & Emily to widow Mary Ann L. (also given as Nancy) MIDDLETON; woman Ann & child Henry Clay 2m old to Hiram McVEIGH for A. W. JOHNSON; woman Jane & child James 4y old to Lovel H. MIDDLETON for J. R. MIDDLETON; woman Hannah to Jos. HORREL; girl Tacy to Chs. KENDAH; woman Rachel to Lovel H. MIDDLETON for himself; boy Thornton to Joseph FLEMING; boy Peyton to Lovel H. MIDDLETON for Chs. MIDDLETON; girl Mima to Thomas MIDDLETON. Divisors: Humphrey B. POWELL, Rich'd COCKRAN.

3Z:251 Date: 15 Jan 1832 [33] RtCt: 15 Jan 1833
Joseph EIDSON, George TURNER & John FRANCIS of Ldn. Bond on EIDSON as Committee of John TRIPLETT an idiot or lunatic.

3Z:252 Date: 2 Jan 1833 RtCt: 14 Jan 1833
Jeremiah W. BRONAUGH & wife Elizabeth H. to William BENTON. Trust using 150a but later found to be 171½a (original trust to Bank of Columbia and Daniel KURTZ and Richard SMITH). Wit: Lewis CARBERY, Edm. BROOKE. CoE for Elizabeth in WashDC. Delv. to BENTON 12 Jan 1836.

3Z:257   Date: 18 Sep 1832   RtCt: 14 Jan 1833
Asa ROGERS (Commr. for Hannah BATTSON dec'd of Ldn) to
William R SWART of Fqr. B/S of 160a where Hannah lived on Little
River (owned jointly by Hannah and sister Jane WEATHERBY of
Fqr who died shortly after Hannah) adj Burr POWELL, Townshend
McVEIGH, Noble BEVERIDGE, John ADAMS.

3Z:261   Date: 20 Sep 1832   RtCt: 14 Jan 1833
William R. SWART & wife Elizabeth of Fqr to James WEEKS of Ldn.
B/S of 160a as above. Wit: A. GIBSON, Robt. BAYLY.

3Z:263   Date: 20 Sep 1832   RtCt: 14 Jan 1833
James WEEKS of Ldn to Humphrey B. POWELL of Ldn. Trust for
debt to William R. SWART of Fqr using above land. Delv. to Asa
ROGERS pr order 7 Feb 1840.

3Z:266   Date: 12 Dec 1832   RtCt: 14 Jan 1833
Jonathan PAINTER & wife Delilah of Ldn to James HARPER of Ldn.
B/S of 6a between short hill & Blue Ridge adj E. GRUBB, George
JACOBS, Christina JACOBS. Wit: Mortimer McILHANEY, John
WHITE.

3Z:268   Date: 12 Dec 1832   RtCt: 14 Jan 1833
Mary STOVEN and Charles J. STOVEN of Fqr to James
McFARLAND of Ldn. B/S of 85a (from reps. of Charles STOVEN
dec'd) adj "Brambleton tract". Delv. to McFARLING 13 Jun 1835.

3Z:269   Date: 2 Jan 1833   RtCt: 14 Jan 1833
Alfred GULICK of Ldn to William GULICK. Trust using Negro girl
Lucy Ann for benefit of his wife Nancy and children conforming to
original intent of Leana GULICK who gave slave to his wife Nancy.

3Z:271   Date: 8 Oct 1832   RtCt: 15 Jan 1833
Joseph SANDERS of Washington Co Ohio to his wife Margaret
SANDERS. PoA for claims to estate of her father Enoch TRIPLETT
of Ldn. Wit: Dudley D. GREEN, P. B. JOHNSON. Ackn. from
SAUNDERS in Morgan Co Ohio.

3Z:273   Date: 8 Oct 1832   RtCt: 15 Jan 1833
James TRIPLETT of Roxbury, Washington Co Ohio (s/o Enoch
TRIPLETT dec'd of Ldn) to Jesse TRIPLETT of Ldn. B/S of int. in
father's estate. Wit: J. WILKIN, P. B. JOHNSON.

3Z:274   Date: 22 Nov 1832   RtCt: 15 Jan 1833
Mary TRIPLETT wd/o Enoch TRIPLETT dec'd, Thomas TRIPLETT,
William TRIPLETT & wife Dorcas, John F. TRIPLETT & wife Nancy,
Jesse TRIPLETT, Reubin TRIPLETT, Henry CLICE & wife Sally late
TRIPLETT, Joseph SANDERS & wife Margaret late TRIPLETT,
Jesse LEWIS (for himself and int. prch/o brother James TRIPLETT)
& wife Elizabeth late TRIPLETT (heirs of Enoch TRIPLETT dec'd) to
John P. DULANY of Ldn. B/S of 147a adj heirs of Samuel MURRY
dec'd, Mrs. LEWIS, Enoch GLASCOCK, Goose Creek. CoE for Sally
CLICE in JeffVa. CoE for Dorcas TRIPLETT in Fqr.

3Z:279 Date: 8 Jan 1833 RtCt: 14 Jan 1833
Rachel FOSTER formerly HIBBS of Mdbg to Benjamin HIBBS of
Guernsey Co Ohio. PoA for rents from James HIBBS as tenent on
126a in Ohio.

3Z:280 Date: 16 Jan 1833 RtCt: 16 Jan 1833
Jacob G. PAXSON of Ldn to James H. CHAMBLIN of Ldn. Trust for
Thomas ROGERS of Ldn as security on numerous bonds using land
where PAXSON now resides (see DBk TTT:273).

3Z:282 Date: 15 Jan 1833 RtCt: 16 Jan 1833
John THOMAS & wife Margaret of Ldn to Peter COMPHER of Ldn.
B/S of 47a adj COMPHER, __ RICKARD. Wit: Samuel M.
EDWARDS, Presley CORDELL. Delv. pr order 23 Nov 1833.

3Z:284 Date: 16 Jan 1833 RtCt: 16 Jan 1833
John THOMAS & wife Margaret of Ldn to George RICKARD of Ldn.
B/S of 21a on Broad run adj Peter COMPHER, heirs of Daniel
STONE, and 2a nr mouth of mill tail race. Wit: Saml. M. EDWARDS,
Presley CORDELL. Delv. pr order 16 Sep 1835.

3Z:287 Date: 16 Jan 1833 RtCt: 16 Jan 1833
George RICKARD of Ldn to Henry W. THOMAS of Ldn. Trust for
debt to John THOMAS using above land. Delv to John THOMAS 8
Apr 1834.

3Z:288 Date: 18 Aug 1832 RtCt: 18 Jan 1833
Thomson F. MASON & wife Betsey C. of AlexDC to George
BEAMER of Ldn. B/S of 238¼a (allotted Betsey as heir of Sarah
PRICE dec'd) on Potomac adj Virginia PRICE d/o Sarah PRICE
dec'd, old road to Heaters ferry, __ HICKMAN, __ CHICHESTER.
Wit: Saml. DAWSON, Geo. PRICE, John J. MATHIAS, Saml. M.
EDWARDS. Delv. to BEAMER 7 Jan 1833.

3Z:291 Date: 20 Aug 1832 RtCt: 18 Jan 1833
George BEAMER of Ldn to Richard H. HENDERSON of Ldn. Trust
for debt to Thomson T. MASON of AlexDC using above land. Wit:
Jno. J. MATHIAS, Elias DAVIS, James McLEAN. Delv. to MASON
20 Apr 1836.

3Z:293 Date: 18 Jan 1833 RtCt: 18 Jan 1833
Emanuel WALTMAN of Ldn to John JANNEY of Ldn. Trust for debt
to Morris OSBURN of Ldn using 25a adj __ FRAZIER, __ MARLOW,
__ EVERHEART, and 6a adj __ EVERHEART (both lots allotted
Jacob WALTMAN in div. of father Jacob WALTMAN dec'd and sold
to Emanuel); also 26a adj __ EVERHEART, and 6a (allotted Elias
WALTMAN in div. and sold to Emanuel); and 38a (allotted
Emanuel). Delv. to OSBURN 24 Apr 1834.

3Z:297 Date: 6 Oct 1832 RtCt: 18 Jan 1833
James BOWLES & wife Elizabeth of Ldn to James W. MACRAE of
Ldn. B/S of 42a where BOWLES resides (as heir of Isaac GIBSON

dec'd) W of new road from Clifton Mill to turnpike road. Wit: Cuthbert POWELL, Benjamin GRAYSON. Delv. pr order 23 May 1835.

3Z:299 Date: 20 Jul 1832 RtCt: 18 Jan 1833
Joseph LEWIS & wife Elizabeth O. of Ldn to James W. MACRAE of Ldn. B/S of 50a on Panther Skin Run part of "Clifton" adj road to Clifton Mills. Wit: Benjamin GRAYSON, Edward HALL. Delv. pr order 23 May 1835.

3Z:300 Date: 18 Jan 1833 RtCt: 21 Jan 1833
Robert MOFFETT & Ellen of Ldn to heirs of Henry GLASGOW dec'd. B/S of lot in Lsbg adj Benjamin SHREVE Sr., Glasgow's brick house. Wit: James RUST, Presley CORDELL.

3Z:302 Date: 10 Dec 1832 RtCt: 23 Jan 1833
James H. BENNET & wife Mary A. of Ldn to John JANNEY of Ldn. Trust for debt to John HOOF of Alex DC using int. in land formerly belonging to his mother where father Charles BENNETT dec'd was tenant. Wit: Edward HALL, Francis W. LUCKETT.

3Z:304 Date: 21 Jan 1833 RtCt: 25 Jan 1833
John BAYLY & Mountjoy BAYLY of Ldn to George BAYLY of FredVa. B/S of int. in 69a (will of Peirce BAYLY Sr. dev. to sons land adj Ariss BUCKNER, leased to Thomas REESE and lease sold to John BLAKER who is now in possession). Delv. pr order 27 Jan 1834.

3Z:306 Date: 2 Jan 1833 RtCt: 29 Jan 1833
William BENTON of Ldn to Richard SMITH (Cashier of Bank of US in WashDC). Trust for debt to U.S. Bank using 171½a (cnvy/b Jeremiah W. BRONAUGH) adj William SMITH, Thomas OUSLEY. Wit: S. SMITH, Mrs. B. VAN ZANDT. Delv. by mail to S. H. SMITH pr order 31 Dec 1835.

3Z:311 Date: 4 Feb 1833 RtCt: 4 Feb 1833
Amos BEALE & wife Elizabeth of Ldn to Saml. M. EDWARDS of Ldn. Trust for debt to Charles B. HAMILTON of Ldn using 105a (cnvy/b David BEALE Jun 1823, DBk FFF:494). Delv. to HAMILTON 10 Apr 1834. Wit: Thomas SAUNDERS, John J. MATHIAS.

3Z:313 Date: 4 Feb 1833 RtCt: 4 Feb 1833
Amos BEALE & wife Elizabeth of Ldn to Enos B. CORDELL of Ldn. Trust for debt to Presley CORDELL of Ldn using 105a (cnvy/b father David BEALE) adj James GREENLEASE, Benjamin WHITE. Wit: John J. MATHIAS, John H. McCABE.

3Z:316 Date: 4 Feb 1833 RtCt: 4 Feb 1833
David LOVETT of Ldn to Amos BEALE of Ldn. Release of trust of Jul 1827 for debt to John TEMPLER & Enos NICHOLS (Admrs of John TEMPLER dec'd) on 105a.

3Z:317 Date: 2 Feb 1833 RtCt: 7 Feb 1833
George W. HENRY of Ldn to Jared CHAMBLIN of Ldn. Trust for debt to Thomas ROGERS of Ldn using one moiety of 90a during his

lifetime in farm of William FOX dec'd dev. to his wife Mary FOX now dec'd (from ct. decree to HENRY as Admr of Elizabeth HENRY dec'd formerly FOX agst John BRADEN & John WRIGHT Admrs of Mary FOX dec'd who was Ex. of William FOX dec'd).

3Z:319   Date: 4 Feb 1833   RtCt: 11 Feb 1833
Joseph WOOD & wife Lydia of Ldn to Addison H. CLARKE of Ldn. Trust for debt to Elizabeth WORSLEY Ex. of John WORSLEY dec'd using 150a adj Asa MOORE dec'd, heirs of Joseph TALBOTT dec'd, heirs of Elijah MYRES, Jonathan MYRES, William FOX dec'd, WOOD, and 80a adj Jonas POTTS, Pompey WHITEN, Stephen BALL, Mahlon JANNEY Jr., new addition to Wtfd, and 12a adj Emanuel NEWCOMER, M. SULLIVAN. Wit: Samuel HOUGH, Presley CORDELL.

3Z:323   Date: 7 Feb 1833   RtCt: 11 Feb 1833
Joseph LEWIS & wife Elizabeth of Ldn to Hamilton LUFBOROUGH of Fqr. Trust for debt to Exor of Richard ROSS dec'd of MontMd using "Clifton" except part sold to James MaCRAE. Wit: Charles LEWIS, Benjamin GRAYSON. Delv. to LOUFBRUGH 1 Apr 1834.

3Z:328   Date: 24 Oct 1831   RtCt: 11 Feb 1833
David GIBSON (Exor of Richard CRUPPER dec'd) to James ROGERS of Ldn. B/S of 118a (given to wife Nancy CRUPPER now died) adj Townshend D. PEYTON, __ TASSEY, __ McCARTY (less 2a used by turnpike road that runs through tract). Delv. to ROGERS 10 Nov 1834.

3Z:329   Date: __ Feb 1833   RtCt: 11 Feb 1833
John YOUNG of Ldn to Abraham SHOEMAKER of Ldn. Trust for benefit of wife Hannah and any children using 92a where he now lives (1/3 in life estate for mother) adj Wm. YOUNG, John ALDRIDGE, John GREGG reps., Betsey HOGUE, farm animals, household items (current debts to Wm. & Alfred WRIGHT, Thomas ROGERS, John PANCOAST). Wit: Wm. CHILTON, Jacob WATERS, Wm. IREY.

3Z:331   Date: 5 Nov 1832   RtCt: 11 Feb 1833
Jesse EVANS & wife Polly/Mary of Ldn to Isaac TALLY of Ldn. B/S of land between them containing a spring of water. Wit: Ebenezer GRUBB, John WHITE. Delv. to TALLY 16 Jun 1834.

3Z:333   Date: __ Dec 1832   RtCt: 11 Feb 1833
Edward CARTER & wife Patsey and Martha w/o Abner CARTER of Ldn to Henry PLASTER Jr. of Ldn. B/S of Lot #3, #4 & #5 nr Union (from div. of William GALLEHER dec'd and cnvy/b heirs) adj James REED, Seth SMITH, William GALLAHER. Wit: Edward HALL, Abner GIBSON. Delv. pr order 11 Jun 1834.

3Z:335   Date: 8 Feb 1833   RtCt: 11 Feb 1833
Yeoman Henry H. HUTCHISON & wife Susan of Ldn to yeoman Isaac PIGGOTT of Ldn. B/S of several lots totaling 106a (cnvy/b

Samuel DUNKIN & Henry PLASTER Sr.) Wit: Edward HALL, A. GIBSON.

3Z:337 Date: 1 Dec 1831 RtCt: 11 Feb 1833
Wallace W. DANIEL & wife Eliza B. of Ldn to James ROGERS of Ldn. B/S of 23a where DANIEL now lives (Lot #6 from div. of father Joseph DANIEL dec'd). Wit: A. GIBSON, Hamilton ROGERS. Delv. to ROGERS 10 Dec 1834.

3Z:339 Date: 15 Jan 1833 RtCt: 11 Feb 1833
William HOGE (and as Exor of Jesse HOGE dec'd and Exor of Isaac NICHOLS dec'd) of Ldn to Sarah DONOHOE of Ldn. Release of trust of Sep 1827 for debt to William HOGE) on 66a adj Glebe of Shelburne Parish (DBk PPP:019). Delv to her son Stephen Joseph DONOHOE 31 Oct 1833.

3Z:340 Date: 13 Apr 1832 RtCt: 14 Feb 1833
David NEER dec'd. Allotment of dower to widow Susannah G. NEER – 68a, reserving to children privilege of waggon road for getting to timber land on W side of short hill.. Commrs. John CONARD, Christian MILLER, George MILLER. Gives plat. From suit of Susannah G. NEER agst Eli SNUKE & wife Sarah Ann, Susannah NEER, Ann NEAR, Elizabeth NEAR, Hannah NEAR & Amos NEAR infant children of David NEAR dec'd.

3Z:343 Date: 11 Feb 1833 RtCt: 11 Feb 1833
William BEVERIDGE, Hugh SMITH & Samuel CHINN. Bond on BEVERIDGE as constable.

3Z:344 Date: __ Feb 1833 RtCt: 12 Feb 1833
Richard H. HENDERSON of Ldn to Mary THORNTON & Sarah WALTERS otherwise called THORNTON (devisees of Charles THORNTON dec'd) of Ldn. B/S of int. of George H. SINCLAIR in land of Samuel SINCLAIR dec'd (suit of Mary & Sarah agst George H. SINCLAIR, for land of Samuel SINCLAIR dec'd which belonged to his son George H. SINCLAIR; suit of Charles THORNTON & wife Sarah a dau. of Samuel SINCLAIR dec'd agst Thomas M. SINCLAIR where THORNTON had purchased int. of George H. without getting a deed, see DBk AAA:027). Delv. to Alfred BELT Exor. of Chs. THORNTON 23 Aug 1838.

3Z:345 Date: 5 Oct 1832 RtCt: 5 Oct 1832
Johnston CLEVELAND, William MERSHON, James L. McKENNA & W. C. SELDEN Jr. of Ldn to John Armstead CARTER of Ldn. B/S of 46¾a (Lot #7 of "Belmont tract" prch/o Ludwell LEE) on Ox road.

3Z:346 Date: 21 Jan 1833 RtCt: 11 Feb 1833
Thomas WHITE of Ldn to Joseph WOOD of Ldn. Release of trust of Oct 1826 for debt to Joshua PUSEY. Wit: Jno. A. BINNS, Chs. G. ESKRIDGE, W. A. POWELL, R. H. HENDERSON.

3Z:347   Date: 15 Jan 1833   RtCt: 12 Feb 1833
Elijah VIOLETT of Fred Va and Charles WRIGHT (Exor. of Phebe VIOLETT dec'd wd/o Elijah VIOLETT dec'd) of Ldn to Hiram SEATON of Ldn. B/S of 70a on Panther Skin adj Amos DENHAM. Delv. to SEATON 15 May 1840.

3Z:349   Date: 28 Jan 1833   RtCt: 14 Feb 1833
Charles SHEPHERD & wife Elizabeth of Ldn to Saml. M. EDWARDS of Ldn. Trust for Samuel M. BOSS & Danl. G. SMITH as endorsers on bank note using lot on S side of Cornwell St in Lsbg (cnvy/b Thomas R. SAUNDERS Nov 1824) adj John G. WATT, William A. POWELL.

3Z:350   Date: 16 Mar 1832   RtCt: 14 Feb 1833
Saml. M. EDWARDS & wife Ann of Ldn to Elizabeth VANDEVANTER of Ldn. B/S of 46a (part of purchase from DIGGS). Wit: Francis W. LUCKETT, John H. McCABE.

3Z:352   Date: 1 Jan 1833   RtCt: 18 Feb 1833
Charles G. ESKRIDGE & wife Margaret of Lsbg to Saml. M. EDWARDS of Lsbg. Trust for debt to Samuel M. BOSS of Lsbg using 20a, 65a & 64a. Wit: John H. McCABE, John J. MATHIAS. Delv. to BOSS 23 Oct 1833.

3Z:354   Date: 16 Mar 1832   RtCt: 14 Feb 1833
Elizabeth VANDEVANTER of Ldn to Samuel M. EDWARDS of Ldn. B/S of 56a (part of allot. as heir of William MAINS dec'd) on NW side of Kittocton Mt. adj Thomas SWANN. Delv. to EDWARDS 3 Oct 1834.

3Z:355   Date: 15 Feb 1833   RtCt: 19 Feb 1833
Mathew ELGIN of Ldn to John A. BINNS of Ldn. Trust for Hiram McVEIGH, Gustavus ELGIN, Wesley McPHERSON, Saml. SIMPSON & Richard ADAMS as security on note to John CHEW using int. in land of father Francis ELGIN dec'd and Negro woman Nancy & her children Sinah and Sarah.

3Z:356   Date: 21 Feb 1833   RtCt: 21 Feb 1833
John MARTIN & wife Mary of Ldn to Edward FRANCIS of Ldn. B/S of lot on E side of King St in Lsbg adj Henry SAUNDERS, Phillip NELSON, __ WILDMAN (DBk UUU:327 [329], subject to life estate of Henry Moore DAVIS). Wit: Presley CORDELL, Saml. M. EDWARDS.

3Z:358   Date: 27 Dec 1832   RtCt: 21 Feb 1833
Newton MURPHEY of Ldn to Mahlon FULTON of Ldn. Trust for debt to Joseph P. McGEATH of Ldn using farm and household items at his home in Bloomfield.

3Z:359   Date: 1 Jan 1833   RtCt: 22 Feb 1833
John MURRY of Ldn to John A. BINNS of Lsbg. Trust for debt to Michael MORRALLE of Lsbg (rent on house & lot nr. Fayette BALL

Esqr) using farm animals, farm and household items. Delv. pr order 18 Feb 1836.

3Z:361   Date: 22 Feb 1833   RtCt: 22 Feb 1833
John P. HALL of Ldn to Marcus D. BAKER of FredVa. B/S of int. in estate of father Enoch TRIPLETT dec'd (from defaulted trust of Jesse TRIPLETT).

3Z:362   Date: 9 Feb 1833   RtCt: 23 Feb 1833
Sarsfield/Sanfield J. FOLEY of BaltMd to mother Sarah FOLEY of BaltMd. B/S of 390a in PrWm and slave men Ceasar & Simon, women Betty & Milly, girls Margaret, Dolly, Milly, Patsey, Lucinda, Sally, Henna, & Ellen, and boys Charles, Sam, Robert, Edmund & George (Sanfield's share as only child of father Presley FOLEY dec'd late of Ldn).

3Z:364   Date: 23 Feb 1833   RtCt: 23 Feb 1833
John HALL Ldn to Adin WHITE and Richard WHITE of Ldn. B/S of 60½a adj Thomas HUGHES, Benj. WHITE (prch/o trustees of Loveless CONWELL).

3Z:365   Date: 29 Oct 1832   RtCt: 25 Feb 1833
Walter ELGIN Jr. & wife Sarah of Wayne Co Ohio to Lewis J. DONOHOE of Ldn. B/S of int. in house & lot on W side of Back St. in Lsbg adj Mrs. BLINCOE (allotted heirs of William HALL dec'd from estate of Josiah HALL dec'd). Wit: Wilson C. SELDEN Jr., Presley CORDELL.

3Z:366   Date: 20 Feb 1833   RtCt: 25 Feb 1833
Thomas HALL & wife Elizabeth and Samuel HALL & wife Mahala Ann of Ldn to John WADE of Ldn. B/S of undivided 1/6th int. in lot on W side of Back St in Lsbg (as above) adj Martha BLINCOE, Peter OATYER, Thomas BIRKLEY. Wit: Wilson C. SELDEN Jr., Presley CORDELL. Delv. to WADE 23 Nov 1833.

3Z:368   Date: 26 Feb 1833   RtCt: 26 Feb 1833
Henry BENEDUM to Edward HAMMAT. Trust for debt to Joseph LAYCOCK & James HIGDON using house & lot on N side of Loudoun St in Lsbg now occupied by widow NEWTON.

3Z:369   Date: 2 Jan 1830   RtCt: 27 Feb 1833
Burr W. HARRISON and Jesse TIMMS (trustees of T. C. QUINLAN & his creditors) to George CARTER. B/S of 213a "Daniels Lott" (excluding 14¼a) S of Goose Creek adj __ POWELL, __MONROE, Elizabeth HARDING. Wit: A. G. WATERMAN, Thomas ROGERS, Erasmus G. HAMILTON. Delv. to CARTER 8 Feb 1839.

3Z:371   Date: 17 Nov 1832   RtCt: 28 Feb 1833
James CURL Jr. & wife Ann of Greene Co Ohio to James CURL of FredVa. PoA for monies from estate of William HOUGH dec'd late of Ldn and estate of his consort Eleanor HOUGH dec'd. Wit: Josiah DAVISSON, David DOUGLASS.

3Z:373 Date: 10 Jan 1833 RtCt: 18 Feb/4 Mar 1833
James THOMAS of Ldn to John FRANCIS of Ldn. Trust for debt to
Enoch FRANCIS & Thomas FRANCIS of Ldn using ¼a lot on
Loudoun St in Lsbg adj Charles GULLAT and 118a below Lsbg
where THOMAS now resides, and farm and household items. Delv.
to FRANCIS 4 Mar 1836.

3Z:374 Date: 18 Dec 1832 RtCt: 28 Feb 1833
Thomas ROGERS & wife Elmina S. of Ldn to Jonathan CARTER of
Ldn. B/S of 111a (from div. George NIXON dec'd in DBk XX:202,
18a Lot #2 to Samuel WHITE, 18a Lot #3 to Jesse HARRIS, 19a Lot
#4 to Joseph WHITE and 19a Lot #5 to William WHITE, 5/9th of lot
all. heirs of Patty TAVENER dec'd, int. in Lot #6, 7a Lot #7 to
George TAVENER Jr., 9a Lot #8 to Henry BELL, 9a Lot #9 to Isaac
BROWN) on Goose Creek where Thomas BISCOE now dec'd lived.
Wit: Francis W. LUCKETT, Tasker C. QUINLAN. Delv. to CARTER
24 Mar 1835.

3Z:376 Date: 29 Jan 1833 RtCt: 4 Mar 1833
George MARKS & wife Mahala of Fqr to William C. PALMER of Ldn.
B/S of ½a (cnvy/b heirs of Joseph LOVETT) adj __ DUNKIN, __
GALLEHER, Isaac BROWN.

3Z:378 Date: 6 Mar 1833 RtCt: 6 Mar 1833
George TURNER to Richard C. McCARTY & Dennis McCARTY of
Ldn. Release of trust of Nov 1831 for debt to James SWART on
200a prop. of father Dennis McCARTY dec'd.

3Z:379 Date: 6 Mar 1833 RtCt: 6 Mar 1833
Thomas ROGERS Dpty Shff for Shff Johnston CLEVELAND to
George RHODES. B/S of 4a (3 leased lots nr Lsbg, from execution
on Archibald M. LYLES). Delv. to RHODES 9 Sep 1836.

3Z:380 Date: 8 Mar 1833 RtCt: 8 Mar 1833
George K. FOX & wife Frances of Ldn to Saml. M. BOSS of Ldn.
B/S of ¼a on S side of Cornwall St Lsbg (see DBk CCC:258) adj
BOSS, __ DOWLING, __ SMITH, William A. POWELL. Wit: Presley
CORDELL, John H. McCABE. Delv. to BOSS 20 Mar 1843.

3Z:382 Date: 8 Sep 1832 RtCt: 9 Mar 1833
Thomas SWANN of WashDC to Richard SMITH cashier of Bank of
US. Trust for debt to Bank of US using 1400a nr Lsbg. Wit: James
ORD, Jno. N. MAULDON. Delv. to SMITH 22 Jun 1835.

3Z:384 Date: 2 Mar 1833 RtCt: 11 Mar 1833
George MILLER & wife Elizabeth (heir of John WALTMAN dec'd) of
Muskingum Co Ohio to Scivilla SLATES of Ldn. B/S of undivided int.
in 48a as dower for widow of John WALTMAN dec'd (now occup. by
Jacob WALTERS who m. widow). Wit: Mortimer McILHANEY, Geo.
W. SHAWEN.

3Z:386 Date: 24 Jan 1833 RtCt: 11 Mar 1833
Jonathan EWERS & wife Mary of Ldn to William BLEAKLEY of Ldn.
B/S of 105a adj Stephen JANNEY, __ ROMINE, __ LODGE. Wit:
Notley C. WILLIAMS, Edward HALL. Delv. to BLAKELY 12 Aug
1833.

3Z:388 Date: 29 Dec 1832 RtCt: 11 Mar 1833
Isaac STEER & wife Elizabeth of Ldn to Samuel PAXSON of Ldn.
B/S of 2 rood lot adj STEER, PAXSON. Wit: Samuel DAWSON,
Geo. W. SHAWEN. Delv. to PAXSON 24 Feb 1847.

3Z:389 Date: 11 Mar 1833 RtCt: 11 Mar 1833
Robert DARNE & wife Fanny/Frances of Ldn to James CAYLOR of
Ldn. B/S of 39a adj Levi HUMMER, Robert HUNTER, old Alexandria
road at Church road. Wit: Wilson C. SELDEN Jr., Presley
CORDELL. Delv. to CAYLOR 7 Nov 1833.

3Z:391 Date: 7 Mar 1833 RtCt: 11 Mar 1833
Leven Ludwell SANDS of Ldn to Vallentine V. PURSELL of Ldn. B/S
of 15a on Katocton Creek, __ PAXSON, and 5a on NW side of
Katocton Mt. (both cnvy/b John RUSE of Seneca Co Ohio).

3Z:392 Date: 1 Feb 1833 RtCt: 11 Mar 1833
William C. PALMER & wife Lucinda of Ldn to A. G. TEBBETTS of
Ldn. B/S of house & ½a in Union (cnvy/b George MARKS) adj Isaac
BROWN. Wit: Notley C. WILLIAMS, Benj. GRAYSON.

3Z:394 Date: 9 Mar 1833 RtCt: 11 Mar 1833
Philip EVERHART of Ldn to John H. BOGAN of Ldn. B/S of 22a adj
Elizabeth EMERY, BOGAN, __ COOPER, and 13a on E side of
Short Hill and __ JANNEY, __ STREAM.

3Z:395 Date: 9 Jan 1832 RtCt: 13 Mar 1832/11 Mar 1833
Keturah BARR (grandd/o George NIXON dec'd) of Ldn to Evan
WILKINSON of Ldn. B/S 15a from undivided estate of grandfather
(allotted to ch/o his dau Hannah BARR who m. Hugh BARR). Wit:
Abner CARTER, Craven WALKER, Saml. HAMMONTREE, Seth
SMITH. Delv. to WILKINSON 6 Dec 1834.

3Z:397 Date: 18 Jan 1833 RtCt: 11 Mar 1833
Elisha KITCHEN of Ldn to Lawson MONEY of Ffx. B/S of 104a adj
__ JENKINS, road from Lanesville to Alexandria. Delv. to MONEY
14 Jan 1834.

3Z:399 Date: 11 Mar 1833 RtCt: 11 Mar 1833
Ariss BUCKNER, Thomas B. MERSHON, James McFARLAN, John
C. TIPPETT, Wm. H. CRAVEN, Horace LUCKETT, Thomas
ROGERS, Asa ROGERS, Wm. THRIFT, Wm. MERSHON, Jacob
SUMMERS, Johnston CLEVELAND & Fielding LITTLETON. Bond
on BUCKNER as Sheriff to collect officers fees.

3Z:399 Date: 11 Mar 1833 RtCt: 11 Mar 1833
Ariss BUCKNER, Thomas B. MERSHON, James McFARLAN, John
C. TIPPETT, Wm. H. CRAVEN, Horace LUCKETT, Thomas

ROGERS, Asa ROGERS, Wm. THRIFT, Wm. MERSHON, Jacob SUMMERS, Johnston CLEVELAND & Fielding LITTLETON. Bond on BUCKNER as Sheriff to collect taxes.

3Z:400 Date: 11 Mar 1833 RtCt: 11 Mar 1833
Ariss BUCKNER, Thomas B. MERSHON, James McFARLAN, John C. TIPPETT, Wm. H. CRAVEN, Horace LUCKETT, Thomas ROGERS, Asa ROGERS, Wm. THRIFT, Wm. MERSHON, Jacob SUMMERS, Johnston CLEVELAND & Fielding LITTLETON. Bond on BUCKNER as Sheriff to collect levies.

3Z:401 Date: 11 Mar 1833 RtCt: 11 Mar 1833
Chilton CRAVEN, Amos GULICK & Mahlon CRAVEN. Bond on Chilton CRAVEN as constable.

3Z:402 Date: 3 Feb 1833 RtCt: 15 Feb 1833
William HAMILTON of Charles Co Md to Burr W. HARRISON (in place of Thomas R. MOTT now dec'd trustee of T. C. QUINLAN). Release of trust of Nov 1824 for debt to William HAMILTON using 798a. Wit: Horace LUCKETT.

3Z:404 Date: 12 Mar 1833 RtCt: 12 Mar 1833
Thomas GRIMES & wife Elizabeth of AlexDC to John LACY of Ldn. B/S of Lot #24 & #30 on Janney St. in new addition to Wtfd. Wit: John H. McCABE, Presley CORDELL. Delv. to LACEY 11 Apr 1836.

3Z:406 Date: 16 Feb 1832 RtCt: 12 Mar 1833
Stephen C. ROSZELL dec'd. Division – divisors George MARKS, James JOHNSTON, Hugh ROGERS & Hugh SMITH chosen by Stephen G., Phebe & Nancy ROSZELL heirs of Stephen C. dec'd and Samuel BROWN rep. of Stephen Wesley ROSZEL by prch/o his right to land where Phebe & Nancy reside – 100a plantation with improvements, claim agst BROWN given up and he can raise dam on Beaverdam as high as he wants without overflowing land but gives up all claims on any land. Stephen G. ROSZEL to get field on E side of Turnpike (with water rights to Phebe & Nancy) and 4a on opposite side of turnpike (or W side of place).

3Z:408 Date: 12 Mar 1833 RtCt: 12 Mar 1833
Michael DERRY, Peter DERRY, Nicholas ROPP & Robert JOHNSON. Bond on Michael DERRY as constable.

3Z:408 Date: 11 Mar 1833 RtCt: 12 Mar 1833
John CARR of Ldn. DoE for slave James POTTER aged abt 40y.

3Z:409 Date: 24 Mar 1830 RtCt: 14 Mar 1833
Joseph VANDEVANTER dec'd. Division – 11a Lot #1 & 26a wood Lot #1 and slave Harry to Washington VANDEVANTER; 43a Lot #2 & 16a wood Lot #2 and slave Charlotte to Eliza Ann VANDEVANTER; 87a Lot #3 and slave James to Isaac VANDEVANTER; 80a Lot #4 and slave Linna to Mary VANDEVANTER; 82a Lot #5 and slave Kitty to Armistead Mason VANDEVANTER, 87a Lot #6 and slave Charles to Gabriel

VANDEVANTER; 77a Lot #7 and slave Adalaide to Cornelius Means VANDEVANTER. Divisors: Presley CORDELL, Jno. BRADEN, Noble S. BRADEN. Slaves Nancy & Lewis to widow Elizabeth VANDEVANTER. Gives plat.

3Z:413   Date: 15 Feb 1833   RtCt: 15 Mar 1833
Thomas WHITE of Ldn to sons James & Thomas WHITE Jr. of Ldn. B/S of 217a (cnvy/b Burr BRADEN & trustees of Nathaniel MANNING dec'd) adj William VERTS, John WRIGHT, Isaac HOLMES, Archibald McDANIEL, Amos BEANS, and 62a (cnvy/b trustees of Nathaniel MANNING dec'd) adj Isaac HOLMES, Sarah NIXON.

3Z:414   Date: 1 May 1832   RtCt: 15 Mar 1833
James COPELAND & wife Sarah of Ldn to Thomas WHITE of Ldn. B/S of 3a (prch/o Nathaniel MANNING dec'd) adj John WRIGHT. Wit: John WHITE, Mortimer McILHANEY. Delv. to WHITE 4 Feb 1842.

3Z:416   Date: 11 Mar 1833   RtCt: 15 Mar 1833
James & Thomas WHITE of Ldn to father Thomas WHITE of Ldn. B/S of 139a adj John WRIGHT, Mortimer McILHANEY, Mary WHITE. Delv. to Thomas WHITE 20 May 1836.

3Z:417   Date: 11 Mar 1833   RtCt: 15 Mar 1833
Thomas WHITE of Ldn to Isaac HOLMES of Ldn. B/S of 3 rood lot (part of prch/o Nathaniel MANNING dec'd) adj Holmes Mill lot, John WRIGHT. Delv. to HOLMES 20 Apr 1835.

4A:001   Date: 3 Jan 1833   RtCt: 13 Mar 1833
William MERSHON (Commr. in Sep 1832 case of Thomas W. ETHOL & wife Sarah G. agst George SHEID) to James WHALEY. B/S of 192a (cnvy/b SHEID May 1819 to trustee) and 65a (cnvy/b SHEID May 1821 to trustee) on Broad Run adj James L. McKENNA, Washington HUMMER.

4A:004   Date: 3 Jan 1833   RtCt: 14 Mar 1833
James WHALEY & wife Amelia to Wm. MERSHON. Trust for debt to Commr. William MERSHON using above land. Wit: John J. MATHIAS, Presley CORDELL. Delv. to MERSHON 10 Dec 1834.

4A:007   Date: 18 Mar 1833   RtCt: 18 Mar 1833
William A. BINNS to Chas. BINNS. Assignment of crop. Wit: Chs. G. ESKRIDGE.

4A:007   Date: 18 Mar 1833   RtCt: 18 Mar 1833
James GARRISON & wife Elizabeth of Ldn to George RICHARDS of Ldn. B/S of 1/6th int. in land of Henry GLASCOW dec'd on S side of Royal St in Lsbg (DBk TTT:298). Wit: Saml. M. EDWARDS, Thos. SAUNDERS.

4A:010   Date: 13 Feb 1833   RtCt: 19 Mar 1833
John UNDERWOOD to W. C. SELDEN Jr. Trust for debt to William THRIFT using – agreement to substitute SELDEN as trustee in deed

their current land, William STOCK. Delv. to Chas. WILLIAMS
ardian of the children 15 Mar 1834.

4A:070 Date: 7 Nov 1832 RtCt: 14 Jan/ 8 Apr 1833
ert ROSE and Christopher ROSE & wife Catharine of Ldn to
phen GARRETT of Ldn. B/S of 3½a on Ketocton Mt. and Goose
ek (part of Robert CARTER's tract). Wit: William BEATTY,
iam H. ROGERS, Samuel N. GALLEHER, Edmund TYLER,
nan SKINNER Sr., John ROSE, Saml. M. EDWARDS. Delv. to
RRETT 3 Oct 1834.

4A:073 Date: 30 Mar 1833 RtCt: 8 Apr 1833
el HINES & wife Sarah of Ldn to Mortimore McILHANY of Ldn.
of 7a where HINES now lives (cnvy/b McILHANY). Wit: James
HANY, John WHITE.

4A:074 Date: 26 Jan 1833 RtCt: 9 Apr 1833
nen WILSON & wife Hannah P. of Ldn to Joshua PANCOAST
n. B/S of 149a on NW fork of Goose Creek adj William
CHER, William SMITH, __ PIGGOTT, Daniel COCKRILL, __
RSON. Wit: Timothy TAYLOR, John SIMPSON.

4A:078 Date: 6 Apr 1833 RtCt: 9 Apr 1833
PURCELL & wife Mary of Ldn to Mahlon WHITE of Ldn. B/S of
on NW fork of Goose Creek adj widow CRAEG, Levi G.
RS, and 13a adj Stephen C. ROSSEL, John HOUGH, John
IDGE, Richard BROWN, Philip VANSICKLER. Wit: John
SON, Timothy TAYLOR. Delv. to __ 23 Sep 1833.

4A:080 Date: 31 Mar 1831 RtCt: 13 Jun 1831
as GORE, Joseph GORE & Joshua OSBURN (Exors of
GORE dec'd) of Ldn to Thomas EMMERSON of Ldn. B/S of
Stephen WILSON, EMMERSON, William SMITH, __
ERILL. Wit: William HOGE, Washington VANDEVENTER,
in F. TAYLOR, Craven POPKINS. Delv. to EMBERSON 25
37.

4A:082 Date: 31 Mar 1831 RtCt: 13 Jun 1831
GORE, Joseph GORE & Joshua OSBURN (Exors of
GORE dec'd) of Ldn to Daniel COCKERILL of Ldn. B/S of
above lot. Wit: William HOGE, Washington
VENTER, Benjamin F. TAYLOR, Craven POPKINS. Delv. to
RILL 12 Aug 1833.

4A:083 Date: 18 Feb 1833 RtCt: 10 Apr 1833
McGUIGGIN & wife Nancy to John HUMPHREY. Trust for
ames JOHNSON using 2 lots in Bloomfield (one cnvy/b
GRAYSON Apr 1829) opp. lot formerly occupied by
CLARK now occupied by Jno. L. GILL and the other adj lot
George MARKS but no deed obtained yet). Ackn. and CoE
JIGGINS in FredVa. Delv. to HUMPHREY 8 Aug 1836.

instead of Wm. JENNERS in previous trust. Wit: Chas. SHREAVE,
A. ADISON, Nicholas OSBURN.

4A:011 Date: 26 Jan 1833 RtCt: 18 Mar 1833
Stephen WILSON & wife Hannah P. of Ldn to William BOLON of
Ldn. B/S of 33a on NW fork of Goose Creek adj __ WHITACRE, __
COOKSEY, __ PIGGOTT, __ PANCOAST, Mary HOWELL, David
SMITH, __ BIRDSALL. Wit: Timothy TAYLOR, John SIMPSON.
Delv. to BOLON 10 Jun 1837.

4A:014 Date: 18 Feb 1833 RtCt: 18 Mar 1833
A. P. BRACKENRIDGE to Thomas ROGERS. Trust for debt to
Charles C. NEWTON using undivided 1/3rd int. in 3a lot nr Lsbg
(subject to life estate of Ann CONNER) adj Rich'd H. HENDERSON,
Charles G. ESKRIDGE, and undivided moiety in ¼a from father
Samuel BRACKENRIDGE who obtained for service during last war
with Gr. Britain, and farm tools. Delv. to ROGERS 28 Jul 1834.

4A:016 Date: 8 Feb 1833 RtCt: 18 Mar 1833
Thomas LITTLETON Jr. to Burr W. HARRISON. Trust for Jno.
LITTLETON as security on bonds using farm and household items.

4A:019 Date: 16 Aug 1832 RtCt: 19 Mar 1833
Susanna SMITH of Ldn to John GEORGE Sr. of Ldn. B/S of 45a adj
__ BOOTHE, Michael EVERHART. Delv. to GEORGE 21 May 1851.

4A:021 Date: 16 Feb 1833 RtCt: 20 Mar 1833
John W. WOOD & wife Ann and mother Mary WOOD of Ldn to
Everitt SAUNDERS of Ldn. B/S of ½a in Lsbg (part of Lot #9 & Lot
#10). Wit: John J. MATHIAS, Presley CORDELL.

4A:023 Date: 9 Dec 1831 RtCt: 20 Mar 1833
James MILLS & wife Ann of Ldn to Everett SANDERS of Ldn. B/S of
½a in Lsbg (cnvy/b Giles HAMMETT Oct 1828) adj Everet
SANDERS, heirs of William HAWK dec'd, Dr. Wilson SELDEN. Wit:
Saml. M. EDWARDS, Jno. ROSE.

4A:026 Date: 21 Mar 1833 RtCt: 21 Mar 1833
William A. BINNS & wife Nancy of Ldn to Benjamin SHREVE Jr. of
Ldn. B/S of 284a (sold by John A. BINNS Jun 1830 to SHREVE,
DBk WW:136, Nancy BINNS now conveys her dower). Wit: F. W.
LUCKETT, Saml. M. EDWARDS. Delv. to SHREVE 9 Dec 1834.

4A:028 Date: 22 Mar 1833 RtCt: 22 Mar 1833
Stephen FOUTY of Ldn to Adin WHITE and Richard WHITE of Ldn.
B/S of lot prch/o Samuel HALL Apr 1832.

4A:029 Date: 22 Mar 1833 RtCt: 22 Mar 1833
Francis S. BOGUE of Lsbg to Thomas ROGERS of Lsbg. Trust for
debt to merchants A. G. WATERMAN and Saml. CAMPBELL using
household items. Delv. to ROGERS 28 Nov 1833.

4A:031   Date: 2 Feb 1830   RtCt: 23 Mar 1833
R. H. HENDERSON and Hugh SMITH to James MOUNT. Release of trust of __ for debt to John PANCOAST with his wife giving up dower rights.

4A:032   Date: 3 Jan 1833   RtCt: 23 Mar 1833
William CARR and Abbe ANDERSON. Agreement – CARR sold lot on Air St. in Lsbg to S. ANDERSON (see DBk VVV:232), will make deed of general warrant.

4A:033   Date: 9 Mar 1833   RtCt: 25 Mar 1833
James WEEKS of Ldn to Stephen G. BAILEY of Mdbg. B/S of Lot #39 & #40 in Mdbg (WEEKS reserves frame shop with chimney). Delv. pr order 5 Dec 1834.

4A:035   Date: 9 Mar 1833   RtCt: 25 Mar 1833
H. B. POWELL to James WEEKS. Release of trust of Sep 1828 for debt to Jacob MANN using Lots #39 & #40 in Mdbg. Elizabeth HAWLING releases although her bond not yet paid.

4A:037   Date: 26 Mar 1833   RtCt: 26 Mar 1833
Mahlon WHITE & wife Margaret of Ldn to John WHITE and Daniel WHITE of Ldn. B/S of undivided 1/5th part of 213a from William WHITE dec'd, adj Isaac HUGHES, Levi WHITE. Wit: John H. MCCABE, Presley CORDELL. Delv. to Daniel WHITE 1 Feb 1866.

4A:039   Date: 30 Mar 1833   RtCt: 30 Mar 1833
Joseph POSTON of Pendleton Co Ky to Elijah PEACOCK of Ldn. B/S of [3a] cnvy/b Lydia HOUGH May 1812 (DBk PP:183).

4A:041   Date: 30 Mar 1833   RtCt: 30 Mar 1833
Amos BEALE of Ldn to Presley CORDELL of Ldn. Release of trust for debt to David BEALE on 306a.

4A:042   Date: 1 Apr 1833   RtCt: 1 Apr 1833
Richard BROWN & wife Elizabeth of Ldn to Gabriel VANDEVENTER of Ldn. B/S of 6a on Catoctin Creek adj Lsbg & Snickers Gap turnpike road, BROWN, VANDEVENTER, Armistead VANDEVENTER. Wit: Francis W. LUCKETT, Saml. M. EDWARDS. Delv. to VANDEVANTER 4 Mar 1835.

4A:044   Date: __ 1833   RtCt: 2 Apr 1833
David JAMES & wife Charlotte of Ldn to Yardley TAYLOR & Stacey TAVENER of Ldn. Trust for debt to John PURCELL using 50a on NW fork of Goose Creek adj Charles TAYLOR, Rufus UPDIKE, Timothy TAYLOR. Wit: Timothy TAYLOR, David REECE.

4A:047   Date: __ 1833   RtCt: 2 Apr 1833
Charles TAYLOR & wife Nancy of Ldn to Yardley TAYLOR & Stacey TAVENER of Ldn. Trust for debt to John PURCELL using 50a adj above. [not signed by Nancy]

4A:050   Date: 11 Mar 1833   RtCt: 2 Apr 1833
Benjamin BIRDSALL of Ldn to Yardley TAYLOR of Ldn. Trust for debt to Stephen WILSON using 151a on NW fork of Goose Creek,

adj Thomas NICHOLS, __ STRIBLING, __ WH BOLON, Lsbg road, Uniontown road. Delv. to

4A:053   Date: 23 Mar 1833   RtCt:
Jonathan WENNER & wife Elizabeth Ann of L WALTMAN of Ldn. B/S of 31a (Lot #6 from di dec'd). Wit: Thomas J. MARLOW, Geo. W. S WALTMAN 7 Jul 1834.

4A:056   Date: 6 Apr 1833   RtCt
William FULTON. Oath as Lt. in 57th Reg Va

4A:057   Date: 6 Apr 1833   RtC
John FULTON. Oath as Ensign in 57th Reg \

4A:057   Date: 1 Oct 1832   RtC
Charles T. MAGILL & wife Mary D., Francis Sarah S., George W. BRONAUGH, Joseph Nancy S., and P. H. W. BRONAUGH of Ldr Ldn. B/S of int. in 179a (from Jeremiah W. rec. from father William BRONAUGH dec'd Dec 1826 to LUCKETT, the others are chil BRONAUGH). Wit: John J. MATHIAS, Pre and CoE for Joseph W. & wife Nancy S. in Jun 1867.

4A:061   Date: 27 Apr 1833   R
John F. BARRETT. Oath as Capt. in 57th

4A:061   Date: 16 Apr 1833   R
Benjamin SHREVE Jr. Oath as Lt. Col. of Brig 2nd Div Va Militia.

4A:062   Date: 27 Mar 1833
Conrad BITZER & wife Catharine of Ldn Ldn. B/S of 152a adj __ SWANK, heirs (PUSEY, heirs of Daniel STONEBURNEI Saml. M. EDWARDS. Delv. to SHAVER

4A:064   Date: 27 Mar 1833
Conrad BITZER & wife Catharine of Ld B/S of 122a adj heirs of Michael BOGE Wit: Jno. J. MATHIAS, Saml. M. EDW/ Apr 1834.

4A:066   Date: 1 Apr 1833
John PURCELL & wife Mary of Ldn to 50a on NW fork of Goose Creek adj T UPDIKE, David JAMES, TAYLOR. Wi REECE. Delv. to TAYLOR 31 Mar 18:

4A:069   Date: 28 Mar 182
Stephen SANDS of Ldn to Thomas G Ann DOWDELL of Ldn by Guardian I

adj
Gu

Ro
Ste
Cre
Wil
Nat
GA

Dan
B/S
McIL

Step
of Lo
HAT
EME

John
13¾a
EWE
ALDR
SIMP

Thoma
Josep
7a adj
COCK
Benjan
Mar 18

Thoma
Josep
10a ad
VANDE
COCKE

Samuel
debt to
Benjami
Richard
(prch/o
for McG

4A:086   Date: 2 Apr 1833   RtCt: 10 Apr 1833
Christian SANBOWER of Ldn to Adam SANBOWER of Ldn. B/S of undivided ½ int. in 23a and 4a allotted wd/o John SANBOWER dec'd

4A:088   Date: 21 Feb 1833   RtCt: 10 Apr 1833
Jane McCABE wd/o Henry McCABE dec'd, John H. McCABE & wife Margaret H. D., Henry M. DOWLING & wife Harriet, Jane H. NEWTON and Mary A. SIMPSON of Ldn to George RUST Jr. of JeffVa. B/S of 12a from dower of Jane McCABE. Wit: John J. MATHIAS, Presley CORDELL, Mortimer MCILHANY, John WHITE.

4A:092   Date: 9 Mar 1833   RtCt: 10 Apr 1833
Jacob SILCOTT & wife Tamer and Craven SILCOTT & wife Elizabeth of Ldn to William GALLAHER of Ldn. B/S of 65a where SILCOTT now resides adj Beaverdam, Amos HIBBS, Isaac COWGILL, Saml. DUNKIN, Joseph GOURLEY. Wit: Edward HALL, Benj'n GRAYSON. Delv. to GALLEHER 25 Sep 1833.

4A:094   Date: 11 Apr 1833   RtCt: 11 Apr 1833
James H. CHAMBLIN to Jacob G. PAXSON. Release of trust of Jan 1833 for debt to Thomas ROGERS on 100a.

4A:095   Date: 19 Sep 1825   RtCt: 15 Apr 1833
Ann NEER wd/o Conrad NEER dec'd, Christian MILLER & wife Sarah, Nathan NEER & wife Eliza, Joseph RUSSELL & wife Ann, Martha NEER, Jesse NEER & Joseph NEER of Ldn (heirs of Conrad dec'd) to Samuel NEER of Ldn. B/S of 46a and 25a on W side of Short Hill. Wit: Craven OSBURN, John WHITE, Ebenezer GRUBB.

4A:099   Date: 11 Apr 1833   RtCt: 11 Apr 1833
Jacob G. PAXSON & wife Mahala of Ldn to Samuel McPHERSON of Ldn. Trust for debt to Ebeneser GRUBB of Ldn using 108a nr Wtfd adj Catoctin Creek, Samuel McPHERSON, Samuel PAXSON, __ STEER, and privileges to spring water of Wm. PAXSON. Wit: George W. SHAWEN, Joshua PUSEY. Delv. to GRUBB 21 Jun 1833.

4A:102   Date: 1 Apr 1833   RtCt: 12 Sep 1833
Philip SWANK & wife Mary of Ldn to William GRAHAM of Ldn. B/S of 20a (part of land from inheritance) adj main road, John VINSEL. Wit: George W. SHAWEN, Thos. J. MARLOW. Delv. to GRAHAM 10 Apr 1834.

4A:104   Date: 11 Apr 1833   RtCt: 12 Apr 1833
Isaac WALKER of Ldn to James H. CHAMBLIN. Trust for debt to Thomas ROGERS using house & lot in Wtfd cnvy/b ROGERS.

4A:107   Date: 11 Apr 1833   RtCt: 15 Apr 1833
Presley WIGGINTON & wife Sarah Ann of Ldn to Jesse NEER of Ldn. Trust for debt to Samuel NEER using 2 lots cnvy/b Samuel

NEER. Wit: Ebenezer GRUBB, John WHITE. Delv. to Jesse NEAR 6 May 1837.

4A:110   Date: 1 Apr 1833   RtCt: 16 Apr 1833
Philip SWANK & wife Mary of Ldn to Conrod R. DOWELL of Ldn. Trust for debt to Conrod BITZER of Ldn using 122a cnvy/b BITZER. Wit: George W. SHAWEN, Thomas J. MARLOW.

4A:115   Date: 1 Apr 1833   RtCt: 16 Apr 1833
John SHAFER Jr. & wife Margaret of Ldn to Conrod R. DOWELL of Ldn. Trust for debt to Conrod BITZER of Ldn using 152a cnvy/b BITZER. Wit: George W. SHAWEN, Thomas J. MARLOW.

4A:119   Date: 17 Apr 1833   RtCt: 17 Apr 1833
Jacob G. PAXSON of Ldn to Samuel PAXSON (trustee of Mahala PAXSON w/o Jacob G.). Trust for benefit of Mahala using 108a nr Wtfd and __ HOUGH, __ STEER, Catoctin Creek; and farm animals, household items, female mulatto Eliza ch/o Henney abt 8y old, mulatto. Delv. to Samuel PAXSON 27 Aug 1833.

4A:122   Date: 19 Apr 1833   RtCt: 20 Apr 1833
Charles B. ALEXANDER & wife Eliza of Ky to James RUST of Ldn and George RUST of JeffVa. B/S of 317a adj __ CARTER, __ GREENUP, __ CARR.

4A:124   Date: 19 Apr 1833   RtCt: 20 Apr 1833
Daniel LOVETT of Ldn to Charles B. ALEXANDER of Ky. B/S of 12a (pr agreement of Dec 1821) on top of hog back mt.

4A:125   Date: 12 Jan 1825   RtCt: 20 Apr 1833
William CLAYTON of Ldn to Amos CLAYTON of Ldn. B/S of ½a on SE side of Lsbg road, adj Jonas FARR.

4A:127   Date: 24 Nov 1824   RtCt: 22 Apr 1833
Israel CLAYTON of Ldn to Amos CLAYTON of Ldn. B/S of 1a on N side of road from Alexandria to Winchester thru Snickers Gap adj Mrs. HOGESON, Amos CLAYTON, N. C. WILLIAMS.

4A:129   Date: 22 Apr 1833   RtCt: 22 Apr 1833
John CARR of Ldn to George RHODES of Ldn. B/S of 3a nr Drye Mill, Tuscarora nr foot of mt., __ CARLILE, road to Nixson's Mill, Middleton SHAW. Delv. to RHODES 9 Apr 1836.

4A:131   Date: 22 Apr 1833   RtCt: 22 Apr 1833
Archibald MAINES of Ldn atty in fact for William MAINES of Ross Co Ohio to George RHODES of Ldn. B/S of 35a (from div. of William MAINES dec'd) on Tuscarora nr foot of Hogback mt., road from RHODES to John NIXSON's mill, __ CARLILE. Delv. to RHODES 9 Sep 1836.

4A:133   Date: 17 Nov 1830   RtCt: 22 Apr 1833
Martha CLAYTON of Ldn to Town'd, Eliza, Washington, Thompson, Jacob, Sarah, Charles Fenton, Catharine & Susan CLAYTON (heirs of Amos CLAYTON dec'd) of Ldn. B/S of 6a on S side of Snickersville adj Martha.

4A:136   Date: 18 Jan 1833   RtCt: 23 Apr 1833
Richard SMITH cashier of Bank of US to Joseph LEWIS of Ldn.
Release of trust of Dec 1821 for debt to Bank of US on 203a
"Clifton" mill land. Wit: R. SMITH, R. S. BRISCOE, N. B. VAN
ZANDT, L. MIFFLIN, Z. W. FAIRMAN.

4A:140   Date: 18 Mar 1833   RtCt: 23 Apr 1833
William T. W. TALIAFERRO & wife Frances of Fqr to Mahlon
GIBSON of Ldn. B/S of 314a "Fermer" adj William C. FITZHUGH,
Vincent MOSS, Daniel THOMAS, Sydnor BAILEY, Thomas
COLSON, Laurence B[A]TTAILLES, heirs of Isaiah HICKS dec'd.
Delv. to GIBSON 10 Jan 1848.

4A:142   Date: 9 Apr 1833   RtCt: 23 Apr 1833
Marcus D. BAKER of FredVa to John P. DULANY of Ldn. B/S of int.
of Jesse TRIPLETT in estate of his father Enoch TRIPLETT (prch/b
BAKER at public auction).

4A:143   Date: 28 Apr 1831   RtCt: 23 Apr 1833
William NOLAND & wife Catharine of Ldn to James SWART of Ldn.
B/S of 1¼a (lot and parts of other lots) in Aldie adj stone bridge on
Little river, Charles F. MERCER, Elias LACEY (on Lot #7). Wit:
Edward HALL, A. GIBSON. Delv. to Col. H. ROGERS Admr dbn of
SWARTS dec'd 11 Nov 1845.

4A:145   Date: __ Apr 1833   RtCt: 24 Apr 1833
Israel WILLIAMS & wife Amelia of Ldn to George W. HENRY of Ldn.
Trust for debt to Joseph POTTERFIELD of Ldn using 93a farm
where WILLIAMS now lives, adj __ HIXSON, Samuel CLAPHAM, __
POTTERFIELD.

4A:148   Date: 19 Sep 1825   RtCt: 25 Apr 1833
Ann NEER wd/o Conard NEER dec'd, Samuel NEER & wife Sarah,
Nathan NEER & wife Eliza, Joseph RUSSELL & wife Ann, Martha
NEER, Jesse NEER & Joseph NEER (heirs of Conrad NEER) of
Ldn to Christian MILLER of Ldn. B/S of 71a adj George MILLER,
John CONARD; and 25a adj __ GRUBB, __ ELLZEY at top of short
hill. Wit: John WHITE, Craven OSBURN, Ebenezer GRUBB. Delv. to
MILLER 12 Aug 1833.

4A:152   Date: 4 Jan 1833   RtCt: 25 Apr 1833
Rebecca HIXSON to Isaac BOWLES. B/S of undivided int. in mill
lots beq. to Rebecca VERNON wd/o Danl. VERNON dec'd. Delv. to
Jas. BOWLES pr order 26 May 1836.

4A:153   Date: 1 Mar 1833   RtCt: 26 Apr 1833
Ariss BUCKNER of Ldn to Daniel KIMBER of Ldn. B/S of 47a on
road from KIMBER's to Log house mill, Benjamin JAMES dec'd,
BUCKNER.

4A:155 Date: 22 Apr 1833 RtCt: 26 Apr 1833
George RHODES & wife Catharine of Ldn to John CARR of Ldn.
B/S of 2a nr drye mill on Tuscarora adj Middleton SHAW. Wit: John
SIMPSON, William CARR.

4A:158 Date: 26 Apr 1833 RtCt: 27 Apr 1833
Thomas RUSSELL to Charles B. HAMILTON Jr. Trust for debt to
William CLENDENING & Jonas P. SCHOOLEY using household
items, crops.

4A:160 Date: 13 Jul 1832 RtCt: 29 Apr 1833
John PANCOAST Jr. of Ldn to John PANCOAST Sr. of Ldn B/S of
149a adj Joshua PANCOAST, Fielding LYNN (cnvy/b Jesse
BURSON). Delv. pr order 14 Oct 1833.

4A:161 Date: 8 Apr 1833 RtCt: 8 Apr/9 Apr/1 May 1833
Thomas ROGERS of Ldn to Jesse RICHARDS of Ldn. Release of
trust of Nov 1829 for debt to Thomas GORE, Joseph GORE &
Joshua OSBURN (Exors. of Joseph GORE dec'd).

4A:163 Date: 13 Apr 1833 RtCt: 2 May 1833
John J. MATHIAS to Chas. G. ESKRIDGE & Edward HAMMAT.
Trust for debt to John GRAY, John H. McCABE, James L. MARTIN,
Saml. STERETT, Wm. MERSHON, Robt. GOVER & B. W. SOWER
using 3a lot in Lsbg (prch/o William CARR), and 13¾a on turnpike
road below Lsbg (prch/o WRIGHT's trustee & Edmund J. LEE), farm
and household items, black woman Pat, note & accts. of Enos
STEPHEN, Thos. SWANN, D. T. MATHIAS, Wm. THRIFT, John
VANDEVENTER assigned to Wm. MERCHANT, Collin AULD, Chas.
B. HAMILTON, Wilson & Dulen, Ann DONAHOE, Peter JACOBS,
James RUS[E?], J. & G. FALLY, Pat'k MILLHOLAND, Jno.
COLEMAN, W. K. ISH, N. S. BRADEN, Thompson F. MASON,
Peter BENNEDUM, Rich'd LOVE., Danl. WARD, Geo. M.
CHICHESTER, Silas WHERRY's estate, H. T. HARRISON, J. T.
NEWTON, Jacob WALTMAN's estate, Jesse BURKS, Chas. G.
ESKRIDGE, J. GARNER, Chas. BINNS, Daniel THOMPSON, Elisha
GLASCOCK, Harry ROBISON, Benj. SHREVE Jr., John MARTIN.

4A:167 Date: 20 Apr 1833 RtCt: 2 May 1833
Millers John J. & Hamilton R. MATHIAS to Chas. G. ESKRIDGE &
Edward HAMMAT. Trust for debt to Hamilton ROGERS, Ann
MASON, John SPINKS, George RICHARDS, George GREGG of
Ldn & Joshua SHELTON of MontMd using 214a, notes and accts –
James DARNE, John VEAL, Aaron DAILEY, Barick CHICK, Jon'o
WALTERS, Westley DOWNES, Levi HALL, Washington HUMMER,
Israel WARNER, George FITCHTER, James MILLS, Ludwell LEE,
John TOWNER, James FLETCHER dec'd, John J. HARDING, John
CRIDLER, William HAMMERLY, Ellis JENKINS, James DOWNS,
Samuel JENKINS, John RYAN, John BINNS, Joseph HOUGH,
Samuel C. SINCLAIR, George W. PRICE.

4A:171   Date: 2 Apr 1833   RtCt: 2 May 1833
John J. & Hamilton R. MATHIAS (insolvent debtors) to Sheriff Ariss
BUCKNER. B/S of 215a and 13¾a (see DBK 4A:163).

4A:172   Date: 4 May 1833   RtCt: 4 May 1833
Wilson C. SELDEN Jr. (trustee of John UNDERWOOD formerly of
Ldn) of Ldn to William THRIFT of Ldn. B/S of undivided int. of
UNDERWOOD land on Lsbg turnpike below Goose Creek in estate
of Samuel UNDERWOOD (cnvy/b Ludwell LEE, and Samuel made
trust to William JENNERS in Jul 1828 for debt to William THRIFT,
see DBk QQQ:427, Wm. JENNERS was out of state so SELDEN
selling instead).

4A:175   Date: 1 Apr 1833   RtCt: 6 May 1833
Burr POWELL & Cuthbert POWELL (trustee of Sarah H. CHILTON)
of Ldn to William ELLZEY of Ldn. B/S of ½a in Lsbg late residence
of William CHILTON. Delv. to ELLZEY 30 Dec 1833.

4A:176   Date: 8 Apr 1833   RtCt: 7 May 1833
Joseph A. LLOYD & wife Margaret F. of Ldn to Michael PLASTER &
John P. JACOBS of Ldn. B/S of ½a (cnvy/b John GALLEHER), ½a
(cnvy/b Mary GALLAHER) and 11a and all int. in dower of Mary
GALLEHER wd/o William GALLAHER dec'd (cnvy/b Samuel
GALLEHER). William BENTON, Edw'd. HALL.

4A:178   Date: 23 Jan 1833   RtCt: 10 May 1833
Hannah JANNEY of Ldn to Jonah SANDS of Ldn. B/S of 3a adj
William NICHOLS, SANDS, Lsbg & Snickers Gap turnpike. Wit:
Thomas NICHOLS, Letitia NICHOLS, Hannah F. NICHOLS. Delv. to
SANDS 14 Jul 1841.

4A:180   Date: 13 Apr 1833   RtCt: 26 Apr/13 May 1833
Isaac WRIGHT & wife Susannah, Daniel T. MATHIAS & wife
Martha, John J. MATHIAS, Hamilton R. MATHIAS, Harriot H.
MATHIAS, Peter MATHIAS & Margaret E. MATHIAS of Ldn to Jane
MATHIAS & Mary Ann MATHIAS of Ldn. B/S of lot at Royal & Back
sts in Lsbg (allotted heirs of Nancy MATHIAS dec'd in div. of Robt.
HAMILTON dec'd) adj heirs of Margaret COOPER, John H.
MONROE. Wit: John H. McCABE, Wilson C. SELDEN Jr.

4A:183   Date: 13 Apr 1833   RtCt: 13 May 1833
Isaac WRIGHT & wife Susannah, Daniel T. MATHIAS & wife
Martha, John J. MATHIAS, Hamilton R. MATHIAS, Harriot H.
MATHIAS, Peter MATHIAS & Margaret E. MATHIAS of Ldn to
Charles GULATT of Ldn. B/S of ½ of 1/8a in Lsbg (allotted heirs of
Nancy MATHIAS formerly HAMILTON from div. of Robt. HAMILTON
dec'd) adj Chas. BINNS on Royal st., heirs of Enos WILDMAN,
Edw'd HAMMAT, James THOMAS. Wit: John H. McCABE, Wilson
C. SELDEN Jr. Delv. to GULLATT 20 Mar 1834.

4A:186 Date: 6 May 1833 RtCt: 13 May 1833
Eli TAVENNER & wife Nancy of Ldn to Israel BURKE of Ldn. B/S of 1a on road from Wtfd to Goose Creek meeting house, adj Hannah JANNEY, Charles B. HAMILTON. Delv. to BURKE 14 Feb 1834.

4A:188 Date: __ 1833 RtCt: 13 May 1833
Isaac NICHOLS Jr. (James HOGUE now dec'd) to Jonathan CARTER. Release of trust of Jan 1824 for debt to Isaac NICHOLS Sr. & Samuel NICHOLS on 192¼a. Delv. to Jonathan's son Francis M. 25 Feb 1848.

4A:190 Date: 13 Mar 1833 RtCt: 13 May 1833
Isaac NICHOLS Jr. (James HOGUE now dec'd) to John RUSE & Sarah CRUZEN formerly Ruse (heirs of Margaret SAUNDERS dec'd). Release of trust of Jun 1825 for debt to Isaac NICHOLS Sr. & Samuel NICHOLS now dec'd.

4A:192 Date: 13 May 1833 RtCt: 13 May 1833
Benjamin JACKSON, John G. HUMPHREY & Stephen McPHERSON. Bond on JACKSON as constable.

4A:193 Date: 13 May 1833 RtCt: 13 May 1833
Joshua PUSEY & John JANNY. Bond on PUSEY as Committee for estate of Esther GRANT.

4A:193 Date: 13 May 1833 RtCt: 13 May 1833
Henry EVANS, Wm. K. ISH & Jesse McVEIGH. Bond on EVANS as Committee for estate of Martha EVANS.

4A:194 Date: __ May 1833 RtCt: 13 May 1833
Nicholas OSBURN to John PHILLIPS & wife Prissilla. Release of trust of Apr 1831 for debt to John BRADEN.

4A:196 Date: 15 Apr 1833 RtCt: 13 May 1833
John PHILLIPS & wife Pressilla of Ldn to David BROWN of Ldn. B/S of 65a (68a less 2a with Nathan GREGG's mill dam and race) adj John BROWN, William BROWN, Samuel PEIRPOINT. Wit: David REECE, Presley CORDELL. Delv. to BROWN 20 Mar 1835.

4A:198 Date: 13 May 1833 RtCt: 13 May 1833
David BROWN & wife Eliza of Ldn to John JANNEY of Ldn. Trust for debt to Abijah JANNEY trustee of Ann HARPER w/o Washington T. HARPER of AlexDC using 25a (see DBk VVV:143), 7a (see DBk VVV:263), above 65a. Wit: John J. MATHIAS, Presley CORDELL. Delv. to JANNY 28 Oct 1836.

4A:202 Date: 28 May 1832 RtCt: 14 May 1833
Motion of May 1833 by Edward CARTER, William BENTON, Price JACOBS, Hiram SEATON & Jno. CRAINE viewed road change from Millsville to Cuthbert POWELL's blacksmith shop from James WARNAL's to intersection of old road at Francis W. LUCKETT – distances increases but road is better. Damages to Francis W. LUCKETT of $.50.

4A:205 Date: 13 May 1833 RtCt: 15 May 1833
Daniel JANNEY to Richard C. McCARTY & Dennis McCARTY.
Release of trust of Nov 1830 for debt to William HOGUE using
interest in land of father Dennis McCARTY dec'd.

4A:207 Date: 28 May 1833 RtCt: 1 Jun 1833
George W. HENRY of Ldn to Jared CHAMBLIN of Ldn. Trust for
debt to Thomas ROGERS of Ldn using ½ int. in farm of William FOX
dec'd now occupied by David SHAWEN & Joseph L. POTTS, and
70a where HENRY now resides with Taylortown Mills.

4A:209 Date: 23 Mar 1832 RtCt: 13 May 1833
Frederick BROOKS & wife Frances of Kanahwa Co Va to Benjamin
RUST of Ldn. B/S of __a (deed from Abraham SKILLMAN to
Thomas BROWN) and __a (deed from George NIXON to Thomas
BROWN) both sold by trustee Samuel B. T. CALDWELL to Chauncy
BROOKS July 1828 (DBk RRR:091).

4A:211 Date: 19 Nov 1832 RtCt: 13 May 1833
Otis DUDLEY & wife Elizabeth of Harpers ferry JeffVA to Patrick
Curren McCABE Harpers ferry JeffVa. B/S of 1000a (cnvy/b
McCABE Apr 1831) adj Ludwell LEE, Thomas L. LEE dec'd. Delv. to
McCABE 14 Jan 1834.

4A:214 Date: 7 May 1833 RtCt: 13 May 1833
William HATCHER & wife Elizabeth of Ldn to Aquila MEAD of Ldn.
B/S of 5a adj George FAIRHURST. Wit: David REECE, Timothy
TAYLOR.

4A:217 Date: 21 Jan 1833 RtCt: 14 May 1833
Nelson GIBSON & wife Emsey Frances of Fqr to John MARTIN of
Ldn. B/S of 15¼a on Goose Creek adj Joshua HOGUE, Ashbys Gap
turnpike bridge (part of tract prch/o Enoch GLASSCOCK by Caleb
RECTOR and cnvy/t GIBSON).

4A:220 Date: 23 Apr 1833 RtCt: 14 May 1833
Yeoman Nelson GIBSON & wife Emsey of Fqr to Caleb RECTOR of
Fqr. B/S of 2 roods (in exchange for 48a) adj Samuel & Joseph
HATCHER, GIBSON, and 73a-74a adj old Alexandria road, Goose
Creek. CoE for Emsey in Ldn by A. GIBSON, Asa ROGERS. Delv.
to RECTOR 21 Sep 1835.

4A:222 Date: 21 Jan 1833 RtCt: 14 May 1833
John MARTIN & wife Frances Ann of Ldn to Gurley HATCHER of
Fqr. Trust for debt to Nelson GIBSON using 15¼a. CoE for Frances
in Fqr.

4A:226 Date: 15 May 1833 RtCt: 15 May 1833
Wm. KING of Lsbg to Thomas ROGERS. Trust for debt to Burr W.
HARRISON & H. T. HARRISON using household items. Delv. to
ROGERS 28 Mar 1835.

4A:228   Date: 25 Jan 1830   RtCt: 16 May 1833
Solomon FILLER of FredMd to Jacob FILLER of Ldn. B/S of 4a (formerly of Jacob FILLER dec'd) adj John WENNER, Michael SANBOWER. Delv. to Jacob FILLER 22 Apr 1836.

4A:230   Date: 1 Oct 1832   RtCt: 16 May 1833
Henry HARDING & wife Margaret of Ldn to Stephen GARRET of Ldn. B/S of 65a on Little river (part of allot. from mother Elizabeth HARDING dec'd) adj Col. James MONROE dec'd, George GULICK, James SWART. Wit: Presley CORDELL, John H. McCABE. Delv. to GARRETT 3 Oct 1834.

4A:232   Date: 13 Mar 1833   RtCt: 17 May 1833
Richard H. HENDERSON of Ldn to Richard, Dennis & Billington McCARTY of Ldn. Release of trust Aug 1828 by Dennis McCARTY now dec'd for debt to Robert J. TAYLOR & Thomson F. MASON of AlexDC on 50a purchased by George McCARTY (Billington was under 21y). Delv. to his son pr order 11 Jun 1836.

4A:234   Date: 29 Jan 1833   RtCt: 17 May 1833
John CAMPBELL & wife Elizabeth of Ldn to Robert COCKERILL, Isaac FALLY, Jesse EVANS, Thomas HOUGH & John EARNEST (trustees of Methodist Episcopal Church) of Ldn. B/S of ½a adj Ebenezer GRUBB, __ MATHEWS (to build house of worship). Wit: Ebenezer GRUBB, John WHITE. Delv. to Jas. GRUBB a trustee 15 Sep 1868.

4A:236   Date: 13 May 1833   RtCt: 17 May 1833
Dennis McCARTY of Ldn to Robert J. TAYLOR of AlexDC. Mortgage using 49a Lot #2 in div. of father Dennis McCARTY dec'd) with detached wood lot. Delv. to TAYLOR 27 Sep 1833.

4A:239   Date: 18 Apr 1832   RtCt: 20 May 1833
James R. COLEMAN of Culpeper Co to James HUNTER of Ffx. Trust for debt to William GUNNELL of Ffx using 220a " Herberts lot" (from div. of James COLEMAN dec'd) adj Johnston J. COLEMAN, Horsepen Run, Thomas DARNES, Richard H. COCKERILL; and slaves Oscar, Jane called Jane ROBINSON & her 3 children Patsey, Mary, Frances and Bronssais, Jane called Jane MORRIS, Sary Ann, Mary Jane called Mary Jane TOMBS, Fanny called Fanny Smith, Mary called Mary SMITH; interest in right of his wife Jane M. late PAGE in pending suit of PAGE's Admr. vs. PATTON &c. Delv. to GUNNELL __ Aug 1833.

4A:242   Date: 1 Apr 1833   RtCt: 20 May 1833
Nancy LOVETT (Feme Solo) of Union to David GALLEHER of Ldn. B/S of 34 24/100 sq poles nr Union (cnvy/b Elizabeth BOLON Feb 1824, DBk GGG:356).

4A:243   Date: 17 May 1833   RtCt: 20 May 1833
Richard C. McCARTY of Ldn to H. B. POWELL of Ldn. PoA for int. in father's estate.

4A:244 Date: 18 May 1833 RtCt: 20 May 1833
Richard C. McCARTY & wife Kezia A. of Ldn to David GALLEHER
of Ldn. B/S of 42a (allotted from div. of Dennis McCARTY dec'd) adj
George W. McCARTY, turnpike road leading to snickers gap, Caleb
N. GALLEHER, Dennis & Billington McCARTY, Goose Creek. Wit:
Hugh SMITH, Asa ROGERS. Delv. to GALLEHER 5 Jun 1837.

4A:246 Date: 1 Feb 1833 RtCt: 20 May 1833
Stephen WILSON & wife Hannah P. of Ldn to Charles TAYLOR of
Ldn. B/S of 31 perches adj TAYLOR. Wit: Timothy TAYLOR, John
SIMPSON. Delv. to TAYLOR 31 Mar 1834.

4A:248 Date: 25 Mar 1829 RtCt: 21 May 1833
Jacob SCRIVER/SHRIVER of Ldn to Adam JACOBS of Ldn. B/S of
40a (Lot #24 & #25) on Short Hill adj __ CLICE, John CONARD.

4A:250 Date: 10 May 1833 RtCt: 22 May 1833
Peter COOPER & wife Nancy, Michael COOPER, Joseph COOPER
& wife Margaret and Daniel COOPER & wife Elizabeth of Ldn to
Elijah PEACOCK of Ldn. B/S of 34a (Daniel's share from Margaret
SAUNDERS dec'd) adj Catoctin Creek. Wit: Geo. W. SHAWEN,
Joshua PUSEY. Delv. to PEACOCK 27 Aug 1833.

4A:252 Date: 23 May 1833 RtCt: 23 May 1833
Robert MOFFETT & wife Ellen of Ldn to Sydnor WILLIAMS of Ldn.
B/S of 41a (Lot #3 by Commrs. from div. of Henry TAYLOR dec'd,
MOFFETT prch/o Sampson RICHARDS & wife Betsy late TAYLOR)
on SE side of Catoctin Creek. Wit: Presley CORDELL, John J.
MATHIAS. Delv. to WILLIAMS 18 Jun 1834.

4A:254 Date: 18 May 1833 RtCt: 27 May 1833
Richard C. McCARTY & wife Keziah A. of Ldn to Jonathan CARTER
Sr. B/S of undivided 1/6th int. in "Mill lot" on Goose Creek and
turnpike road to Snickers Gap at bridge. Wit: Hugh SMITH, Asa
ROGERS. Delv. to Asa JACKSON pr order 15 Aug 1839.

4A:256 Date: 27 Mar 1833 RtCt: 27 May 1833
William J. McKINNEY & wife Rebecca late GREGG (d/o Aaron
GREGG, grandd/o William GREGG) of Montgomery Co Ohio to
Robert MOFFETT of Ldn. B/S of ¼ int. (from father Aaron) of
Rebecca in land dev. to widow of William GREGG dec'd and 1/4th
int. in part of her brother Rezin GREGG. Wit: James RUSSELL,
Saml. BINCKLEY. Delv. to MOFFETT 14 Feb 1835.

4A:258 Date: 24 May 1833 RtCt: 29 May 1833
William H. CRIDER of Ldn to Fielding LITTLETON of Ldn. Trust for
debt to Asa ROGERS using int. in house & lot in Mdbg (late prop. of
Frederick CRIDER dec'd) on main st adj Oliver DENHAM, Noble
BEVERIDGE.

4A:260 Date: 30 May 1833 RtCt: 30 May 1833
William P. FOX of Ldn to Edward THOMPSON. B/S in trust for
benefit of wife Esther FOX of int. in estate of Esther's father Mortho

SULLIVAN dec'd and from deed by SULLIVAN to Isaac LAROWE in trust for wife and children dated Jan 1813. Delv. to Braden E. FOX pr order 14 Apr 1849.

4A:261 Date: 20 Apr 1834 [33] RtCt: 30 May 1833
William P. FOX of Ldn to Edward THOMPSON. Trust to THOMPSON for notes etc. using farm animals and crops. Wit: THOMPSON 25 Dec 1840.

4A:262 Date: 1 Jun 1833 RtCt: 3 Jun 1833
Amos GULICK & wife Sarah Matilda of Ldn to David F. BEALL of Ldn. B/S of 1 moiety of ½a in Mt. Gilead (cnvy/b William P. EATON in 1829). Wit: John SIMPSON, Hugh SMITH.

4A:264 Date: 3 Jun 1833 RtCt: 3 Jun 1833
Amos GULICK to John SIMPSON. Trust for debt to John VANSICKLER using writing obligations from John TAYLOR, Robert E. BEALL, James KITTLE, Ezra BOLON, Manly ATWELL, John SIMPSON, Edward TILLETT & James TAVENER, Manly ATWELL to Bernard McCORMICK, James RUSK, Abram SULLIVAN, Bernard PURCELL, William LICKEY, John PYOTT, Andrew BIRDSALL, Isaac CONWELL.

4A:266 Date: 1 Jun 1833 RtCt: 3 Jun 1833
Amos GULICK & wife Sarah Matilda of Ldn to Henry H. HAMILTON of Ldn. Trust for debt to Noble BEVERIDGE using house & 1½a now occupied by Alfred GULICK adj George GULICK, and any int. in estate of father Moses GULICK dec'd. Wit: Jno. SIMPSON, Hugh SMITH. Delv. to BEVERIDGE 15 Jun 1833.

4A:268 Date: 12 Mar 1832 RtCt: 13 Mar/5 Jun 1833
John JANNEY & Saml. M. BOSS of Ldn to John H. MONROE of Ldn. Release of trust of May 1830 for debt to Samuel M. BOSS using house & lot in Lsbg.

4A:269 Date: 5 Jun 1833 RtCt: 5 Jun 1833
Amos GULICK of Ldn to William WRIGHT of Ldn. Trust for debt to David F. BEALL using interest, accts. goods, etc. of Amos GULICK & Co., David F. BEALL & Co, Amos GULICK & Enoch G. DAY, and household items. Delv. to WRIGHT 18 Jun 1839.

4A:272 Date: 15 May 1833 RtCt: 6 Jun 1833
Hamilton ROGERS (signed as Jr.) of Ldn to Amos WHITACRE of Ldn. B/S of undivided ½ of 173a cnvy/t ROGERS by WHITACRE as Exor. of Alice WHITACRE dec'd, adj __ COOKSEY, __ PIGGOTT, __ BOLON, __ BIRDSALL, heirs of Francis STRIBLING.

4A:274 Date: 16 May 1833 RtCt: 6 Jun 1833
Hamilton ROGERS (signed as Jr.) to Yardley TAYLOR & Thomas NICHOLS Esqr. Trust for debt to Amos WHITACRE using above land.

4A:276 Date: 2 Oct 1832 RtCt: 3 Oct 1832/10 Jun 1833
Andrew GRAHAM of Ldn to Saml. M. EDWARDS of Ldn. Trust for debt to John GRAY & Saml. HOUGH of Ldn using 169a part of "Beaverdam tract" cnvy/b HOUGH Sep 1832.

4A:278 Date: 22 Mar 1833 RtCt: 10 Jun 1833
John YOUNG dec'd. Division – 18a Lot #1 to widow Lowis YOUNG as dower; 18a Lot #2 to cnvy/b David YOUNG to John YOUNG with life estate to widow; 34a Lot #3 to John YOUNG & 18a Lot #4 cnvy/b heirs of Elizabeth BURKETT to John YOUNG. Heirs William YOUNG & George YOUNG, shares of David YOUNG and heirs of Elizabeth BURKITT late YOUNG purchased by John YOUNG, William YOUNG and George YOUNG jointly before division. Also divides personal estate. Divisors: Thos. NICHOLS, Yardley TAYLOR, Daniel JANNEY. Gives plat.

4A:280 Date: 9 Feb 1833 RtCt: 10 Jun 1833
Edward BRADFIELD, John CROZER & Adah WINDER residents of Columbiana Co Ohio and Sarah GALAWAY resident of Stark Co Ohio (heirs of Susanna CARTER dec'd of Ldn) to William LONGSHORE of Columbiana Co Ohio. PoA to receive from James HILL of Ldn int. in 79a from estate of Susanna dec'd held by dower by his wife Elizabeth HILL late WOODFORD wd/o William WOODFORD Jr. dec'd. Wit: Jesse UNDERWOOD, Joseph THOMPSON. Delv. to Hill 9 Sep 1833.

4A:282 Date: 6 Apr 1833 RtCt: 10 Jun 1833
Adam SANBOWER & wife Christina to Thomas J. MARLOW. Trust for debt to Adam KERN using 57a cnvy/b Manuel WALTMAN Jun 1825 on Potomac River below landing at Berleen ferry; 16a cnvy/b Exors of above adj __ BOOTH at NE end of short hill; and 81a cnvy/b Christian SANBOWER adj __ WENNER, __ MARLOW, __ LOWERY. Wit: Thomas J. MARLOW, Geo. W. SHAWEN. Delv. to KERN 4 Apr 1842.

4A:285 Date: 15 Aug 1827 RtCt: 10 Jun 1833
James F. NEWTON of Ldn to Joseph T. NEWTON of Ldn. Trust for debt to Commrs. Humphrey PEAKE & George WISE using 56a on Goose Creek (Lot #11 of late Ricketts & Newton). Wit: Jas. HANSBROUGH Sr., Rich'd H. LOVE, David RICKETTS.

4A:287 Date: 15 Aug 1827 RtCt: 16 Aug 1827/10 Jun 1833
Joseph T. NEWTON of Ldn to Humphrey PEAKE of AlexDC. Trust for debt to Commrs. Humphrey PEAKE & Geo. WISE using 97a Lot #3 and 1a Lot #5 on turnpike road adj NEWTON. Wit: James F. NEWTON, Rich'd H. LOVE, Jas. HANSBROUGH Sr.

4A:288 Date: 5 Jan 1833 RtCt: 10 Jun 1833
John CROZIER & wife Eleanor, Edward BRADFIELD & wife Margaret and Edah WINDSOR of Columbiana Co Ohio, Sarah GALLOWAY of Stark Co Ohio, and William PENQUITE & wife Keziah of Fqr to James HILL of Ldn. B/S of undivided 1/5th int. in

land which Elizabeth HILL late WOODFORD w/o James has a life estate (as dower from former husband William WOODFORD dec'd, and after her death to heirs of Susanna CARTER dec'd m/o of William WOODFORD dec'd). Wit: Jesse UNDERWOOD, Joseph THOMPSON. Delv. to HILL 9 Sep 1833.

4A:290 Date: 3 Apr 1833 RtCt: 10 Jun 1833
Joseph BRADFIELD & wife Elizabeth of Warren Co Ohio and Benjamin BRADFIELD of Columbiana Co Ohio to James HILL of Ldn. B/S of undivided 2/8th of 1/7th int. 79a as above (4A:288). Wit: Notley C. WILLIAMS, Roger CHEW. Delv. to HILL 9 Sep 1833.

4A:292 Date: 30 Apr 1833 RtCt: 10 Jun 1833
William NOLAND & wife Catharine of Ldn to James SWART of Ldn. B/S of 139a (NOLAND cnvy/t SWART Jan 1824 adj ADAMS, GULICK, MERCER & NOLAND now BERKLEY with Catharine's CoE in Aug 1824, but neglected to put husband's name on it). Wit: H. SMITH, Asa ROGERS.

4A:294 Date: 28 Jan 1833 RtCt: 10 Jun 1833
Yeoman Edward CARTER & wife Patsey and Martha E. CARTER w/o Abner CARTER of Ldn to Gent. George W. NORRIS of Ldn. B/S of 1a with 2-story brick house in Union now occ. by Abner CARTER adj Joseph GARDNER (occ. by H. EVANS), John C. GREEN, John & James McPHERSON. Wit: A. GIBSON, Edward HALL.

4A:295 Date: 26 Mar 1833 RtCt: 10 Jun 1833
John BOGER (of Michael) of Ldn to Samuel BOGER of Ldn. B/S of 40¼a (Lot #5 from div. of Michael BOGER dec'd) adj __ FAWLEY, __ CARNES. Delv. to grantee 20 Oct 1865.

4A:297 Date: 14 Jun 1833 RtCt: 14 Jun 1833
John MARTIN, Saml. M. BOSS & Saml. STERRETT. Bond on MARTIN as constable.

4A:298 Date: 14 Jun 1833 RtCt: 14 Jun 1833
Edward HAMMAT, Saml. M. BOSS & Jas. L. MARTIN. Bond on HAMMAT as constable.

4A:298 Date: 26 May 1833 RtCt: 10 Jun 1833
Saml. LAYCOCK. Oath as 2nd Lt. in 2nd Reg of artillery Va Militia.

4A:299 Date: 20 May 1833 RtCt: 10 Jun 1833
Francis SHREVE. Oath as Captain of artillary Va Militia.

4A:299 Date: 21 May 1833 RtCt: 10 Jun 1833
Thomas WHALEY. Oath as Ensign of 57th Reg 6th Brig 2nd Div Va Militia.

4A:299 Date: 20 May 1833 RtCt: 10 Jun 1833
Hamilton ROGERS. Oath as Colonel of 57th Reg 6th Brig 2nd Div Va Militia.

4A:299 Date: __   RtCt: 10 Jun 1833
Amos CARR. Qualified as Ensign in 57th Reg of Infantry 6th Brig 2nd Div of Va Militia.

4A:300 Date: 11 Jun 1833 RtCt: 11 Jun 1833
H. SMITH (Commr. in decree of Nov 1831 James SURGHNOR agst Selden HARRISON & Addison HARRISON) of Ldn to John S. DIVINE of Ldn. B/S of house & lot in Mdbg (from estate of Nancy HARRISON dec'd).

4A:300 Date: 11 Jun 1833 RtCt: 11 Jun 1833
John S. DIVINE to John SURGHNOR (trustee of Harriet P. SURGHNER). Trust for benefit of Harriet P. SURGHNOR w/o James SURGHNOR using above house & lot.

4A:301 Date: 11 Jun 1833 RtCt: 11 Jun 1833
John S. DIVINE of Ldn to Hugh SMITH of Ldn. Trust for debt to Commr of Hugh SMITH using house & lot in Mdbg as above.

4A:303 Date: 24 Dec 1831 RtCt: 28 Dec 1831/10 Jun 1833
James IDEN of Ldn to H. B. POWELL. Trust for debt to Hugh SMITH using 125a on Goose Creek adj Isaac GOCHENOUR. Wit: A. GIBSON, Horace LUCKETT, Burr WEEKS, Thomas J. NOLAND.

4A:304 Date: 24 Dec 1831 RtCt: 28 Dec 1831/10 Jun 1833
H. B. POWELL to James IDEN. B/S of 125a (from defaulted trust of Mar 1822 from John IDEN for debt to Burr POWELL Exor. of Leven POWELL dec'd and Dpty Shff Hugh SMITH) on Goose Creek adj Isaac GOCHENOUR. Wit: A. GIBSON, Burr WEEKS, Horace LUCKETT, Thomas J. NOLAND.

4A:305 Date: 1 May 1833 RtCt: 10 Jun 1833
Samuel HOUGH & wife Jane G. of Ldn to Elijah PEACOCK & Andrew GRAHAM of Ldn. B/S of 7a from "Beaverdam tract" adj Wm. HOUGH, GRAHAM, and 4a adj GRAHAM, PEACOCK. Wit: Geo. W. SHAWEN, Joshua PUSEY. Delv. to GRAHAM 30 Jul 1835.

4A:308 Date: 29 Dec 1832 RtCt: 10 Jun 1833
Samuel PAXSON & wife Martha of Ldn to Isaac STEER of Ldn. B/S of 1a adj STEER. Wit: Saml. DAWSON, Geo. W. SHAWEN. Delv. to STEER 7 Aug 1835.

4A:309 Date: 17 Apr 1830 RtCt: 10 Jun 1833
Andrew B. McMULLIN & wife Nancy of Ldn to James SWART of Ldn. B/S of ½ of 2a "Meed Town" (late prop. of William SILVER sold under trust by Gerard L. W. HUNTER) now occupied by Philip WINKOOP. Wit: John SIMPSON, William CARR.

4A:311 Date: 22 Apr 1833 RtCt: 10 Jun 1833
Edward COCHRAN of Ldn to Townshend McVEIGH of Ldn. Trust for Samuel IDEN of Ldn as security using household items.

4A:312 Date: 25 Oct 1832 RtCt: 10 Jun 1833
Jacob SUMMERS & wife Elizabeth of Ldn to Townsend McVEIGH of Ldn. B/S of 200a where SUMMERS resides (cnvy/b Henry F.

LUCKETT Jan 1832) adj Jesse McVEIGH, __ McCARTY, __ FAIRFAX, Hugh ROGERS, Lsbg road, __ CRUPPER. Wit: Wm. B. HARRISON, A. GIBSON. Delv. to McVEIGH 24 Sep 1833.

4A:314 Date: 8 Jun 1833 RtCt: 10 Jun 1833
Amos GULICK of Mt. Gilead to Fielding LITTLETON of Mdbg. Trust for debt to William N. McVEIGH using household items purchased at sale of Alfered GULICK's prop. by const. Wm. BEVERIDGE. Wit: Chas. TURNER, Jas. W. SMITH, Jas. H. McVEIGH.

4A:315 Date: 11 Jun 1833 RtCt: 11 Jun 1833
Isaac HARRIS Sr. & wife Sarah of Ldn to Thomas SANDERS of Ldn. B/S of 110a adj __ BENEDUM, SANDERS (cnvy/b Walter ELGIN Jr. Dec 1828). Wit: Saml. M. EDWARDS, John H. McCABE. Delv. to SAUNDERS 3 Dec 1834.

4A:318 Date: 12 Jun 1833 RtCt: 12 Jun 1833
Saml. M. EDWARDS & wife Ann of Ldn to William CLINE of Ldn. B/S of 2a "Cottage Lot" W of Lsbg on N side of Market St. adj Rich'd H. HENDERSON, Chas. BINNS, Mrs. SAUNDERS (cnvy/b John G. WATT Jan 1824, DBk III:284) with privilege of spring water. Wit: Francis W. LUCKETT, Wilson C. SELDEN Jr. Delv. to CLINE 18 Oct 1833.

4A:319 Date: 11 Jun 1833 RtCt: 13 Jun 1833
Thornton F. OFFUTT of Ldn to Perrin WASHINGTON of FredVa. Release of trust of Oct 1831 for debt to Thomas DRAKE using stone house & lot in Snickersville. Delv. to CLINE 18 Oct 1833.

4A:320 Date: 14 Jun 1833 RtCt: 14 Jun 1833
John WILSON & wife Sarah of JeffVa to Jesse BESICKS and Henly BESICKS (legatees of Priscilla BESICKS dec'd) of Ldn. B/S of 1½a (paid by Priscilla while alive) adj David DANIEL, William CARR. Wit: Geo. RICHARDS.

4A:321 Date: 14 Jun 1833 RtCt: 15 Jun 1833
Sarah C. HAMILTON w/o Charles B. HAMILTON. CoE for deed of Apr 1831. Delv. to Joseph MEAD 23 Aug 1833.

4A:321 Date: 23 May 1833 RtCt: 15 Jun 1833
Sydnor WILLIAMS & wife Mary S. of Ldn to Joseph MEAD & Benjamin MOFFETT of Ldn. Trust for debt to Robert MOFFETT of Ldn using 41a adj Geo. W. HENRY, __ RATLIFF, __ POTTERFIELD, __ HAMILTON. Wit: Geo. W. SHAWEN, William SLATER. Delv. to MOFFETT 10 Jun 1839.

4A:324 Date: 1 Jun 1833 RtCt: 18 Jun 1833
Nathan COCHRAN & wife Mary Pleasant late McGAVACK (d/o Patrick McGAVACK) of Muskingum Co Ohio to Israel T. GRIFFITH of Ldn. B/S of part of Lot #6, #7 & #8 from div. of Mary's grandfather Patrick McGAVICK dec'd (cnvy/b Asa MOORE & Henry BURKETT) on main street in Wtfd. Wit: William HOLMES, Austin HENSLA. Delv. pr order 15 Jul 1835.

4A:327 Date: 18 Jun 1833 RtCt: 18 Jun 1833
George W. HENRY of Ldn to Jesse OXLEY of Ldn. LS of farm now in poss. of Joseph L. POTTS (awarded HENRY as his int. as tenant by the curtesy in land of former wife Elizabeth late FOX for 10y).

4A:327 Date: 19 Jun 1833 RtCt: 19 Jun 1833
Amos GULICK (insolvent debtor) of Ldn to Sheriff Ariss BUCKNER of Ldn. B/S of undivided int. in estate of father Moses GULICK dec'd subject to trusts for debt to Benj. DAVIS & Noble BEVERIDGE.

4A:328 Date: 20 Jun 1833 RtCt: 20 Jun 1833
Thomas WHITE Jr. of Ldn to James WHITE of Ldn. B/S of 2 tracts cnvy/b Thomas Sr. Feb 1833 (using land cnvy/b James jointly with Thos. Jun 1833).

4A:330 Date: 15 Jun 1833 RtCt: 20 Jun 1833
Thomas WHITE Sr. and James WHITE & wife Elizabeth R. of Ldn to Thomas WHITE Jr. of Ldn. B/S of interest in 158a occupied by Philip MORGAN adj James MERCHANT, James ROACH, Mortimer McILHANY and 18a on E side of short hill adj Thomas Sr., Mortimer McILHANY, "garlic level tract", George COOPER (both dev. by James NIXON dec'd to heirs of dau. Jane). Wit: Geo. W. SHAWEN, Mortimer McILHANY.

4A:331 Date: 20 Jun 1833 RtCt: 20 Jun 1833
Thomas WHITE Jr. of Ldn to George SMITH and Daniel T. CRAWFORD of Ldn. B/S of 158a (DBk EE:140) and 18a (as above, both dev. by James NIXON dec'd to heirs of his dau. Jane WHITE dec'd).

4A:333 Date: 19 Jun 1833 RtCt: 21 Jun 1833
Caleb C. SUTHERLAND to S. M. EDWARDS. Trust for Saml. M. BOSS & E'd. E. COOK as endorsers on bank note using rent due from John MURRAY for lots adj Lsbg.

4A:334 Date: 4 May 1833 RtCt: 21 Jun 1833
John ALDER & wife Mary of Ldn to Curtis GRUBB of Ldn. B/S of 216 sq poles adj GRUBB. Wit: Geo. W. SHAWEN, Joshua PUSEY. Delv. to GRUBB 5 Jun 1834.

4A:335 Date: 1 Apr 1833 RtCt: 21 Jun 1833
Richard H. HENDERSON & wife Orra Moore of Ldn to Ebenezer GRUBB Jr. of Ldn. B/S of 141a adj Henry SHORT, Reuben HIXSON, Sandford RAMEY, Thomas DAVIS, Margaret SANDERS, 12¼a nearly adj, and 37a (dev. by Cornelius SHAWEN dec'd to sons George W. SHAWEN and David SHAWEN, then in trust to HENDERSON). Wit: Saml. M. EDWARDS, Edw'd E. COOKE. Delv. to GRUBB 28 Nov 1833.

4A:338 Date: 20 Jun 1833 RtCt: 29 Jun 1833
Nehemiah M. ROWLES & wife Sarah of Ann Arundel Co Md to Amos JANNEY of Ldn. B/S of undivided 1/9th of 4/15th int. in 495a (from his uncle Edmond JENNINGS dec'd) nr short hill adj Samuel

KALB, N. BRADEN, David AXLINE, heirs of __ THRASHER. Wit: David B. FERGUSON, Wm. ASHMAN. Ackn. in BaltMd.

4A:339   Date: 8 Apr 1833   RtCt: 25 Jun 1833
Madison GALLAWAY and Charles L. NOLAND of Ldn to James HILL of Ldn. Trust for debt to Martha CLAYTON of Ldn using wheat machion [machine]. Wit: Thornton WALKER, Wm. CLAYTON, Catharine LUKE.

4A:341   Date: 12 Nov 1832   RtCt: 29 Jun 1833
Francis SIMPSON & wife Deborah of Ldn to Asa BROWN of Ldn. Trust for debt to John HUNT Sr. of Ldn using ¼a in Hllb (cnvy/b Isaac HOUGH to John HUNT May 1820) adj William CLENDENING, Thomas LESLIE. Wit: Thomas BROWN. Delv. to BROWN 24 Jul 1837.

4A:342   Date: 20 Jun 1833   RtCt: 29 Jun 1833
Joshua J. ROWLES & wife Harriot of BaltMd to Amos JANNEY of Ldn. B/S of 1/9th of 4/15th int. in 495a (of Edmond JINNINGS dec'd with 1/9th left to heirs of Candy ROWLES) adj Samuel KALB, N. BRADEN, David AXLINE, E. THRASHER. Wit: David B. FERGUSON, Wm. ASHMAN.

4A:344   Date: 29 Jun 1833   RtCt: 1 Jul 1833
James GARRISON to Archibald M. KITZMILLER. LS for 5y of house and lot at Market & King sts in Lsbg now in tenure of GARRISON store occupied by H. T. HARRISON, house by __ CORDELL, shop by T. W. BROOKS, and shop by __ PARRETT excepted. Wit: Saml. CAMPBELL.

4A:345   Date: 29 Jun 1833   RtCt: 1 Jul 1833
Archibald M. KITZMILLER of Ldn to James GARRISON. B/S of int. in estate of Martin KITZMILLER dec'd (in consideration of LS above). Delv. to GARRISON 20 Nov 1835.

4A:346   Date: 29 Jun 1833   RtCt: 5 Jul 1833
Samuel HOUGH & wife Jane G. of Ldn to Charles G. ESKRIDGE. Trust for debt to Israel T. GRIFFITH of Ldn using 59a adj Wtfd, Fairfax meeting house lot (see DBk TTT:001), and strips of land from others, and two 4a (see DBk YYY:149) nr Wtfd adj Dr. McCABE, Asa MOORE dec'd. Wit: George W. SHAWEN, Joshua PUSEY. Delv. pr order 15 Jul 1835.

4A:350   Date: 9 Oct 1832   RtCt: 5 Jul 1833
Dr. Charles G. EDWARDS & wife Deborah, George L. LACKLAND & wife Eliza, John M. EDWARDS & wife Mary and Mrs. Elizabeth WHERRY of Ldn to Samuel HOUGH of Ldn. B/S of 436a "Goshen" or "Edwards ferry tract" on Potomac and Goose Creek (WHERRY reserves right of dower and rents during her life) adj Ricketts & Newton, Dulin & Saunders. Wit: George W. SHAWEN, Joshua PUSEY, John H. McCABE, Presley CORDELL. Ackn. and CoE for LACKLANDs in St. Louis Co Missouri. Delv. to HOUGH 20 Jan 1836

4A:354   Date: 1 Jun 1833   RtCt: 6 Jul 1833
Joshua OSBURN (Commr. in case of John NICHOLS agst Charity
NICHOLS) of Ldn to Thomas S. STONE of Ldn. B/S of 2a (from
estate of James NICHOLS the elder dec'd) nr blue ridge mt. on Lsbg
& Snickersville turnpike rd. adj Thomas OSBURN. Calvin
THATCHER, H. ELLIOTT, Nathaniel NICHOLS. Delv. to STONE 9
Jan 1834.

4A:356   Date: 4 Jul 1833   RtCt: 8 Jul 1833
Thomas L. ORR and Asa ROGERS (sole distributees of Mary A.
ORR dec'd). Ackn. receipt of bond on Jno. R. COOKE Esqr of
Winchester for last settlement by Wm. Alexander POWELL Admr.
dbn of Mary A. ORR dec'd.

4A:356   Date: 8 Jun 1833   RtCt: 8 Jul 1833
John STEPHENSON. Oath as Lt. in 57th Reg Va Militia.

4A:356   Date: 8 Jul 1833   RtCt: 8 Jul 1833
Levi COOKSEY & wife Elizabeth of Ldn to Saml. M. EDWARDS of
Ldn. Trust for debt to Charles B. HAMILTON of Ldn using 7a and 3a
(see DBk SSS:407 and ZZZ:203).

4A:358   Date: 1 Mar 1833   RtCt: 19 Jul 1833
Thomas P. COLEMAN of AlexDC to William D. NUTT of AlexDC.
B/S of int. in prop. of George COLEMAN dec'd late of AlexDC (from
execution agst Thomas J. NOLAND). Delv. to A. ADDISON pr order
9 Sep 1833.

4A:360   Date: 1 Mar 1832   RtCt: 9 Jul 1833
Richard H. HENDERSON (Exor of Sally L. AISQUITH dec'd) of Lsbg
to William B. TYLER of Lsbg. B/S of house & lot on Market St in
Lsbg (prch/o William JOHNSON) adj __ SAUNDERS. Delv. to
TYLER 1 Jan 1837.

4A:361   Date: 17 Jul 1833   RtCt: 17 Jul 1833
Jared CHAMBLIN to George W. HENRY. Release of trust of Feb
1833 for debt to Thomas ROGERS using int. in farm of William FOX
dec'd dev. to Mary FOX now dec'd.

4A:362   Date: 20 Jul 1833   RtCt: 22 Jul 1833
Elizabeth DAVIS of Ldn to granddaughter Mary Eliza POWER d/o
Thos. POWER. Gift of household items. Wit: Saml. M. EDWARDS.

4A:363   Date: 29 Jan 1833   RtCt: 24 Jul 1803
Thomas SANDERS (Exor of Presley SANDERS dec'd) of Ldn to
Nicholas MONEY of Ldn. B/S of 55a adj John ROSE (formerly Clear
OXLEY) at foot of mt. Delv. to MONEY 25 Sep 1833.

4A:365   Date: 10 Sep 1832   RtCt: 25 Jul 1833
Flavious J. BRADEN of Natches Mississippi to Elizabeth SULLIVAN
of Ldn. B/S of house & ½a in Wtfd on side of hill now occupied by
Henry BODINE (dev. by father Jos. BRADEN dec'd 1814) adj
Edward DORSEY, Negro woman Risby. Wit: G. W. HOUGH, D.
CONRAD, Isaac WALKER.

4A:367 Date: 29 Jan 1833 RtCt: 25 Jul 1833
Nicholas MONEY & wife Ann to Saml. M. EDWARDS. Trust for debt to Thomas SANDERS (Exor of Presley SAUNDERS dec'd) using 55a on Catoctin Mt. (see 4A:363). Wit: Presley CORDELL, John H. McCABE. Delv. to SAUNDERS 23 Apr 1835.

4A:370 Date: 4 Jan 1833 RtCt: 27 Jul 1833
James VERNON & wife Nancy, Mary IDEN late VERNON wd/o Jonah IDEN, Asa TRAYHORN & wife Elizabeth late VERNON, Abraham VERNON & wife Mary and Elizabeth HARLAN to Isaac BOWLES. B/S of int. in "Mill lots" of Daniel VERNON dec'd (as heirs). Wit: William SCOTT, Isaac M. LANNING of Gurnsey Co. Ohio and Notley C. WILLIAMS, E. B. GRADY in Ldn. Delv. to Jas. BOWLES pr order 26 May 1836.

4A:373 Date: 4 Jan 1833 RtCt: 27 Jul 1833
James VERNON & wife Nancy, Mary IDEN late VERNON wd/o Jonah IDEN, Asa TRAYHORN & wife Elizabeth late VERNON, Abraham VERNON & wife Mary and Elizabeth HARLAN to Mordecai THROCKMORTAN. B/S of int. in 20a (from estate of Daniel VERNON dec'd) on S side of Blue ridge (prch/o Walter LANGLEY Feb 1827) adj __ CHEW, __ URTON. Wit: William SCOTT, Isaac M. LANNING of Gurnsey Co. Ohio and Notley C. WILLIAMS, E. B. GRADY in Ldn. Delv. to J. B. YOUNG pr order 29 Aug 1836.

4A:375 Date: 4 Jan 1833 RtCt: 27 Jul 1833
David GIBSON, Eli GIBSON, Rebecca HIXSON, Abner GIBSON & wife Susanna E., Hamilton ROGERS & wife Nancy late HIXSON and Burr POWELL & wife Catharine (reps of int. of Levi GIBSON) to Mordecai THROCKMORTAN. B/S of int. in 20a (from estate of Daniel VERNON dec'd beq. to wife Rebecca now dec'd) as above. Wit: Notley C. WILLIAMS, Ed. HALL, John SIMPSON.

4A:379 Date: 1 Jun 1833 RtCt: 27 Jul 1833
Isaac BOWLES of Ldn to Isaac NICHOLS of Ldn. B/S of 8a on NW fork of Beaverdam Creek adj Samuel PUGH, Sarah TRAHERN, Isaac NICHOLS. Wit: Alpheus GIBSON, Alfred WRIGHT, William YOUNG.

4A:380 Date: 27 Jul 1833 RtCt: 29 Jul 1833
John SURGHNOR of Ldn to George RICHARDS of Ldn. Trust for John MARTIN as security on note to Robert ELGIN using house and lot on S side of Royal St in Lsbg (DBk FFF:115), int. in Jacob TOWNER's Lot #2 on Royal St (DBk KKK:360), house on W side of King st. now occ. up SURGHNOR as a work shop (DBk XXX:054), house & lot on N side of Loudoun St. now occ. by Peter GUIDER, house & lot on S side of Market St. occ. by Harry BRANT a free man of color.

4A:382 Date: 4 May 1833 RtCt: 31 Jul 1833
Curtis GRUBB & wife Harriot/Harriet of Ldn to John ALDER of Ldn. B/S of 108 sq poles adj GRUBB, __ HOOE, __ LITTLE on Laurel Hill

nr "the Narrows". Wit: Geo. W. SHAWEN, Joshua PUSEY. Delv. to ALDERS 14 Jun 1838.

4A:384   Date: 31 Jul 1833   RtCt: 31 Jul 1833
Frederick D. DECK to George RICHARDS. Trust for debt to John A. McCORMICK using farm animals, farm and household items. Delv. to McCORMICK 14 Feb 1835.

4A:386   Date: 2 Aug 1833   RtCt: 2 Aug 1833
James GARRISON & Edward SHACKLETT. List of prop. purchased at sale of John SURGHNOR on 15 [?] Aug 1833 to satisfy debts to John MARTIN – household items totaling $202.99¼. GARRISON and SHACKLETT lend this amt. to Mary E. SURGHNOR, John H. SURGHNOR, Sally E. SURGHNOR, Mary E. SUMMERS, Emily E. SUMMERS & Samuel SUMMERS (ch/o of SURGHNOR & wife) for their comfort.

4A:388   Date: 2 Aug 1833   RtCt: 2 Aug 1833
William D. DRISH to Jesse TIMMS, Charles G. ESKRIDGE & Erasmus G. HAMILTON. Trust for debt to George CARTER of Oatlands using lot on W side of King St. in Lsbg (part of Lot #19 & #20 cnvy/b John LITTLEJOHN Jul 1793, DBk V:43) adj late prop. of __ McCOWAT, __ FADLEY, Dr. CLAGGETT. Delv. to TIMMS by direct. of G. CARTER __.

4A:391   Date: 27 Jul 1833   RtCt: 3 Aug 1833
Elijah PEACOCK & wife Ann and Andrew GRAHAM & wife Mary of Ldn to William H. HOUGH of Ldn. B/S of 6a on Beaverdam Creek adj GRAHAM, HOUGH. Wit: C. B. HAMILTON Jr., Joshua PUSEY. Delv. 6 Aug 1835 to N. S. BRADEN pr order.

4A:393   Date: 7 May 1833   RtCt: 8 Aug 1833
James STROTHER to Saml. HOUGH. Trust for debt to Charles G. EDWARDS using farm animals, farm and household items, Negro boy Livi STINGER, crops.

4A:395   Date: 25 Jul 1833   RtCt: 9 Aug 1833
James HIXSON & wife Mary of Ldn to Benjamin HIXSON of Ldn. B/S of 19¾a on S side of Little River (cnvy/b Benjamin) and 84½a on Little River adj James HIXSON, Lewis BERKLEY, Hugh SMITH. Wit: Abner GIBSON, Asa ROGERS. Delv. to Ben. HIXSON 5 Jan 1836.

4A:398   Date: 25 Jul 1833   RtCt: 9 Aug 1833
James HIXSON of Ldn to Benjamin HIXSON of Ldn. Articles of agreement concerning payment for sale of above land.

4B:001   Date: 25 Jul 1833   RtCt: 9 Aug 1833
Benjamin HIXSON & wife Tacy of Ldn to James HIXSON of Ldn. B/S of 23a Lot #7 in div. of Joseph DANIELS dec'd. Wit: Abner GIBSON, Asa ROGERS.

4B:002 Date: 25 Jul 1833 RtCt: 9 Aug 1833
James HIXSON & wife Mary of Ldn to Sandford RODGERS of Ldn.
B/S of 163a (prch/o MASON's heirs) adj William ROGERS, __
HARRISON. Wit: Abner GIBSON, Asa ROGERS. Delv. to B.
ROGERS pr order ?P:407, 23 Feb '66.

4B:003 Date: 5 Aug 1833 RtCt: 10 Aug 1833
James BROWN of Ldn to Charles BINNS of Ldn. Mortgage of farm
items. Delv. to BINNS 28 Feb 1834.

4B:003 Date: 10 Aug 1833 RtCt: 10 Aug 1833
Charles BINNS of Ldn to Eli OFFUTT of Ffx. Trust for benefit of
Hannah BINNS w/o Charles using Negro Jinney aged 52y, Tom abt
50y, Levi 30y, Joe 49y, Emma 27y, Solomon abt 52y, Middleton abt
52y, carriage and horses. Delv. to Hannah BINNS 30 Sep 1833.

4B:004 Date: 10 Aug 1833 RtCt: 10 Aug 1833
Charles BINNS & wife Hannah of Ldn to John GRAY and Robert
BENTLEY of Ldn. B/S of 230a now in poss. of Charles W. D. BINNS
(224a cnvy/b father Charles BINNS dec'd, DBk R:017, and 6a
cnvy/b William A. BINNS, DBk DDD:082). Wit: Saml. M. EDWARDS,
John J. MATHIAS.

4B:005 Date: 10 Aug 1833 RtCt: 10 Aug 1833
Benjamin SMITH & wife Sarah A. E./Sally late BLINCO of Ldn to
John ROSE of Ldn. Trust for benefit of Sarah A. E. using undivided
1/6th int. in estate of father Sampson BLINCO dec'd subject to
widow's dower. Wit: Francis W. LUCKETT, Wilson C. SELDEN Jr.

4B:006 Date: 2 Aug 1833 RtCt: 10 Aug 1833
Samuel HAMMONTREE of Ldn to Michael PLASTER of Ldn. Trust
for debt to Noble BEVERIDGE, A. G. TIBBITTS, James JOHNSON,
George KILE, Jacob SILCOTT, William GALLEHER, James
DUNKEN, John P. JACOBS, Mortica THOGMORTON, Samuel
BECK, George PETTETT, George KEEN, Thomas DORMAN,
Fielden LITTLETON, Seth SMITH, John THOMPSON, Marques
DISHMAN, Peter GREGG, Thomas N. JONES of Ohio, George
TURNER, Banister STEPHENS, William BLUNDREN, Elisha
BLUNDREN & Winefred BLUNDREN orphan ch/o John & Sarah
BLUNDREN dec'd to be paid to George HAMMONTREE, William C.
PALMER using house & lot in Union where he lives and household
items. Delv. to PLASTER 21 Feb 1835.

4B:008 Date: 10 Aug 1833 RtCt: 10 Aug 1833
Abel JANNEY & wife Lydia of Ldn to Daniel G. SMITH of Ldn. B/S of
110a (cnvy/b Jonathan TAYLOR Sr. (dec'd) & wife Ann to Jonas
JANNEY Sr. & wife Ruth) adj Wm. PIGGOTT, James HATCHER, __
PANCOAST, Jonas JANNEY. Wit: Notley C. WILLIAMS, H. T.
HARRISON. Delv. to SMITH 11 Feb 1836.

4B:009 Date: 10 Aug 1833 RtCt: 10 Aug 1833
Daniel G. SMITH & wife Eliza of Ldn to Thomas NICHOLS & John JANNEY of Ldn. Trust for debt to Abel JANNEY using above land. Wit: Notley C. WILLIAMS, John ROSE.

4B:011 Date: 12 Jul 1833 RtCt: 12 Aug 1833
Geo. W. HENRY. Oath as Colonel in 56th Reg of infantry 6th Brig 2nd Div Va Militia.

4B:011 Date: 12 Aug 1833 RtCt: 12 Aug 1833
Dean JAMES. Oath as Major in 57th Reg 2nd Div 6th Brig Va Militia.

4B:011 Date: 12 Aug 1833 RtCt: 12 Aug 1833
John J. JANNEY s/o Thomas JANNEY dec'd. Receipt of full payment from Seth SMITH his Guardian by Exors of father's Admr.

4B:012 Date: 31 May 1833 RtCt: 12 Aug 1833
Tailor Benedict PADGETT & wife Eleanor of Union to Henry PLASTER Jr. of Union. B/S of 56 sq poles which was exchanged. Wit: William BENTON, Ludwell LUCKETT.

4B:013 Date: 15 Jan 1833 RtCt: 12 Aug 1833
James VIOLET of FredVa and Charles WRIGHT of Ldn (Exors of Phebe VIOLET dec'd wd/o Elijah VIOLET dec'd) to John VIOLET (trustee for his sister Jememia BISHOP). B/S of 13a (from land of Elijah VIOLET dec'd).

4B:013 Date: 1 Aug 1832 RtCt: 14 Aug 1833
Samuel D. LESLIE of Ldn to Nathan NEAR of Ldn. B/S of 23½a adj Joshua OSBURN, heirs of __ McILHANY, Wm. POTTS. Delv. to his son 11 Apr 1838 pr order.

4B:014 Date: 21 Apr 1833 RtCt: 17 Aug 1833
Cyrus BURSON of Ldn to John BURSON of Ldn. B/S of 134a (former prop. of Joseph BURSON dec'd cnvy/t Cyrus) adj Thomas HUMPHREY, Samuel PUGH. Delv. to John BURSON 13 Apr 1835.

4B:015 Date: 24 Jun 1833 RtCt: 17 Aug 1833
Morris HUMPHREY & wife Mary Ann of Jackson Co Ohio to Thomas M. HUMPHREY of Ldn. B/S of undivided $1/6^{th}$ int. in land of Jesse HUMPHREY dec'd allotted as dower to widow Mary (sold Oct 1827 to Cyrus BURSON who sold to Thomas M. without deed). Wit: Timothy RATCLIFF, John RATCLIFF.

4B:017 Date: 12 Aug 1833 RtCt: 17 Aug 1833
David F. BEALL of Ldn to children Robert E. BEALL, David L. BEALL (<21y) & Mary C. E. BEALL (<21y). Gift of 54a where David F. now lives (prch/o Abijah JANNEY, DBk NN:234) and slave Jane & her 2 children Maria & Susan, farm animals, farm and household items (for support of David F.) Wit: William S. DUGGON, Alfred WRIGHT, W. G. WRIGHT. Delv. to Robt. E. BEALL pr order 4 Jun 1840.

4B:018 Date: 19 Aug 1833 RtCt: 22 Aug 1833
Howell DAVIS to Noble BEVERIDGE. B/S of land from trust of May 1831 Amos GULICK for debt to Benjamin DAVIS. Delv. to BEVERIDGE 9 Jan 1837.

4B:019 Date: 2 Jun 1833 RtCt: 16 Aug 1833
Dinah ROGERS, John HOLMES, Thomas ROGERS & wife Elmina, Arthur ROGERS & wife Hannah, Elijah HOLMES & wife Elizabeth, Samuel ROGERS and Hamilton ROGERS Jr. of Ldn and Hugh ROGERS & wife Mary and Joseph ROGERS & wife Mary of Belmont Co Ohio to Thomas HUGHES of Ldn. B/S of 79a (cnvy/b William D. DIGGS and Catharine DIGGS to Hamilton ROGERS) adj James GREENLEES. Wit: F. A. F. CARTER, John PERRY Jr., William R. SHIELDS, William HOLMES Jr., Benjamin W[H]ITE, Francis W. LUCKETT, Saml. M. EDWARDS. Delv. to HUGHES 20 Aug 1836.

4B:021 Date: 2 Jun 1833 RtCt: 16 Aug/24 Aug 1833
Dinah ROGERS wd/o Hamilton ROGERS dec'd, John HOLMES who m. Mary ROGERS (now dec'd), Arthur ROGERS & wife Hannah, Hamilton ROGERS Jr. (of Ldn) and Hugh ROGERS & wife Mary and Joseph ROGERS & wife Mary of Belmont Co Ohio (heirs of Hamilton ROGERS dec'd) to Thomas ROGERS, Samuel ROGERS & Elijah HOLMES who m. Elizabeth ROGERS (other heirs). B/S of 215a adj Elijah HOLMES, Richard TAVENNER, GREENLEESE. Wit: F. A. F. CARTER, John PERRY Jr., William R. SHEILDS, William HOLMES Jr., Benjamin WHITE, Timothy TAYLOR, Jas. McILHANY.

4B:023 Date: 16 Aug 1833 RtCt: 24 Aug 1833
Joseph WOOD & wife Lydia of Ldn to Yardley TAYLOR of Ldn. Trust for debt to Isaac NICHOLS, William PIGGOTT, William HOGE and Thomas HATCHER using 12a (prch/o Pompey WHITEN Mar 1815), 15a (prch/o James MOORE May 1816) and 80a (prch/o James MOORE, Asa MOORE & John WILLIAMS Exors. of Mahlon JANNEY dec'd Mar 1817). Wit: Joshua PUSEY, David REECE. Delv. to PIGGOTT 27 Nov 1843.

4B:025 Date: 27 Nov 1829 RtCt: 24 Aug 1833
Daniel EACHES of Ldn to Jesse RICHARDS of Ldn. B/S of int. in land on Pantherskin allotted as dower of widow of John GIBSON (cnvy/b Amos GIBSON & wife Hannah, Elisha JANNEY & wife Mary, John JANNEY, Mahlon GIBSON & Hugh SMITH & wife Elizabeth May 1823, DBk GGG: 250). Wit: Thomas ROGERS, Gourley R. HATCHER, Caleb RECTOR.

4B:026 Date: 17 Oct 1829 RtCt: 24 Aug 1833
Humphrey B. POWELL to Daniel EACHES. Trust for debt to Joseph GORE, William RICHARDS, Henry S. TAYLOR Exor. of Margaret MEAD, James BROWN & Thomas EACHES using int. in land & mill occupied by Jesse RICHARDS formerly of John GIBSON. Wit:

Ferdinando BOLON, Craven POPKINS, Th. ROGERS, Joshua B.
DUNKIN, Gourley REEDER, John LOVETT, C. L. CLOWES, Thos.
J. BENNETT, D. BROWN.

4B:027 Date: 20 Mar 1833 RtCt: 26 Aug 1833
James LOVE & wife Susannah of Ldn to Eli PIERPOINT of Ldn. B/S
of int. in land occupied by Eli PIERPOINT (as heirs of Elizabeth
LOVE & Sarah LOVE late dec'd) and undivided $1/8^{th}$ part of L/L in
same tract (prch/o Benjamin DANIEL an heir of James LOVE Sr.
dec'd). Wit: Fenton M. LOVE, Mary R. LOVE., James McILHANY,
David REECE. Delv. to PAIRPOINT 18 Mar 1835.

4B:028 Date: 28 Feb 1833 RtCt: 26 Aug 1833
James LOVE & wife Susannah, Eli A. LOVE & wife Sarah Ann and
John P. LOVE of Ldn to Eli PIERPOINT of Ldn. B/S of $1/8^{th}$ int. in
L/L of land PIERPOINT now occupies (inherited by Thomas LOVE
from father's estate less dower then cnvy/t Benjamin DANIEL by
deed of gift then sold to LOVE. Wit: John WHITE, Mortimer
McILHANY. Delv. to PAIRPOINT 18 Mar 1835.

4B:030 Date: 25 Mar 1833 RtCt: 26 Aug 1833
Charles F. DOWNES & wife Esther, Joseph GRUBB & wife Mary,
James DANIEL and Hannah DANIEL of Ldn to Eli PIERPOINT of
Ldn. B/S of int. in land (as heirs of Sarah LOVE & Elizabeth LOVE)
where PIERPOINT lives. Wit: John WHITE, James McILHANY.
Delv. to PEIRPOINT 18 Mar 1835.

4B:031 Date: 16 Mar 1833 RtCt: 26 Aug 1833
Craven BROWN & wife Mariah and Lydia LOVE of Ldn to Eli
PIERPOINT of Ldn. B/S of int. in land (as heirs of Sarah LOVE &
Elizabeth LOVE) where PIERPOINT lives. Wit: Jas. McILHANY,
Presley CORDELL. Delv. to PEIRPOINT 18 Mar 1835.

4B:032 Date: 30 Jan 1833 RtCt: 26 Aug 1833
John P. LOVE and Eli A. LOVE & wife Sarah Ann of Ldn to Eli
PIERPOINT of Ldn. B/S of int. in land (as heirs of Sarah LOVE &
Elizabeth LOVE ch/o James LOVE Sr. dec'd) where PIERPOINT
lives. Wit: John WHITE, Mortimer McILHANY. Delv. to PEIRPOINT
18 Mar 1835.

4B:033 Date: 11 Apr 1833 RtCt: 26 Aug 1833
Thomas ROGERS (as Commr. in case of Sep 1832 George W.
CHAMBERS & wife Emeline formerly SMALLWOOD agst George
TAVENNER & wife Sarah late SMALLWOOD, John THOMAS,
Joseph POSTON, John TOWNER & wife Sarah Ann late
SMALLWOOD, Philip REED & wife Amanda late SMALLWOOD and
Eleanor SMALLWOOD) to Isaac WALKER. B/S of house and lot in
Wtfd (former prop. of Leven SMALLWOOD dec'd occupied by
Mess'rs WALKERS as a store room and by John A. MOORE as a
dwelling (cnvy/b Asa MOORE to SMALLWOOD Sep 1810, DBk
NN:68) adj Lydia HOUGH, John WILLIAMS. Delv. to WALKER 27
Apr 1835.

4B:034   Date: 26 Aug 1833   RtCt: 26 Aug 1833
Charles BINNS & wife Hannah of Ldn to William CARR of Ldn. B/S
of 130a where John HULLS formerly lived adj B. SHREVE Jr.,
Charles B. ALEXANDER, Wm. CARR, Walter ELGIN, Andrew
GRIMES (then lived). Wit: Saml. M. EDWARDS, John J. MATHIAS.
Delv. to CARR 9 Apr 1835.

4B:035   Date: 10 Aug 1833   RtCt: 26 Aug 1833
Jacob G. PAXSON of Ldn to Isaac WALKER of Wtfd. Trust for debt
to William WILSON using thrashing machine. Wit: John WILLIAMS,
William WILLIAMS, Isaac WILSON.

4B:036   Date: 27 Aug 1833   RtCt: 27 Aug 1833
Jacob G. PAXSON & wife Mahala to Charles G. ESKRIDGE and
John A. CARTER. Trust for debt to Samuel PAXSON, Thomas
ROGERS & Fleming HIXSON using 108a nr Wtfd (cnvy/b William
PAXSON) adj __ HOUGH, Samuel PAXSON, and farm animals,
household items. Wit: Saml. M. EDWARDS, Francis W. LUCKETT.

4B:038   Date: 27 Aug 1833   RtCt: 27 Aug 1833
Samuel PAXSON (trustee of Mahala PAXSON) of Ldn to Jacob G.
PAXSON of Ldn. B/S of above 108a, etc.

4B:039   Date: 29 Aug 1833   RtCt: 30 Aug 1833
Richard H. HENDERSON (Commr. in case of Robert JOHNSON &
wife Malinda late MILLS agst Alexander CORDELL Admr. of Elias
THRASHER dec'd and Lydia RAMEY Exor. of Sanford RAMEY
dec'd who was security of Admr and heirs of Elias THRASHER
dec'd, Sept 1832) of Ldn to Robert JOHNSON of Ldn. B/S of 276a
where JOHNSON lives and 45 a in occupation of widow of Elias
THRASHER dec'd.

4B:040   Date: 31 Aug 1833   RtCt: 31 Aug 1833
Elijah KENT (insolvent debtor) to Sheriff Ariss BUCKNER. B/S of int.
in land on NW side of Loudoun St in Lsbg leased by KENT of
William CARR, adj Saml. HARPER.

4B:040   Date: 2 Sep 1833   RtCt: 2 Sep 1833
William D. DRISH of Ldn to John CURRY of Ldn. BoS for Negro Ann
supposed to be 9y old on 24 Dec next (see BoS from Presley
SAUNDERS to Joseph MEAD) until she arrives at 30y when she
and increase to be freed.

4B:041   Date: 2 Sep 1833   RtCt: 2 Sep 1833
Samuel HOUGH Esqr of Ldn to Charles G. ESKRIDGE of Ldn. Trust
for debt to John WILLIAMS Guardian of Hannah MENDENHALL
using 76a (91a prch/o Stephen HIXSON less 15a sold to G. W. &
David SHAWEN). Delv. to Wm. RUSSELL pr order 12 Sep 1836.

4B:042   Date: __ 1830   RtCt: 4 Sep 1833
Joseph WALTMAN of FredMd to Emanuel WALTMAN of Ldn. B/S of
5a (from Jacob WALTMAN dec'd) adj __ BUCKINGHAM. Delv. to __
16 Jun 1834.

4B:043 Date: 8 Apr 1828 RtCt: 6 Sep 1833
Thomas BURGEE Sr. & wife Eleanor of Md to Marthey GARRETT (d/o Thomas). Gift of 110a (prch/o Nicholas GARRETT). Wit: Wm. MURPHEY, Philemon S. MACKELFRESH.

4B:044 Date: 10 Aug 1833 RtCt: 7 Sep 1833
Charles BINNS & wife Hannah of Ldn to daus. Ann Alexander BINNS and Elizabeth Douglas BINNS. B/S of houses & lots and 2a on Cornwell St (perfecting deed of Aug 1832 cnvy/t Nancy & Elizabeth houses and lots in Lsbg now occupied by Charles BINNS) and slave men Adam and Titus, children Letty & Jack, household items (long list). Wit: William ELLZEY, Saml. M. EDWARDS. Delv. to Ann & Eliz'th. BINNS 1 Mar 1834.

4B:048 Date: 29 Aug 1833 RtCt: 7 Sep 1833
John H. McCABE to Christopher FRYE. B/S of 14a and 22a (from defaulted trust of Jan 1831 from Robert CAMPBELL dec'd for debt to FRYE). Delv to S. M. EDWARDS who is transacting business for M. FRYE Exor. of C. FRYE dec'd 26 Jan 1836.

4B:049 Date: __ Sep 1833 RtCt: 7 Sep 1833
Nancy MORRIS of Ldn to Charles B. HAMILTON and Vallentine V. PURCEL. Mortgage of household items as security for Thomas MORRIS dec'd Guardian of a legacy from Aquilla WILLETT dec'd to daus. Lucinda, Keziah and Sophronia. Wit: Lyman LANE, Saml. PURSELL Jr.

4B:049 Date: 9 Sep 1833 RtCt: 9 Sep 1833
John YOUNG & wife Hannah and Abraham SHOEMAKER of Ldn to Thomas NICHOLS Esqr and Yardly TAYLOR. Trust for debt to William YOUNG, Swithen NICHOLS and Joshua PANCOAST using 92a with 1/3 life estate to mother (John YOUNG made trust to Abraham SHOEMAKER for benefit of Hannah and children, SHOEMAKER owes SWITHEN).

4B:051 Date: 14 Aug 1833 RtCt: 8 Sep 1833
Christian MILLER & wife Sarah of Ldn to Jonah HATCHER of Ldn. B/S of 6a on W side of short hill adj William POTTS, and 233a adj other lot adj __ GRUBB, __ DOWLING. Wit: William CLENDENING, John WHITE. Delv. to HATCHER 31 Aug 1835.

4B:052 Date: 1 Apr 1829 RtCt: 12 Oct 1829/9 Sep 1833
William DERRY of Ldn to Michael WIARD of Ldn. Trust for debt to Jacob DERRY using 72a on W side of Short Hill where DERRY lives adj Christian NISEWANGER, John CUNNARD, Absalom VANVACTER, John NISEWANGER, Mathias PRINCE. Wit: Robert JOHNSON, Jacob STREAM, David DERRY. Delv. to WIARD pr order __.

4B:054 Date: 9 Sep 1833 RtCt: 9 Sep 1833
George W. MOCK (Exor of Jacob MOCK dec'd) of Ldn to Samuel B. HARRIS of Ldn. B/S of undivided ½ of 2a (owned by Jacob dec'd

and Henry RUSSELL) adj William WRIGHT, road from Wtfd to Nolands Ferry.

4B:055   Date: Jul 1827   RtCt: 10 Sep 1833
Ricketts & Newton. Survey and plat of land – 118a Lot #1; 327a Lot #2; 97a Lot #3; 66a Lot #4; 1a Lot #5; 10a wood Lot #6; 12a wood Lot #7; 11a wood Lot #8; 10a wood Lot #9; 8a wood Lot #10; 56a wood Lot #11; 93a Lot #12.

4B:057   Date: 7 Sep 1833   RtCt: 9 Sep 1833
William J. DRISH of Ldn to Notley C. WILLIAMS. Trust for benefit of wife Martha L. DRISH and any children using yearly rents from farm formerly owned by Mathew ADAM dec'd.

4B:058   Date: 17 Aug 1833   RtCt: 9 Sep 1833
John CONNER. Qualified as Lt. in 57th Reg of infantry 6th Brig 2nd Div Va Militia.

4B:058   Date: 17 Aug 1833   RtCt: 9 Sep 1833
James WILLIAMS. Qualified as Ensign in 57th Reg of infantry 6th Brig 2nd Div Va Militia.

4B:058   Date: 9 Sep 1833   RtCt: 9 Sep 1833
Garrison B. FRENCH, Timothy TAYLOR Sr. & Charles TAYLOR. Bond on FRENCH as constable.

4B:059   Date: 13 May 1833   RtCt: 9 Sep 1833
On motion of Levi G. EWERS of Apr 1833 to have road opened from north fork road to Narcissa GHEEN and John WRIGHT to road from Ewer's mill to Snickers Gap turnpike. Charles TAYLOR, Joshua NICHOLS & Abraham SKILLMAN viewed and reported – from Narcissa GHEEN and John WRIGHT to nr Edward BOLEN to Henry BROWN intersecting old road thru Mary McINTYRE, David YOUNG to Levi G. EWERS' mill then to Snickers Gap turnpike. Of great importance as mill road to church, blacksmith shop, market and labour. $215 damages to Narcissa GHEEN.

4B:061   Date: 13 May 1833   RtCt: 9 Sep 1833
On motion of Levi G. EWERS of Apr 1833 to have road opened from north fork road to Narcissa GHEEN and John WRIGHT to road from Ewer's mill to Snickers Gap turnpike. Charles TAYLOR, Joshua NICHOLS & Abraham SKILLMAN viewed and reported – same as above. $27.50 damages to Edward BOLEN.

4B:063   Date: 8 Aug 1833   RtCt: 9 Sep 1833
Motion of Emanuel WALTMAN of Oct 1830 to have road from Berlin Ferry on Potomack to intersect road from Newtown to John EVERHEART's Mill at corner between Thomas J. MARLOW and Joseph MILLER. John MOORE, John EVERHEART & John GEORGE viewed and reported – from Ferry down old road thru Susan WALTMAN, Emanuel WALTMAN her Guardian and thru Margaret WALTMAN E. WALTMAN also her Guardian to old road thru Jacob SMITH and wood lot of Jonathan WENNER to Adam

SANBOWER wood land to Jonathan WENNER with old road thru Jacob SMITH, Thomas BUCKINGHAM, then to Thomas J. MARLOW then to Joseph MILLER to old road from Newtown to John EVERHEART's mill. $20 damages to Jacob SMITH.

4B:065   Date: 8 Aug 1833   RtCt: 10 Sep 1833
Motion of Emanuel WALTMAN of Oct 1830 to have road from Berlin Ferry on Potomack to intersect road from Newtown to John EVERHEART's Mill at corner between Thomas J. MARLOW and Joseph MILLER. John MOORE, John EVERHEART & John GEORGE viewed and reported – as above. $4.50 damages to Margeret WALTMAN.

4B:067   Date: 8 Aug 1833   RtCt: 10 Sep 1833
Motion of Emanuel WALTMAN of Oct 1830 to have road from Berlin Ferry on Potomack to intersect road from Newtown to John EVERHEART's Mill at corner between Thomas J. MARLOW and Joseph MILLER. John MOORE, John EVERHEART & John GEORGE viewed and reported – as above. $6.00 damages to Ann SANBOWER.

4B:069   Date: 8 Aug 1833   RtCt: 10 Sep 1833
Motion of Emanuel WALTMAN of Oct 1830 to have road from Berlin Ferry on Potomack to intersect road from Newtown to John EVERHEART's Mill at corner between Thomas J. MARLOW and Joseph MILLER. John MOORE, John EVERHEART & John GEORGE viewed and reported – as above. $3.66 damages to Christian SANBOWER.

4B:071   Date: 8 Aug 1833   RtCt: 10 Sep 1833
Motion of Emanuel WALTMAN of Oct 1830 to have road from Berlin Ferry on Potomack to intersect road from Newtown to John EVERHEART's Mill at corner between Thomas J. MARLOW and Joseph MILLER. John MOORE, John EVERHEART & John GEORGE viewed and reported – as above. $30 damages to Thomas J. MARLOW.

4B:072   Date: 7 Sep 1833   RtCt: 10 Sep 1833
Jacob G. PAXSON & wife Mahala J. of Ldn to George RUST Jr. of JeffVa. B/S of 108a nr Wtfd (cnvy/b William PAXSON Nov 1829) adj __ HOUGH, Saml. PAXSON. Wit: George W. SHAWEN, Joshua PUSEY.

4B:074   Date: 9 Sep 1833   RtCt: 10 Sep 1833
Charles BINNS, Chs. W. D. BINNS & Chs. G. ESKRIDGE. Bond on Charles BINNS as Clerk of the Court.

4B:074   Date: 9 Sep 1833   RtCt: 9 Sep 1833
Jesse TIMMS & Johnston CLEVELAND. Bond on TIMMS as Commissioner of the revenue for 1st District.

4B:074 Date: 9 Sep 1833 RtCt: 9 Sep 1833
Jesse McVEIGH & John G. HUMPHREY. Bond on McVEIGH as Commissioner of the revenue for 2nd District.

4B:075 Date: 6 May 1833 RtCt: 24 Sep 1833
Joseph MILLER & wife Mary Ann of Ldn to Emanuel WALTMAN of Ldn. B/S of 6a (Lot #4 in div. of Jacob WALTMAN dec'd to Mary Ann) on Potomac. Wit: Geo. W. SHAWEN, Thomas J. MARLOW. Delv. to WALTMAN 7 Jul 1834.

4B:076 Date: 10 Sep 1833 RtCt: 9 [10?] Sep 1833
Samuel McPHERSON, Charles G. ESKRIDGE & John A. CARTER to Jacob G. PAXSON. Release of trust of Aug 1831 for debt to Ebenezer GRUBB Jr., Samuel PAXSON, Thomas ROGERS & Fleming HIXSON.

4B:078 Date: 2 Sep 1833 RtCt: 9 Sep 1833
William T. HOUGH & wife Louiza of Ldn to William VIRTZ Jr. of Ldn B/S of 21a (from will of mother & grandfather William HOUGH dec'd) adj Charles B. HAMILTON, __ DAVISSON, Elizabeth HOUGH. Wit: Thomas J. MARLOW, John WHITE. Delv. to VIRTS 5 Mar 1834.

4B:079 Date: 9 Sep 1833 RtCt: 10 Sep 1833
John GEORGE, Jacob SMITH & Susan(nah) SMITH of Ldn to Emanuel WALTMAN of Ldn. Release of trust of Aug 1824 for debt to Jacob & Susannah SMITH (DBk HHH:377).

4B:079 Date: 3 Sep 1833 RtCt: 11 Sep 1833
William MOORE & wife Elizabeth of Ldn to William H. HOUGH of Ldn. B/S of 34a (beq. by Wm. HOUGH dec'd to son John (now dec'd), 1 share from will of Jane HOUGH dec'd and part of share of 13a she prch/o Curtis GRUBB & wife Harriet) adj John WOLFORD, Elijah PEACOCK, Wm. VIRTZ. Wit: George MARLOW, Mortimer McILHANY. Delv. to HOUGH 5 May 1846.

4B:081 Date: 11 Sep 1833 RtCt: 11 Sep 1833
James GARRISON & wife Elizabeth to Burr W. HARRISON & Wm. D. DRISH. Trust for debt to Joseph COX and sons George W. COX & James G. COX partners using lot at King & Market Sts in Lsbg adj Henry CLAGETT, __ MARTIN, __ DRISH (cnvy/b Jno. McCORMICK, etc. Mar 1828). Wit: Henry T. HARRISON, Jno. J. MATHIAS. Delv. to Joseph COX 30 Oct 1834.

4B:082 Date: 11 Sep 1833 RtCt: 12 Sep 1833
Richard F. PAYTON & wife Virlinda of Butler Co Ohio and Townshend D. PAYTON & wife Sarah M. of Ldn to Henry T. HARRISON of Ldn. B/S of 265a on E side of Little River adj Asa ROGERS, T. McVEIGH, Noble BEVERIDGE (part of prch/o Francis HERIFORD dec'd by Townshend). Wit: Hugh SMITH, Asa SMITH. Delv. to HARRISON 11 Jan 1839.

4B:084   Date: __ Sep 1833   RtCt: 13 Oct 1833
Charles G. ESKRIDGE to James SINCLAIR, Everitt SAUNDERS, Wilson C. SELDEN Jr., John MARTIN, Edward HAMMATT & James L. MARTIN. B/S of Lot #3 & 86½a Lot #7 in Lsbg (from defaulted trust of Apr 1832 from John J. MATHIAS). Gives plat of 9 lots. Delv. to HAMMAT 18 Aug 1836.

4B:086   Date: 16 Sep 1833   RtCt: 16 Sep 1833
Thomas ROGERS (Commr. in May 1833 case of Thomas PHILIPS agst Amey TAYLOR) of Ldn to Thomas PHILIPS of Ldn. B/S of undivided ½ of Moore & Phillips tanyard in Wtfd.

4B:086   Date: 1 Aug 1833   RtCt: 16 Sep 1833
William NICHOLS & wife Cassandra of Ldn to George GRIMES of Ldn. B/S of 67a on NW fork of Goose Creek (cnvy/b Jonah SANDS). Wit: David REECE, Presley CORDELL. Delv. to GRIMES 25 Feb 1834.

4B:088   Date: 16 Sep 1833   RtCt: 16 Sep 1833
William RUSSELL & wife __ of Ldn to Thomas PHILLIPS of Ldn. B/S of 61a on E side of Short Hill mt. adj John VINCEL, __ POTTERFIELD (cnvy/b PHILLIPS and Joseph BOND 14 Sep 1833).

4B:088   Date: 14 Sep 1833   RtCt: 16 Sep 1833
Thomas PHILLIPS surviving partner of Moore & Phillips, Thomas PHILLIPS and Joseph BOND (Exors of Asa MOORE dec'd partner) of Ldn to William RUSSELL of Ldn. B/S of 61a as above. Delv. to RUSSELL 28 May 1841.

4B:089   Date: 16 Sep 1833   RtCt: 16 Sep 1833
Thomas PHILLIPS and Joseph BOND (Exors of Asa MOORE dec'd) to Asa M. BOND. B/S of undivided int. in Moore & Phillips tanyard in Wtfd.

4B:090   Date: 24 Jul 1832   RtCt: 16 Sep 1833
Thomas PHILLIPS and Joseph BOND (Exors of Asa MOORE dec'd) and Thomas PHILLIPS of Ldn to William RUSSELL of Ldn. B/S of 6a in Wtfd adj J. H. McCABE, meeting house lot, E side of road from Wtfd to Factory (Lot #1 cnvy/b Saml. M. EDWARDS for David JANNEY to Moore & Phillips from decree of May 1824). Delv. to RUSSELL 27 Sep 1836.

4B:091   Date: 17 Sep 1833   RtCt: 17 Sep 1833
William EVERHEART of Ldn to Burr W. HARRISON of Ldn. Trust for debt to John LESLIE using 10a in German Settlement.

4B:093   Date: 11 Sep 1833   RtCt: 17 Sep 1833
John LESLIE & wife Rachel of Ldn to William EVERHEART of Ldn. B/S of 10a in German Settlement (formerly belonging to Robert BRADEN now dec'd). Wit: Francis W. LUCKETT, Henry T. HARRISON. Delv. pr order 17 Jan 1834.

4B:093 Date: 18 Sep 1833 RtCt: 19 Sep 1833
Samuel McPHERSON & wife Mary of Ldn to William B. STEER of Ldn. Trust for William H. HOUGH & William SUMMERS of Ldn as security for Sarah NIXON & Rebecca KENWORTHY using 5a "McPHERSON's Mill" on little Catoctin creek adj Isaac STEER. Wit: George W. SHAWEN, Joshua PUSEY. Delv. to STEER 9 May 1835.

4B:095 Date: 19 Sep 1833 RtCt: 19 Sep 1833
Charles BINNS to Charles W. D. BINNS. BoS for slave for life Lewis JACKSON in consideration for $50 loaned to John A. BINNS to purchase clover seed for Charles last spring and a lot on Loudoun St in Lsbg now occupied by Thomas FLOWERS adj Charles GULLATT, estate of George ROWAN. Wit: Chs. G. ESKRIDGE. Delv. to C. W. D. BINNS 10 Oct 1834.

4B:096 Date: 19 Sep 1833 RtCt: 19 Sep 1833
Charles W. D. BINNS to Charles BINNS. Memorandum: will make Charles a perfect title for property above. Delv. to C. W. D. BINNS 10 Oct 1834.

4B:096 Date: 19 Sep 1833 RtCt: 19 Sep 1833
Ann GOVER to George HEAD. Trust of int. from father Samuel GOVER dec'd in house & lot in Wtfd and household items. Ann about to marry William GARNER and wants to control int. for benefit of her son Edwin GOVER.

4B:097 Date: 18 Sep 1833 RtCt: 20 Sep 1833
Samuel C. LUCKETT & wife Mary B. of Ldn to Charles B. HAMILTON Jr. (br/o Mary B.) of Ldn. B/S of undivided 1/4th int. (subject to life estate of Winefred HAMILTON) in 105a "Ogden farm" of their father John HAMILTON dec'd (cnvy/b by James McILHANY trustee of Andrew OGDEN). Wit: George W. SHAWEN, William SLATER. Delv. to HAMILTON 24 Mar 1834.

4B:098 Date: 2 Aug 1833 RtCt: 20 Sep 1833
George W. SHAWEN & wife Jane of Ldn to Charles B. HAMILTON Jr. of Ldn. B/S of undivided 1/4th int. (subject to life estate of Winefred HAMILTON) in 105a "Ogden farm" of their father John HAMILTON dec'd (cnvy/b by James McILHANY trustee of Andrew OGDEN). Wit: William SLATER, Joshua PUSEY. Delv. to HAMILTON 24 Mar 1834.

4B:099 Date: 3 Sep 1833 RtCt: 21 Sep 1833
Humphrey B. POWELL to Asa Rogers. B/S of 21½a "Mill Hill" (from defaulted trust of Aug 1830 from Augustus P. F. LAURENS for debt to T. D. PAYTON) on Little River. Delv. to ROGERS pr verbal order 30 Aug 1851.

4B:100 Date: 1 Aug 1832 RtCt: 23 Sep 1833
Thomas BROWN & wife Amelia A. of Ldn to Benjamin RUST of Ldn. B/S of int. in two lots sold by Samuel T. CALDWELL as trustee to

Chauncey BROOKS July 1828 (DBk RRR:091). Wit: John WILSON, Jesse HUDSON.

4B:101 Date: 8 Aug 1833 RtCt: 23 Sep 1833
Kemp F. COCKE & wife Amanda M. of Fqr to Samuel RECTOR of Ldn. B/S of int. in land of Amanda's father Joseph HATCHER, adj Gourley REEDER, Price JACOBS, Jonas LOVETT. Delv. to RECTOR 19 Feb 1835.

4B:102 Date: 20 Apr 1833 RtCt: 23 Sep 1833
Richard ASBURY & wife Nancy B. of RichVa to Isaac LEADHAM of Ldn. B/S of 198a S of turnpike from Aldie to Alexandria (dev. by grandfather Henry ASBURY dec'd) on Elk licking run adj John JAMES, Lewis HUTCHISON dec'd, Dean JAMES, __ SWART, Newton KEENE. Wit: Jas. M. STIFF, Wm. CRABB, Robt. STIFF. Delv. to LEADHAM 5 Dec 1843.

4B:103 Date: __ 1833 RtCt: 23 Sep 1833
John PURCELL & wife Mary of Ldn to David JAMES of Ldn. B/S of 50a on NW fork of Goose Creek adj Charles TAYLOR, Rufus UPDIKE, __ OSBURN. Wit: Timothy TAYLOR, David REECE.

4B:105 Date: 9 Nov 1813 RtCt: 9 Nov 1813/24 Sep 1833
Colin AULD and James SANDERSON of AlexDC to William NOLAND of Ldn. B/S of 400a nr Gum Spring adj __ HYLER, Stephen ROZELL, Benjamin JAMES, _ FAIRFAX, John SPENCER Jr., __ RUSSELL. Wit: Thos. SWANN, Edm. J. LEE, R. J. TAYLOR.

4B:106 Date: 14 Jul 1832 RtCt: 24 Sep 1833
Alexander ANDERSON of Culpeper Co Va to John H. WOOD of Culpeper Co Va. Trust for debt to William DUNKIN and Franklin & Addison TURNER of Culpeper Co Va using farm animals, household items.

4B:107 Date: 23 Sep 1833 RtCt: 24 Sep 1833
John MIDDLEBURG/MITTEELBURGER & wife Christiana to William CULLISON. B/S of 20a on paved road from Lsbg to Alexandria adj blacksmith shop; and 15a; and 16a adj __ UNDERWOOD on paved road from Lsbg to Alexandria adj blacksmith (except 1a with house sold to John WATERS by __ LEE). Wit: Ludwell LEE, Wilson C. SELDEN.

4B:108 Date: 13 Jul 1833 RtCt: 25 Sep 1833
Sarah SYPHERD and Ann SANBOWER bound to Adam KARNE Exor of Magdalina SHOVER dec'd. KARNE paid Sypherd Admx wwa of Catharine SANBOWER dec'd legacy and bond in case other debts arise that SYPHERD will refund part of legacy. Wit: Thos. J. MARLOW.

4B:109 Date: 24 Sep 1833 RtCt: 25 Sep 1833
Jacob G. PAXSON to David SHAWEN. Trust for debt to Noble S. BRADEN and Lydia RAMEY using household items. Delv. pr order 20 Feb 1834.

4B:110 Date: 25 Sep 1833 RtCt: 25 Sep 1833
Hannah LOVETT and William GALLEHER of Ldn to John LOVETT
of Ldn. Release of trust of Mar 1828 on ¼ of estate of father Joseph
LOVETT (from deed of partition with her 3 brothers). John has given
her security. Wit: Seth SMITH, Henry H. HUTCHISON, Robert S.
FULTON.

4B:111 Date: 9 Mar 1832 RtCt: 26 Sep 1833
Craven SILCOTT & wife Elizabeth of Ldn to Banister P. STEVENS.
B/S of ¼a adj Thomas GALLEHER, Daniel LOVETT, He[n]ry
PLASTER. Wit: Benjamin GRAYSON, Edward HALL.

4B:112 Date: 25 Sep 1833 RtCt: 26 Sep 1833
Jacob SILCOTT & wife Tamer of Ldn to Aquila GLASSCOCK of Fqr.
B/S of 125¼a adj Thomas LITTLETON, John P. DULANY, Robt. &
Mahlon FULTON, Beaverdam, Samuel RICHARDS. Wit: William
BENTON, Ludwell LUCKETT. Delv. to GLASCOCK 24 Apr 1834.

4B:113 Date: 7 Jun 1833 RtCt: 26 Jun/26 Sep 1833
Francis F. KING of Ldn to John B. YOUNG of Ldn. Trust for debt to
Benjamin JACKSON of Ldn using farm animals, household items.
Wit: Geo. D. ALDER, Roger CHEW. Delv. to YOUNG 29 Mar 1834.

4B:114 Date: 6 Sep 1833 RtCt: 326 Sep 1833
John G. HUMPHREY (Commr. in ct. case) of Ldn to Francis T.
GRADY of Ldn. B/S of 16a of Evan THOMAS dec'd (cnvy/b
Phinehas THOMAS) adj Lsbg road, __ JANNY, __ SANDS, William
LODGE. Delv. to Francis W. LUCKETT at request of GRADY 1 Dec
1835.

4B:114 Date: 13 Aug 1833 RtCt: 28 Sep 1833
George W. HOUGH to Samuel M. EDWARDS and Richard H.
HENDERSON. B/S of legacy (lien on land) from Cornelius SHAWEN
dec'd (willed money to dau Mary Catherine w/o HOUGH to be paid
by Exors. Geo. W. SHAWEN & David SHAWEN who received real
estate, after death of Mary SHAWEN m/o Mary Cath'e residue sold
to EDWARDS & HENDERSON).

4B:116 Date: 13 Aug 1833 RtCt: 28 Sep 1833
Mary SHAWEN to Samuel M. EDWARDS & Richard H.
HENDERSON. B/S of int. in annuity from real estate (from husband
Cornelius SHAWEN dec'd directive to Exors George W. SHAWEN &
David SHAWEN to pay annual sum for life in lieu of dower of land,
see div. of land to David DBk PPP:341). Wit: S. HOUGH, Hamilton
ROGERS, Isaac WALKER. Delv. to EDWARDS 28 Aug 1841.

4B:117 Date: 31 Aug 1833 RtCt: 28 Sep 1833
John PAXSON & wife Ann of Ldn to Samuel M. EDWARDS and
Richard H. HENDERSON of Ldn. B/S of int. in above from Ann's
father Cornelius SHAWEN dec'd (mill tract now rented to Elijah
PEACOCK and other lots totaling 140a). Wit: William ELLZEY,
Francis W. LUCKETT. Delv. to EDWARDS 28 Aug 1841.

4B:118 Date: 30 Sep 1833 RtCt: 30 Sep 1833
Samuel HALL Sr. & wife Charity of Ldn to Adin WHITE and Richard
WHITE of Ldn. B/S of 70a (Lot #3 in div. of Josiah HALL dec'd) adj
__ CARUTHERS, William HOLMES, Thomas HUGHES. Wit: W. C.
SELDEN Jr., Presley CORDELL.

4B:120 Date: 2 Oct 1833 RtCt: 3 Oct 1833
Jonas LOVETT & wife Nancy J. of Ldn to Joseph CARR of Ldn. B/S
of 115a (dev. from Joseph LOVETT dec'd) where they now reside
(see DBk RRR:170 [QQQ:170]). Wit: Ludwell LUCKETT, William
BENTON. Delv. to CARR 9 Jun 1834.

4B:121 Date: 2 Oct 1833 RtCt: 3 Oct 1833
William GALLEHER to Joseph LOVETT. Release of trust of Mar
1828 for debt to Hannah LOVETT using 115a from father Joseph
LOVETT dec'd. Wit: L. LUCKETT, Wm. BENTON.

4B:122 Date: 22 Oct 1831 RtCt: 5 Oct 1833
Jared POTTS & wife Lucinda of Boon Co Missouri to Norval
OSBURN of Ldn. B/S of undivided 1/9th int. in 258a from Nathan
POTTS dec'd on Little Catocton on S of Blue Ridge mt. adj David
POTTS, William POTTS, heirs of James McILHANEY. Wit: James
ROBERTS. Delv. to OSBORNE 12 Sep 1836.

4B:123 Date: 12 Apr 1830 RtCt: 5 Oct 1833
Joshua POTTS and Samuel D. LESLIE of Ldn to Norval OSBURN
of Ldn. B/S of 175a from Nathan POTTS dec'd (Norval owns 2/3rd of
land, Joshua gets 2/9th and Samuel gets 1/9th now divided). Delv. to
OSBORNE 12 Sep 1836.

4B:125 Date: 7 Oct 1833 RtCt: 7 Oct 1833
Henson MONROE to John H. MONROE. Trust for debt to Henry
MONROE using farm animals, farm and household items, crops.

4B:126 Date: 1 Jun 1833 RtCt: 10 Oct 1833
Gunnell DARNE and Corbin DARNE (sons of John DARNE dec'd) to
mother Hannah DARNE wd/o John dec'd. B/S of int. in Negroes they
have at death of mother and marriage of sister Elizabeth DARNE.
Wit: Isaiah SIMMS, Robert DARNE.

4B:127 Date: 12 Oct 1833 RtCt: 12 Oct 1833
George W. HENRY & wife Dewanna B. of Ldn to Charles G.
ESKRIDGE of Ldn. Trust for debt to John WILLIAMS of Ldn using
land where HENRY now resides from div. of Taylortown estate of
John HAMILTON dec'd.

4B:128 Date: 16 Feb 1833 RtCt: 14 Oct 1833
Thomas BRADFIELD, William BRADFIELD, John BRADFIELD,
John BURSON and William NOWLING of Columbiana Co Ohio and
Abraham SLACK of Start Co Ohio (heirs of Susanna CARTER dec'd
late of Ldn) to William LONGSHORE of Columbiana Co Ohio. PoA
to received money from James HILL of Ldn as int. in 79a from estate
of Susanna dec'd held as dower by wife Elizabeth HILL late

WOODFORD wd/o William WOODFORD Jr. dec'd. Wit: Jonathan MORRIS, Joseph THOMPSON, Wm. VAN DUYN.

4B:129   Date: 16 Feb 1833   RtCt: 14 Oct 1833
Thomas BRADFIELD & wife Hannah, William BRADFIELD & wife Sarah, John BURSON & wife Mary, William NOWLING & wife Ann and John BRADFIELD of Columbiana Co Ohio and Abraham SLACK of Stark Co Ohio to James HILL of Ldn. B/S of undivided 6/7th of 79a which Elizabeth HILL formerly WOODFORD w/o James has life estate as dower from late husband William WOODFORD dec'd. Wit: Jonathan MORRIS, Joseph THOMPSON, Wm. VAN DUYN, Samuel RHODES. Delv. to HILL 3 Nov 1834.

4B:132   Date: 2 Oct 1833   RtCt: 14 Oct 1833
Bailey PADGET & wife Harriet T. of Ffx and Elizabeth PADGET of Ldn to Ann AKERS of Ldn. B/S of 112a (deed of settlement cnvy/b John DESKINS to Mary TEBBS in 1748, recorded in Pr Wm, and Feb 1763 cnvy/b James TEBBS who m. Mary TEBBS to Francis PADGET). Wit: Robt. BAYLY, Wm. B. HARRISON.

4B:134   Date: 21 Sep 1833   RtCt: 14 Oct 1833
David F. BEALL of Ldn to Rebecca CRAIG of Ldn. B/S of ½a Lot #28 in Mt. Gilead on Loudoun St adj Mrs. Ure HANDY's heirs.

4B:135   Date: 28 Sep 1833   RtCt: 14 Oct 1833
Clarinda FRENCH of Ldn to Joseph HOUGH of Ldn. B/S of 22a (Lot #2 from div. of land of Wm. HOUGH dec'd willed to son Thomas and after his death to his children) adj John WILLIAMS, Joseph HOUGH, and 8a (Lot #5 in div.) Delv. to HOUGH 31 Dec 1833.

4B:136   Date: 9 Apr 1830   RtCt: 14 Oct 1833
Caldwell CARR to Elizabeth GIBSON. Release of trust of Mar 1821 for debt to Isaac NICHOLS Jr., Stephen WILSON, Abner GIBSON, etc.

4B:137   Date: 31 Dec 1832   RtCt: 14 Oct 1833
Reuben MURRY of Fqr to son Alfred MURRY of Fqr. Gift of 104a (from Catharine MURRY dec'd late w/o Reuben and m/o Alfred who willed 104a inherited from father Thomas CHINN dec'd to her son Alfred). Delv. to Saml. & A. MURRY pr mail 18 Feb 1830 [?] pr order.

4B:138   Date: 14 Oct 1833   RtCt: 14 Oct 1833
Peyton TAYLOR of Ldn to Asa ROGERS of Ldn. Trust for debt to Joseph TAYLOR using household items.

4B:138   Date: 14 Oct 1833   RtCt: 14 Oct 1833
Redding HUTCHISON, Wm. AMBLER & William WHALEY. Bond on HUTCHISON as Committee for estate of Lewis HUTCHISON a lunatic.

4B:139   Date: 19 Sep 1833   RtCt: 14 Oct 1833
Bernard McCORMICK. Qualified as Capt. in 2nd Reg artillery 6th Reg 2nd Div Va Militia.

4B:139 Date: 20 Sep 1833 RtCt: 14 Oct 1833
James WHITE. Qualified as Ensign in 56th Reg 6th Brig 2nd Div Va Militia.

4B:139 Date: 28 Sep 1833 RtCt: 15 Oct 1833
On motion of 13 Jun 1833 by George M. CHICHESTER to have road opened from Lsbg to a point on Potomac. Thomas BIRKBY, John H. McCABE, John MARTIN, John THOMAS & John JANNY viewed route and recommended beginning at market st to river on land of Chichester, passing thru land of Dr. Wilson C. SELDEN, heirs of Aaron SANDERS dec'd (Thomas R. SANDERS, Fanny WHITE, Curtis R. SANDERS, Aaron R. SANDERS, Susan R. SANDERS, Catherine R. SANDERS & Alcinda SANDERS, and CHICHESTER. $530 damages to Wilson C. SELDEN. Gives plat.

4B:144 Date: 15 Oct 1833 RtCt: 15 Oct 1833
Eleanor DRISH of Ldn to William D. DRISH of Ldn. B/S of int. in estate of late husband John DRISH dec'd (agreed that William would pay Eleanor in lieu of dower rights to land). Wit: Thos. WRIGHT, Arch'd HENDERSON Jr., Wilson J. DRISH. Delv. to W. D. DRISH 2 Jan 1834.

4B:145 Date: 26 Apr 1833 RtCt: 17 Oct 1833
James VIOLET of Frederick to James BOWLES of Ldn. B/S of 8½a (in decree of Mar 1833, Violet in place of John MARTIN named as trustee for George GIBSON) adj Joseph LEWIS' "Clifton". Delv. to BOWLES 28 Jan 1836.

4B:146 Date: 26 Jan 1833 RtCt: 23 Oct 1833
Stephen WILSON & wife Hannah P. of Ldn to Lot TAVENER of Ldn. B/S of 136a on NW fork of Goose Creek adj __ BOLON, __ WHITACRE, __ COOKSEY, __ TAYLOR, __ ZIMMERMAN, __ PANCOAST, __ SMITH. Wit: Timothy TAYLOR, John SIMPSON. Delv. to TAVENNER 14 Feb 1837.

4B:148 Date: 18 Oct 1833 RtCt: 23 Oct 1833
Richard C. McCARTY of Ohio to brother Dennis McCARTY of Ldn. B/S of 4a on Snickers Gap turnpike road (½ of 8a from Dennis McCARTY Sr. dec'd allotted to their sister Caroline G. McCARTY and cnvy/b her to her brothers). Wit: John FIELD, Geo. W. McCARTY.

4B:148 Date: 7 Jun 1833 RtCt: 23 Oct 1833
Lott TAVENER & wife Phebe of Ldn to William PIGGOTT of Ldn. B/S of 41a on Beaverdam (from Jonah TAVENER dec'd) on Snickers Gap turnpike road adj heirs of Samuel NICHOLS, Jesse TAVENER, Sarah TRAHERN, __ BOWLES. Wit: David REECE, Timothy TAYLOR.

4B:150 Date: 4 Oct 1833 RtCt: 24 Oct 1833
Edward TILLETT & wife Elizabeth of Ldn to Hannah TILLETT of Fqr. B/S of 1/4th int. in 130a (subject to dower of Hannah, formerly prch/b

James TILLETT since dec'd father of Edward from Catherine BERKLEY dated Oct 1810) adj Rich'd VANPELT, Sarah ELLZEY, place formerly held by Richard KEENE. Wit: William ELLZEY, Presley CORDELL.

4B:151   Date: 26 Jan 1830   RtCt: 25 Oct 1833
Stephen WILSON & wife Hannah P. of Ldn to Benjamin BIRDSALL of Ldn. B/S of 151a adj NW fork of Goose Creek, Thomas NICHOLS, __ STRIBLING, __ WHITACRE, __ SPENCER, David SMITH, Joel CRAVEN. Wit: Timothy TAYLOR, John SIMPSON. Delv. to BIRDSALL 11 Mar 1831.

4B:152   Date: 8 Apr 1833   RtCt: 25 Oct 1833
Benjamin BIRDSALL of Ldn to Elizabeth and Hannah BIRDSALL of Ldn. B/S of 80a on Beaverdam Creek adj Mahlon CRAVEN, __ GARRETT, __ HOGE.

4B:153   Date: 26 Oct 1833   RtCt: 26 Oct 1833
Jeremiah CULLISON & wife Rebecca of Ldn to Joseph HAVENNER of Ldn. B/S of 216¼a (dev. by will of Jeremiah CULLISON dec'd) adj __ McKINNEY, __ VEALE (see DBk MMM:090). Wit: Samuel M. EDWARDS, Wilson C. SELDEN Jr.

4B:155   Date: 15 May 1833   RtCt: 28 Oct 1833
Amos WHITACRE (Exor of Alice WHITACRE dec'd) of Ldn to Hamilton ROGERS of Ldn. B/S of 173a (cnvy/b TIDBALL of FredVa) adj __ COOKSEY, __ PIGGOTT, __ BOLON, __ BIRDSALL, heirs of Francis STRIBLING. Delv. to ROGERS 8 Jan 1836.

4B:156   Date: 12 Oct 1833   RtCt: 28 Oct 1833
Joseph W. BRONAUGH & wife Nancy S. of Ldn to Ludwell LUCKETT of Ldn and William C. ELLGIN of Upperville Fqr. Trust for debt to Francis W. LUCKETT, John L. POWELL, John MORGAN, Robert L. ARMISTEAD, William O. CHILTON, Daniel S. KERFORT, Isaac NICHOLS, Thomas FRAZIER, Emma HICKS, Kimble HICKS, Thomas G. SETTLE, William RUST, Thomas TRUSSELL, John GLASCOCK using 128a adj Peter GREGG, William BENTON and 36a wood lot adj P. H. W. BRONAUGH (both allotted in div. of Wm. BRONAUGH dec'd except 15a sold to Ludwell LUCKETT); and household items. Wit: Asa ROGERS, William BENTON. Delv. to LUCKETT 22 Sep 1834.

4B:158   Date: 28 Oct 1833   RtCt: 29 Oct 1833
Charles L. POWELL and Archibald HENDERSON Jr. (Commrs. in ct. decree in mortgage from Martin BRENT to Charles BENNET) to John P. DULANY. B/S of 80a (96a less 16a sold to Hiram SEATON).

4B:159   Date: 22 Aug 1833   RtCt: 30 Oct 1833
Robert BENTLEY & wife Kitty L. of Ldn to John GRAY of Ldn. B/S of int. in 230a (cnvy/b Charles BINNS & wife Hannah Aug 1833 to BENTLEY and GRAY). Wit: William ELLZEY, Henry T. HARRISON.

4B:159 Date: 17 Sep 1833 RtCt: 1 Nov 1833
Joseph FREDD & wife Hannah to Ebenezer JACKSON. Trust for Benjamin JACKSON as security on note to Hugh SMITH Esqr. using 94a where FREDD resides Wit: Roger CHEW, Edw'd. B. GRADY.

4B:161 Date: 1 Nov 1833 RtCt: 1 Nov 1833
George RICHARDS & John ROSE to President and directors of Literary fund. Bond on RICHARDS as treasurer.

4B:161 Date: 22 Aug 1833 RtCt: 2 Nov 1833
Joseph FRED Jr. & wife Hannah, Thomas FRED & wife Rachel, John VANSICKLE & wife Mahaly late FRED and Euphamia FRED single woman of Ldn to John TORBERT of Ldn. B/S of 4/9th int. in 100a (cnvy/b Samuel BUTCHER to Samuel TORBERT dec'd May 1790 and then dev. to father Thomas TORBERT & wife Elizabeth then to their 9 children, Thomas FRED owning 11a as his 1/9th) adj Thomas A. HEREFORD. Wit: Edward B. GRADY, Roger CHEW. Delv. to TORBERT 27 Jan 1835.

4B:163 Date: 26 Oct 1833 RtCt: 2 Nov 1833
Elijah PEACOCK & wife Ann of Ldn to Jacob GOODHEART of Ldn. B/S of 34a (share of Daniel COOPER & wife Elizabeth) adj Michael COOPER, Catocktin Creek. Wit: George W. SHAWEN, William CLENDENING.

4B:165 Date: 2 Nov 1833 RtCt: 2 Nov 1833
William CARR of Ldn to Susan FICHTER & her children Peggy, Sally & George. L/L (on 4 lives) of land between James MARTAIN and Samuel HARPER.

4B:165 Date: 1 Nov 1833 RtCt: 5 Nov 1833
Henry CLAGETT of Ldn to William GILMORE of Ldn. B/S of 100a adj __ LOVE, __ CARTER, __ GILMORE; and 13a adj Bernard HOUGH (lots cnvy/b Joshua PUSEY).

4B:166 Date: 12 Sep 1833 RtCt: 5 Nov 1833
James ALEXANDER & wife Jane of Ldn to John HARDY of Ldn. B/S of 3a adj Cuthbert POWELL, Chrisley MILEY. Wit: Cuthbert POWELL, Thomas M. COLSTON.

4B:167 Date: 10 Oct 1833 RtCt: 7 Nov 1833
Martha GARRETT of FredMd to Edward HAMMETT of Ldn. B/S of 110a (cnvy/b Thomas BURGEE Sr. Apr 1828, also see DBk FF:403). Wit: P. S. McELFRESH, Z. T. WINDSOR. Delv. to HAMMATT 23 Nov 1836.

4B:169 Date: 21 Oct 1833 RtCt: 9 Nov 1833
Thomas SWANN of Ldn to Erasmus G. HAMILTON of Ldn. Trust for debt to John P. SMART of Ldn using slaves Alfred aged abt 14y, Jane d/o Betsy aged 15y, Sandy s/o Betsy aged 13y, Fenton s/o Eliza aged 10y, Catherine aged 16y.

4B:170   Date: 11 Nov 1833   RtCt: 11 Nov 1833
William ELLZEY of Ldn to Charles LEWIS of Ldn. B/S of 18a adj __
RUSSELL, __ McCARTY, __ ASHTON (See DBk RRR:105).

4B:171   Date: __ 1833   RtCt: 11 Nov 1833
Humphrey B. POWELL to Horace LUCKETT. Release of trust of
May 1828 for Gourley REEDER & Jonah TAVERNER as securities
using 172a.

4B:172   Date: 20 Mar 1833   RtCt: 11 Nov 1833
Lewis AMBLER & wife Sarah/Sally of Guernsea Co Ohio to Andrew
HUTCHISON of Ldn. B/S of 88a on Elk lick run, old Alex'a road. Wit:
Daniel BICHARD, Nicholas BAILHACHE.

4B:173   Date: 28 Oct 1833   RtCt: 11 Nov 1833
Daniel COCKERILL. Qualified as Lt. Colonel of 56th Reg of Infantry
6th Brig 2nd Div Va Militia.

4B:173   Date: 11 Nov 1833   RtCt: 11 Nov 1833
James SWART dec'd. Renunciation of will by widow Elizabeth
SWART. Wit: William NOLAND, William ROSE Jr.

4B:174   Date: __ 1833   RtCt: 11 Nov 1833
George D. SMITH. Receipt of payment in full from Mrs. Ann
SAUNDERS late EKART Guardian of his wife Martha L. late
GREGG (and Exor. of Elisha GREGG dec'd and of George GREGG
dec'd).

4B:174   Date: 12 Oct 1833   RtCt: 12 Nov 1833
Mahlon JANNEY & wife Rachel of Ldn to Elijah JAMES of Ldn. B/S
of 107a (cnvy/b David REESE Exor of Thomas TRIBBEY dec'd Jan
1830, DBk TTT:088) free of dower right of Mary TRIBBY wd/o
Thomas dec'd who is also now dec'd. Wit: Presley CORDELL, Saml.
M. EDWARDS.

**4B:175   Date: 16 Aug 1791   RtCt: 13 Feb 1792/14 Jan 1793/12
Nov 1833**
Bryan FAIRFAX and Thomas FAIRFAX of Ffx to William GUNNELL
of Ldn. B/S of 200a and 476a in Cameron Parish. Wit: John MOSS,
Thos. GUNNELL, Jesse MOORE, Henry GUNNELL Jr., Robt.
GUNNELL. Delv. to Geo. GUNNELL 23 May 1834.

4B:177   Date: 8 Jun 1833   RtCt: 13 Nov 1833
Nelson EVERHART & wife Elizabeth of Ldn to Michael DERRY,
William ADAMS, Jesse BATEMAN, Presley WIGGINTON & Horatio
COE (trustee of Methodist Episcipol Church). B/S of ¾a adj
TEMORY [DEMORY?] to build house of worship. Wit: Thos. J.
MARLOW, E. GRUBB. Delv. to M. DERRY 31 Nov 1836.

4B:179   Date: 9 Nov 1833   RtCt: 13 Nov 1833
Amos NEAR & wife Eliza of Ldn to Michael DERRY of Ldn. B/S of
undivided 1/6th of 230a (from father David NEAR dec'd) including
dower int., adj Philip COONS, John CONARD, James NEAR. Wit:

William CLENDENING, Thomas J. MARLOW. Delv. to DERRY 31 Nov 1836.

4B:181   Date: 10 Apr 1833   RtCt: 13 Nov 1833
James UNDERWOOD & wife Susannah late NEAR, Eli SNOOK & wife Sarah Ann, Amos NEAR & wife Eliza of JeffVa to John NEAR of Ldn. B/S of 1a (John NEAR prch/o David NEAR dec'd). Delv. to Fielding LITTLETON pr order 12 Nov 1835.

4B:182   Date: 13 Nov 1833   RtCt: 13 Nov 1833
John LONG, Jno. GEORGE & John BOOTH. Bond on LONG as Committee for estate of Mary MULL Sr. an insane person.

4B:183   Date: 14 Nov 1833   RtCt: 14 Nov 1833
Elijah PEACOCK. Oath as Major in 56th Reg Va Militia.

4B:183   Date: 9 Nov 1833   RtCt: 14 Nov 1833
Joseph CRAWFORD of Lower Providence Township, Montgomery Co Pa to John TORBERT of Ldn. PoA for monies, especially from James TORBERT of Ldn or John JANNEY Esqr. attorney with mortgage and bond agst James. Wit: J. W. EVANS, Ph. S. MARKLEY.

4B:184   Date: 14 Dec 1832   RtCt: 10 Apr 1833
David LOVETT of Ldn to Hiram BROWN and Sarah BROWN of Ldn. Release of trust of May 1828 for debt to Swithin NICHOLS.

4B:185   Date: 9 Sep 1833   RtCt: 9 Oct/6 Dec 1833
Albert G. WATERMAN of PhilPa late of firm Johnson, Waterman & Co, merchants of PhilPa to Richard H. HENDERSON of Ldn and Benjamin W. RICHARDS of PhilPa. Trust for debt to R. H. HENDERSON using lot in Lsbg cnvy/b Robert J. TAYLOR Sep 1830. Wit: John BINNS, Saml. BADGER. Delv. to HENDERSON Apr 1840.

4B:187   Date: 12 Nov 1833   RtCt: 15 Nov 1833
Elijah JAMES & wife Sarah of Ldn to Saml. M. EDWARDS of Ldn. Trust for debt to Philip OTTERBACK of WashDC using 107a. Wit: W. C. SELDEN Sr., Francis W. LUCKETT. Delv. to EDWARDS 8 Apr 1837.

4B:189   Date: 14 Nov 1833   RtCt: 15 Nov 1833
Wilson J. DRISH & wife Martha L. of Ldn to Arch'd HENDERSON of Ffx. Trust for debt to John GRAY, Gray Campbell & Co, John J. HARDING, Robert BENTLEY, Anthony ADDISON, Daniel G. SMITH, James SINCLAIR, Walter M. ELGIN, Todd & Co. using int. in 14a from estate of John DRISH dec'd adj Dr. SELDEN, heirs of STONEBURNER; and 1/3 of mother's dower; and household items. Wit: Wilson C. SELDEN, Jno. J. MATHIAS. Delv. to HENDERSON Mar 1834.

4B:191   Date: 25 Apr 1833   RtCt: 20 Nov 1833
James SWART & wife Elizabeth of Ldn to dau. Mary Ann WALKER of Ldn. Gift of undivided int. in 87½a (share of James and Manley -

Nov 1821 Charles Fenton MERCER of Aldie cnvy/t SWART during lifetime and to son James SWART Jr. and infant Manly SWART 112a on Bull run mt. at Bartons branch; Manly died in infancy). Wit: Asa ROGERS, Hugh SMITH.

4B:192   Date: __ Sep 1833   RtCt: 22 Nov 1833
John A. BINNS of Ldn to John ROSE of Ldn. Trust to discharge embarassing debts and for benefit of wife Mary Maria BINNS using Negro Betsey & her 2 daus. Sally Greenfield aged abt 30m and Mary Catherine an infant in arms and Charlotte sister to Betsey aged abt 16y but very infirm & sickly and 3 houses & lots, 1 vacant lot in Lsbg and 2 other lots nr Goose Creek with wife agreeing to relinq. dower on these lots.

4B:193   Date: 21 Nov 1833   RtCt: 22 Nov 1833
John JANNEY of Ldn to William HOLMES of Ldn. B/S of int. in 161a of father Charles BENNETT dec'd (from defaulted trust of Mar 1828, DBk RRR:021, from John HOOF and James H. BENNETT) and 1/10th int. in leased land.

4B:193   Date: 26 Jan 1833   RtCt: 22 Nov 1833
John M. MOORE of Fqr to Albert A. ASHBY of Fqr. Trust for debt to Peter ADAMS of Fqr using farm animals, farm and household items.

4B:194   Date: 10 Oct 1833   RtCt: 23 Nov 1833
Samuel CORDELL & wife Catherine of Ldn to Samuel FILLER of Ldn. B/S of 12½a (Lot #2 in div. of Adam CORDELL dec'd) on Catoctin Creek. Wit: C. B. HAMILTON Jr., Wm. SLATER. Delv. to FILLER 9 Sep 1834.

4B:195   Date: 18 Nov 1833   RtCt: 23 Nov 1833
Jacob DIVINE of Ldn to James TIPPETT of Ldn. Trust for debt to John DODD using house & lot (<¼a) in Wtfd opposite Sarah HOUGH and adj __MOORE, __ PHILLIPS; and farm animals, household items.

4B:197   Date: 26 Aug 1833   RtCt: 25 Nov 1833
Thomas FRED, John C. GREEN, James JOHNSON, Thomas MOUNT, Thornton F. OFFUTT, Sydnor BAILEY & Craven VANHORN to Samuel HAMMONTREE. Release of trust of Jun 1830 (to Craven VANHORN) using house & lot in Union and household items.

4B:197   Date: 11 May 1833   RtCt: 27 Nov 1833
Michael COOPER, Joseph COOPER, Margaret COOPER and Daniel COOPER & wife Elizabeth of Ldn to Peter COOPER & wife Nancy of Ldn. B/S of 12a adj __ PEACOCK and 7a adj __ GOODHEART (from Margaret SAUNDERS dec'd). Wit: George W. SHAWEN, Joshua PUSEY. Delv. to COOPER 2 Apr 1836.

4B:199   Date: 12 Nov 1833   RtCt: 27 Nov 1833
John JANNEY & wife Alcinda S. of Lsbg and Mary JANNEY of Hllb to Benjamin RUST Jr. of Ldn. B/S of 65a on Beaverdam Creek adj

Benjamin RUST Jr., John VANSICKLE. Wit: Presley CORDELL, Saml. M. EDWARDS, James McILHANEY, John WHITE. Delv. to RUST 25 Feb 1850.

4B:200   Date: 25 Apr 1833   RtCt: 28 Nov 1833
James SWART & wife Elizabeth of Ldn to Lucinda SKILLMAN of Ldn. B/S of 166a adj Thomas ASBURY, Jeremiah FOSTER nr mt. road (from tract prch/o Benjamin BULLETT by Peter ROSZELL) and 20a. Wit: Asa ROGERS, H. SMITH. Delv. to Abraham? SKILLMAN 2 Apr 1839.

4B:201   Date: 24 Aug 1833   RtCt: 30 Nov 1833
Charles BINNS & wife Hannah of Ldn to James GARRISON of Ldn. B/S of lot on Liberty St in Lsbg adj BINNS, Joseph HILLIARD. Wit: William ELLZEY, Wilson C. SELDEN Jr.

4B:203   Date: 30 Sep 1833   RtCt: 30 Nov 1833
James GARRISON & wife Elizabeth to Joseph HILLIARD. Assignment of int. in above lot. Wit: Presley CORDELL, Saml. M. EDWARDS. Delv. to HILLIARD 7 Apr 1838.

4B:204   Date: __ Oct 1833   RtCt: 2 Dec 1833
Charles G. ESKRIDGE of Ldn to William CLINE of Ldn. B/S of 13a (from defaulted trust of Apr 1832 from John J. MATHIAS) on turnpike road adj __ WRIGHT, __ FICHTER. Delv. to CLINE 6 May 1834.

4B:205   Date: 23 Nov 1833   RtCt: 30 Nov 1833
George PRICE & wife Elizabeth of Ldn to Richard H. HENDERSON of Ldn. Trust for debt to Bazil GORDON of Falmouth (bonds of Elizabeth late CLAPHAM), etc. using (all belonging to Elizabeth) 200a with mill on Goose Creek, 148a, 21a and 411a "Kentuck" (dev. by her father John JOHNSON dec'd) and 170a where they reside; and Negroes James (blacksmith), Ben, Jesse, Bill, King, Easter, Amey, Maria and child Sam, Edie, Elias, Nathan, Alfred, Hiram, Daniel, Robert, Wilson, Flora, John Fenton, Joe, Jane w/o Jim the blacksmith, Georgiana, Emily, Rose, Adeline, Little Elias, Henry, Tom, Mary, Tabitha & her child Betsey, Jim Fisher, Simon Fisher, old Poll, Harriet, Middleton, (Bill Shaver, Henry, Phill, Madison, Frederick who are now runaway); and farm and household items. Wit: Saml. DAWSON, George MARLOW. Delv. to R. H. H. 15 Apr 1837.

4B:208   Date: 7 Feb 1833   RtCt: 7 Dec 1833
Presley WIGGINTON & wife Sarah Ann to Richard GRUBB. Trust for debt to Ebenezer GRUBB using 6a (prch/o Samuel NEAR) where WIGGINTON resides adj George MILLER, John CONARD, Daniel CRIM. Wit: George Wm. WOLFORDE, John GRUBB, William CLENDENING, John WHITE. Delv. to E. GRUBB Exor. of Ebenezer GRUBB dec'd 27 Jun 1838.

4B:210 Date: 8 Oct 1833 RtCt: 9 Dec 1833
Philip SWANK & wife Mary of Ldn to Peter STUCK of Ldn. B/S of 37a adj John BOGER, heirs of Daniel STONE dec'd. Wit: George W. SHAWEN, William SLATER. Delv. to STUCK 21 Apr 1845.

4B:211 Date: __ RtCt: 9 Dec 1833
Widow Elizabeth SAUNDERS and Washington SAUNDERS, William SAUNDERS, Benjamin SAUNDERS, Philip SANDERS, James SANDERS & Elizabeth SANDERS the younger ch/o James SAUNDERS dec'd. DoE for Negro man slave Jesse upwards of 40y old. Wit: David BEALE, Amos BEALE, Joel NIXON.

4B:212 Date: 21 Nov 1833 RtCt: 9 Dec 1833
Enos NICHOLS. Oath as Captain in 2nd Reg of Cavalry 6th Brig 2nd Div Va Militia.

4B:212 Date: 21 Nov 1833 RtCt: 9 Dec 1833
Conrad R. DOWELL. Oath as 2nd Lt. in 2nd Reg of Cavalry 6th Brig 2nd Div Va Militia.

4B:212 Date: 9 Dec 1833 RtCt: 9 Dec 1833
Samuel ROGERS of Ldn. DoE for slave Catharine aged abt 35y.

4B:213 Date: 9 Dec 1833 RtCt: 9 Dec 1833
Craven OSBURN of Ldn. DoE for slave Amos.

4B:213 Date: 2 Dec 1833 RtCt: 10 Dec 1833
Edward M. COE dec'd. Division – 50a Lot #1 and wood Lot #1 to widow Mary COE as dower; 21a Lot #2 and 9a wood Lot #2 to Elizabeth Ann COE; 21a Lot #3 and 9a wood Lot #3 to Reubin COCKERILL & wife Mary E.; 31a Lot #4 and 9a wood Lot #4 to Emily Jane COE. Divisors: John SIMPSON, French SIMPSON, William LICKEY. Gives plat.

4B:215 Date: 10 Nov 1832 RtCt: 10 Dec 1833
Thomas GHEEN & wife Catharine of Perry Co Ohio to Peter and Nathan SKINNER of Ldn. B/S of 17¼a (except ¼a for burial ground) nr Aldie (prch/o Commrs. for William EVANS dec'd Feb 1828) adj __ MERCER. Wit: Henry ROBERTS, Jacob SUMMERS. Delv. to SKINNER 31 Aug 1846.

4B:217 Date: 29 Nov 1832 RtCt: 10 Dec 1833
Absalom NEWKIRK & wife Elizabeth late TAILOR, Thomas CAPEHART & wife Mary late SKINNER, Susan CONDEN late SKINNER, Samuel BOWMAN & wife Emily late SKINNER, Richard A. SKINNER & wife Eliza and Daniel McCRAY & wife Harriet late SKINNER of Warren Co Ohio to Peter SKINNER of Ldn. B/S of int. in land of Cornelius SKINNER dec'd prch/o Exors of Joseph CROSS dec'd. Wit: Richard TAYLOR, Mary CONDEN. Delv. to Peter SKINNER 1 Apr 1839.

4B:219 Date: 2 Nov 1833 RtCt: 10 Dec 1833
Caldwell CARR & wife Cornelia of Fqr to James GREENLEASE of Ldn. B/S of 100a adj __ COLEMAN. Delv. to GREENLEESE 1 Jul 1834.

4B:220 Date: 2 Nov 1833 RtCt: 10 Dec 1833
James GREENLEASE & wife Catharine to Charles L. POWELL. Trust for debt to Caldwell CARR using above 100a. Wit: John H. McCABE, Presley CORDELL. Delv. to Carr 11 Aug 1834.

4B:222 Date: 28 Aug 1833 RtCt: 11 Dec 1833
Samuel NEAR & wife Sarah of Ldn to George ABEL Jr. of Ldn. B/S of 3a (prch/o Vallentine JACOBS) between Blue Ridge and Short Hill adj E. GRUBB; and 8a wood lot (prch/o Thomas KIDWELL) adj __ PURCELL, George KOONCE. Wit: Ebenezer GRUBB, William CLENDENING. Delv. to Abel 20 Feb 1835.

4B:224 Date: __ Dec 1832 RtCt: 11 Dec 1833
Thomas ROGERS (Commr. in case of Benjamin SHREVE Jr. Admr of Daniel TRUNDLE dec'd and James TRUNDLE agst Charles SHEPHERD Admr. of James SHEPHERD dec'd and his heirs) to Benjamin SHREVE Jr. B/S of 38a (Lot #3 allotted James SHEPHERD in his lifetime from Charles Shepherd dec'd) adj heirs of James LEWIS dec'd; and 10a wood lot. Delv. to SHREVE 6 Feb 1835.

4B:225 Date: 20 Nov 1833 RtCt: 11 Dec 1833
Joseph W. BRONAUGH to Ludwell LUCKETT and Richard O. GRAYSON. Trust for debt to William A. STEPHENSON & Co. using 165a, horse, household items. Delv. to GRAYSON 24 Nov 1834.

4B:227 Date: 8 Oct 1833 RtCt: 12 Dec 1833
John M. ANDERSON (insolvent debtor) & wife Malinda and Sheriff William COOKE Esqr. of FredVa to Washington G. SINGLETON (trustee of Malinda ANDERSON). Trust for debt to James KEENAN and Harrison Waller BOWERS of FredVa (case of Harriet BOWERS, James KEENAN, George W. BOWERS & Harrison Waller BOWERS agst John M. ANDERSON for rents) using house & lot in Union (descended to Melinda ANDERSON as heir of Reubin TRIPLETT dec'd) and interest in house & lot in Winchester now occupied by ANDERSON held as dower of late Adam BOWERS dec'd.

4B:230 Date: 6 Dec 1833 RtCt: 9 Dec 1833
Thomas ROGERS (Commr. in Sept 1832 case of DRAKEs agst Jesse CARTER) to James McGEATH & wife Margaret late DRAKE, Townsend J. JURY & wife Mary Ann late DRAKE and John TAVENER & wife Urah late DRAKE. B/S of land [101½a, see DBk 2U:375] cnvy/b George TAVENER Jr. to Jesse CARTER Jul 1816 less 15a formerly cnvy/t Samuel PEUGH.

4B:231   Date: 15 Aug 1827   RtCt: 17 Aug 1827/9 Dec 1833
Commrs. Humphrey PEAKE and George WISE (decree of Sup. Ct. of Alexandria) to Joseph T. NEWTON of Ldn. B/S of 97a Lot #3 of Ricketts & Newton and 1a Lot #5. Wit: Rich. H. LOVE, Jas. HANSBROUGH Sr., James F. NEWTON.

4B:232   Date: 9 Dec 1833   RtCt: 12 Dec 1833
Richard H. HENDERSON of Ldn to Charles TURNER of Ldn. B/S of undivided int. in estate of Moses GULICK dec'd f/o Alfred (from defaulted trust of Aug 1832 from Alfred GULICK, DBk 3Y:262).

4B:233   Date: __ 1833   RtCt: 13 Dec 1833
Margaret WALTMAN of Ldn to Emanuel WALTMAN of Ldn. B/S of 36a from div. of Jacob WALTMAN dec'd. Delv. to E. WALTMAN 7 Jul 1834.

4B:234   Date: 8 Nov 1833   RtCt: 17 Dec 1833
James GARRISON & wife Elizabeth of Ldn to Isaac VANDEVANTER of Ldn. B/S of 19a adj Arch'd MAINS, Joseph CAVANS dec'd. Wit: Presley CORDELL, Saml. M. EDWARDS.

4B:235   Date: 28 Sep 1833   RtCt: 21 Dec 1833
John LOVETT & wife Naomi of Ldn to George KEEN of Ldn. B/S of 130a adj __ GALLEHER nr Bethesda meeting house, Henry PLAISTER Jr., __ BRONAUGH, Jonathan LOVETT. Wit: William BENTON, Ludwell LUCKETT. Delv. to KEEN 25 Jun 1835.

4B:237   Date: 1 Dec 1832   RtCt: 23 Dec 1833
Isaiah B. BEANS & wife Elizabeth to Richard TAVENER, James TIPPETT, Fielding BROWN, Nathan NICHOLS and Joseph B. FOX (trustees of Methodist Episcopal Church). B/S of ½a adj Jno. HEATON, BEANS; to erect house of worship. Wit: John WHITE, Jacob SHUTT, Richard K. LITTLETON, James McILHANEY.

4B:240   Date: 24 Dec 1833   RtCt: 24 Dec 1833
Amos FOUCH of Ldn to Isaac HALLING of Ldn. Trust for debt to Burr W. HARRISON using 25a (dev. by will of Thomas FOUCH) adj Enoch FRANCIS, Catherine HARRISON. Delv. to Amos FOUCH 5 May 1836.

4B:241   Date: 21 Oct 1833   RtCt: 27 Dec 1833
Sarah ELLZEY of Ldn to George RHODES of Ldn. B/S of 23a nr Lsbg adj Charles BINNS, Jacob FADELY, RHODES (including lots under lease by Mrs. Nancy THOMAS of 3a, lately by FITCHTER or LYLE of 5a, lately by FITCHTER of 13a, and by Robt. CAMPBELL's devisees of 10a, all 5y renewable). Wit: Isaiah CHAPPEL. W. ELLZEY, Christopher HOWSER. Delv. to RHODES 9 Sep 1836.

4B:242   Date: 23 Nov 1833   RtCt: 27 Dec 1833
Sarah ELLZEY (Admx wwa of Elizabeth ELLZEY and Mary ELLZEY dec'd) of Ldn to Philip HOWZER of Ldn. B/S of 175a adj __ OATYEAR, __ PAYTEN, __ FOUCH, __ LEFEVRE. Delv. to HOUSER 15 May 1834.

4B:243 Date: 18 Sep 1833 RtCt: 27 Dec 1833
Charles Fenton DOWNES & wife Hester/Esther of Ldn to Joseph
GRUBB of Ldn. B/S of int. of Elizabeth LOVE dec'd in land of estate
of John LOVE dec'd. Wit: James McILHANY, John WHITE.

4B:244 Date: 28 Dec 1833 RtCt: 28 Dec 1833
Fenton VANDEVANTER of Ldn to Archibald MAINS of Ldn. B/S of
50a (Lot #1 in div. of Wm. MAINS dec'd) adj Mrs. RICE, Ellis
WILLIAMS, Benjamin BROWN, MAINS. Wit: A. M. KITZMILLER.
Delv. to Mains 9 Apr 1834.

4B:245 Date: 4 Oct 1833 RtCt: 31 Dec 1833
David Fendall BEALL of Ldn to Samuel THOMPSON of Ldn. B/S of
62a on NW fork of Goose Creek, and __ NICHOLS, James BEANS,
David SMITH (prch/o Levi WILLIAMS & David SMITH).

4B:246 Date: 11 Sep 1829 RtCt: 14 Sep 1829/1 Jan 1834
Christiana WRIGHT wd/o Samuel WRIGHT dec'd, Anthony
WRIGHT & wife Sarah, William STREAM & wife Pleasant, John
WRIGHT & wife Sarah, Nancy HURDLE, Samuel WRIGHT & Lewis
WRIGHT of Ldn to John CONARD·of Ldn. B/S of 131a (cnvy/b
David LOVETT Mar 1811 to Samuel WRIGHT) and Ezekiel POTTS,
Thomas LESLIE. Wit: Craven OSBURN, John WHITE. Confirmation
by Lewis WRIGHT, now 21y old, on 1 Jan 1834. Delv. to CONARD
3 Dec 1836.

4B:247 Date: 30 Dec 1833 RtCt: 1 Jan 1834
Joseph LEWIS & wife Elizabeth O. of Ldn to Jacob FAULEY of Ldn.
B/S of 10a on E side of Catoctin mt. (part of land cnvy/b Fleming
HIXSON) adj Israel WILLIAMS, road from Taylor Town to Lsbg. Wit:
William BENTON, Benj'a. GRAYSON.

4B:249 Date: 30 Sep 1833 RtCt: 1 Jan 1834
Daniel POTTERFIELD & wife Mary of Ldn to William WENNER of
Ldn. B/S of 3/8tha (cnvy/b Ishmael VANHORN) adj __ DERRY. Wit:
William SLATER, Thos. J. MARLOW. Delv. to WENNER 8 Oct 1834.

4B:250 Date: 12 Oct 1833 RtCt: 1 Jan 1834
Adam WEVER/WEAVER & wife Lydia of JeffVA to Elizabeth E. W.
BALCH of FredMd. B/S of Lot #45 at SW corner of Cornwall & King
Sts in Lsbg. Wit: James HITE, William BUTLER.

4B:251 Date: 3 Dec 1833 RtCt: 1 Jan 1834
Richard TAVENNER & wife Nancy to James TIPPETT, Samuel B.
HARRIS, Taliafaro M. McILHANY, Joseph B. FOX, John WHITE,
Frederick A. DAVISSON, Mortimer McILHANY & Absolam KALB
(trustees of Methodist Episcopal Church). B/S of 1½a nr Snickers
Gap turnpike road nr James TAVENNER's stable; to build house of
worship. Wit: Thomas J. MARLOW, David REECE.

4B:253 Date: 31 Dec 1833 RtCt: 3 Jan 1834
Uriel GLASSCOCK & wife Nancy of Ldn to James RUST of Ldn.
Trust for debt to Morris OSBURN using 189a adj __ FRANCIS, __

GOUCHENOUR, Mrs. POWELL, William J. BRONAUGH, Joseph LANE dec'd. Wit: Ludwell LUCKETT, William BENTON. Delv. to RUST 13 Feb 1840.

4B:254 Date: 17 Aug 1833 RtCt: 3 Jan 1834
George W. HENRY & wife Dewanner of Ldn to Charles G. EDWARDS of Ldn. B/S of undivided 1/4th int. in "Ogden farm" of John HAMILTON dec'd subject to life estate of widow Winefred HAMILTON (from deed of James McILHANY trustee of Andrew OGDEN to John HAMILTON) as 97¾a Lot #1 and 5a Lot #2. Wit: Saml. DAWSON, William SLATER.

4B:255 Date: 5 Jan 1834 RtCt: 7 Jan 1834
Thomas ROGERS (Commr. in ct. decree of Sep 1832 case of John GEORGE, Ebenezer GRUBB, Exors of Jacob VERTZ dec'd agst George SHOVER Admr. of Simon SHOVER dec'd who was Admr. of Adam SHOVER dec'd, Christian SANBOWER surv. Admx of Adam SHOVER dec'd & heirs of Simon SHOVER dec'd) to Adam HEFFNER of Ldn. B/S of 47½a (Lot #3 in div. of Adam SHOVER dec'd, DBk GGG:436) and 4a Lot #9. Delv. to HEFFNER 5 Apr 1843.

4B:256 Date: 5 Jan 1834 RtCt: 7 Jan 1834
Adam HEFFNER of Ldn to James H. CHAMBLIN of Ldn. Trust for debt to Commr of Thomas ROGERS using above land. Delv. to ROGERS 25 Mar 1834.

4B:257 Date: 18 Sep 1832 RtCt: 8 Jan 1834
Walter ELGIN & wife Sarah, Joseph CARR & wife Mary, William HALL & wife Eliza Ann and Lewis J. DONOHOE & wife Delila of Ldn to Joel NIXON of Ldn. B/S of 38a adj Mary BEATY, Benjamin WHITE, NIXON, John NIXON s/o George (including 15a HALL cnvy/t NIXON) Wit: Wilson C. SELDEN Jr., Presley CORDELL, Samuel M. EDWARDS, Henry T. HARRISON. Delv. to NIXON 8 Mar 1835.

4B:259 Date: 18 Sep 1832 RtCt: 8 Jan 1834
Walter ELGIN & wife Sarah, Joseph CARR & wife Mary, William HALL & wife Eliza Ann and Lewis J. DONOHOE & wife Delila of Ldn to Adin WHITE and Richard WHITE of Ldn. B/S of 38a adj Josiah HALL, Joel NIXON (1/5th of land originally held by Richard WHITE dec'd). Wit: Wilson C. SELDEN Jr., Presley CORDELL, Saml. M. EDWARDS, Henry T. HARRISON. Delv. to A. H. ROGERS 13 Dec 1865.

4B:262 Date: 31 Dec 1832 RtCt: 8 Jan 1834
John G. HUMPHREY & wife Mary, Abraham VICKERS & wife Mariah, and John G. HUMPHREY as agent for William RICHARDS Jr. & wife Margaret of Ldn to Abner CARTER of Ldn. B/S of 115a on Goose Creek (where VICKERS now resides) adj __ WORNALD, __ HALL, heirs of __ MURRY, Edward CARTER. Wit: Edward HALL, Benj. GRAYSON. Delv. pr order 28 Sep 1837.

4B:263 Date: 7 May 1833 RtCt: 8 Jan 1834
Abner CARTER & wife Martha E. of Ldn to James S. CARTER of Culpeper Co. B/S of 115a on Goose Creek where Abner now resides adj __ WORNALD, __ HALL, heirs of Samuel MURRY, Edward CARTER. Wit: Edward HALL, William BENTON.

4B:265 Date: 9 Dec 1833 RtCt: 9 Jan 1834
Erasmus G. HAMILTON and Charles G. ESKRIDGE of Ldn to Wilson Cary SELDON of Exeter. Release of trust of Dec 1825 for debt to George CARTER of Oatlands.

4B:266 Date: 10 Jan 1834 RtCt: 10 Jan 1834
Charles BINNS of Ldn to Samuel M. EDWARDS and George LEE of Ldn. Trust for debt to Thomas ROGERS and Richard H. HENDERSON of Ldn using 240a adj Mrs. TILLETT, __ SWANN, Moses BUTLER, Isaac CROSSBY, old poor house, __ CLINE, __ HENDERSON. Delv. to BINNS 6 Sep 1836.

4B:267 Date: 1 Jan 1834 RtCt: 1 Jan 1834
List of property sold by Dpty Sheriff J. CHAMBLIN for Aris BUCKNER for execution by Abeleno HOLE and purchased by Samuel STERRETT who sold to Joseph MEAD. Wit: John FULTON, Jno. W. KAYLOR.

4B:268 Date: 1 Jan 1834 RtCt: 1 Jan 1834
Joseph MEAD to Abeleno HOLE. Loan of above property for 3 years.

4B:268 Date: 21 Jun 1833 RtCt: 13 Jan 1834
George W. SEVERS (Marshall of Winchester Dist. Ct.) to William HOUGH and Thomas NICHOLS of Ldn. B/S of 100a (land of Andrew REED dec'd father of Deft. Samuel in case of Dec 1825 Bank of Valley agst Samuel REED) adj Thomas MARKS, Lewis ELLZEY.

4B:269 Date: 7 Sep 1833 RtCt: 13 Jan 1834
Province McCORMICK of FredVa to Humphrey SHEPHERD of Ldn. Release of trust of Jan 1826 for debt to William CASTLEMAN.

4B:270 Date: 13 Jan 1834 RtCt: 13 Jan 1834
John L. PARSON. Qualified as 2nd Lt. 2nd Reg of artillery 6th Brig 2nd Div Va Militia.

4B:271 Date: 9 Jan 1834 RtCt: 14 Jan 1834
Israel DYER of Ldn to Bailey R. GLASCOCK of Fqr. Trust for debt to Joshua T. HOPE using household items.

4B:272 Date: 8 Nov 1833 RtCt: 14 Jan 1834
William WIRE & wife Catharine of Clinton Co Ohio to Jonathan WENNER of Ldn. B/S of 60 sq poles (cnvy/b Harman HINZERLING's heirs) adj James & Wm. HOYS. Wit: Jacob SHOEMAKER, Pricilla SHOEMAKER. Delv to WENNER 1 Aug 1834.

4B:273   Date: 13 Jan 1834   RtCt: 14 Jan 1834
Joseph MORRISON of Ldn to James MERCHANT of Ldn. B/S of 90a adj Mortimer McILHANEY, John STATLER, George SMITH (cnvy/b Frederick A. DAVISON Oct 1831). Delv. 8 Mar 1882.

4B:274   Date: 6 Jan 1834   RtCt: 14 Jan 1834
James MERCHANT & wife Mary of Ldn to Thomas WHITE of Ldn. Trust for debt to Joseph MORRISON using 90a. Wit: John WHITE, William CLENDENING. Delv. to MORRISON 10 May 1836.

4B:276   Date: 6 Jan 1834   RtCt: 14 Jan 1834
James MARCHANT [MERCHANT] & wife Mary of Ldn to Joseph MORRISON of Ldn. B/S of undivided 1/11th of 206a from will of Archibald MORRISON dec'd. Wit: William CLENDENING, John WHITE. Delv. to MORRISON 10 May 1836.

4B:277   Date: 30 Mar 1833   RtCt: 14 Jan 1834
George HAMMOND & wife Mary of Ldn to James MARCHANT/MERCHANT of Ldn. B/S of 3½a on SW side of Short Hill (formerly of Francis McKAMIE dec'd). Wit: James McILHANEY, John WHITE. Delv. to ? MERCHANT one of the Exors. of grantee pr order DBk 5R:049.

4B:279   Date: 13 Jan 1834   RtCt: 14 Jan 1834
Jane MORRISON d/o Archibald MORRISON dec'd of Ldn to Edward MORRISON of Ldn. B/S of undivided 2/11th (her share and share prch/o sister Rachel LESLIE) of "upper place" farm of Archibald MORRISON dec'd.

4B:280   Date: 30 Dec 1833   RtCt: 1 Jan 1834
Joseph LEWIS & wife Elizabeth O. of Ldn to George MARLOW of Ldn. B/S of 26a on E side of Catocton mt. (formerly owned by Leonard ANSELL cnvy/b Fleming HIXON) adj Israel WILLIAMS, __ DIXON. Wit: William BENTON, Benjamin GRAYSON. Delv. to MARLOW 11 Apr 1836.

4B:281   Date: 30 Aug 1833   RtCt: 15 Jan 1834
Josiah CONWELL & wife Ann and Jonathan CONWELL of Gournsey Co Ohio and Elizabeth CONWELL of Gurnsey Co Ohio (heirs of Elizabeth CONWELL w/o Loveless CONWELL) to James HIGDON of Ldn. B/S of 2a and Peter BENEDUM, Charles BINNS, Joseph MEAD (sold to Isaac CONWELL by Loveless CONWELL, DBk FFF:__ and WWW:__). Wit: Joseph EDIE, Peter UMSTOT.

4B:283   Date: 25 Apr 1832   RtCt: 15 Jan 1834
Loveless CONWELL & wife Elizabeth, Isaac CONWELL & wife Margaret, Jacob CONWELL & wife Sarah of Ldn, Israel BOLEN & wife Ellen, Mary CONWELL, Jonathan CONWELL & Elizabeth CONWELL of Mus. Co Ohio and Josiah CONWELL & wife Ann of Gurnsey Co Ohio to James HIGDON of Ldn. B/S of 2a as above.

4B:285 Date: 25 Nov 1833 RtCt: 15 Jan 1834
Jacob F. McCARL & wife Elizabeth (d/o John WILSON dec'd who was s/o Ebenezer WILSON dec'd and neice and heir of Asa WILSON dec'd a s/o Ebenezer dec'd) of Tuscarawas Co Ohio to William CLENDENING of Ldn. B/S of undivided int. in 130a of Ebenezer WILSON dec'd where Hannah WILSON now resides, between Blue ridge mt. and Short Hill adj heirs of Thomas HOUGH, Jacob SHUTT, Jesse EVANS, Robert COCKERILL, John CAMPBELL. Wit: John WHITE, James McILHANEY. Delv. pr order DBk UUU:153, 21 Oct 1834.

4B:286 Date: 17 Aug 1833 RtCt: 15 Jan 1834
John MARLATT & wife Hannah (d/o John WILSON dec'd who was s/o Ebenezer WILSON dec'd and neice and heir of Asa WILSON dec'd a s/o Ebenezer dec'd) of JeffVa to William CLENDENING of Ldn. B/S of undivided int. in 130a as above. Delv. pr order DBK UUU:153., 21 Oct 1834.

4B:287 Date: 8 Jan 1834 RtCt: 19 Jan 1834
Caleb N. GALLEHER & wife Lucinda of Ldn to Horace LUCKETT of Ldn. B/S of 48a on Goose Creek on N side of Snickers Gap turnpike road adj heirs of William HARDING. Wit: Hugh SMITH, Asa ROGERS. Delv. to LUCKETT 24 Sep 1834.

4B:289 Date: 18 Jan 1834 RtCt: 21 Jan 1834
William EVERHART to Jesse NEAR and George SAUNDERS. Trust to Absalom KALB and Samuel KALB Exors. of John KALB for benefit of Susanna EVERHEART w/o Wm. using int. 10a with mill (DBk 4B:093) in German Settlement (Susanna EVERHEART willed 1/8th of estate of father John KALB dec'd).

4B:291 Date: 2 Jan 1833 RtCt: 22 Jan 1834
William T. HOUGH & wife Louiza of Ldn to John WOLFORD of Ldn. B/S of 22a adj land left HOUGH by mother and grandfather William HOUGH, William VIRTS, __ DAVISSON. Wit: Thomas J. MARLOW, John WHITE. Delv. to WOLFORD 27 Aug 1846.

4B:292 Date: 10 Jan 1834 RtCt: 24 Jan 1834
Mary BALL of Ldn to Ebenezer GRUBB Jr. of Ldn. B/S of ¼a at NW corner of land cnvy/b John A. BINNS to Peter SAUNDERS (15 Apr 1811, DBk NN:470). Signed by Mary BALL and Samuel BALL. Delv. to GRUBB 5 Jun 1834.

4B:293 Date: 25 Jan 1834 RtCt: 27 Jan 1834
James DOWNS of Ldn to Abner WILLIAMS of Ldn. Trust for debt to Saml. HOUGH and Wesley DOWNS using farm and household items. Delv. to WILLIAMS 5 Jan 1836.

4B:294 Date: 18 Jan 1834 RtCt: 29 Jan 1834
Thomas B. LOVE to Joseph TAYLOR. Trust for debt to Vallentine V. PURSEL & V. V. & S. PURSEL using undivided int. of 217a adj Richard ADAMS, Samuel RUSSELL, Jacob COST dec'd, James

BEST, Thos. GREGG & William WILSON. Delv. to V. V. PURSEL 9 Jul 1834.

4B:296   Date: 21 Nov 1833   RtCt: 30 Jan 1834
Cuthbert POWELL & wife Catharine of Ldn to Joseph LEWIS of Ldn. B/S of 7a POWELL, nr house of LEWIS. Wit: Abner GIBSON, Hugh SMITH.

4B:297   Date: 1 Feb 1834   RtCt: 1 Feb 1834
Wilson J. DRISH (insolvent debtor) of Ldn to Sheriff Ariss BUCKNER. B/S of int. in estate of father John DRISH, int. in real estate of Mathew ADAMS dec'd father of his wife. Delv. to Dpty Shff LITTLETON 28 Apr 1834.

4B:297   Date: 3 Feb 1834   RtCt: 3 Feb 1834
George K. FOX of Lsbg to John MARTIN of Lsbg. Trust for debt to Saml. M. BOSS using household items.

4B:299   Date: 3 Feb 1834   RtCt: 3 Feb 1834
Jacob SHAEFFER of Ldn to Samuel DAWSON of Ldn. B/S of undivided 11th interest in 186a of George RAZOR dec'd (from defaulted trust of Oct 1829 from Jacob RAZOR & wife Dorcas for debt to James HOOPER, DBk TTT:023). Delv. to Chs. GASSAWAY 28 Nov 1846.

4B:300   Date: 5 Feb 1834   RtCt: 5 Feb 1834
Lewis RUSE of Ldn to Charles B. HAMILTON. Mortgage using household items. Delv. pr order 8 Apr 1850.

4B:301   Date: 23 Sep 1833   RtCt: 6 Feb 1834
Enos PURCEL, Bernard PURCEL and Edmund/Edwin PURCEL of Ldn to John HESKITT, Conrad BITZER, James COPELAND, Richard COPELAND and Joseph BENNETT (elders of Baptist Meeting at Kittocton) of Ldn. B/S of 1a adj meeting , Dr. James HEATON, Catocton Creek.

4B:302   Date: 15 Jan 1834   RtCt: 6 Feb 1834
John A. BINNS & wife Mary Maria of Ldn to Charles BINNS of Ldn. B/S of lot on Loudoun St in Lsbg (cnvy/b William DODD, June 1830, DBk UUU:011).

4B:303   Date: 6 Jan 1834   RtCt: 6 Feb 1834
Charles BINNS Sr. of Ldn to John ROSE of Ldn. Trust for benefit of Anna Rose BINNS & Charles BINNS Jr. infant ch/o Mary Maria BINNS using int. in trust of Jun 1824, DBk HHH:160.

4B:303   Date: 6 Feb 1833   RtCt: 6 Feb 1834
John A. BINNS surv. trustee (Josiah L. DREAN being dec'd) to William W. KITZMILLER. B/S of leased lot on Loudoun St in Lsbg dev. by Mathew WEATHERBY to Richard H. LEE as trustee of Episcopal congregation of St. James Church (from defaulted trust of John CRIDLER, DBk VVV:237).

4B:304   Date: 24 May 1830   RtCt: 7 Feb 1834
David RICKETTS & wife Elizabeth of Ffx to Wesley S. McPHERSON
of Ldn. B/S of 8a (Lot #10 from case of John STUMP and David
RICKETTS vs. John T. NEWTON) called mill seat at Tuscarora and
Goose Creek; and 3a Lot #12.

4B:306   Date: 25 Nov 1833   RtCt: 8 Feb 1834
John S. MAGILL (Marshall of Sup. Ct. Winchester, case of Jun 1831
suit of Lydia PANCOAST agst Lydia NICHOLS) to John ALDRIDGE
of Ldn. B/S of 135a "Greggsville (paid to William HOGUE & Thomas
HATCHER Exors. of Isaac NICHOLS) adj George YOUNG, William
YOUNG, __ NICHOLS, __ WILKINSON.

4B:307   Date: __ 1830   RtCt: 8 Feb 1834
Yardley TAYLOR trustee, Isaac NICHOLS, William HOGE & William
PIGGOTT of Ldn to Andrew BIRDSALL of Ldn. Release of trust of
May 1827 for debt to Isaac NICHOLS on 187a.

4B:308   Date: __ Sep 1833   RtCt: 8 Feb 1834
John A. BINNS & wife Mary M. of Ldn to William CARR of Ldn. B/S
of 3a wedge on N side of Secolin claimed by Charles B.
ALEXANDER under Ragans Patent cnvy/b Alexander to William A.
BINNS Jun 1827 then to John A. Delv. to CARR 9 Apr 1835.

4B:309   Date: 12 Dec 1833   RtCt: 10 Feb 1834
Benjamin RUST & wife Frances of Ldn to Yardley TAYLOR of Ldn.
Trust for debt to Bernard TAYLOR using 99a on Beaverdam Creek
(cnvy/b Bernard TAYLOR). Wit: William BENTON, Timothy
TAYLOR. Delv. to TAYLOR 28 Mar 1836.

4B:311   Date: 6 Feb 1834   RtCt: 10 Feb 1834
Hendley BESIX of Ldn to David CARR of Ldn. Trust for debt to
William CARR using 2a where BESIX now lives (formerly of his
mother Prescilla BESSIX). Delv. to CARR 21 Sep 1835.

4B:312   Date: 27 Dec 1833   RtCt: 10 Feb 1834
Elijah BROOKS of Ldn to Joseph MEAD of Ldn. Trust for debt to
Benjamin SHREVE of Ldn using farm animals, crops. Wit: James
DAVIS, Nathan EDMUND.

4B:313   Date: 7 Dec 1833   RtCt: 10 Feb 1834
John POSTON of Ldn to Thomas ROGERS of Ldn. Trust for debt to
Chs. G. ESKRIDGE using farm animals, farm and household items,
crops on farm of Christopher FRYE. Delv. to ESKRIDGE 29 Jul
1836.

4B:314   Date: 10 Feb 1834   RtCt: 10 Feb 1834
Mary BELTZ of Ldn. DoE for slave Maria West aged abt 20y.

4B:314   Date: 7 Jan 1834   RtCt: 10 Feb 1834
Gustavus ELGIN of Ldn. DoE for slave Luke Norris.

4B:314   Date: 11 Feb 1834   RtCt: 11 Feb 1834
Jas. W. SMITH, Hugh SMITH and Geo. C. POWELL. Bond on
SMITH as constable.

4B:314 Date: 11 Feb 1834 RtCt: 11 Feb 1834
E. B. JAMES, David JAMES and Stephen T. CONARD. Bond on James as committee for estate of Dempsey CARTER an insane person.

4B:315 Date: 17 Apr 1832 RtCt: 12 Nov 1832/10 Mar 1834
George THOMAS of WashDC to Lewis F. MANKIN of Ldn. B/S of 419a on broad run adj Wm. AMBLE, M. & E. FRENCH, __ HARRISON. Wit: J. CLEVELAND, Saml. O'BANION, Johnston J. COLEMAN. Delv. to MANKINS 7 Feb 1838.

4B:316 Date: 16 Mar 1833 RtCt: 16 Sep 1833/10 Feb 1834
Thomas PHILLIPS and Joseph BOND to William RUSSELL. Release of trust of Feb 1830 for debt to Daniel JANNEY and William NICHOLS.

4B:317 Date: 20 Sep 1833 RtCt: 10 Feb 1834
Samuel McPHERSON & wife Mary of Ldn to Henry RUSSELL and John WILLIAMS of Ldn. Trust for debt to Samuel PAXSON & William RUSSELL of Ldn using 3a nr Wtfd with merchant mill & house (former prop. of Robert BRADEN, see DB YYY:186). Wit: David REECE, S. HOUGH.

4B:318 Date: 24 Sep 1833 RtCt: 10 Feb 1834
Levi COOKSEY & wife Elizabeth of Ldn to Bernard TAYLOR of Ldn. B/S of 7a adj Samuel IDEN. Wit: Timothy TAYLOR, David REECE. Delv. to TAYLOR 27 Jan 1835.

4B:320 Date: 2 Jun 1832 RtCt: 10 Feb 1834
Jacob WALTERS & wife Margaret of Ldn to Adam JACOBS of Ldn. B/S of 2a Lot #28 on W side of short hill. Wit: Mortimer McILHANY, Geo. W. SHAWEN. Delv. to JACOBS 8 Feb 1836.

4B:321 Date: 26 Oct 1833 RtCt: 10 Feb 1834
Jesse RICHARDS & wife Eleanor of Ldn to Dr. Thomas W. SMITH of Upperville Fqr. B/S of undivided int. in 80a of John GIBSON dec'd allotted to widow Elizabeth as dower; and int. of David E. BROWN & Mahlon GIBSON in 1½a with house occ. by Elizabeth by lease of Jun 1819, DBk BBB:169.

4B:322 Date: 16 Jan 1834 RtCt: 11 Feb 1834
Samuel BUTCHER of Wood Co Va to John H. BUTCHER and Edward B. GRADY of Ldn. B/S of 2a where Ebenezer Baptist Meeting House stands (dev. by father Samuel BUTCHER dec'd) for house of worship.

4B:324 Date: 1 Jun 1833 RtCt: 10 Feb 1834
Joseph CARR & wife Mary late HALL and William HALL & wife Eliza of Ldn to John WADE of Ldn. B/S of 2/6th int. (allotted in div. of Josiah HALL dec'd to reps of William dec'd) in house & lot on W side of Back St in Lsbg adj Mrs. BLINCOE, __ DRAIN, __ OATYER, __ BIRKBY. Wit: Wilson C. SELDEN Jr., Presley CORDELL.

4B:326   Date: 11 Feb 1834   RtCt: 11 Feb 1834
Charles BINNS & wife Hannah of Ldn to James L. MARTIN of Ldn.
B/S of 3 lots prch/o Benjamin WOODLEY dec'd with dwelling house.

4B:327   Date: 6 May 1833   RtCt: 12 Feb 1834
Lewis J. DONOHOE & wife Delilah late HALL of Ldn to John WADE
of Ldn. B/S of 2/6th int. (allotted in div. of Josiah HALL dec'd to reps
of William dec'd) in house & lot on W side of Back St in Lsbg adj
Mrs. BLINCOE, __ DRAIN, __ OATYER, __ BIRKBY. Wit: Saml. M.
EDWARDS, Henry T. HARRISON.

4B:328   Date: 4 Feb 1834   RtCt: 13 Feb 1834
John Thomas HUTCHISON and William HUTCHISON & wife Martha
L. of Ldn to Andrew HUTCHISON of Ldn. B/S of 66a on old
Alexandria road. Chas. LEWIS, Wm. B. HARRISON.

4B:329   Date: 13 Feb 1834   RtCt: 13 Feb 1834
Bernard McCORMICK of Ldn to Townsend J. JURY of Ldn. Trust for
debt to Joseph P. McGEATH using household items. Delv. to JURY
25 Sep 1834.

4B:330   Date: 14 Feb 1834   RtCt: 14 Feb 1834
Usher SKINNER to William B. TYLER. Trust for debt to Peter
SKINNER using slave boys George and Howard.

4B:331   Date: 10 Sep 1833   RtCt: 15 Feb 1834
Delilah BREWER & her husband William BREWER and Elizabeth
ROBERTS & her husband Henry H. ROBERTS (daus. of Samuel
HOUGH) to brother William S. HOUGH. PoA for monies from
William HOUGH dec'd (formerly of Ldn who died at the year of 1814
and beq. to son Samuel HOUGH & his children). Ackn in Todd Co
Ky for grantors. Oath from Samuel HOUGH in Belmont Co Ohio that
Delilah & Elizabeth are his children.

4B:333   Date: 15 Feb 1834   RtCt: 15 Feb 1834
John A. BINNS of Ldn to Archibald M. KITZMILLER & Charles W. D.
BINNS. Trust for debt to John ROSE, Charles BINNS Sr. & Anna
Rose BINNS (infant ch/o John A. using int. in slaves cnvy/b
Benjamin W. PERRY (also sold Anna's Negro boy Lewis). Delv. to
C. BINNS 30 Jul 1836.

4B:334   Date: 12 Feb 1834   RtCt: 17 Feb 1834
John A. BINNS to C. W. D. BINNS. Agreement for hire of slave
Charlotte. Delv. to C. W. D. BINNS 28 Apr 1834.

4B:334   Date: 30 Dec 1833   RtCt: 19 Feb 1834
Mahlon GIBSON & wife Elenora of Ldn to Robert L. ARMISTEAD of
Fqr. Trust for debt to William T. W. TALIAFERRO of Fqr using 34a
"Femen" tract where they reside. Wit: John B. ARMISTEAD, Josiah
TIDBALL.

4B:336   Date: 18 Sep 1833   RtCt: 20 Feb 1834
Richard H. HENDERSON to Joseph HOCKINGS. B/S of 35a (from
defaulted trust of Jan 1826 from William COE & wife Catharine for

debt to Samuel CARR, descended to Catharine from brother Menan COE dec'd). Delv. to HAWKINS 27 Mar 1837.

4B:337   Date: 14 Sep 1834   RtCt: 21 Feb 1834
Thomas LOVE of Montgomery Co Indiana to Eli PIERPOINT of Ldn. B/S of int. in land entitled to John, Sarah and Elizabeth LOVE dec'd ch/o James LOVE Sr. dec'd; and 1/8th of 1/3rd int. in lease of farm where PIERPOINT resides and 1/8th of L/L. Wit: Francis MILLER, P. M. CURREY. Delv. to PEIRPOINT 18 Mar 1835.

4B:338   Date: 21 Feb 1834   RtCt: 22 Feb 1834
James LOVE of Ldn to James D. LOVE, Fenton M. LOVE & Mary R. LOVE of Ldn. B/S of int. in real estate of Henry NICHOLS dec'd which fell to Lydia NICHOLS afterwards Lydia GREGG w/o Nathan GREGG, now both dec'd.

4B:339   Date: 25 Feb 1834   RtCt: 25 Feb 1834
John F. BARRETT to Saml. M. EDWARDS. Trust for debt to Jane D. WILDMAN using stove and horse. Delv. pr order 9 Feb 1837.

4B:340   Date: 14 Sep 1830   RtCt: 27 Feb 1834
Samuel HAMMAT of Ldn to Daniel McCARTY a free man of colour of Ldn. B/S of 10a (Lot #9, DBk OOO:337 [335]).

4B:341   Date: 27 Feb 1834   RtCt: 27 Feb 1834
Daniel McCARTY of Ldn to Wesley S. McPHERSON of Ldn. B/S of 10a as above. Wit: Saml. M. EDWARDS. Delv. to grantee 16 Feb 1870.

4B:342   Date: 25 Dec 1833   RtCt: 28 Feb 1834
Ludwell LAKE & wife Agnes of Ldn to Samuel SIMPSON of Ldn. B/S of 250a (cnvy/b Benj. R. LACEY Jan 1832) adj Maj. POWELL, __ SKINNER, __ CURRELL, __ SWART. Wit: A. GIBSON, Hugh SMITH.

4B:344   Date: 20 Feb 1834   RtCt: 1 Mar 1834
Ananias ORRISON to Samuel M. EDWARDS. Trust for debt to Rich'd H. HENDERSON Exor. of Thomas R. MOTT dec'd using farm animals, farm and household items.

4B:344   Date: 8 Nov 1833   RtCt: 4 Mar 1834
George BROOKS & wife Rachel of BaltMd to Joseph BROOKS of BaltMd. B/S of int. in estate of Edmund JENNINGS dec'd (George BROOKS & Joseph BROOKS sons of William BROOKS of BaltMd & Elizabeth BROOKS his wife now dec'd, Edmund JENNINGS dec'd of Ldn dev. to his sister Elizabeth BROOKS & children shares in his estate in Va & Md). Wit: Stephenson ARCHER.

4B:346   Date: __ 1833   RtCt: 4 Mar 1834
George W. HOUGH & wife Mary C. and Pleasant E. HOUGH of Ldn to Jesse T. SAPPINGTON of Ldn. B/S of 20 perch lot in Wtfd adj Fleming HIXON, __ BRADEN. Wit: Geo. W. SHAWEN, Joshua PUSEY. Delv. to SAPPINGTON 9 May 1837.

4B:347   Date: 31 Dec 1832   RtCt: 5 Mar 1834
Edward FRANCIS & wife Ann E. B. of Ldn to Jane D. WILDMAN of
Ldn. B/S of undivided share of house & lot on NW corner of King &
Royal Sts. in Lsbg (cnvy/t Ann late HAMILTON by her grandfather
Charles BENNETT). Wit: Presley CORDELL, Saml. M. EDWARDS.

4B:349   Date: 22 Feb 1834   RtCt: 7 Mar 1834
James B. BISCOE of Ldn to Silas BEATTY of Ldn. Trust for debt to
Thomas W. DORMAN of Ldn using books.

4B:350   Date: 7 Mar 1834   RtCt: 7 Mar 1834
John CRIDLER of Ldn to Arch M. KITZMILLER. Trust for John H.
MONROE and James BRADY of Ldn as security on bond to Mrs.
Belinda PERRY using horse and wagon.

4B:351   Date: 5 Mar 1834   RtCt: 8 Mar 1834
James UNDERWOOD & wife Susannah to P. C. McCABE. Trust for
debt to Joseph L. RUSSELL using household items the dower of
Susannah from estate of late husband David NEAR dec'd. Wit:
William CLENDENING, Peter DERRY, John McCARTY.

4B:353   Date: 10 Mar 1834   RtCt: 10 Mar 1834
Charles T. MAGILL of Ldn to Ludwell LUCKETT of Ldn. Trust for
John S. MAGILL of FredVa as security to various debts using
household items dev. by will of brother Archibald MAGILL dec'd, and
14a cnvy/b William NAYLOR nr Romney Hampshire Co Va, int. in
tavern leased to him by Mrs. Eleanor PEERS in Lsbg, and int. as
tenant by curtesy to land on Big Kanawha in Mason Co Va dev. to
wife Mary D. by her father William BRONAUGH Sr. dec'd.

4B:355   Date: 31 Aug 1833   RtCt: 10 Mar 1834
William NICHOLS (s/o Samuel NICHOLS) & wife Catherine of Ldn to
Jonas JANNEY (s/o Jonas JANNEY) of Ldn. Trust for debt to
Mahlon CRAVEN of Ldn using 127a on Beaverdam Creek cnvy/b
CRAVEN. Wit: John SIMPSON, Timothy TAYLOR.

4B:357   Date: 8 Mar 1834   RtCt: 10 Mar 1834
Alexander MONEY of Mdbg to Townshend McVEIGH of Ldn. Trust
for debt to H. & J. H. McVEIGH using farm and household items.
Delv. pr order 20 Aug 1836.

4B:358   Date: 25 Jan 1830   RtCt: 10 Mar 1834
Richard COCHRAN of Ldn to Noble BEVERIDGE of Ldn. B/S of Lot
#22 in Mdbg with brick store house and log house.

4B:359   Date: 9 Oct 1833   RtCt: 10 Mar 1834
Joseph W. BRONAUGH & wife Nancy S. of Ldn to Ludwell
LUCKETT of Ldn. B/S of 15a (wood lot from div. [of William
BRONAUGH dec'd]). Wit: Francis W. LUCKETT, William BENTON.
Delv. to LUCKETT 22 Sep 1834.

4B:361   Date: 10 Jun 1833   RtCt: 10 Mar 1834
William PIGGOTT & wife Mary of Ldn to Jonathan TAVENER of Ldn.
B/S of 41a (from Jonah TAVENER dec'd) on Snickers Gap turnpike

road adj heirs of Samuel NICHOLS, Jonah TAVENER, Jesse TAVENER, Sarah TREHERN, __ BOWLES. Wit: David REESE, Timothy TAYLOR. Delv. to Jonathan TAVENER 20 Feb 1835.

4B:362 Date: 18 Jan 1834 RtCt: 10 Mar 1834
Vallentine V. PURCEL & wife Mary of Ldn to John SCHOOLEY of Ldn. B/S of 7a on Catoctin Creek adj John ROBINSON. Wit: James McILHANEY, Timothy TAYLOR.

4B:364 Date: 15 Feb 1834 RtCt: 10 Mar 1834
John KILE & wife Winefred of Ldn to William BENTON of Ldn. B/S of 56a on Goose Creek adj BENTON. Wit: Ludwell LUCKETT, Asa ROGERS. Delv. to BENTON 2 Jan 1836.

4B:365 Date: 18 Jan 1834 RtCt: 10 Mar 1834
Valentine V. PURCEL & Townsend HEATON to Elijah JAMES & wife Sarah. Release of trust of Mar 1829 for debt to Joseph TAYLOR & wife Lydia using 93a.

4B:366 Date: 10 Mar 1834 RtCt: 10 Mar 1834
Elias POOL of Ldn to Archibald M. KITZMILLER of Ldn. Trust for Michael MORRALLEE and John A. BINNS as security on bond to John MOCK using farm animals, farm and household items. Delv. to KITZMILLER 7 Nov 1834.

4B:367 Date: 10 Mar 1834 RtCt: 10 Mar 1834
Jacob WATERS, Chas. B. HAMILTON Jr. & Emanuel WALTMAN. Bond on WATERS as constable.

4B:368 Date: 10 Mar 1834 RtCt: 10 Mar 1834
William G. WRIGHT, William GILLMORE & Charles TURNER. Bond on WRIGHT as constable.

4B:368 Date: 10 Mar 1834 RtCt: 10 Mar 1834
William ROSE Jr., William ROSE Sr. & John SIMPSON. Bond on William ROSE Jr. as constable.

4B:369 Date: 10 Mar 1834 RtCt: 10 Mar 1834
Joseph HOCKINGS, Jesse TIMMS, Jesse McVEIGH & John SIMPSON. Bond on Joseph HAWKINS as constable.

4B:369 Date: 10 Mar 1834 RtCt: 10 Mar 1834
Ariss BUCKNER, Charles LEWIS, Johnston CLEVELAND, William THRIFT, James H. CHAMBLIN, Thomas ROGERS, Samuel ROGERS, Feilding LITTLETON, Horace LUCKETT, Burr WEEKS, Wm. MERSHON, John S. EDWARDS & Samuel M. EDWARDS. Bond on BUCKNER as Sheriff to collect levies.

4B:370 Date: 10 Mar 1834 RtCt: 10 Mar 1834
Ariss BUCKNER, Charles LEWIS, Johnston CLEVELAND, William THRIFT, James H. CHAMBLIN, Thomas ROGERS, Samuel ROGERS, Feilding LITTLETON, Horace LUCKETT, Burr WEEKS, Wm. MERSHON, John S. EDWARDS & Samuel M. EDWARDS. Bond on BUCKNER as Sheriff to collect officer fees.

4B:370 Date: 10 Mar 1834 RtCt: 10 Mar 1834
Ariss BUCKNER, Charles LEWIS, Johnston CLEVELAND, William THRIFT, James H. CHAMBLIN, Thomas ROGERS, Samuel ROGERS, Feilding LITTLETON, Horace LUCKETT, Burr WEEKS, Wm. MERSHON, John S. EDWARDS & Samuel M. EDWARDS. Bond on BUCKNER as Sheriff to collect taxes.

4B:371 Date: Jan 1834 RtCt: 10 Mar 1834
William MCKNIGH[T]. Oath as Lt. in artillery of Va Militia.

4B:371 Date: 10 Mar 1834 RtCt: 10 Mar 1834
Thomas J. MARLOW. DoE for slave Samuel James abt 35y old.

4B:372 Date: 7 Feb 1834 RtCt: 11 Mar 1834
James SWART dec'd. Allotment of dower of widow Elizabeth SWART – Court order dated 9 Dec 1833, from 522¾a home tract on Little River, 50a on Little River turnpike road, 9a on Goose Creek nr Johnson's Ford, lot with buildings in Mdbg, lot with buildings in Aldie, lot with buildings on Snickers Gap turnpike road, undivided ½ of house in Mudtown. Dower of 194a including mansion from Little River tract. Divisors: Chas. TURNER, David HIXSON. Gives plat.

4B:375 Date: 11 Mar 1834 RtCt: 11 Mar 1834
John WEADON, Eli McVEIGH & Wm. C. PALMER. Bond on WEADON as constable.

4B:375 Date: 17 Feb 1834 RtCt: 11 Mar 1834
Edward M. BAKER to William G. NEWMAN. Trust for debt to Henry F. LUCKETT using household items. Delv. pr order 4 Mar 1835.

4B:377 Date: 4 Aug 1832 RtCt: 21 Aug 1832/12 Mar 1834
L. P. W. BALCH of FredMd to Robert COE of Ldn. B/S of 42¾a with stone mill (from defaulted trust of Feb 1826 from Elizabeth C. COE now TRIPLETT). Wit: Burnard PURSEL, Robert CURRY, Wm. COE Jr., Wm. BARR, Wm. COE. Delv. to COE 8 Apr 1835.

4B:378 Date: 20 Feb 1834 RtCt: 12 Mar 1834
James Battaile LEWIS (adult heir) and Thomas A. MOORE (Commr. in suit of Feb 1834 of Joseph LEWIS agst Admx Mary LEWIS and infant heirs of John H. LEWIS dec'd – Fisher Ames, Charles Henry, John Berkley, Mary Jane, Magnus Muse, Joseph Newton, Robert and William Hierome Thomas LEWIS) to Joseph LEWIS. B/S of 140a where Jeremiah PURDOM resided in Mar 1822, part of Piedmont. Delv. pr order 8 Aug 1834. Ackn. of MOORE in JeffVa.

4B:379 Date: 20 Sep 1833 RtCt: 12 Mar 1834
David FULTON & wife Phebe of Ldn to Charles L. POWELL of Ldn. Trust for debt to Robert FULTON using 1/5th int. in 145a of father David FULTON Sr. dec'd subject to widow's dower, adj Cuthbert POWELL, Herod THOMAS. Wit: Thomas M. COLSTON, Cuthbert POWELL. Delv. to Robert S. FULTON 12 Nov 1835.

4B:380 Date: 19 Feb 1834 RtCt: 12 Mar 1834
Joseph LEWIS & wife Elizabeth O. of Ldn to Daniel BOLAND of Ldn.
B/S of 139a adj BOLAND, John CRIM, Simon SHOEMAKER. Wit:
William BENTON, Edward HALL. Delv. to BOLAND 30 Jun 1835.

4B:382 Date: 24 Feb 1834 RtCt: 12 Mar 1834
John RICHARDSON & wife Mary of FredVa to John P. SMART of
Ldn. B/S of int. in "Big Spring Mill" (cnvy/b George M.
CHICHESTER). Delv. to SMART 1 Jan 1835.

4B:383 Date: 11 Mar 1834 RtCt: 12 Mar 1834
John MOSS of Ldn to Jacob WILDMAN of Ldn. B/S of 2a adj MOSS,
Murphey C. SHUMATE.

4B:384 Date: 14 Mar 1834 RtCt: 14 Mar 1834
Ludwell LEE of Ldn to Ellen M. R. LEE. Gift of slaves Betsy w/o
Philip BOOTH & their daus. Betsy & Jane.

4B:384 Date: __ 1834 RtCt: 15 Mar 1834
George W. HENRY (insolvent debtor) to Sheriff Ariss BUCKNER.
B/S of int. in 100a of William FOX dec'd nr Wtfd (life estate subject
to lease for years to Jesse OXLEY) and undivided 1/4th int. in
"Ogden farm" of John HAMILTON dec'd subject to life estate of
widow Winefred HAMILTON.

4B:385 Date: 14 Mar 1834 RtCt: 17 Mar 1834
William RIGHT/WRIGHT of Ldn to Samuel PUGH/PEUGH (trustee
for infant Ury Jane BROWN) of Ldn. Trust for debt to BROWN using
farm animals, household items. Delv. pr order 20 Sep 1834.

4B:386 Date: 20 Jan 1834 RtCt: 20 Mar 1820
John FRED & wife Mary, William LIVINGSTON & wife Dardania of
Belmont Co Ohio to John TOLBERT of Ldn. B/S of 1/9th int. in 100a
cnvy/b Samuel BUTCHER to Samuel TORBERT dec'd May 1790
(dev. by Samuel to father Thomas TORBERT dec'd & wife
Elizabeth, then to their 9 children – John FRED & Dardania w/o
LIVINGSTON desc from Thomas FRED Sr. dec'd who m. Elizabeth
TORBERT d/o Thomas & Elizabeth) adj Thomas A. HEREFORD.
Wit: Ammon EWERS, Jane MINK. Delv. to TORBERT 27 Jan 1835.

4B:387 Date: 21 Mar 1834 RtCt: 24 Mar 1834
Robert RUSSELL of Ldn to Henry FRAZIER of FredMd. B/S of 211a
- tract adj Anthony AMOND, __ SHAFER, __ CORDELL, Peter
COMPHER, and tract on W side of Cotoctin Mt. adj Peter FRY. Wit:
Thos. J. MARLOW, Wm. Slater.

4B:389 Date: 21 Mar 1834 RtCt: 24 Mar 1834
Henry FRAZIER of FredMd to Henson MARLOW of FredMd. Trust
for debt to Robert RUSSELL using 196a from above. Wit: Thos. J.
MARLOW, Wm. SLATER.

4B:390 Date: 4 Mar 1834 RtCt: 24 Mar 1834
Conrad R. DOWELL and James McILHANY of Ldn to Robert
RUSSELL of Ldn. B/S of 3/7th of "Taylortown tract" (from defaulted

trust of Dec 1827 from Conrad BITZER). Delv. to RUSSELL 15 Dec 1834.

4B:391 Date: 24 Mar 1834 RtCt: 24 Mar 1834
William ELGIN of Ldn to Ignatius ELGIN of Ldn. B/S of undivided int. dev. by Gustavus ELGIN dec'd to sons Francis and William. Delv. to Ignatius 30 Jul 1835.

4B:392 Date: 18 Jan 1834 RtCt: 24 Mar 1834
Edwin C. BROWN to Phebe R. DONOHOE. Release of trust of Feb 1825, DBk III:339, and of Feb 1826, DBk LLL:377.

4B:392 Date: 22 Mar 1834 RtCt: 26 Mar 1834
Joseph LESLIE of Ldn to Samuel D. LESLIE of Ldn. B/S of 33a adj Samuel on great road. Delv. to grantee 3 Dec 1855.

4B:393 Date: 17 Feb 1834 RtCt: 29 Mar 1834
Jacob WATERS of Ldn to Amos JANNEY of Ldn. Trust for debt to John JANNEY using 40a adj dower of widow of John WALTMAN, SLATES & EVERHEART, heirs of Jacob EVERHART; and ¼ of 30a dower to widow of John WALTMAN (cnvy/b John MOORE & Jacob EVERHEART Aug 1827), and 30a & 7a (cnvy/b David WALTMAN Jan 1829), and David WALTMAN's int. in widow's dower.

4B:395 Date: 2 Jul 1833 RtCt: 27 Mar 1834
Amos JANNEY & wife Mary Ann of Ldn to Susannah C. ROWLES of Ldn. B/S of 20a (prch/o Adam HOUSHOLDER) adj Daniel COOPER, Curtis GRUBB. Wit: Thomas J. MARLOW, Mortimer McILHANEY.

4B:397 Date: 9 Jan 1834 RtCt: 27 Mar 1834
Thomas J. ROWLES (s/o Candall ROWLES) & wife Edy of Anne Arundel Md to Amos JANNEY of Ldn. B/S of 1/9th of 4/15th of 496a of Edmund JENNINGS dec'd on E side of short hill. Wit: Rich'd PHELPS, Joel HOPKINS.

4B:398 Date: 20 Feb 1834 RtCt: 27 Mar 1834
Amos JANNEY of Ldn to Jerome B. WRIGHT and John EVERHEART of Ldn. B/S of 4a (part of prch/o of William ELLZEY) on E side of short hill adj Sam. BAKER, Jo. DAVIS, Wm. KEYS, A. JANNEY. Delv. to WRIGHT 14 Mar 1836.

4B:399 Date: 27 Feb 1834 RtCt: 27 Mar 1834
John L. HATCHER and Rachel HATCHER wd/o Noah HATCHER dec'd of Ldn to Thomas E. HATCHER of Ldn. B/S of ½ of tract cnvy/b William BEANS dec'd to Noah HATCHER dec'd. Delv. to Thomas E. HATCHER 16 Dec 1834.

4B:400 Date: 15 Apr 1830 RtCt: 28 Mar 1834
Elizabeth Taliaferro BRYARLY w/o Samuel BRYARLY of FredVa to daus. Ann Sarah Armistead of Fqr and Frances Barne Taliafero. Gift of 2/3 of 200a "Femeu?" (1/3rd to each) adj Wm. C. FITZHUGH, Vincent MORSE, Sydnor BAILEY, Lawrence BATTAILE, J. HICKS, __ COLSTON. Francis to pay annual annuity, Elizabeth can live with

her in Upperville area if Samuel dies. Wit: Robt. L. ARMISTEAD, John CARTER.

4B:402   Date: 27 Mar 1834   RtCt: 28 Mar 1834
Jonah NICHOLS & wife Fanny of Ldn to Yardley TAYLOR & Mahlon K. TAYLOR. Trust for debt to Mahlon WALTERS using 213a adj __ SANDS, Conrad R. DOWELL, William NICHOLS, William BROWN. Wit: David REECE, Timothy TAYLOR. Delv. pr order 3 Sep 1837.

4B:404   Date: 28 Mar 1834   RtCt: 28 Mar 1834
Enoch G. DAY of Ldn to Isaac EATON of Ldn. Trust for debt to John W. DAY of Anne Arundel Co Md, Henry F. LUCKETT of Ldn using household items.

4B:406   Date: 12 Jun 1833   RtCt: 28 Mar 1834
Betsey TEBBS of Dumfries PrWm to son Foushe TEBBS & wife Margaret of Ldn. Release of trust of Aug 1824 in PrWm.

4B:407   Date: 27 Mar 1834   RtCt: 28 Mar 1834
Mahlon WALTERS & wife Elizabeth of Ldn to Jonah NICHOLS of Ldn. B/S of 213a adj Mahlon K. TAYLOR, William NICHOLS, turnpike road, Conrad R. DOWELL, William BROWN. Wit: David REESE, Timothy TAYLOR. Delv. to NICHOLS 26 Mar 1836.

4B:409   Date: 29 Mar 1834   RtCt: 29 Mar 1834
Michael MORALLEE of Lsbg to Richard H. HENDERSON of Lsbg. Trust for debt to merchants Samuel B. LARMOUR & Joseph MANDEVILLE of AlexDC using house (tavern) & lot on N side of Market St in Lsbg now occup. by Samuel HARPER and house & lot on N side of Loudoun St occup. by MORALLEE. Delv. to HENDERSON 30 Mar 1835.

4B:410   Date: __   RtCt: 14 Apr 1834
Patrick B. MILHOLLEN/MILHOLLAND & wife Malinda of Ldn to Mathew MITCHELL of Lsbg. B/S of part of Lot #16 in Lsbg adj James GARNER. Wit: Saml M. EDWARDS, Abiel JENNERS.

4B:412   Date: 12 Mar 1834   RtCt: 31 Mar 1834
William GREGG & wife Elizabeth of Ldn and Mary GREGG, Phebe GREGG, Asenith GREGG, Aaron GREGG & wife Elizabeth, Mahlon GREGG & wife Emily to Silas GARRETT. B/S of 10a Lot #1 & 6a Lot #2 in div. of Joseph GREGG dec'd. Wit: Notley C. WILLIAMS, Edward B. GRADY. Delv. to Silas GARRETT 28 Mar 1837.

4B:414   Date: 12 Nov 1833   RtCt: 31 Mar 1834
Lewis GRIGSBY & wife Malinda of Ldn to Andrew HEATH of Ldn. B/S of 115a adj John TURLEY's spring branch, road from *Babtist* meeting house to Gum Spring, John SPENCER, Benjamin JAMES. Wit: Charles LEWIS, John BAYLY.

4B:415   Date: 12 Feb 1834   RtCt: 1 Apr 1834
Solomon RUSE & wife Tabitha of Ldn to Thomas ROGERS of Ldn. B/S of 15a adj John IREY, Elijah HOLMES, Hamilton ROGERS,

George GRIMES. Wit: David REESE, James McILHANEY. Delv. to ROGERS 17 Jul 1837.

4B:416   Date: 1 Apr 1834   RtCt: 2 Apr 1834
George RICHARDS of Ldn to John A. BINNS of Ldn (who requested cnvy/t James SINCLAIR of Ldn). B/S of __a from decree in Sup. Ct. Winchester and household items (from defaulted trust of Nov 1827 from Moses BUTLER, DBk PPP:190). Delv. to James SINCLAIR 12 Aug 1836.

4B:417   Date: 4 Apr 1834   RtCt: 4 Apr 1834
Charles T. MAGILL (insolvent debtor) to Sheriff Ariss BUCKNER. B/S of int. in real estate of father Charles MAGILL Sr. dec'd and of brother Archibald MAGILL dec'd, and int. in 14a in Hampshire Co. adj __ ROMNEY and int. as tenant by curtesy to land dev. to his wife Mary D. MAGILL from her father William BRONAUGH Sr. dec'd and land on Big Kanawha in Mason Co Va.

4B:418   Date: 1 Apr 1833   RtCt: 11 Apr 1834
Amos JANNEY & wife Mary Ann of Ldn to John DAVIS of Ldn. B/S of 6¾a (prch/o William ELLZEY) adj Benjamin GRUBB, Philip EVERHEART, __ BAKER, Wm. KEYS. Wit: George W. SHAWEN, Thomas J. MARLOW.

4B:420   Date: 11 Apr 1834   RtCt: 11 Apr 1834
Sidney H. SHAW of Ldn to George RICHARDS of Ldn. Trust for debt to Henry T. HARRISON using undivided int. in house & lot on SE corner of Loudoun & King Sts in Lsbg now occupied by William H. JACOBS (from estate of John SHAW dec'd). Delv. to RICHARDS 3 Dec 1845.

4B:421   Date: 18 Mar 1834   RtCt: 12 Apr 1834
Nathan GREGG & wife Susan R. of Ldn to Absalom BEANS of Ldn. Trust for debt to John L. HATCHER using 34a on S fork of Kittocton Creek (part of Lot #3 in div. of Samuel GREGG dec'd allotted to Thomas E. HATCHER & wife) adj BEANS, and 38a Lot #4 from div. Wit: David REESE, James McILHANEY.

4B:423   Date: 20 Dec 1833   RtCt: 14 Apr 1834
Samuel THOMPSON & wife Amelia of Ldn to Thomas & Joshua HATCHER of Ldn. Trust for debt to John PANCOAST Jr. using 62a on N fork of Goose Creek. Wit: Timothy TAYLOR, David REECE.

4B:425   Date: 8 Apr 1834   RtCt: 14 Apr 1834
William C. BROWN to V. V. PURCELL. Trust for debt to Jonah NICHOLS Exor of Rebecca LOVE dec'd using 142a prch/o LOVE. Delv. to NICHOLS 26 Mar 1836.

4B:426   Date: 26 Mar 1834   RtCt: 14 Apr 1834
French THOMPSON & wife Nancy of Ldn to Greenbarry THOMPSON. Trust for debt to Mary Ann SINGLETON using 100a leased land (granted 1793 by Denny FAIRFAX to Henry STICKLE, now in poss. of French) and farm animals, farm and household

items. Wit: Cuthbert POWELL, Thomas M. COLSTON. Delv. pr order 15 Jul 1834.

4B:428   Date: 12 Apr 1834   RtCt: 14 Apr 1834
Joshua B. OVERFIELD & wife Anna of Ldn to Samuel DAWSON of Ldn. B/S of undivided 1/11th share of Philip RAZOR as heir of George RAZOR dec'd (cnvy/b by John H. BUTCHER Jun 1819) adj George PRICE, Sarah CHICHESTER, Truman GORE. Wit: Roger CHEW, Thomas M. COLSTON.

4B:429   Date: 17 May 1832   RtCt: 14 Apr 1834
Samuel HOUGH & wife Jane G. of Ldn to John WAR of Ldn. B/S of 7a and adj ¾a lot (cnvy/b Zachariah DULANEY & Noble S. BRADEN trustees of Thomas DONALDSON Apr 1827) adj __ JENNERS, Nicholas MONEY. Wit: Joshua PUSEY, George W. SHAWEN. Delv. to WAR 28 Aug 1834.

4B:430   Date: 29 Mar 1834   RtCt: 14 Apr 1834
Jesse GOVER & wife Miriam G. of Ldn to Ephraim SCHOOLEY of Ldn. B/S of house & ¼a lot in Wtfd former prop. of John MORROW (cnvy/b Richard H. HENDERSON Mar 1830). Wit: Chas. B. HAMILTON Jr., David REECE. Delv. to SCHOOLEY 30 Jul 1842.

4B:431   Date: 14 Apr 1834   RtCt: 14 Apr 1834
William HOGE of Ldn to Ludwell LUCKETT & wife Ann C. of Ldn. Release of trust of Nov 1827 for debt to Isaac NICHOLS Sr. using interest in estates of William BRONAUGH dec'd & his son Jeremiah W. BRONAUGH dec'd.

4B:432   Date: 30 Jan 1834   RtCt: 14 Apr 1834
Lydia PATTERSON wd/o Robert PATTERSON dec'd of Fqr to Samuel RECTOR of Fqr. LS of 1a in Millsville (during her lifetime, where Robert dec'd formerly lived) adj RECTOR, Wm. BENTON, John LLOYD. Wit: Asa ROGERS.

4B:433   Date: 20 Mar 1834   RtCt: 15 Apr 1834
John C. GREEN (f/o Triplett C.) to Edward HALL. Trust for debt to Triplett C. GREEN (int. under will of John CAMPBELL dec'd late of Frederick Co in 60a "Stone house place" in Frederick Co from Dr. Taliaferro STRIBLING, assigned as loan) using Negro man James, horse, household items.

4B:435   Date: 4 Mar 1834   RtCt: 15 Apr 1834
John C. GREEN of Ldn to James JOHNSTON of Ldn. B/S of ¾a (2 lots with houses occup. by GREEN, prch/o Josiah GREGG and JOHNSTON) in Union and 7a lot on NW side of Union (prch/o Moses BROWN). Delv. pr order 8 Feb 1836.

4B:436   Date: 15 Feb 1834   RtCt: 15 Apr 1834
Andrew J. HOSKINSON of Ldn to sons Robert J. HOSKINSON and Thomas W. HOSKINSON. Gift of all his personal estate – farm animals, farm and household items.

4B:437   Date: 28 Mar 1834   RtCt: 14 Apr 1834
John L. HATCHER to Thomas E. HATCHER Exor. of Noah
HATCHER dec'd. Receipt and acknowledgement.

4B:437   Date: 10 Apr 1827   RtCt: 15 Apr 1834
Francis TRIPLETT of Fqr to Presley SAUNDERS of Ldn. B/S of ¾a
lot leased to David WATHERLY nr Lsbg between lot of Isaac free
man of colour and lot he sold to Jacob WILLIAMS free man of colour
but now belongs to Gen. Geo. RUST. Wit: Wm. CLINE, Peter
GREGG.

4B:438   Date: 17 Apr 1834   RtCt: 17 Apr 1834
William W. KITZMILLER of Lsbg to John A. BINNS of Lsbg. Trust for
debt to George FOSTER of Lsbg using lot on Loudoun St. in Lsbg
(cnvy/b John A. BINNS surv. trustee of John A. BINNS & Josiah L.
DREAN from John CRIDLER for benefit of KITZMILLER) and int. in
"tan yard" lot from father Martin KITZMILLER dec'd. Delv. to
FOSTER 8 Sep 1834.

4B:439   Date: 14 Dec 1833   RtCt: 18 Apr 1834
Benjamin BROWN & wife Anne of Ldn to Archibald MAINS of Ldn.
B/S of 1a on Catocton Mt. adj BROWN, MAINS, Ellis WILLIAMS.
Wit: Henry T. HARRISON, Presley CORDELL.

4B:441   Date: 22 Feb 1834   RtCt: 18 Apr 1834
Andrew S. ANDERSON & wife Eleanor of Ldn to William NETTLE of
Ldn. B/S of lot in Wtfd (cnvy/b Wm. PAXSON) adj John WILLIAMS,
Edward DORSEY, __ SMALLWOOD. Wit: Joshua PUSEY, S.
HOUGH. Delv. to NETTLE 19 Jun 1835.

4B:442   Date: 30 Dec 1833   RtCt: 21 Apr 1834
Joseph LEWIS & wife Elizabeth O. of Ldn to John DIXON of Ldn.
B/S of 11a (cnvy/b Fleming HIXSON) adj __ FAWLEY, George
MARLOW. Wit: William BENTON, Benjamin GRAYSON. Delv. to
DIXON 28 Nov 1835.

4B:444   Date: 28 Dec 1833   RtCt: 28 Apr 1834
Samuel McPHERSON & wife Mary of Ldn to Isaac STEER of Ldn.
Trust for debt to Isaac STEER using 7a part of McPHERSON's mill
on Catocton Creek and 5a wood land on Cotocton Creek, STEER,
William PAXSON. Wit: David REESE, Saml. HOUGH. Delv. to
STEER 7 Aug 1835.

4B:445   Date: 21 Apr 1834   RtCt: 28 Apr 1834
Jacob FADELY & wife Mary of Ldn to Mary A. NEWTON of Ldn. B/S
of lot on W side of Liberty St in Lsbg adj William HEAD, __
CALDWELL. Wit: Wilson C. SELDEN Jr., Presley CORDELL. Delv.
to NEWTON 21 Feb 1852.

4B:447   Date: 7 Apr 1834   RtCt: 29 Apr 1834
George TAVENER of Ldn to Richard O. GRAYSON of Ldn. Trust for
debt to James JOHNSTON using farm animals, farm and household
items.

4B:448   Date: 28 Apr 1834   RtCt: 29 Apr 1834
John A. BINNS of Ldn to Charles BINNS of Ldn. Assignment of int. in deed of trust by John A. BINNS to A. KITZMILLER & C. W. BINNS for benefit of John ROSE, DBk 4B:333. Delv. to BINNS 1 Aug 1836.

4B:448   Date: 1 May 1834   RtCt: 1 May 1834
Charles BINNS of Ldn to Richard H. HENDERSON and Samuel M. EDWARDS of Ldn. Trust for debt to Samuel M. BOSS of Ldn using 46a W of Lsbg on Lsbg & Snickers Gap turnpike road and Richard H. HENDERSON, George RHODES, Christopher FRYE.

4B:449   Date: 2 May 1834   RtCt: 2 May 1834
Miriam HOLE (insolvent debtor) of Ldn to Sheriff Ariss BUCKNER. B/S of dower which Levi HOLE prch/o Exors of Jacob JANNEY dec'd, DBk RR:052 and DBk LL:422).

4B:450   Date: 9 Apr 1834   RtCt: 9 May 1834
William J. BRONAUGH (Guardian of his infant children) of DC and Francis W. LUCKETT of Ldn to Ludwell LUCKETT of Ldn. B/S of children's int. in 179a (Jeremiah W. BRONAUGH dec'd in Dec 1826 cnvy/t Francis W. LUCKETT int. from father's estate for payment of debts and 1/7th balance at mother's death to children of BRONAUGH, ct. decreed to sell land). Wit: James GETTYS, Thomas D. GOZZLER.

4B:452   Date: 9 May 1834   RtCt: 9 May 1834
Isaac CONWELL of Muskingum Co Ohio to John NORRIS of Ldn. LS of house & lot on NW corner of Markett & Back Sts in Lsbg. Wit: Arch. M. KITZMILLER.

4B:453   Date: __ Jan 1834   RtCt: 12 May 1834
William JAMES to Jonathan BEARD. Trust for William MERSHON & William SAFFER as security for bond to Rich'd H. HENDERSON using 133a late prop. of Jacob JAMES dec'd adj Timothy PADGETT, Reubin SETTLES' heirs.

4B:454   Date: 17 Jun 1833   RtCt: 12 May 1834
James McILHANY & wife Margaret of Ldn to Jonathan HEATON of Ldn. B/S of 23a adj McILHANY, HEATON. Wit: John WHITE, William CLENDENING. Delv. to HEATON 25 Jun 1834.

4B:455   Date: 12 May 1834   RtCt: 12 May 1834
William HEATH of Ldn to Archibald M. KITZMILLER. Trust for debt to Samuel HARPER using Negro woman Ann now in poss. of HEATH & her son George.

4B:457   Date: 5 Nov 1833   RtCt: 12 May 1834
David LOVETT of Ldn to Simon SHOEMAKER Sr., Michael WIARD & Daniel POTTERFIELD (trustees of Presbyterian Church in German Settlement). B/S of 2a adj LOVETT, Daniel HOUSHOLDER, Mary BONTZ (except ground where BONTZ's chimney now stands). Wit: Philip EVERHEART, Adam

POTTERFIELD, Daniel MILLER Jr. Delv. to POTTERFIELD 12 Sep 1836.

4B:457 Date: 12 May 1834 RtCt: 12 May 1834
Joshua HATCHER of Ldn to William HATCHER of Ldn. B/S of 1/5th of ½ int. in 134a farm where Rebecca HATCHER died adj Goose Creek meeting house, George FAIRHIRST, Yardly TAYLOR, Jesse HIRST.

4B:458 Date: 23 Jan 1834 RtCt: 12 May 1834
David ORRISON. Oath as Lt. in 56th Reg of infantry 6th Brig 2nd Div Va Militia from 30 Nov 1833.

4B:459 Date: 18 Sep 1833 RtCt: 13 May 1834
George GIBSON. Oath as Capt. in Va Militia.

4B:459 Date: 26 Mar 1834 RtCt: 19 Apr 1834
Hamilton STEWART & wife Jane Ann of Brownsville Fayette Co Pa to Allen KRAMER of Pittsburg Pa. B/S of Lot #35, #36, #37 & #38 (3a) in Lsbg (allotted Jane Ann STEWART and James William STEWART & wife Paulina in right of mother Rebecca d/o William WRIGHT, also see DBk TT:135 and XXX:381). Wit: Wm. JACKMAN, Robert ROGERS.

4B:461 Date: 21 Apr 1834 RtCt: 13 May 1834
Isaac FRY & wife Hannah of Ldn to Benjamin JACKSON of Ldn. Trust for debt to Stephen McPHERSON and George KEEN of Ldn using 1a where FRY lives (cnvy/b Isaac COWGILL). Wit: Edward HALL, Roger CHEW. Delv. to JACKSON 10 Aug 1836.

4B:463 Date: 6 Feb 1834 RtCt: 13 May 1834
John MOORE & wife Catharine of Ldn to William JACOB and Emanuel WENNER of Ldn. B/S of 107½a (cnvy/b Christopher BURNHOUSE Apr 1815) adj __ MULL. Wit: William SLATER, William CLENDENING. Delv. pr order 12 Aug 1837.

4B:464 Date: 26 Sep 1833 RtCt: 13 May 1834
Lott TAVENER & wife Phebe of Ldn to Samuel McGETH/McGEATH of Ldn. B/S of 18a on Beaverdam Creek adj old Snickers Gap road, heirs of Samuel NICHOLS, Jonathan TAVENER, __ DILLON, Uniontown road, John PANCOAST Jr., David YOUNG. Wit: David REESE, Timothy TAYLOR. Delv. to MEGEATH 22 May 1844.

4B:466 Date: 16 May 1834 RtCt: 16 May 1834
Thomas ROGERS of Ldn (as Commr. in Sup. Ct. suit of Apr 1834 of John JANNEY agst Alexander CORDELL & wife Diana and Zachariah DULANEY) to John JANNEY of Ldn. B/S of 101a (cnvy/b Sandford RAMEY to Zachariah DULANY in trust for Diana CORDELL Feb 1828) adj Sandford RAMEY, Margaret SAUNDERS, George W. SHAWEN.

4B:466 Date: 2 May 1834 RtCt: 17 May 1834
Henry SAUNDERS and Adelia North SAUNDERS of New London, New London Co Connecticut to Presley SAUNDERS of Ldn. B/S of

lot with stone dwelling house on N side of Loudoun St in Lsbg (see DBk PPP:129) adj Michael MORRALLEE. Wit: Saml. G. J. DeCAMP, Jac. AMMEN.

4B:468 Date: 17 May 1834 RtCt: 19 May 1834
Presley SAUNDERS & wife Mary of Ldn to William TORRISON of Ldn. B/S of above lot. Wit: Henry T. HARRISON, Presley CORDELL. Delv. to TORRISON 13 May 1836.

4B:469 Date: 7 Mar 1834 RtCt: 19 May 1834
Thomas S. LEWIS of Ldn to John BOGER of Ldn. Trust for debt to Ann Jane Maria ADAMS of Ldn using farm animals, farm and household items. Wit: Geo. W. SHAWEN.

4B:470 Date: 21 Apr 1834 RtCt: 20 May 1834
Caroline ROWLES and Harriet ROWLES (ch/o Candas ROWLES) of Annerendle Co Md to Amos JANNEY of Ldn. B/S of undivided 2/9th of 4/15th int. in 496a farm of Edmund JENNINGS dec'd nr E side of short hill. Wit: William WARFIELD, Jas. B. LATIMER.

4B:471 Date: 17 May 1834 RtCt: 21 May 1834
George RUST & wife Maria C. of JeffVa to James MUNROE and Mordecai M. NOAH of NY City. Trust for debt to Uriah P. LEVY (Lt. in Navy) using 503a on Potomac adj Gen. T. MASON, and 42a nr Lsbg adj S. GRAY, S. G. McCABE, and 44a on road from Lsbg to Nolands Ferry adj Dr. SELDEN.

4B:475 Date: 6 Aug 1833 RtCt: 23 May 1834
James L. McKENNA of Ffx to Phillip R. FENDALL of WashDC. Trust for debt to dau Elizabeth Ann Fitzhugh Randolph McKENNA as her Guardian and Mrs. Portia HODGSON of AlexDC using Negro slaves Lucy aged 55y, Anna aged 28y and her children George aged 8y, Maria aged 6y and Abner aged 4y, Lucinda aged 26y and her children Nancy aged 9y, Henry aged 6y and Washington aged 2y, Charlotte aged 19y, Charles Cook aged 24y, Joe Cook aged 22y, and an orphan child named Eliza aged 8a (all are descendents of first named Lucy, and were a gift to Ann Fitzhugh Randolph the m/o Elizabeth Ann Fitzhugh Randolph McKENNA). Wit: Guy ATKINSON, Chs. A. ATKINSON, R. L. CAMPBELL, B. A. LEE, L. S. BECK, Richard HANDLEY. Delv. to FENDELL 22 Apr 1835.

4B:477 Date: 19 Apr 1833 RtCt: 27 May 1834
Charles B. ALEXANDER & wife Eliza of Breckenridge Co Ky to James RUST of Ldn and George RUST Jr. of JeffVa. B/S of 317a adj __ CARTER, __ GREENUP, __ CARR. Delv. to James RUST 16 Mar 1837.

4B:479 Date: 6 Mar 1834 RtCt: 30 May 1834
William BRADFIELD of Ldn to Samuel LODGE of Ldn. Release of trust of Mar 1832, DBk XXX:255, for benefit of suit of Loudoun CROZIER agst PENQUITE) using prop. of Susanna CARTER dec'd. Delv. to LODGE 7 Jan 1835.

4B:480   Date: 28 May 1834   RtCt: 29 May 1834
William W. KITZMILLER to Jared CHAMBLIN. Trust for Samuel M.
BOSS, James GARRISON, James GARNER, John MARTIN,
Michael MORRALLEE, John H. MONROE, Thomas ROGERS &
Samuel STERRET as endorsers on note to Joseph MEAD using
animals hides, wagon, Negro man Richard, the unexpired term of
Negro girl Matilda. Delv. to CHAMBLIN 27 Oct 1834.

4B:481   Date: 31 May 1834   RtCt: 31 May 1834
Samuel HALL to Ldn to Chas. SHREVE of Ldn. Trust for debt to
William HALL of Ldn using 81a adj Daniel LOVETT, __ CARR (dev.
by father William HALL dec'd).

4B:482   Date: 8 Apr 1834   RtCt: 2 Jun 1834
Jonah NICHOLS (Exor of Rebecca LOVE dec'd) of Ldn to William C.
BROWN of Ldn. B/S of 142a adj __ SMITH, BROWN, James LOVE.
Delv. to BROWN 6 Oct 1834.

4B:483   Date: 8 Nov 1833   RtCt: 2 Jun 1834
William NICHOLS & wife Cassandra of Ldn to Soloman RUSE of
Ldn. B/S of 70a on NW fork of Goose Creek adj Joseph TAVENER,
NICHOLS, __ GRIMES, __ HATCHER. Wit: James McILHANY,
David REECE. Delv. pr order 1 Sep 1841.

4B:485   Date: 2 May 1834   RtCt: 2 Jun 1834
John SMITLEY of Ldn to James & William HOEY of Ldn. BoS for
farm animals, household items.

4B:485   Date: 3 Jun 1834   RtCt: 3 Jun 1834
Samuel ROGERS of Ldn to Elijah HOLMES of Ldn. B/S of ½ of his
undivided 1/3rd int. in 215a "Valley tract" (see 4B:021).

4B:486   Date: 4 Jun 1834   RtCt: 4 Jun 1834
Elijah HOLMES & wife Elizabeth of Ldn to Samuel ROGERS of Ldn.
B/S of undivided 1/9th int., subject to life estate of Dinah ROGERS,
in 157a "valley tract" farm where Hamilton ROGERS dec'd resided
adj George GRIMES, Joseph TAVENER, Richard TAVENER. Wit:
Francis W. LUCKETT, Samuel M. EDWARDS.

4B:487   Date: 5 Jun 1834   RtCt: 5 Jun 1834
Jesse TIMMS and Richard H. HENDERSON of Lsbg to Samuel M.
BOSS of Lsbg. B/S of house & lot at King & Cornwell Sts in Lsbg
(from defaulted trust of Apr 1829 from William KING) adj Robert
BENTLEY, John JANNEY. Delv. to BOSS 15 Jul 1834.

4B:488   Date: 5 Jun 1834   RtCt: 5 Jun 1834
Samuel M. BOSS & wife Elizabeth F. to Jesse TIMMS and Rich'd H.
HENDERSON. Trust for debt to George CARTER of Oatlands using
above house & lot. Wit: Presley CORDELL, John H. McCABE. Delv.
to CARTER 6 Oct 1837.

4B:489   Date: 10 May 1834   RtCt: 5 Jun 1834
Taliafarro M. McILHANY & wife Ann of Ldn to John WRIGHT and
Mortimer McILHANY of Ldn. Trust for debt to of Ebenezer GRUBB

of Ldn using 400a (clear of incumberance of dower of Margaret McILHANY) dev. by father John McILHANY dec'd. Wit: John WHITE, William CLENDENNING. Delv. to E. GRUBB Exor. of Ebenezer GRUBB dec'd 27 Jun 1838.

4B:491   Date: 24 May 1834   RtCt: 9 Jun 1834
James S. EDWARDS. Oath as Lt. in 57th Reg of infantry 6th Brig 2nd Div Va Militia.

4B:491   Date: 13 May 1834   RtCt: 9 Jun 1834
Daniel COCKRILL. Oath as Colonel of 56th Reg of infantry 6th Brig 2nd Div Va Militia.

4B:491   Date: 7 Sep 1833   RtCt: 9 Jun 1834
Enos BEST. Oath as Captain in Va Militia.

4B:491   Date: 14 May 1834   RtCt: 9 Jun 1834
Thomas MERSHON. Oath as Lt. of infantry in Va Militia.

4B:491   Date: 16 May 1834   RtCt: 9 Jun 1834
Gabriel VANDEVANTER. Oath as Major in 56th Reg infantry 6th Brig 2nd Div Va Militia.

4B:492   Date: 15 May 1834   RtCt: 9 Jun 1834
Conrad R. DOWELL. Oath as 1st Lt. in 2nd Reg of Cavalry 6th Brig 2nd Div Va Militia.

4B:492   Date: 18 Apr 1834   RtCt: 9 Jun 1834
George RICHARDSON. Oath as Lt. in 132nd Reg 6th Brig Va Militia.

4B:492   Date: 15 May 1834   RtCt: 9 Jun 1834
Emanuel WALTMAN. Oath as Lt. Colonel of 56th Reg Va Militia.

4B:492   Date: 2 Jun 1834   RtCt: 9 Jun 1834
John H. McCABE & wife Margaret H. D. of Ldn to Samuel M. EDWARDS of Ldn. Trust for debt to Samuel M. BOSS using 5a and adj 29a nr Lsbg, 8a (less ¼a sold to James STEADMAN) and 20a adj Wtfd (see DBk XXX:079 [?]), 2½a lot on Market St in Lsbg, undivided 1/3rd int. in lots held by mother Mrs. Jane McCABE as dower from Henry McCABE dec'd. Wit: Wilson C. SELDEN, Presley CORDELL. Delv. to S. M. BOSS 13 Jul 1834.

4B:494   Date: 2 Jun 1834   RtCt: 9 Jun 1834
John H. McCABE of Ldn to Saml. M. EDWARDS of Ldn. Trust for benefit of his wife Margaret H. D. using Negro woman slave Susan until she is 25y old, household items.

4B:495   Date: 16 Jan 1834   RtCt: 9 Jun 1834
James ROGERS & wife Martha late HAWLING of Ldn to Hamilton ROGERS of Ldn. B/S of 127a Lot #4 in div. of estate of William HAWLING dec'd, DBk QQQ:252 [249]) and undivided int. in 89a Lot #1 assigned to brother William HAWLING, and undivided int. in 20a Lot #5 assigned to brother William HAWLING now dec'd. Wit: Abner GIBSON, Asa ROGERS.

4B:496 Date: 9 Jun 1834 RtCt: 9 Jun 1834
William ROSE Jr., William ROSE & John T. SIMPSON. Bond on
William Jr. as constable.

4B:497 Date: 17 May 1834 RtCt: 9 Jun 1834
John LLOYD & wife Harriet/Anne H. of AlexDC to Charles L.
POWELL & wife Silena (d/o LLOYD) of Ldn. Gift of 28a nr Mdbg adj
__ RECTOR, Goose Creek (cnvy/b trustee Richard H.
HENDERSON Jun 1826).

4B:498 Date: 17 May 1834 RtCt: 17 May 1834
George RICHARDS of Ldn to Lloyd NOLAND (pr request of Charles
G. EDWARDS) of Ldn. B/S of int. rents from Nolands Ferry and 50a
adj Ferry and rents from nearby island (from defaulted trust of Jun
1832 from Thomas S. HAMERSLY for debt to EDWARDS, DBk
YYY:143). Delv. pr order 8 Dec 1838.

4B:499 Date: 9 Jun 1834 RtCt: 9 Jun 1834
William HEATH of Ldn to Fleming HIXON of Ldn. Trust for debt to
William HOLMES using undivided int. in 110a derived by marriage
with Diadama PAXSON wd/o of William PAXSON Jr. dec'd & dau. of
David LACEY dec'd, adj Euphemia MANNING, Isaac
VANDEVANTER, Joshua PUSEY. Delv. to HOLMES 26 Feb 1835.

4B:500 Date: 7 Jun 1834 RtCt: 9 Jun 1834
Enoch G. DAY of Ldn to Robert T. LUCKETT of Ldn. Trust for debt
to Henry F. LUCKETT using horses, right in Mt. Gilead school
house, farm items, crops. Delv. pr order 26 Sep 1834.

4B:501 Date: 24 May 1834 RtCt: 9 Jun 1834
Conrad BITZER and Jesse SILCOTT of Ldn to Jacob SILCOTT of
Ldn. Release of trust of Apr 1827 to BITZER using 65a.

4B:502 Date: 8 Mar 1834 RtCt: 9 Jun 1834
Catherine NISEWANGER of Ldn to Henry N. HOLMES, John W.
HOLMES, Elizabeth E. HOLMES, Jos. D. HOLMES, Jacob F.
HOLMES, James A. HOLMES & Edward C. HOLMES heirs of
Catharine HOLMES dec'd. B/S of int. in 14a from div. of estate of
Henry NISEWANGER.

4B:503 Date: 9 Jun 1834 RtCt: 9 Jun 1834
Thomas J. MARLOW. DoE for slave Moses Johnson aged abt 32y.

4B:504 Date: 9 Jun 1834 RtCt: 9 Jun 1834
Edward THOMPSON, Harrison RUSSELL & Jacob WALTMAN.
Bond on THOMPSON as constable.

4B:504 Date: 9 Jun 1834 RtCt: 9 Jun 1834
Samuel WALTMAN of Ldn to Jacob WATERS of Ldn. B/S of 38½a
Lot #2 from div. of John WALTMAN dec'd, and int. in dower land of
mother after her death.

4B:505 Date: 1 Mar 1834 RtCt: 10 Jun 1834
Benjamin SHREVE and Wesley McPHERSON. Division from ct.
case – 122a Lot #1 to heirs of Chas. THRIFT dec'd; 95a Lot #2 to

Benjamin SHREVE. Divisors: John LITTLETON, John M. WILSON, George RHODES. To remain in effect unless infant defendants within 6m of attaining age show cause to the contrary. Gives plat.

4B:507 Date: 11 Jun 1834 RtCt: 11 Jun 1834
James CAYLOR, John J. COLEMAN, William WHALEY & William MERSHON. Bond on CAYLOR as constable.

4C:001 Date: 11 Jun 1834 RtCt: 11 Jun 1834
John ATTWELL to Charles WRIGHT. Trust for debt to W. & A. WRIGHT using 1/12th int. in 141a where Jesse ATTWELL lives, adj Abraham SKILLMAN Sr., Mrs. Narsisa GHEEN, Philip VANSICKLER. Wit: John SIMPSON, Robert COE, E. HAMMAT.

4C:002 Date: 24 Feb 1834 RtCt: 13 Jun 1834
Gideon HOUSHOLDER of Ldn to Curtis GRUBB of Ldn. Release of trust of Sep 1830 for debt to Adam HOUSHOLDER & wife Sarah of Clark Co Ohio. Wit: John HEATON, John JUDY. Delv. to GRUBB 3 Aug 1835.

4C:004 Date: 17 May 1834 RtCt: 16 Jun 1834
Presley SAUNDERS & wife Mary of Ldn to Simon SMALE of Ldn. B/S of lot adj SMALE (prch/o Henry SAUNDERS May 1834). Wit: Henry T. HARRISON, Presley CORDELL.

4C:005 Date: 10 May 1834 RtCt: 18 Jun 1834
Stephen T. CONARD & wife Vashti of Ldn to Thomas S. STONE of Ldn. B/S of 12a (sold by Commr. Joshua OSBURN for heirs of James NICHOLS the elder dec'd reserving water rights for Adah CUNARD) adj Jefferson C. THOMAS, Samuel LODGE, Thomas STONE's tanyard, heirs of Edward CUNARD. Wit: Roger CHEW, Thomas M. COLSTON. Delv. to STONE 31 Jan 1835.

4C:007 Date: 19 Jun 1834 RtCt: 19 Jun 1834
Samuel McPHERSON & wife Mary to William B. STEER and William H. HOUGH. Trust for debt to Joshua PUSEY, John & Daniel WINE (Exors of Jacob WINE dec'd and Catharine WINE dec'd), William STEER, Washington MYRES, John STATLER, Henry RUSSELL, Israel McGARVICK, Saml. JARBO, Jacob CRIM, David SHRIVER, John GRAY, Jacob SHRIVER & John WILLIAMS using 2a and mill (prch/o Isaac STEER) abt 2m NW of Wtfd. Wit: George W. SHAWEN, C. B. HAMILTON Jr. Delv. to STEER 9 May 1835.

4C:012 Date: 19 Jun 1834 RtCt: 19 Jun 1834
Samuel McPHERSON to Jonah STEER. Trust for Wm. B. STEER as security on note to Washington MYRES, Wm. RUSSELL & William H. HOUGH as security on bank notes using household items. Delv. to Jonah STEER 14 Apr 1835.

4C:013 Date: 19 Jun 1834 RtCt: 19 Jun 1834
Samuel McPHERSON & wife Mary to William B. STEER & William H. HOUGH. Trust for debt to Farmers & Mechanic Bank using interest in Wtfd Mill and 3a lot with mansion prch/o jointly with

Edward BOND in 1832 of Thomas PHILLIPS. Wit: George W. SHAWEN, Charles B. HAMILTON. Delv. to STEER 9 May 1835.

4C:016   Date: 23 Jan 1834   RtCt: 20 Jun 1834
James GARRISON & wife Elizabeth of Ldn to Charles A. JOHNSTON of Ldn. B/S of lot on Market St in Lsbg adj jail lot, church lot, Edward HAINES. Wit: A. M. KITZMILLER, Rob. BENTLEY, Wilson C. SELDEN Jr., Presley CORDELL. Delv. to JOHNSTON 27 Jun 1835.

4C:017   Date: 24 Jan 1834   RtCt: 20 Jun 1834
Charles A. JOHNSTON to Archibald M. KITZMILLER. Trust for debt to James GARRISON using above lot. Wit: Rob. BENTLEY, Saml. J. TEBBS.

4C:019   Date: __ 1834   RtCt: 27 Jun 1834
Presley SAUNDERS, Everitt SAUNDERS & James RUST of Ldn to Samuel M. EDWARDS of Ldn. Release of trust of Dec 1825 for security as Committee on estate of Susanna ANSELL an idiot (see DBk NNN:149). Land has been sold to Isaac HARRIS.

4C:020   Date: 1 Mar 1834   RtCt: 27 Jun 1834
Samuel M. EDWARDS & wife Ann of Ldn to Isaac HARRIS of Ldn. B/S of lot with tannery on S side of Royal St in Lsbg (see DBk NNN:235). Wit: John H. McCABE, Presley CORDELL.

4C:022   Date: 1 Mar 1834   RtCt: 27 Jun 1834
Isaac HARRIS & wife Sarah of Ldn to Samuel M. EDWARDS of Ldn. B/S of house & lot on S side of Loudoun St (see DBk AA:170). Wit: Presley CORDELL, John H. McCABE. Delv. to EDWARDS 3 Aug 1837.

4C:024   Date: 1 May 1834   RtCt: 30 Jun 1834
Daniel WILSON & wife Rosanna and John ETHELL & wife Mary (wives are d/o Philip MOUL dec'd late of Ldn) of Licking Co Ohio to David CONARD of Ldn. B/S of undivided 1/5th of 28a (perfecting deed) where George MOUL f/o Philip now dec'd formerly lived (MOUL cnvy/t Anthony CONARD f/o David in 1812, DBk OO:318, who cnvy/t David). Wit: Edward CONNELLY, Jacob ROBB.

4C:026   Date: 8 May 1832   RtCt: 30 Jun 1834
Thomas CASTLEMAN & wife Martha P. late TAYLOR to James WHITE. Gift of int. in estate of Josiah WHITE dec'd (from trust to P. McCORMICK for debt to Martha P.) for benefit of Ann Eliza TAYLOR (w/o Geo. W. TAYLOR, d/o Josiah WHITE dec'd, dau-in-law of Martha P.) and her children. CoE for Martha P. in FredVa. Delv. to Josiah R. WHITE pr order 24 Apr 1837.

4C:028   Date: 16 May 1834   RtCt: 1 Jul 1834
Robert RAY and Nathaniel PRIME of NY City to George RUST Jr. of Harpers Ferry JeffVa late of Ldn. Release of trust of May 1824, DBk HHH:130. Wit: Oliver M. LOUNDS, James HOPSON.

4C:030   Date: 25 Jun 1834   RtCt: 2 Jul 1834
George RICKARD to Gideon HOUSHOLDER. Trust for debt to
George SLATER, Peter COMPHER, Daniel HOUSHOLDER,
Michael FRYE, George COOPER, Simon SHOEMAKER Sr., John
GEORGE & Philip BOGAR using 150a (cnvy/b John MARTIN Apr
1814). Wit: Seth D. ROBERTSON, George KABRICK, G. W.
GRIFFITH. Delv. to HOUSHOLDER 28 Aug 1835.

4C:032   Date: 21 Jun 1834   RtCt: 2 Jul 1834
Stephen GREGG, Smith GREGG & Thomas GREGG of Ldn to
Nathan GREGG & Gabriel VANDEVANTER of Ldn. Trust for debt to
David RUSE & Charles B. HAMILTON (Exors of Nathan GREGG
dec'd) using 172a cnvy/b Exors. Delv. to VANDEVANTER 18 Sep
1843.

4C:034   Date: 20 May 1834   RtCt: 2 Jul 1834
David RUSE & Charles B. HAMILTON (Exors of Nathan GREGG
dec'd) of Ldn to John BRADEN of Ldn. B/S of 131a former prop. of
Nathan dec'd) adj Mary FOX, Lambert MYRES. Delv. pr order 2 May
1842.

4C:036   Date: 1 May 1834   RtCt: 5 Jul 1834
Christopher FRYE & wife Margaret of Ldn to Jacob FADELY of Ldn.
B/S of 2a on W side of Lsbg ad FRYE, FADELY, William CARR. Wit:
Henry T. HARRISON, Presley CORDELL. Delv. to Fenton
FADELEY __.

4C:038   Date: 28 Mar 1834   RtCt: 7 Jul 1834
Anna GOODIN late BIRDSALL and Elizabeth BIRDSALL of Ldn to
Mary BIRDSALL of Ldn. B/S of undivided 1/3rd of 1/8th int. (from
father Whitson BIRDSALL dec'd to his 8 children with right of dower
to widow Rachel BIRDSALL, cnvy/b Noah HATCHER Mar 1805) on
Cotocton Creek. Delv. to Mary BIRDSALL 31 Dec 1838.

4C:040   Date: 28 Jun 1834   RtCt: 9 Jul 1834
Stephen REED of Ldn to Joseph TAYLOR of Ldn. Trust for debt to
Vallentine V. PURSEL and V. V. & S. PURSEL using farm animals,
farm and household items.

4C:041   Date: 28 Jun 1834   RtCt: 9 Jul 1834
Eli BOLAN & wife Lydia of Ldn to Conrad R. DOWELL of Ldn. Trust
for debt to V. V. & S. PURSEL using black boy named Hiram. Wit:
Jas. McILHANEY, Timothy TAYLOR. Delv. to V. V. PURCELL 4 Nov
1834.

4C:043   Date: 13 May 1831   RtCt: 14 Jul 1834
John CARR of Ldn to Benjamin GRUBB of Ldn. Release of trust of
Apr 1830 from George RICKARD (who later sold to Benjamin
GRUBB) for debt to John WORSLEY on 153a, DBk TTT:286.

4C:045   Date: 30 Jun 1834   RtCt: 14 Jul 1834
James D. McPHERSON. Qualified as Lt. of 2nd Reg of artillery 6th
Brig 2nd Div Va Militia.

4C:045 Date: 12 Jun 1834 RtCt: 14 Jul 1834
Powell SHRY. Oath as Capt. of infantry in Va Militia.

4C:046 Date: 14 Jul 1834 RtCt: 14 Jul 1834
James W. TIMMS, Jesse TIMMS & James GARRISON. Bond on
James W. TIMMS as constable.

4C:046 Date: 14 Jul 1834 RtCt: 14 Jul 1834
G. A. MORAN (insolvent debtor) of Ldn to Sheriff Ariss BUCKNER.
B/S 295a leased land where he resides (for executions by William
H. CRAVEN, Thos. D. MULLER assignee of James CAYLOR).

4C:047 Date: 14 Jul 1834 RtCt: 14 Jul 1834
Sheriff Ariss BUCKNER to Jacob WALTMAN. B/S of int. in 100a nr
Wtfd (allotted insolvent George W. HENRY from estate of William
FOX dec'd) and undivided 1/4th int. of HENRY in 100a "Ogden
Farm" of John HAMILTON dec'd subject to life estate of widow
Winifred HAMILTON. Delv. to WALTMAN 21 Apr 1835.

4C:049 Date: __ May 1834 RtCt: 15 Jul 1834
Sheriff Ariss BUCKNER to Eleanor DRISH of Ldn. B/S of undivided
int. of insolvent Wilson J. DRISH in estate of Mathew ADAMS dec'd.

4C:050 Date: 16 Jul 1834 RtCt: 18 Jul 1834
Levi WINEGARDNER of Ldn to Joshua PUSEY of Ldn. Trust for
debt to Sanford J. RAMEY using notes, horses & wagon, int. in
estate of Catharine COMPHER dec'd.

4C:051 Date: 14 Jun 1834 RtCt: 18 Jul 1834
John SARBAUGH & wife Elizabeth of Ldn to Powel SRYE of Ldn.
Trust for debt to Philip HEATER using 4a where SARBAUGH now
resides adj John WENNER, Michael SANBOWER, Adam CARN,
Adam HEFNER. Wit: Charles B. HAMILTON, William SLATER.
Delv. to Henry S. WUNDER Admr of HEATER dec'd 2 Mar 1836.

4C:054 Date: 14 Jul 1834 RtCt: 18 Jul 1834
Ludwell LUCKETT of Ldn to Francis W. LUCKETT (trustee for
benefit of Mary D. MAGILL). B/S of int. in land in Mason Co Va on
great Kenhawa river dev. to Mary D. MAGILL by her father William
BRONAUGH (from defaulted trust of Mar 1834 from Charles T.
MAGILL h/o Mary D.)

4C:055 Date: 15 Jul 1834 RtCt: 22 Jul 1834
William CLINE & wife Margaret of Ldn to Thornton F. OFFUTT of
Ldn. B/S of ¼a in Snickersville now in possession of Charles
CARPENTER (sold by Robert BRADEN dec'd to Fielder BURCH but
no deed has been executed) adj William CLAYTON, Amos
CLAYTON. Wit: Henry T. HARRISON, Presley CORDELL.

4C:057 Date: 15 Jul 1834 RtCt: 22 Jul 1834
Thornton F. OFFUTT & wife Eliza of Ldn to Presley CORDELL of
Ldn. Trust for debt to William CLINE using land prch/o CLINE. Wit:
D. McGEORGE, James STEPHENSON. Delv. to CLINE 1 Jun 1835.

4C:059 Date: 30 Jun 1834 RtCt: 23 Jul 1834
John C. NEWTON & wife Margaret and Alexander P.
BRACKENRIDGE & wife Elizabeth S. of Ldn to Charles G.
ESKRIDGE of Ldn. B/S of int. in 3a (cnvy/b Robert PERFECT to
Charles BINNS for Robt NEWTON & wife Ann during their lives and
after divided between children John C. NEWTON, Elizabeth Lee
NEWTON & Robert C. NEWTON, see DBk GG:422 and HH:311).
Wit: Saml. M. EDWARDS, Presley CORDELL.

4C:062 Date: 28 Jul 1834 RtCt: 28 Jul 1834
Jonathan MILBOURNE & wife Sarah of Ldn to Jared CHAMBLIN &
Isaac VANDEVANTER of Ldn. Trust for debt to David CARR &
Gabriel VANDEVANTER Admrs. of John CARR dec'd using 15a on
Ketoctin mt. adj David MILBOURNE (willed to Sarah by Benjamin
SAUNDERS). Wit: Saml. M. EDWARDS, Presley CORDELL. Delv.
to CHAMBLIN 10 Mar 1840.

4C:063 Date: 29 Jul 1834 RtCt: 29 Jul 1834
William HEATH (insolvent debtor) to Sheriff Ariss BUCKNER. B/S of
int. in land from estate of David LACEY dec'd adj Isaac
VANDEVANTER, Mrs. MANNING, Wm. HOLMES, Joshua PUSEY.
Wit: Presley CORDELL, John JANNEY, E. HAMMAT, T. A. W.
EDWARDS.

4C:064 Date: 8 Jul 1834 RtCt: 1 Aug 1834
Burr W. HARRISON & John JANNEY (Commrs. in suit of May 1832
of Riggs & Peabody agst Admr. and heirs of Joshua BEARD dec'd)
to Edward HAMMATT. B/S of house & lot on King St in Lsbg
(formerly occ. by Joseph BEARD) adj heirs of Alexander
SUTHERLAND, John MATTHIAS dec'd. Delv. to HAMMAT 24 Apr
1835.

4C:065 Date: 4 Aug 1834 RtCt: 4 Aug 1834
John RYON to Jno. A. BINNS & Michael MORRALLEE. Trust for
debt to MORRALLEE using farm and household items. Delv. pr
order 3 Dec 1834.

4C:066 Date: 1 Jul 1830 RtCt: 7 Aug 1834
Richard H. HENDERSON (Commr. in case of Daniel LOVETT agst
Craven P. LUCKETT reps of Christopher GREENUP dec'd) of Ldn
to Daniel LOVETT of Ldn. B/S of 164a (patented to GREENUP Apr
1788) adj Craven PEYTON, Robert FOWKE.

4C:067 Date: 1 Aug 1834 RtCt: 7 Aug 1834
Tunis TITUS of Ldn to William D. DRISH of Ldn. Trust for debt to
Geo. M. CHICHESTER using farm animals, farm and household
items. Wit: R. H. HENDERSON. Delv. to R. G. BOWIE 25 Sep 1837.

4C:068 Date: 10 Jun 1833 RtCt: 10 Jun 1833/7 Aug 1834
Richard H. HENDERSON, Humphrey POWELL & Jesse TIMMS of
Ldn to Mary ALLBRITAIN, William D. DANIEL, Hannah MARKS,
Wallace DANIEL, Martha BEATY, Humphrey DANIEL & Tacy

DANIEL (ch/o Joseph DANIEL dec'd). Release of trust of Jul 1824 for debt to George CARTER using 150a.

4C:069   Date: 12 Sep 1832   RtCt: 7 Aug 1834
Charles G. ESKRIDGE of Ldn to Samuel HOUGH of Ldn. Release of trust of Nov 1827 for debt to John GRAY on 184a.

4C:070   Date: 30 Jul 1834   RtCt: 11 Aug 1834
Lovell H. MIDDLETON and Thomas P. MIDDLETON & wife Mary of Ldn to Humphrey B. POWELL of Ldn. Trust for debt to Charles L. POWELL using 28a on Goose Creek adj __ RECTOR. Wit: Abner GIBSON, Hugh SMITH.

4C:073   Date: 14 Mar 1833   RtCt: 11 Aug 1834
Burr W. McKIM & wife Catharine of Ldn to Daniel WINE of Ldn. B/S of 2a (cnvy/ Thomas PHILIPS and Exors of Asa MOORE dec'd) adj Wm. HOUGH, John HOUGH dec'd. Wit: Mortimer McILHANY, Geo. W. SHAWEN. Delv. to WINE 25 Oct 1837.

4C:074   Date: 3 Jul 1834   RtCt: 11 Aug 1834
Washington MYERS & wife Margaret to David REECE. Trust for debt to John BRADEN using land prch/o BRADEN.

4C:076   Date: 6 Sep 1833   RtCt: 11 Aug 1834
John G. HUMPHREY & wife Mary and Abraham VICKERS & wife Maria of Ldn and John G. HUMPHREY atty in fact for Wm. RICHARDS Jr. & wife Margaret late of Ldn to Edward HALL of Ldn. B/S of 72a on Goose Creek adj HALL, William VICKERS, heirs of Enoch TRIPLETT, Abner CARTER, heirs of Mrs. LEWIS. Wit: Ludwell LUCKETT, William BENTON.

4C:078   Date: 11 Aug 1834   RtCt: 11 Aug 1834
Richard COCHRAN of Mdbg to Humphrey B. POWELL of Ldn. Trust for debt to Hiram McVEIGH & Co, Beveridge & Smith using houses, stables & lot where COCHRAN lives adj Jno. BRADY. Delv. to POWELL 26 Sep 1835.

4C:079   Date: 11 Dec 1833   RtCt: 11 Aug 1834
Bernard TAYLOR (Exor of William TOMLINSON dec'd) of Ldn to Benjamin RUST of Ldn. B/S of 99a (formerly of Wm. TOMLINSON dec'd) on Beaverdam adj Abraham SKILMAN, __ BROWN, __ SAGER. Delv. to RUST 28 Feb 1850.

4C:081   Date: 3 Jul 1834   RtCt: 11 Aug 1834
John BRADEN & wife Mary of Ldn to Washington MYERS of Ldn. B/S of 34a (cnvy/b Exors of Nathan GREGG dec'd) adj Mary FOX, BRADEN. Wit: David RUSE, Joshua PUSEY.

4C:083   Date: 5 Apr 1834   RtCt: 11 Apr 1834
Joseph MILLER & wife Mary Ann, Joseph MILLER as Admr. of John ROPP dec'd, Margaret WALTMAN and Susan Ann WALTMAN of Ldn to Nicholas ROPP of Ldn. B/S of land between short hill and Blue Ridge where ROPP resides which was leased to Jacob REAP

by Battaille MUSE agent for Sarah FAIRFAX Mar 1796. Wit: Thomas J. MARLOW, George W. SHAWEN.

4C:084 Date: 11 Aug 1834 RtCt: 11 Aug 1834
Dpty Sheriff James Henry McVEIGH for Sheriff Ludwell LEE to James LOVE of Ldn. B/S of int. in lot in Hllb then occupied by Thomas LOVE Jr. (from insolvent debtor Benjamin DANIEL of Ldn held in right of his former wife Jane d/o James LOVE dec'd).

4C:085 Date: 21 Jul 1834 RtCt: 11 Aug 1834
Lewis TORRISON. Oath as Lt. in 56th Reg of infantry of the line in 6th Brig 2nd Div of Va Militia.

4C:086 Date: 11 Aug 1834 RtCt: 11 Aug 1834
Joseph R. COCKERILL. Oath as Ensign in 56th Reg of infantry 6th Brig 2nd Div Va Militia.

4C:086 Date: 11 Aug 1834 RtCt: 12 Aug 1834
Richard COCHRAN of Ldn to H. B. POWELL of Ldn. Trust for debt to H. B. POWELL, etc. using "Capitol Hill" with 6a adj subject to ground rents and trust, 13a adj other lot (prch/o Maj'r B. POWELL), 2½a lots prch/o heirs of HALE – with coach shop, blacksmith shop, dwelling house, lots and house now occupied by COCHRAN adj John BRADY, lot with brick house prch/o John L. DAGG, farm animals, farm and household items, Negro boys Townshend & Joe. Wit: Samuel R. ADAMS, Wm. H. ROGERS, J. H. COCKRAN. Delv. to POWELL 26 Sep 1835.

4C:089 Date: 17 May 1834 RtCt: 12 Aug 1834
Michael DERRY to George B. STEPHENSON. Trust for debt to William ANDERSON and W & S. B. Anderson Co. using Lot #2 & #4 prch/o Amos NEAR, farm animals, wagons. Delv. pr order 28 Oct 1841.

4C:090 Date: 12 Aug 1834 RtCt: 12 Aug 1834
John HAMILTON and Charles B. HAMILTON of Ldn and John WHITE of Ldn. Agreement on straightening the lines between their property.

4C:091 Date: 18 Jul 1834 RtCt: 12 Aug 1834
Archibald N. DOUGLAS of Ldn. Receipt for full settlement from brother Charles DOUGLAS of Ldn as Exor of Hugh DOUGLAS dec'd Admr of Margaret DOUGLAS dec'd Admr. & Guardian of Lewis F. DOUGLAS and his own Guardian.

4C:092 Date: 24 May 1832 RtCt: 13 Aug 1834
William COE & wife Elizabeth late COPELAND of Union Co Indianna to Andrew COPELAND of Ldn. B/S of 1/18th int. in 202¾a of Andrew COPELAND Sr. dec'd on NW side of short hill between Blue Ridge (beq. to sons Andrew, Bennett & David but div. never made and David died and Elizabeth is entitled to 1/6th of his share).

4C:094   Date: 8 Oct 1831   RtCt: 13 Aug 1834
Bennet COPELAND & wife Mary of Franklin Co Indiana and William
McQUARD & wife Nancy late COPELAND, Maria COPELAND, Eliza
COPELAND of Union Co Indiana and Nancy COPELAND of Ldn to
Andrew COPELAND of Ldn. B/S of ½ int. in above 202¾a.

4C:095   Date: 14 Aug 1834   RtCt: 14 Aug 1834
James BEST. Qualified as Ensign in 56th Reg 6th Brig 2nd Div of Va
Militia.

4C:096   Date: 14 Aug 1834   RtCt: 14 Aug 1834
Jesse TRIBBY. Qualified as Capt. in 56th Reg 6th Brig 2nd Div Va
Militia.

4C:096   Date: 14 Aug 1834   RtCt: 14 Aug 1834
Arch. M. KITZMILLER, M. MORRALLEE, Wm. W. KITZMILLER,
John H. MONROE & James GARNER. Bond on Arch. M.
KITZMILLER as Admr. of Samuel STERRETT dec'd to indemnify
Thos. SAUNDERS as security with Lydia STERRETT.

4C:097   Date: 14 Aug 1834   RtCt: 14 Aug 1834
Joshua HATCHER of Ldn to Thomas HATCHER of Ldn. B/S of 1/5th
int. in 213a farm of Samuel HATCHER dec'd adj William NICHOLS,
William PIGGOTT, Jesse HIRST, Swithen NICHOLS, Soloman
RUSE.

4C:097   Date: 28 Jul 1834   RtCt: 19 Aug 1834
James GARNER and John Nicholas KLINE of Ldn to Philip
NELSON of Ldn. Release of trust of Apr 1831 for debt to John N.
KLINE using house & lot in Lsbg. Wit: Saml. M. EDWARDS.

4C:098   Date: 23 Aug 1834   RtCt: 25 Aug 1834
Patty/Martha CLAYTON of Ldn to William CLAYTON of Ldn. B/S of
57 sq poles nr Snickersville on N side of Snigers Gap turnpike road
adj Mordicai THROCKMORTON.

4C:099   Date: 23 Aug 1834   RtCt: 25 Aug 1834
William CLAYTON of Ldn to John B. YOUNG of Ldn. B/S of above
lot.

4C:101   Date: 27 Aug 1834   RtCt: 27 Aug 1834
Eliza GLASGOW of Ldn to Samuel M. EDWARDS of Ldn. Trust for
debt to Samuel M. BOSS using undivided 1/6th int. in real estate in
Lsbg of father Henry GLASGOW dec'd. Delv. to BOSS 30 Oct 1834.

4C:103   Date: 28 Aug 1834   RtCt: 28 Aug 1834
Jesse HOLMES with acknowledgment by Elizabeth HOLMES,
Samuel HOGE & wife Mary, William HOLMES Jr., Isaac HOLMES &
wife Hannah, Thomas NICHOLS & wife Emily and Lot HOLMES of
Ldn to deed made 28 Apr 1828 to Elijah HOLMES of Ldn. B/S of
52a (cnvy/b Hamilton ROGERS) adj "Diggs Valley", heirs of
Hamilton ROGERS.

4C:104   Date: 28 Aug 1834   RtCt: 28 Aug 1834
Jesse HOLMES (heir of Joseph HOLMES dec'd) in ackn. as above of Ldn to deed made 28 Apr 1828 to William SMITH of Ldn. B/S of 144a on NW fork of Goose Creek adj Mary CANBY, Thomas HUGHES, Joseph CLOWS, Eli JANNEY (prch/o John WILKS 1771 by William HOLMES and dev. to son Joseph). Delv. to SMITH 29 Sep 1835.

4C:105   Date: 21 Apr 1834   RtCt: 30 Aug 1834
Charles WILLIAMS (Commr in case of Nov 1832 Charles WILLIAMS & wife Mary, Isaac S. CRAVEN, Eleanor V. CRAVEN & Thomas G. DOWDLE agst Elizabeth E. DOWDLE & Mary Ann DOWDLE) to John THOMAS of Lsbg. B/S of 131a (see VV:074). Delv. to THOMAS 12 Dec 1834.

4C:106   Date: 21 Apr 1834   RtCt: 30 Aug 1834
John THOMAS to Samuel M. EDWARDS. Trust for debt to Commr. Charles WILLIAMS using above 131a. Delv. to Thomas pr order 24 Jul 1840.

4C:108   Date: 21 May 1834   RtCt: 8 Sep 1834
Charles L. POWELL & wife Selina of Ldn to Lovell H. MIDDLETON and Thomas P. MIDDLETON of Ldn. B/S of 28a adj Mdbg road, __ RECTOR, Goose Creek. Wit: Cuthbert POWELL, Thomas M. COLSTON. Delv. to Lovell H. MIDDLETON 19 Jun 1835.

4C:110   Date: 8 Aug 1834   RtCt: 8 Sep 1834
Charles TURNER & wife Matilda to H. B. POWELL. Trust for debt to Lovell H. MIDDLETON & Thomas P. MIDDLETON using 28a as above. Wit: A. GIBSON, Hugh SMITH. Delv. to Lovell H. MIDDLETON 19 Jun 1835.

4C:112   Date: 8 Aug 1834   RtCt: 8 Sep 1834
Charles TURNER & wife Matilda of Ldn to H. B. POWELL of Ldn . Trust for debt to Lovell H. MIDDLETON & Thomas P. MIDDLETON using undivided int. of Matilda from father Moses GULICK dec'd and 1/3 int. prch/b TURNER under trust from Alfred GULICK to Richard H. HENDERSON, adj Townshend PEYTON, Horace LUCKETT, George GULICK. Wit: A. GIBSON, Hugh SMITH. Delv. to L. H. MIDDLETON 21 Apr 1840.

4C:114   Date: 18 Aug 1834   RtCt: 8 Sep 1834
Mahlon TAVENNER & wife Mary Ann of Ldn to Jonathan TAVENER of Ldn. B/S of 55a n Beaverdam Creek (part of Mahlon's share from father Jonah TAVENER dec'd). Wit: Edward HALL, Ludwell LUCKETT. Delv. to Jonathan TAVENER 20 Feb 1835.

4C:116   Date: 23 Aug 1834   RtCt: 8 Sep 1834
George RHODES Jr. Qualified as 2nd Lt. in 2nd Reg of Cavalry 6th Brig 2nd Div Va Militia.

4C:117   Date: 8 Sep 1834   RtCt: 8 Sep 1834
Landon WORTHINGTON. Qualified as Ensign in infantry of the line in 57th Reg 6th Brig 2nd Div Va Militia.

4C:117   Date: 6 Sep 1834   RtCt: 8 Sep 1834
William RICE. Qualified as Lt. in 57th Reg Infantry of the line in 6th Brig 2nd Div Va Militia.

4C:117   Date: 8 Sep 1834   RtCt: 8 Sep 1834
Jesse McVEIGH & James H. McVEIGH. Bond on Jesse as Commissioner of the revenue for the 2nd District.

4C:118   Date: 8 Sep 1834   RtCt: 8 Sep 1834
Jesse TIMMS & George CARTER. Bond on TIMMS as Commissioner of the revenue for the 1st District.

4C:118   Date: 13 Oct 1834   RtCt: 13 Oct 1834
Charles BINNS (Clerk of the Court) & Charles W. D. BINNS. Bond on Charles as Clerk to pay into treasury all taxes.

4C:119   Date: 12 Sep 1834   RtCt: 12 Sep 1834
David McGAHY of Ldn to William McGAHY of Ldn. B/S of land where David now resides (cnvy/b Thomas GASSAWAY Dec 1823, DBk GGG:370). Wit: Geo. RICHARDS, Edmund TYLER.

4C:120   Date: 9 Sep 1834   RtCt: 12 Sep 1834
Thomas SAUNDERS (Exor of Michael SHRYOCK dec'd) to Burr W. HARRISON. B/S of 464a on Goose Creek adj Wm. ELLZEY, Rich'd VANPELT, __ WORKMAN, __ BALL. Delv. to HARRISON 27 Jun 1835.

4C:121   Date: 3 Jul 1834   RtCt: 12 Sep 1834
Thornton F. OFFUTT & wife Eliza of Ldn to William H. McCULLOUGH of Ldn. B/S of ¼a (½ of lot cnvy/b Thomas ROGERS as Commr in case of OFFUTT agst Elizabeth CLAYTON wd/o Amos CLAYTON dec'd May 1832, DBk YYY:023) on S side of Snickers Gap turnpike. Wit: Roger CHEW, Ludwell LUCKETT.

4C:122   Date: 27 May 1834   RtCt: 15 Sep 1834
John WIRTZ of FredMd to John GEORGE of Ldn. B/S of 44a (Lot #4 in div. of Jacob WIRTZ dec'd) adj __ LEWIS, __ ROLLER, __ EVERHART. Delv. to GEORGE 28 Apr 1838.

4C:123   Date: 5 Apr 1834   RtCt: 18 Sep 1834
Jacob CRUSEN & wife Sarah of Ldn to John RUSE Jr. of Ldn B/S of 34¾a (½ of tract of Margaret SAUNDERS dec'd) adj __ KALB, __ HAMILTON, __ GRAHAM. Wit: Geo. W. SHAWEN, Charles B. HAMILTON.

4C:125   Date: 7 Jun 1834   RtCt: 22 Sep 1834
John ROSE to Richard W. STONESTREET & Eleanor STONESTREET. Release of trust of Jun 1827 for John G. & Dewanna WATT, DBk OOO:224 and OOO:244). Wit: F. W. LUCKETT, Presley CORDELL.

4C:126   Date: 5 May 1834   RtCt: 22 Sep 1834
Isaac FOUCH Sr. of Ldn to brother Amos FOUCH (to provide support and education of his children) of Ldn. Gift of 16a and 6a wood Lot #6 on Goose Creek (as heir of brother Temple FOUCH late of PrWm). Wit: Isaac FOUCHE Jr., Emily FOUCHE, John G. BRACK. Delv. to Amos FOUCH 11 Feb 1835.

4C:128   Date: 9 Jun 1834   RtCt: 22 Sep 1834
Richard W. STONESTREET & wife Eleanor of Ldn to William CARR of Ldn. B/S of 2a (cnvy/b John G. WATT Jun 1827). Wit: Newton KEENE, Presley CORDELL. Delv. to CARR 3 Jun 1837.

4C:129   Date: 11 May 1831   RtCt: 22 Sep 1834
James McILHANY to Richard GRUBB. Trust for debt to Ebenezer GRUBB using 302a (allotted in div. of father's estate) occupied of Stephen GREGG adj McILHANY, Edward POTTS, Charles J. KILGOURE, Morris OSBURNE. Delv. to Ebenezer GRUBB Exor. of E. GRUBB dec'd 27 Jun 1838.

4C:130   Date: 12 Aug 1834   RtCt: 22 Sep 1834
Philip HUNT & wife Mary of Belmont Co Ohio, John GRIGSBY & wife Sarah of Muskingum Co Ohio, Amos WHITACRE & wife Lydia of Ldn, Daniel COCKERILL & wife Esther of Ldn and John HANDLEY & wife Hannah of Licking Co Ohio (heirs of Giles CRAVEN dec'd) to Charles TAYLOR and Timothy TAYLOR Jr. B/S of 79½a (in lieu of former deed which is lost) on NW fork of Goose Creek adj Joel CRAVEN, Thomas NICHOLS, __ EVANS, __ HOGUE. Wit: David RUSE, James McILHANEY. Delv. to Timothy TAYLOR Jr. pr direction of C. BINNS 27 Jun 1835.

4C:134   Date: 12 Dec 1833   RtCt: 23 Sep 1834
Arthur S. ROBERTSON & wife Mahala of Perry Co Ohio to Edmund ALLEN of Ldn. B/S of int. in dower of Mary LYDER wd/o Lewis LYDER dec'd. Wit: John DODDS, Benjamin D. POE. Delv. to ALLEN 22 Dec 1834.

4C:135   Date: 10 Sep 1834   RtCt: 23 Sep 1834
Mahlon FULTON & wife Jane S. of Bloomfield to Robert S. FULTON of Ldn. B/S of undivided ½ of 98a (conveyed jointly, DBk CCC:335) adj George KEENE, Amos HIBBS, Samuel RICHARDS. Wit: Benjamin GRAYSON, Thomas M. COLSTON. Delv. to Robert S. FULTON 14 Jun 1837.

4C:137   Date: 10 Sep 1834   RtCt: 23 Sep 1834
Robert S. FULTON & wife Sarah of Ldn to Mahlon FULTON of Ldn. B/S of undivided ½ of 6a (conveyed jointly, DBk CCC:335). Wit: Benjamin GRAYSON, Thomas M. COLSTON.

4C:138   Date: 24 Sep 1831   RtCt: 14 Aug/23 Sep 1834
William RICHARDS Jr. & wife Margaret of Ldn to John G. HUMPHREY of Ldn. PoA. Wit: Edmund ALLEN, John D. SHANK, Thornton WALKER. Delv. to grantee 17 May 1855.

4C:139   Date: 22 Sep 1834   RtCt: 23 Sep 1834
Benjamin JOHNSON of Ldn to Francis JOHNSON of Ldn. BoS for
farm animals, farm and household items. Wit: John JONES Sr.,
John JONES Jr., Fenton JOHNSON.

4C:139   Date: 13 Sep 1834   RtCt: 24 Sep 1834
Stacy J. TAVENER & wife Pleasant of Ldn to Humphrey
SHEPHERD of Ldn. B/S of 138a on NW fork of Beaverdam and Eli
TAVENER, heirs of Jonah TAVENER, turnpike road, Gabriel
McGEATH, Garret WALKER, Sophia WALTERS. Wit: John
SIMPSON, David REESE.

4C:141   Date: 23 Sep 1834   RtCt: 24 Sep 1834
Samuel HALL & wife Mahala Ann of Ldn to William HALL of Ldn.
B/S of 81a (dev. by father William HALL Sr.) adj David CARR,
Daniel LOVETT. Wit: William CARR, Presley CORDELL. Delv. to
grantee 13 Feb 1837.

4C:143   Date: 24 Jul 1834   RtCt: 24 Sep 1834
Fielding LITTLETON (Commr. in suit of Apr 1834 of Joel Z.
HARPER survivor of William HARPER & HARPER late merchant
agst Thomas CLOVES & Charles S. CLOVES & Isaac BROWN) to
James H. BENNETT now of Ldn. B/S of house & lot in Union
occupied by Isaac BROWN Sr.

4C:144   Date: 24 Jul 1834   RtCt: 25 Sep 1834
James H. BENNETT & wife Mary A. of Union to Thomas ROGERS.
Trust for debt to Commr. Fielding LITTLETON using above lot &
house. Wit: Edward HALL, Ludwell LUCKETT. Delv. to ROGERS 11
Jul 1838.

4C:146   Date: 21 May 1833   RtCt: 26 Sep 1834
Nathan SEEVERS (Commr. in suit of Jun 1831 of LYDER,
PANCOAST etc. agst Lydia NICHOLS etc.) to William SMITH of
Ldn. B/S of 22a "meeting house lot" nr Goose Creek meeting house
adj __ ZIMMERMAN. Delv. to SMITH 29 Sep 1835.

4C:147   Date: 8 Aug 1834   RtCt: 26 Sep 1834
Lovell H. MIDDLETON and Thomas P. MIDDLETON & wife Mary of
Ldn to Charles TURNER of Ldn. B/S of 24a (with 4a more in creek)
adj Mdbg road, Goose Creek, __ Rector. Wit: A. GIBSON, Hugh
SMITH.

4C:149   Date: 13 Oct 1819   RtCt: 13 Oct 1823/29 Sep 1834
James MONROE (Exor. of Joseph JONES dec'd) & wife Eliza to
James SWART. B/S of 283½a (agreement reached on payment,
sale made by JONES to SWART, cnvy/b Joseph JONES s/o Joseph
dec'd on 20 Mar 1806). Wit: Geo. HAY, William BENTON, James
PHILLIPS, Thos. SWANN, W. NOLAND, C. F. MERCER. Ackn. by
MONROE in WashDC

4C:151 Date: 16 Jul 1823 RtCt: 12 Aug 1823/29 Sep 1834
Charles Fenton MERCER of Aldie and Samuel TODD of Aldie.
Exchange of 10a lot (MERCER prch/o Mathew RUST) on Bull run
mt. nr Aldie with 10a (TODD prch/o Levi BARTON Aug 1815) on Bull
run mt. adj Amos FERGUSON, __ TORBERT.

4C:152 Date: 27 Sep 1834 RtCt: 29 Sep 1834
John WINCEL & wife Mary late BOGER of Ldn to Philip BOGAR of
Ldn. B/S of 21a (Lot #6 in div. of Michael BOGER dec'd). Wit:
William SLATER, C. B. HAMILTON Jr. Delv. to BOGER 4 Feb 1846.

4C:154 Date: 28 Jul 1834 RtCt: 30 Sep 1834
Thomas ROGERS to A. P. BRACKENRIDGE. Release of trust of
Mar 1833 for debt to Charles C. NEWTON, DBk 4A:014).

4C:155 Date: __ Aug 1833 RtCt: 1 Oct 1834
John THOMAS to Thomas SAUNDERS. Release of trust of 1830 for
debt to Aaron HARLAN on house & lot in Wtfd.

4C:156 Date: 22 Sep 1834 RtCt: 2 Oct 1834
Daniel LOVETT of Ldn to Henry PLAISTER Jr. of Ldn. B/S of house
& ¼a in Union adj LOVETT, PLAISTER.

4C:157 Date: 6 Oct 1833 RtCt: 6 Oct 1834
George DERRY & wife Eliza of Ldn to Jacob SARBAUGH of Ldn.
B/S of 2a on S side of Short Hill adj Michael EVERHEART (cnvy/b
John WINSEL Jun 1830, DBk UUU:059). Wit: William ELLZEY,
Saml. M. EDWARDS. Delv. to SARBAUGH 20 Mar 1837.

4C:158 Date: 20 Sep 1834 RtCt: 6 Oct 1834
William JOHNSON & wife Margaret of Ldn to Charles G. ESKRIDGE
of Ldn. B/S of ½ of 9a nr Lsbg (cnvy/b James GARNER Jan 1811).
Wit: William ELLZEY, Presley CORDELL.

4C:160 Date: 1 Aug 1834 RtCt: 7 Oct 1834
Charles MOFFETT & wife Ellen of Pittsilvania Co Va now in Ldn to
Josiah MOFFETT. PoA for int. in estate of Michael SHRYOCK
dec'd. Wit: Saml. M. EDWARDS, Charles W. MOFFETT.

4C:160 Date: 8 Oct 1834 RtCt: 8 Oct 1834
Richard H. HENDERSON to James B. DUNKIN (who recently
removed to Rappahannock Co) and who conveys land Benjamin
JACKSON of Ldn. B/S of int. (9a) in land the late prop. of Nancy
CLARKE late CLAYTON d/o William CLAYTON the elder dec'd
(from defaulted trust of Jul 1819 from John HOFFMAN, DBk
ZZ:459).

4C:161 Date: 8 Oct 1834 RtCt: 8 Oct 1834
Richard W. A. POWER of Ldn to Mary BRABHAM of Ldn. Gift of a
cow.

4C:162 Date: 20 Feb 1834 RtCt: 10 Oct 1834
James Battaile LEWIS adult heir of John H. LEWIS dec'd and
Thomas A. MOORE (Commr for infant heirs Fisher Ames LEWIS,
Charles Henry LEWIS, John Berkley LEWIS, Mary Jane LEWIS,

Magnus Muse LEWIS, Joseph Newton LEWIS, Robert LEWIS and William Hierome Thomas LEWIS) to Joseph LEWIS. Release of trust Mar 1822 for debt to heirs of John H. LEWIS using 140a. Ackn. of James B. LEWIS in JeffVa.

4C:164 Date: 1 Oct 1834 RtCt: 10 Oct 1834
James RUST & wife Sally to Richard H. HENDERSON, Jesse TIMMS & John JANNY of Ldn. Trust for debt to George CARTER of Oatlands using 147a. Wit: Henry T. HARRISON, Hamilton ROGERS.

4C:167 Date: 20 Sep 1834 RtCt: 13 Oct 1834
William COOPER & wife Elizabeth to David WIRE. Trust for debt to John SOUDER Guardian of Elizabeth Margaret COOPER using 28a adj __ RUSSELL, __ HICKMAN. Wit: William SLATER, George W. SHAWEN.

4C:169 Date: 1 Sep 1834 RtCt: 10 Oct 1834
Peter GREGG to Hugh SMITH. Trust for debt to James IDEN using 119¼a adj Goose Creek, Wm. BRONAUGH, __ GOCHNAUER.

4C:171 Date: 14 Jun 1834 RtCt: 13 Oct 1834
Yeoman Samuel RECTOR & wife Anne V. of Ldn to Price JACOBS of Ldn. B/S of undivided 48a (2/5th of 72a - former dower of Hannah wd/o Joseph HATCHER and at her death to children Mary who m. Caleb RECTOR, Emzey who m. Nelson GIBSON, Gourley R. HATCHER, Amanda M. who m. Kemp COCKE and Anne V. who m. Samuel RECTOR, Samuel purchased COCKEs share). Wit: A. GIBSON, Hugh SMITH. Delv. to Seth SMITH 14 Mar 1837.

4C:174 Date: 10 May 1834 RtCt: 13 Oct 1834
Stephen T. CONARD & wife Vashti and Elwood B. HALL of Ldn to Edward HALL of Ldn. B/S of 100a in Ldn and JeffVa at summit of Blue Ridge adj William BERKLEY, Thomas KIRKPATRICK (part of grant of Dec 1788 to John HOUGH); and 74a (part of grant of Jan 1771 to William BERKLEY) on Blue Ridge adj Joseph THOMAS, Richard THATCHER, Col. Thomas HUMPHREY. Wit: Roger CHEW, Thomas M. COLSTON. Delv. pr order 2 Apr 1835.

4C:176 Date: 16 Sep 1834 RtCt: 13 Oct 1834
Isaac TALLY & wife Elizabeth of Ldn to Jonathan PAINTER of Ldn. B/S of lot with spring of water (cnvy/b Robert COCKRILL) and adj 40½a (cnvy/b Jesse EVANS). Wit: William CLENDENING, John WHITE. Delv. to grantee 18 Apr 1870.

4C:178 Date: 15 Sep 1834 RtCt: 13 Oct 1834
Jonathan WENNER & wife Elizabeth Ann of Ldn to William WENNER, Jacob WENNER & Emanuel WENNER of Ldn. B/S of 11a (Lot #6 in div. of William WENNER dec'd) and 1a (lot #6 at foot of short hill). Wit: Thomas J. MARLOW, Charles B. HAMILTON. Delv. pr order of Wm. WENNER 18 Mar 1835.

4C:180   Date: 31 Mar 1834   RtCt: 13 Oct 1834
Phebe SKINNER, Gabriel SKINNER & wife Elizabeth, Samuel
SKINNER & wife Elizabeth, William R. ELLIS & wife Rebecca,
Nancy SKINNER, Betsey SKINNER, Sarah SKINNER, Mary
SKINNER, Robert SKINNER, Fanny SKINNER, Jane SKINNER and
Alexander SKINNER to William BEVERIDGE. B/S of 10a adj
Townsend McVEIGH, Silas BEATY, __ DISHMAN, Mdbg road. Wit:
A. GIBSON, Hugh SMITH.

4C:182   Date: 13 Oct 1834   RtCt: 13 Oct 1834
George RICHARDS & John ROSE to Pres. & Directors of Literary
Fund. Bond on RICHARDS as treasurer.

4C:182   Date: 9 Oct 1834   RtCt: 14 Oct 1834
Ephraim SCHOOLEY & wife Tacy of Ldn to Eli L. SCHOOLEY of
Ldn. B/S of 74¼a (part of tract of Reubin SCHOOLEY dec'd) on
road from Lsbg to Wtfd adj __ SANDFORD, __ PUSEY. Wit: Saml.
M. EDWARDS, Presley CORDELL. Delv. to Eli L. SCHOOLEY 30
Oct 1843.

4C:184   Date: 1 Oct 1834   RtCt: 16 Oct 1834
John W. WOOD & wife Ann S. and Mary WOOD wd/o Mack WOOD
dec'd of Ldn to George RICHARDS & Samuel M. BOSS of Ldn.
Trust for debt to William CARR using lot on NW corner of Loudoun &
Back Sts. in Lsbg. Wit: Presley CORDELL, John J. MATHIAS. Delv.
to RICHARDS 7 Feb 1838.

4C:186   Date: 16 Oct 1834   RtCt: 16 Oct 1834
John ATWELL of Ldn to William LICKEY of Ldn. Trust for debt to
Mandly ATWELL using 141a where Jesse ATWELL now lives adj
Abraham SKILLMAN Sr., Narcissa GHEEN, Philip VANSICKLER.
Delv. to Manly ATWELL 18 Feb 1835.

4C:187   Date: 30 Oct 1834   RtCt: 23 Oct 1834
El(ea)ner McFARLAND of Greene Co Pa (for herself and in name of
her 2 children William & Cephas McFARLAND) and John
McFARLAND, James McFARLAND, Catherine McFARLAND &
Jesse McFARLAND ch/o of Elnor McFARLAND to David REESE.
Release of REESE as Exor (Thomas TRIBBY dec'd willed to his
child Elner McFARLAND int. and at her death to her children). Delv.
to REESE 11 Jan 1836.

4C:189   Date: 27 Aug 1834   RtCt: 23 Oct 1834
William McFARLAND & Cephas McFARLAND of Butler Co Ohio to
Ellinor McFARLAND of Green Co Pa. PoA to receive funds from
David REESE Admr. of William TRIBBY dec'd of Ldn. Delv. to
REECE 11 Jan 1836.

4C:189   Date: 19 Jul 1834   RtCt: 25 Oct 1834
Albert GREEN of Ldn to David P. FULTON of Ldn. Trust for debt to
William FULTON of Ldn using horse. Wit: William TEMPLER,
Ignatius NORRIS.

4C:191 Date: 27 Oct 1834 RtCt: 27 Oct 1834
Reuben COCKERILL & wife Mary Ellen of Ldn to John S.
EDWARDS of Ldn. Trust for debt to John COCKERILL of Ldn using
int. in land allotted to wife in div. of Edward M. COE dec'd (DBk
4B:213) and int. in dower of Mary COE wd/o of Edward M. COE
dec'd, and farm and household items. Wit: Henry T. HARRISON,
John J. MATHIAS. Delv. to John COCKERILL 14 Dec 1838.

4C:192 Date: 11 Aug 1834 RtCt: 31 Oct 1834
Malcolm C. KIRK & wife Mary Ann and William J. SPENCE & wife
Elizabeth to Samuel M. BOSS and Burr W. HARRISON. B/S of Lot
#9 at Loudoun & Church Sts. in Lsbg now in possession of
HARRISON. Ackn. by SPENCE in Licking Co Ohio. Ackn. by KIRK
in JeffVa. Delv. to BOSS 20 Mar 1843.

4C:195 Date: 5 Mar 1834 RtCt: 1 Nov 1834
Daniel ADAMS & wife Susan of Ldn to Peter ADAMS of Ldn. B/S of
int. in Lot #7 in div. of Peter COMPHER dec'd allotted to Abigail late
COMPHER w/o James ADAMS, adj John STOUTSENBERGER.
Wit: George W. SHAWEN, Charles B. HAMILTON. Delv. to __ 6 Jul
1837.

4C:196 Date: 1 Nov 1834 RtCt: 3 Nov 1834
Philip HEATER & wife Mary of Ldn to George RUST Jr. of JeffVa.
B/S of 161a adj __ ELGIN, __ CONARD, __ COCKE; and 21a adj
Westwood T. MASON, Thompson MASON (both cnvy/b Mahlon
JANNEY). Wit: Thomas J. MARLOW, C. B. HAMILTON. Delv. to
RUST 13 Dec 1836.

4C:198 Date: 28 Oct 1834 RtCt: 10 Nov 1834
John HOLLINGSWORTH & wife Elizabeth of Belmont Co Ohio to
Thomas JAMES of Ldn. B/S of 11a on Goose Creek (formerly
owned by George NICHOLS) adj JAMES, dower of Ann NICHOLS,
Charles KILGORE; and int. in 40a dower of Ann NICHOLS. Wit:
Asenath A. HOGE, Charles Wililam [William] GEATH? Delv. to
JAMES 11 Jan 1836.

4C:200 Date: 10 Nov 1834 RtCt: 10 Nov 1834
Samuel ELGIN & wife Susannah late WIRTS of Ldn to John
CUNARD of Ldn. B/S of 43a Lot #2 in div. of Jacob WIRTS dec'd in
German Settlement. Wit: Hamilton ROGERS, John J. MATHIAS.
Delv. to CUNARD 11 Apr 1835.

4C:202 Date: 1 Sep 1832 RtCt: 10 Nov 1834
Benjamin GRAYSON & wife Nancy of Ldn to Richard O. GRAYSON
of Ldn. B/S of 219a on road to Upperville adj George NOBLE, John
RICHARDS, William RICHARDS, Henry CARTER, road to Clifton
Mill, John P. DULANY, Matthew CARPENTER. Wit: Cuthbert
POWELL, Thomas M. COLSTON.

4C:204   Date: 27 Feb 1830   RtCt: 21 Jan/10 Nov 1834
Eliza D. PEYTON of Ldn to William ELLZEY of Ldn. B/S of 83a
(cnvy/b John McKINLY & Mary ARMISTEAD Sep 1825, DB
LLL:001, and by Sarah ELLZEY to PEYTON Feb 1830). Wit: L.
ELLZEY, V. PEYTON, Isaiah CHAPPELL, Wm. W. ELLZEY.

4C:205   Date: 30 Aug 1817   RtCt: 10 Nov 1834
Joseph MALIN & wife Ann to Henry EVANS. Relinquishment of int.
in estate of William EVANS dec'd and int. claimed by will from
William PERL now dec'd and int. in dower right at the decease of
wife's mother Martha EVANS. Wit: James MOSES, Margaret
PATERSON. Ackn. from Jefferson Co Ohio.

4C:207   Date: 3 Nov 1834   RtCt: 10 Nov 1834
Thornton WALKER to Perin WASHINGTON. Release of trust of May
1832 for Thornton F. OFFUTT and Stephen T. CONARD as security.

4C:208   Date: 8 Nov 1834   RtCt: 10 Nov 1834
Andrew HEATH of Ldn to Matthew P. LEE of Ldn. B/S of 115a adj
John TURLEY's spring branch, road from Baptist meeting house to
Gum Spring, John SPENCER, Benjamin JAMES (now claimed by
Sampson TURLEY). Delv. to LEE 8 Jul 1835.

4C:209   Date: 10 Nov 1834   RtCt: 10 Nov 1834
Samuel CRAVEN. Oath as Lt. of Cavalry in 2nd Reg 2nd Div.

4C:210   Date: 11 Nov 1834   RtCt: 11 Nov 1834
George H. ALDER & Nathan NICHOLS. Bond on ALDER as
constable.

4C:210   Date: 19 Aug 1833   RtCt: 12 Nov 1834
John HARRIS & wife Elizabeth to Sheriff Burr POWELL. B/S of lot in
Mdbg adj Noble BEVERIDGE, Burr POWELL. Ackn. by HARRIS in
Rappahannock Co Va.

4C:212   Date: 22 Sep 1834   RtCt: 12 Nov 1834
Israel P. THOMPSON (Exor of Jonah THOMPSON dec'd late of
AlexDC) to Anthony ADDISON & William MERSHON of Ldn. B/S of
33a with grist and saw mill (from defaulted trust of Mar 1834 from
James L. McKENNA). Delv. to MERSHON 7 Jun 1837.

4C:213   Date: 12 Nov 1834   RtCt: 12 Nov 1834
John L. GILL, Joseph P. McGEATH, Fielding LITTLETON & Isaac
G. BOWLES. Bond on GILL as constable.

4C:214   Date: __ Nov 1834   RtCt: 11 Nov 1835
Mahlon MYRES of Ldn to Edmund COLEMAN of Ldn. Trust for debt
to Lydia COLEMAN using farm animals, farm and household items.
Delv. to Edm'd. W. COLEMAN 13 Feb 1835.

4C:216   Date: __ 1834   RtCt: 11 Nov 1834
William WHALEY of Ldn to John J. COLEMAN of Ldn. B/S of 70 late
prop. of father Levi WHALEY dec'd (as ordered in case of Mar 1831
James WHALEY agst William WHALEY) on Broad run adj Wilson C.
SELDEN Jr., James L. McKENNA.

4C:217   Date: 13 Nov 1834   RtCt: 13 Nov 1834
Joshua HATCHER of Ldn to Isaac PIGGOTT of Ldn. B/S of 80a "Greenway" with mill and stone dwelling on S fork Creek of Beaverdam adj Gourley REEDER, South fork meeting house.

4C:217   Date: 27 Oct 1834   RtCt: 20 Nov 1834
John SCHOOLEY & wife Sarah of Ldn to Israel T. GRIFFITH of Ldn. B/S of 58a (part of land of Reubin SCHOOLEY dec'd cnvy/t John Sep 1826, DBk NNN:018). Wit: Henry T. HARRISON, Presley CORDELL. Delv. pr order 15 Jul 1835.

4C:219   Date: 14 Nov 1834   RtCt: 20 Nov 1834
John CONARD of Ldn to George SMITH, John SMITH, Jacob FILLER & Jesse PORTER (trustees of St. Paul's Evangelical Lutheran Church). B/S of ¼a between Short Hill and Blue Ridge adj road from Harpers Ferry to Hllb, Ebenezer GRUBB; to build a church. Delv. to John SMITH 17 Mar 1857.

4C:221   Date: 10 Oct 1834   RtCt: 21 Nov 1834
William A. POWELL & wife Lucy P. of Ldn to James RUST of Ldn. B/S of 133a (Lot #2 in div. of estate of Leven POWELL Jr., DBk BBB:015) adj __ HANDY, __ OUSLEY, __ BURSON, __ REECE; and 94a (Lot #3 & #4 in div., see DBk TTT:099). Wit: Henry T. HARRISON, Presley CORDELL. Delv. to RUST 21 Aug 1839.

4C:223   Date: 10 Oct 1834   RtCt: 21 Nov 1834
James RUST & wife Sarah of Ldn to Burr W. HARRISON & Charles G. ESKRIDGE of Ldn. Trust for debt to William A. POWELL using above land. Wit: Henry T. HARRISON, Presley CORDELL. Delv. to POWELL 9 Apr 1835.

4C:226   Date: 14 Nov 1834   RtCt: 21 Nov 1834
Ebenezer GRUBB of Ldn to George SMITH, John SMITH, Jacob FILLER & Jesse PORTER (trustees of St. Paul Evangelical Lutheran Church). B/S of ¼a between short hill & Blue ridge adj John CONARD. Wit: Wm. SLATER, Wm. CLENDENING Sr. Delv. to John SMITH 17 Nov 1857.

4C:227   Date: 15 Nov 1834   RtCt: 22 Nov 1834
Joshua COOPER & wife Catharine of Ldn to William PEACOCK of Ldn. B/S of 3a adj __ UMBAUGH, COOPER, PEACOCK, and 5a. Wit: Charles B. HAMILTON, Geo. MARLOW. Delv. to PEACOCK 30 Nov 1836. (Plat recorded in Plat Book No. 2, Page 96)

4C:229   Date: 26 Nov 1834   RtCt: 26 Nov 1834
James ORANGE and Susan FICHTER. Marriage Contract – FICHTER has L/L from William CARR on N side of Loudoun St in Lsbg and various household items to be held in trust for her by George TURNER.

4C:231   Date: 10 Sep 1816   RtCt: 27 Nov 1834
John HOPKINS & wife Cornelia of Hill and Dale, FredVa to James L. McKENNA of AlexDC. Trust for debt to Bank of Alexandria using

250a in Piedmont on Short Hill formerly leased to Abram Sulley FRANK; and 227½a (cnvy/b Abram BROWN May 1814) adj __ SNICKERS, __ HAMPTON, Major Lawrence LEWIS. Wit: Ann C. LEE, Lucy Lyons HOPKINS, Absalom RENINGTON.

4C:233   Date: 20 Nov 1834   RtCt: 27 Nov 1834
Henry W. THOMAS to John THOMAS. B/S of 23a on Broad run adj Peter COMPHER with merchant mill (from defaulted trust from George RICKARD). Delv. to Jno. THOMAS by Henry W. THOMAS 23 Apr 1835.

4C:235   Date: 20 Jul 1833   RtCt: 27 Nov 1834
Vallentine JACOBS of Boon Co Indiana to Jesse PORTER of Ldn. PoA for sale of 2 lots on E side of Blue Ridge adj Jesse NEAR, widow HALL, widow KOONSE occupied by Presley WIGGINTON. Wit: Benjamin TITUS, David ROSS.

4C:237   Date: 13 Mar 1832   RtCt: 29 Nov 1834
Saml. DAWSON & Fayette BALL of Ldn to Thomas SWANN of WashDC. B/S of __a prch/o Stephen BALL (from defaulted trust of Charles P. TUTT to George M. CHICHESTER & William T. T. MASON, with DAWSON & BALL substituted in suit). Delv. to SWANN 9 Apr 1835.

4C:238   Date: 1 Sep 1834   RtCt: 31 Nov 1834
James IDEN & wife Margarett of Ldn to Peter GREGG of Ldn. B/S of 119¼a on Goose Creek adj William BRONAUGH, __ GOCHNAUER. Wit: A. GIBSON, Asa ROGERS. Delv. to GREGG 13 Nov 1844.

4C:240   Date: 15 Nov 1834   RtCt: 1 Dec 1834
Joshua COOPER & wife Catharine of Ldn to Edward THOMPSON of Ldn. B/S of 57a adj __ HOUGH, __ FULTON, __ UMBAUGH (deducting 17½a COOPER conveyed as 8a to William PEACOCK, 3a to Sarah FELMY, 2a to John HIGHTON, 2½a to __ GILMORE, 2a to __ COLE). Wit: Chas. B. HAMILTON, Geo. MARLOW. Delv. to THOMPSON 14 Aug 1837.

4C:242   Date: 15 Nov 1834   RtCt: 1 Dec 1834
Joshua COOPER & wife Catharine of Ldn to John HEIGHTON of Ldn. B/S of 2a where HEIGHTON now resides on E side of Kittockton Mt. Wit: Chas. B. HAMILTON, Geo. MARLOW. Delv. to HEIGHTON 14 Mar 1836.

4C:244   Date: 22 Nov 1824 [34?]   RtCt: 2 Dec 1834
Mary F. SPENCE of PrWm to John CURLEY of Ldn. B/S of 50a adj __ MOTT, James MONROE dec'd, Goose Creek. Delv. to CURLEY 20 Jan 1835.

4C:245   Date: __ Nov 1834   RtCt: 5 Dec 1834
Thomas D. ALLNUTT of Ldn to George A. GEESLING of Ldn. Trust for debt to John P. SMART of Ldn using slave Anthony abt 58y old, Harry abt 42, Hagar 32, William 26, Charity 24, George 22, Sandy

18, Agnes 16, Seely 14, Jim 12, Mulatto 12, Mary 8, Patience 19, Eliza 13, Bill 6, Charles 2, farm animals, farm and household items. Wit: John H. ALLNUTT, Periander L. BUSSARD, James L. ALLNUTT. Delv. to SMART 25 Feb 1835.

4C:247   Date: 9 Aug 1834   RtCt: 8 Dec 1834
Daniel BROWN & wife Ann of Ldn and Mahlon CRAVEN of Knox Co Ohio (trustee in marriage contract between Daniel BROWN & Ann WATKINS of 25 May 1825) to Joel CRAVEN of Ldn. B/S of 13a on NW fork of Goose Creek adj Isaac HOGE, Levi WILLIAMS, Giles CRAVEN. Wit: S. W. HILDRETH, Thos. IRVINE. Delv. to Joel CRAVEN 10 Aug 1835.

4C:250   Date: 13 Sep 1834   RtCt: 8 Dec 1834
Joshua NICHOLS & wife Naomi of Ldn to Daniel COCKERILL of Ldn. B/S of 11a on NW fork of Goose Creek adj David SMITH, William BOLAN. Wit: John SIMPSON, David REESE. Delv. to COCKERILL 6 Feb 1837.

4C:252   Date: 6 Nov 1834   RtCt: 8 Dec 1834
Sydnor WILLIAMS of Ldn to John HICKMAN of Ldn. B/S of 16a (Lot #6 from div. of father's estate) on E side of Cotocton Mt. Delv. to HICKMAN 14 Apr 1835.

4C:254   Date: 15 May 1834   RtCt: 8 Dec 1834
Abraham SKILLMAN Sr. & wife Delilah H. to Charles WRIGHT. B/S of 1 1/8a adj WRIGHT, __ ATWELL, __ BROWN. Wit: John SIMPSON, Notley C. WILLIAMS.

4C:256   Date: __ Oct 1834   RtCt: 24 Oct//10 Nov/8 Dec 1834
Charles WRIGHT of Ldn to John ATWELL of Ldn. Release of trust of Jun 1834 for debt to W. & A. WRIGHT (DBk 4C:001) on 141a. Wit: Hamilton BROWN, Mahlon BALDWIN, Jesse ATTWELL.

4C:257   Date: 25 Oct 1834   RtCt: 14 Dec 1834
Everitt SAUNDERS & wife Susan B. of Lsbg to Edmund J. LEE of AlexDC. B/S of 17a on N side of Lsbg Turnpike road, adj house occupied by Samuel DAILEY (exchanged adj lots). Gives plat. Wit: John J. MATHIAS, Presley CORDELL. Delv. to LEE 31 Jan 1835.

4C:260   Date: 10 Dec 1834   RtCt: 17 Dec 1834
William W. KITZMILLER of Lsbg to John THOMAS of Lsbg. Trust for James GARRISON, James GARNER, Michael MORRALLEE & Lydia STERRETT of Lsbg as security on note to Samuel M. BOSS using hides, horse, farm and household items, note of Samuel THOMPSON of DC. Delv. to THOMAS 24 Aug 1835.

4C:262   Date: 15 Nov 1834   RtCt: 19 Dec 1834
Joshua COOPER & wife Catharine of Ldn to Sarah FELMY of Ldn. B/S of 3a on E side of Cotoctin Mt. now occupied by FELMY. Wit: Chas. B. HAMILTON, Geo. MARLOW. Delv. pr order 25 Mar 1847.

4C:264   Date: 8 Oct 1834   RtCt: 22 Dec 1834
Richard TRANARA/TRENARY & wife Matilda late SETTLE of Frederick Co to Thomas SETTLE of Ldn. B/S of 1/6th int. in 134½a of Reubin SETTLE Jr. dec'd. Wit: Robert CUNNINGHAM, John THARP, Nelson SETTLE.

4C:264   Date: 24 Dec 1834   RtCt: 27 Dec 1834
David CARR & John H. MONROE of Ldn to Richard H. HENDERSON of Ldn. B/S of house & lot on Loudoun St in Lsbg late prop. of Bernard HOUGH now dec'd (from defaulted trust of Bernard HOUGH) adj. Mrs. Lucy BALL.

4C:265   Date: 24 Dec 1834   RtCt: 27 Dec 1834
Richard H. HENDERSON of Lsbg to James GARNER & John H. MONROE of Lsbg. B/S of house & lot on Loudoun St. in Lsbg as above. Delv. to MONROE pr order from GARNER 4 Jan 1836.

4C:266   Date: 24 Dec 1834   RtCt: 27 Dec 1834
James GARNER & John H. MONROE agree with R. H. HENDERSON Exor. of James SWART dec'd that above house & lot shall stand as security.

4C:267   Date: 27 Dec 1834   RtCt: 29 Dec 1834
William HUNTER of Ldn to Michael FRY of Ldn. Trust for debt to Michael ARNOLD of Ldn using farm animal, household items.

4C:269   Date: 12 Oct 1831   RtCt: 31 Dec 1834
Francis W. LUCKETT (Commr. to sell land of Thomas RUSSELL dec'd) to William CHAMBLIN. B/S of 125 (Samuel DUNKIN and Joshua B. DUNKIN originally purchased but sold to CHAMBLIN before conveyance) on Beaverdam adj William REEDER. Wit: Price JACOBS, J. SILCOTT, Moses BROWN. Delv. pr order __.

4C:271   Date: 24 Dec 1834   RtCt: 1 Jan 1835
Samuel HARPER & wife Margaret of Ldn to Hester STEWART of Ldn. B/S of lot on N side of Loudoun St in Lsbg (cnvy/b Peter FICHTER) adj __ EMBERSON, James GARNER. Wit: Wilson C. SELDEN Jr., Presley CORDELL.

4C:272   Date: 1 Jan 1835   RtCt: 2 Jan 1835
Unah HUNT of Ldn to Francis SIMPSON of Ldn. B/S of 15a (from father John HUNT dec'd) adj Major HUNT, Eli HUNT, Thomas CARR.

4C:273   Date: 13 Sep 1834   RtCt: 5 Jan 1835
Edward JENKINS & wife Philena of Md to Burr W. HARRISON of Ldn. Trust for debt to John W. DAVIS of 75a adj Stephen BEARD, William WARFORD, Abraham WARFORD, William ALLEN, and 100a DAVIS, BEARD, __ FERGUSON. Wit: Robert BAYLY, Charles LEWIS. Delv. to DAVIS 13 Jul 1835.

4C:276   Date: 1 Oct 1833   RtCt: 8 Jan 1835
Hamilton ROGERS & wife Mary late HAWLING of Ldn to John SPINKS of Ldn. B/S of 459¾a (late prop. of William HAWLING

dec'd) on Potomac adj George SINCLAIR. Wit: Henry T. HARRISON, Presley CORDELL. Delv. to SPINKS 7 Feb 1835.

4C:278 Date: 1 Oct 1834 RtCt: 8 Jan 1835
John SPINKS of Ldn to Richard H. HENDERSON of Ldn. Trust for debt to Hamilton ROGERS using above 459¾a. Delv. to HENDERSON 11 Oct 1836.

4C:279 Date: 9 Jan 1835 RtCt: 9 Jan 1835
Presley K. DORSEY of Ldn to Joseph HOUGH of Ldn. Trust for debt to HOUGH using hose, desk, bed.

4C:280 Date: 30 Dec 1834 RtCt: 12 Jan 1835
Robert RAY and Nathaniel PRIME of NY City to Charles B. HAMILTON Jr. of Ldn. Release of trust Dec 1824 from John HAMILTON for debt to Nathaniel PRIME, DBK JJJ:272) using 630. HAMILTON died leaving children Charles B. HAMILTON Jr., Jane W. SHAWEN w/o Geo. W. SHAWEN, Dewan[n]a B. HENRY w/o Geo. W. HENRY and Mary B. HAMILTON. Other children sold shares to Charles B. (DBk XXX:038). Wit: O. M. LOUNDS.

4C:282 Date: 30 Dec 1834 RtCt: 12 Jan 1835
Robert RAY and Nathaniel PRIME of NY City to Elijah JAMES of Ldn. Release of trust of Dec 1824 of John HAMILTON for debt to Nathaniel PRIME, DBk JJJ:272 on 630a on Potomac. Widow Winefred HAMILTON and children sold 157a to JAMES, DBk VVV:266. (see above deed). Wit: O. M. LOUNDS.

4C:284 Date: 30 Dec 1834 RtCt: 12 Jan 1835
Robert RAY and Nathaniel PRIME of NY City to Joseph MEAD of Ldn. Release of trust of Dec 1824 of John HAMILTON for debt to Nathaniel PRIME, DBk JJJ:272 on 630a on Potomac. Widow Winefred HAMILTON & children sold 225a to MEAD, DBk VVV:331. (see above deeds). Wit: O. M. LOUNDS.

4C:287 Date: 11 Oct 1834 RtCt: 12 Jan 1835
Thomas VICKERS to William CLENDENNING Jr. Trust for debt to Daniel CRIM using 10a adj Ebenezer GRUBB, John CONARD, Presley WIGGINTON.

4C:289 Date: 21 Jun 1834 RtCt: 12 J an 1835
David REESE & Charles B. HAMILTON (Exors of Nathan GREGG dec'd) of Ldn to Stephen GREGG, Smith GREGG & Thomas GREGG of Ldn. B/S of 172a "Mill Farm" on Kittocton below Smith shop. Delv. pr order 22 Jun 1847.

4C:291 Date: 15 Dec 1834 RtCt: 12 Jan 1835
Jacob SHUTT & wife Caroline Frances of Ldn to Edward DOWLING of Ldn. B/S of 8a adj __ CHAMBLIN, __ DEMORY, DOWLING. Wit: John WHITE, William CLENDENING. Delv. 6 Jun 1849 to Philip DERRY who m. DOWLING's only child.

4C:293   Date: 1 Dec 1834   RtCt: 12 Jan 1835
George KEENE to Moses BROWN. Release of trust for debt to
Samuel DUNKIN assigned to Richard H. HENDERSON.

4C:294   Date: __ 1835   RtCt: 12 Jan 1835
George W. HENRY of Ldn to Israel WILLIAMS & wife Amelia of Ldn.
Release of trust of Apr 1833 (DBk 4A:145) for debt to Joseph
POTTERFIELD using 93a.

4C:295   Date: 12 Jan 1835   RtCt: 12 Jan 1835
Lewis F. MANKIN, Chs. LEWIS & William MERSHON. Bond on
MANKIN as constable.

4C:296   Date: 10 Dec 1834   RtCt: 14 Jan 1835
Isaac NICHOLS of Allen Co Ohio and Benjamin F. TAYLOR of Ldn
to Thomas ROGERS Admr. wwa of John HATCHER. Bond that
NICHOLS, who m. Hannah HATCHER d/o Noah HATCHER dec'd
will refund if further debts are owed. Wit: J. CHAMBLIN.

4C:297   Date: 24 May 1834   RtCt: 12 Jan 1835
Sarah ELLZEY (Admx wwa of Elizabeth ELLZEY & Mary ELLZEY
dec'd) of Ldn to Isaac WORKMAN of Ldn. B/S of 145a adj __
HOSKINSON, __ SHRYOCK. Wit: L. ELLZEY, W. ELLZEY, M. P.
HARRISON.

4C:299   Date: 23 Nov 1833   RtCt: 15 Jan 1835
Sarah ELLZEY (Admx wwa of Elizabeth ELLZEY & Mary ELLZEY
dec'd) of Ldn to Henry MOFFETT of Ldn. B/S of 145a adj __
SHRYOCK, __ WORKMAN, __ HOSKINSON. Wit: L. ELLZEY, M.
P. HARRISON, W. ELLZEY, John M. HARRISON. Delv. to
MOFFETT 20 Jun 1835.

4C:301   Date: 24 May 1834   RtCt: 15 Jan 1835
Isaac WORKMAN & wife Sarah Jane of Ldn to John M. HARRISON
(in trust for Henry MOFFETT) of Ldn. Trust for debt to Sarah
ELLZEY using 145a above. Wit: L. ELLZEY, Wm. ELLZEY, M. P.
HARRISON, Sarah ELLZEY. Delv. to MOFFETT 20 Jun 1835.

4C:302   Date: 2 Jan 1835   RtCt: 8 Jan 1835
Charles BINNS & wife Hannah of Ldn to George RUST Jr. of JeffVa.
B/S of 46a (see DBk BBB:428) adj __ HEREFORD, __ THORNTON,
__ RHODES, road to Coblers Gap. Wit: William ELLZEY, Henry T.
HARRISON. Delv. to Saml. M. EDWARDS pr direction of George
RUST 2 Dec 1837.

4C:304   Date: 5 Apr 1834   RtCt: 15 Jan 1835
John DAVIS & wife Mary of Ldn to Jesse NEER of Ldn. B/S of 6¾a
(prch/o Amos JANNEY) adj Benjamin GRUBB, S'm BAKER, Wm.
KEYS, __ BOGAN. Wit: Thos. J. MARLOW, William CLENDENING.
Delv. to NEER 24 Feb 1846.

4C:306   Date: 6 Nov 1834   RtCt: 15 Jan 1834
John MOORE & wife Elizabeth, James G. MOORE & wife Dorinda,
Elija(h) MOORE & wife Fanny and Robert MOORE & wife Christina

of Muskingum Co Ohio to Benjamin MOORE of Muskingum Co Ohio. PoA to sell estate of Joseph MOORE dec'd late of Perry Co Ohio (children John, James G., Benjamin, Elija & Robert purchased rights of widow Cloe).

4C:308   Date: 31 Dec 1828   RtCt: 15 Jan 1835
Richard H. HENDERSON of Ldn to William WHITE of Ffx. B/S of 47a nr Hllb (from defaulted trust of Jun 1824 from Jozabed WHITE, land from div. of father Josiah WHITE dec'd).

4C:309   Date: 16 Jan 1835   RtCt: 16 Jan 1835
John Lewis SULLIVAN to Samuel SULLIVAN. Trust for debt to Elizabeth SULLIVAN using int. in estate of father Murtho SULLIVAN dec'd, farm animals, crops, household items. Delv. to Elizabeth SULLIVAN 9 Jun 1843.

4C:311   Date: 25 Dec 1834   RtCt: 17 Jan 1835
Isaac NICHOLS to Seth SMITH & wife Anne. Release of trust for debt to Isaac NICHOLS and Joseph GORE (DBk TT:301).

4C:312   Date: 28 Oct 1834   RtCt: 21 Jan 1835
Josiah BURCHET of Ldn to Charles B. HAMILTON of Ldn. BoS for 19½a of wheat crop on Samuel PAXSON's farm. Wit: John L. PARSONS, Eli TAVENER. Delv. to Jas. H. CHAMBLIN by dir. of HAMILTON on __.

4C:313   Date: 22 Jan 1835   RtCt: 23 Jan 1835
John CAMBELL & wife Polly/Mary of Ldn to William SIMPSON of Ldn. LS of 104 sq poles (original LS from James HEREFORD to Patrick CAVANS Aug 1798) on road from Lsbg to the Dry Mill. Wit: John H. McCABE, John J. MATHIAS.

4C:315   Date: 22 Jan 1835   RtCt: 23 Jan 1835
William SIMPSON of Ldn to Samuel HARPER. Assignment of interest in above lease.

4C:315   Date: 9 Jan 1835   RtCt: 23 Jan 1835
John NIXON Jr. & wife Casander/Cassandra of Ldn to James HIGDON of Ldn. B/S of 20a & 8a wood lot (allotted in div. of father George NIXON dec'd. Wit: Henry T. HARRISON, Presley CORDELL. Delv. to HIGDON 20 Apr 1843.

4C:317   Date: 14 Dec 1833   RtCt: 23 Jan 1835
Mary McGARVICK of Muskingum Co Ohio to brother William WRIGHT of Ldn. B/S of undivided 1/8th int. in 200a of father Patterson WRIGHT on little Catocton Creek adj Samuel PAXTON, William PAXSON. Wit: Peter HOLMES, Jos. W. CROWN. Delv. to Wm. WRIGHT 24 Sep 1844.

4C:319   Date: 23 Jan 1835   RtCt: 23 Jan 1835
Emanuel WALTMAN of Ldn to Jacob SMITH & John EVERHEART of Ldn. Trust for debt to brother Joseph WALTMAN using 225a where Emanuel lives (from father Jacob WALTMAN dec'd).

4C:320   Date: 22 Jan 1835   RtCt: 24 Jan 1835
William D. DRISH, Robert BENTLY & John GRAY to Eleanor
PEERS. Release of trust of Jul 1827 to Otho R. BEATTY (who has
since died) on house & lot in Lsbg.

4C:321   Date: 26 Sep 1834   RtCt: 26 Jan 1835
Yeoman Price JACOBS & wife Catharine of Ldn to yeoman Elijah
ANDERSON of Ldn. B/S of 61a (allotted in div. of William REEDER
dec'd to daus. & children of dec'd dau. Sarah HATCHER, see III:252
[2T:251?]) adj William CHAMBLIN, Edward HALL. Delv. pr order 31
Jul 1835. Wit: Edward HALL, Ludwell LUCKETT.

4C:323   Date: 18 Jan 1834   RtCt: 27 Jan 1835
Malcom HORTON & Margaret A. of Buncombe Co NC to David B.
DENHAM and Charles T. DENHAM of Ldn. B/S of undivided 1/8th
int. in 35a from Amos DENHAM dec'd (exclusive of dower rights of
widow Amey DENHAM and claim by heirs of John ARMISTEAD in
right of mother Mrs. ARMISTEAD dec'd) on Goose Creek. Wit: A.
GIBSON, Asa ROGERS. Delv. to David B. DENHAM 9 Feb 1836.

4C:325   Date: 26 Jan 1835   RtCt: 28 Jan 1835
Francis LUCAS and William LUCAS (coloured men) of Ldn to
Joseph WOOD of Ldn. Mortgage of horses and wagons. Wit: Jas.
LAMBON, Joseph WOOD Jr., Josiah BENNETT.

4C:326   Date: 3 Dec 1834   RtCt: 30 Jan 1835
Richard C. McCARTY of Perry Co Ohio to James B. WILSON of
Ldn. B/S of int. in 76a on Goose Creek where mother Margaret
McCARTY now lives held as dower from Dennis McCARTY dec'd.
Delv. to WILSON 10 Apr 1835.

4C:328   Date: 9 Jan 1835   RtCt: 30 Jan 1835
Thomas ROGERS(Admr wwa of Eleanor PEERS dec'd) of Ldn to
Daniel G. SMITH of Ldn. B/S of house & lot. Delv. to SMITH 12 Oct
1841.

4C:329   Date: 12 May 1834   RtCt: 3 Feb 1835
John R. COOKE of Frederick Co to Richard H. HENDERSON . Trust
for debt to Alexander S. TIDBALL using 438a on Rocky branch adj
Henry S. COOKE. Delv. to HENDERSON 19 Jun 1837.

4C:331   Date: 28 Jan 1835   RtCt: 3 Feb 1835
Nathaniel SEVERS (late Dpty Marshall of Winchester Ct. in case of
John LLOYD agst Fleet SMITH and Daniel BROWN, Apr 1830) to
Richard H. HENDERSON of Ldn. B/S of 80a with grist and saw mill
(from defaulted trust of Feb 1810 by BROWN) on Goose Creek.
Delv. to HENDERSON 20 Jan 1836.

4C:332   Date: 26 Dec 1834   RtCt: 5 Feb 1835
George PRICE & wife Elizabeth to John P. SMART. B/S of 50a with
"Elizabeth Mill" (former prop. of Samuel CLAPHAM dec'd) on Goose
Creek (also see 2Y:323). Wit: Samuel M. EDWARDS, Francis W.
LUCKETT.

4C:334   Date: 26 Dec 1834   RtCt: 5 Feb 1835
John P. SMART to Rich'd H. HENDERSON. Trust for debt to
George PRICE using above mill and 50a. Delv. to HENDERSON 25
Jul 1835.

4C:335   Date: 30 Jan 1835   RtCt: 6 Feb 1835
James GARRISON & wife Elizabeth of Lsbg to Richard H.
HENDERSON and Jesse TIMMS of Ldn. Trust for debt to George
CARTER of Oatlands using lot at Market & King Sts. in Lsbg (prch/o
John McCORMICK) now occupied by H. H. HARRISON and Enos B.
CORDELL. Wit: Joshua PUSEY, Presley CORDELL.

4C:339   Date: 11 Oct 1834   RtCt: 6 Feb 1835
Daniel CRIM & wife Mary of Ldn to Thomas VICKERS of Ldn. B/S of
10a between Short Hill and Blue Ridge (part of allotment to Christian
JACOBS in div. of Peter JACOBS dec'd and sold to CRIM) adj __
CONARD, __ GRUBB, __ WIGGINTON. Wit: Mortimer McILHANEY,
William CLENDENING. Delv. to VICKERS 31 Dec 1836.

4C:341   Date: 1 Dec 1834   RtCt: 9 Feb 1835
Charles LEWIS (Exor of Joseph LEWIS Sr. dec'd) to Matthew P.
LEE. B/S of 304a (purchased by John L. BERKLEY who died before
conveyance, BERKLEY's will dev. to son Rufus BERKLEY who sold
to LEE) on N fork of Broad run adj Joshua LEE. Delv. to LEE 7 Jul
1835.

4C:342   Date: 4 Dec 1834   RtCt: 9 Feb 1835
William DULANEY of Ldn to Presley WIGGINTON of Ldn. Trust for
debt to Jesse PORTER using 16a where DULANEY resides on E
side of Blue Ridge (cnvy/b Vallentine JACOBS by agent Jesse
PORTER). Delv. to WIGGINTON 21 Sep 1835.

4C:344   Date: 23 Jan 1835   RtCt: 9 Feb 1835
John BOYD to H. B. POWELL. Trust for debt to Elizabeth BOYD
using house and 7/8a lot in Mdbg on N side of Washington St.
where John resides. Delv. to POWELL 12 Dec 1836.

4C:346   Date: 1 Dec 1834   RtCt: 9 Feb 1835
Charles LEWIS to Matthew P. LEE & wife Ann late BERKLEY. B/S
of 10a on S fork of Broad Run at Springfield or the Gum Spring
(LEWIS sold to John L. BERKLEY now dec'd who willed to Ann
LEE) adj road from Gum Spring to Lsbg, Nat. S. ODEN, Sudley Mill
road. Wit: Nathaniel S. ODEN, Melville B. HUTCHISON, Robert W.
ROGERS. Delv. to LEE 7 Jul 1835.

4C:347   Date: 29 Dec 1834   RtCt: 9 Feb 1835
James H. CHAMBLIN & Thomas ROGERS to Isaac WALKER.
Release of trust of Apr 1833 for debt to Thomas ROGERS using
house & lot.

4C:349 Date: 15 Jan 1835 RtCt: 9 Feb 1835
Matthew P. LEE & wife Ann of Ldn to Alexander D. LEE of Ldn. B/S of 36a adj Joshua LEE, Broad run, James McFARLAND. Wit: Chas. LEWIS, John BAYLY, Joshua LEE. Delv. to A. D. LEE 2 Apr 1841.

4C:350 Date: 15 Jan 1835 RtCt: 9 Feb 1835
Matthew P. LEE & wife Ann of Ldn to Joshua LEE of Ldn. B/S of 150a on road from Lsbg to Gum Spring. Wit: Chas. LEWIS, John BAYLY, Alexander D. LEE. Delv. to Joshua LEE 30 Aug 1836.

4C:351 Date: 15 Jan 1835 RtCt: 9 Feb 1835
Joshua LEE & wife Theodocia of Ldn to Matthew P. LEE of Ldn. B/S of 102a (part of tract cnvy/b Henry T. HARRISON) adj John L. BERKLEY dec'd. Wit: Chas. LEWIS, John BAYLY, Alexander D. LEE. Delv. to Matthew P. LEE 7 Jul 1835.

4C:353 Date: 9 Feb 1835 RtCt: 9 Feb 1835
Charles LEWIS (Commr. in suit of Aug 1834 of Vincent LEWIS, Vincent LEWIS 2nd, Susan LEWIS, Catharine DARNE, Martha LEWIS, __ LESTER & wife Eliza late LEWIS, Samuel HANCOCK & wife Jane late LEWIS, James Battaile LEWIS, Fisher A. LEWIS, Charles H. LEWIS, John H. LEWIS, Mary J. LEWIS, Margaret M. LEWIS, Joseph E. N. LEWIS, Robert V. LEWIS, William F. LEWIS by Charles LEWIS their next friend, Thomas B. LEWIS, Charles L. LEWIS, James M. LEWIS, __ BRYANT & wife Sarah J. late LEWIS and Mary LEWIS wd/o John LEWIS dec'd agst Charles DOUGLAS and Archibald N. DOUGLAS) to Archibald N. DOUGLAS of Ldn. B/S of int. in 188a (former prop. of James M. LEWIS dec'd cnvy/t him by Betsey TEBBS, DBk WW:157) and 37½a (cnvy/b Charles SHEPHERD, DBk ZZ:277) and 37½a (cnvy/b Leven W. SHEPHERD, DBk DDD:317). Wit: Jno. L. EDWARDS.

4C:355 Date: 15 Jan 1835 RtCt: 9 Feb 1835
Matthew P. LEE & wife Ann of Ldn to James McFARLAND of Ldn. B/S of 11a on N fork of Broad Run adj Alex'r D. LEE. Wit: Chas. LEWIS, John BAYLY, Alexander D. LEE. Delv. to McFARLAND 13 Jun 1835.

4C:356 Date: 7 Aug 1834 RtCt: 9 Feb 1835
Thomas WRIGHT. Oath as Ensign in 132nd Reg Va Militia.

4C:357 Date: 28 Jan 1835 RtCt: 9 Feb 1835
Charles ELGIN dec'd. Division of slaves – court order dated 14 Jan 1835 – Robert, James & Nace (old man) to widow's dower; Joshua to Charles W.; Harriet to Isabella; Emily to John Gustavus; George & Joe (Veney) to Francis Wilson; Charles Fenton & Maria to Armistead Mason. Divisors: Charles DOUGLAS, George MARLOW, Alfred BEST, Benj. JACKSON. From case of Charles W. ELGIN agst Wm. D. DRISH, Tilghman GORE & wife Rowena late ELGIN Admr. of Charles ELGIN dec'd, John S. ELGIN, Armistead M. ELGIN, Isabella ELGIN & Francis W. ELGIN.

4C:358 Date: 9 Feb 1835 RtCt: 9 Feb 1835
William BEVERIDGE, Hugh SMITH & Lovel H. MIDDLETON. Bond on BEVERIDGE as constable.

4C:359 Date: __ Sep 1834 RtCt: 10 Feb 1835
William H. McCULLOUGH of Ldn to Benjamin TOMBLINSON. Trust for debt to Thornton F. OFFUTT using ¼a in Snickersville (cnvy/b OFFUTT) on turnpike road adj heirs of Amos CLAYTON dec'd.

4C:361 Date: 11 Feb 1835 RtCt: 12 Feb 1835
John W. THAYER of Ldn to Henry H. HAMILTON of Ldn. Trust for debt to Noble BEVERIDGE using farm animals, household items, Negro man Harrison & girl Caroline, crops. Delv. to BEVERIDGE 10 Mar 1835.

4C:362 Date: 1 Nov 1834 RtCt: 11 Mar 1835
Vincent L. LEWIS and Rebecca MACHEN of Simpson Co Ky (heirs of Thos. MACHEN dec'd) to William B. LEWIS of WashDC. PoA. Delv. to Chs. LEWIS by Wm. MERSHON 4 Mar 1833 [35?].

4C:364 Date: 10 Feb 1835 RtCt: 11 Feb 1835
George AMICK of Ldn to John JANNEY of Ldn. B/S of 1/11th int. in 37a Lot #11 (div. of Michael BOGAR dec'd allotted Mary now dec'd w/o Samuel AMICK dec'd) adj heirs of Frederick COOPER dec'd.

4C:365 Date: 1 Jan 1835 RtCt: 11 Feb 1835
George PRICE & wife Elizabeth of Ldn to Basil NEWMAN of Ldn. B/S of 119a on Goose Creek (cnvy/t Samuel CLAPHAM dec'd by Patrick McINTYRE) adj James NEWTON dec'd, Samuel HOUGH, John P. SMART's mill lot. Wit: Francis W. LUCKETT, Samuel HOUGH.

4C:367 Date: 5 Feb 1835 RtCt: 11 Feb 1835
Bazil NEWMAN of Ldn to Richard H. HENDERSON of Ldn. Trust for debt to George PRICE using above 119a.

4C:368 Date: 10 Feb 1835 RtCt: 11 Feb 1835
John S. EDWARDS (Commr. in case of Samuel TILLETT Admr. of Edward TILLETT dec'd agst John A. BINNS Jr.) to Samuel TILLETT of Ldn. B/S of life estate int. of Sarah BINNS in house & lot.

4C:369 Date: 24 Dec 1833 RtCt: 13 Feb 1835
Mary E. POWELL, William Alex'r POWELL & wife Lucy, John L. POWELL & wife Maria L., Abner GIBSON & wife Susan Elizabeth and Alfred H. POWELL to Uriel GLASSCOCK. B/S of 133a adj Daniel REESE, Daniel BROWN, Cabin branch nr bridge over S fork of Beaverdam, GLASSCOCK. Ackn. of John L. POWELL & wife & Susanna E. GIBSON in Fqr. Wit: Cuthbert POWELL, Henry T. HARRISON. Delv. to GLASSCOCK 2 May 1835.

4C:373 Date: 2 Feb 1835 RtCt: 13 Feb 1835
Townsend McVEIGH & wife Keron H. of Ldn to Hiram McVEIGH of Ldn. B/S of Lot #47 & #48 in Mdbg (See DBk SSS:457). Wit: A.

GIBSON, Hugh SMITH. Delv. to Js. H. McVEIGH pr order 13 Nov 1835.

4C:375   Date: 4 Sep 1834   RtCt: 13 Sep 1834/16 Feb 1835
Daniel COOPER of Ldn to Fleming HIXON of Ldn. Trust for debt to Peter COMPHER, William WIRTS, William STEER, Simon SHOEMAKER, George SAUNDERS, Elijah PEACOCK & John SHOEMAKER using 26a (prch/o Noah HIXON) adj __ COMPHER, Catharine HIXON, __ REMEY; and farm animals, farm and household items.

4C:379   Date: 3 Jan 1834   RtCt: 14 Feb 1835
Colin AULD to Presley CORDELL. Release of trust of __ 18__ to Samuel M. EDWARDS for debt to AULD, DBk TTT:113, using lot in Lsbg. Wit: John RAMSEY.

4C:380   Date: 14 Feb 1835   RtCt: 14 Feb 1835
Charles William ELGIN (s/o Charles ELGIN dec'd late of Ldn) of BaltMd to Richard H. HENDERSON of Ldn. Trust for debt to Tilghman GORE using undivided 1/5th int. in land of father subject to dower of mother now w/o GORE. Delv. to HENDERSON 3 Jun 1837.

4C:382   Date: 15 Jul 1834   RtCt: 18 Feb 1835
Thomas J. NOLAND to Lewis BERKLEY. B/S of 228a (from defaulted trust of Jan 1821 from Arthur ORRISON, DBk CCC:044).

4C:383   Date: 1 Oct 1834   RtCt: 19 Feb 1835
Michael LYNN of Ldn to Fielding TAVENER of Ldn. Trust for debt to Joseph P. McGEATH of Ldn using farm and household items. Wit: Norval SILCOTT. Delv. pr order 23 Mar 1836.

4C:385   Date: 1 Jan 1835   RtCt: 20 Feb 1835
Nimrod CUMINS of Ldn to Jonathan TAVENER of Ldn. Trust for debt to Jos. P. McGEATH using household items. Delv. pr order 23 Mar 1836.

4C:387   Date: 10 Jan 1835   RtCt: 20 Feb 1835
John BROWN of Kalamazoo Co Michigan to Jonathan TAVENER of Ldn. PoA .

4C:388   Date: 2 Jan 1835   RtCt: 15 Jan/17 Jan/20 Feb 1835
Richard H. HENDERSON & Samuel M. EDWARDS of Ldn to Charles BINNS of Ldn. Release of trust of May 1834, DBk 4B:448, for debt to Samuel M. BOSS using 46a. Delv. to BINNS 21 Jul 1835.

4C:390   Date: 9 Feb 1835   RtCt: 21 Feb 1835
Joshua NICHOLS & wife Naomi of Ldn to Thomas NICHOLS of Ldn. B/S of 10a (part of prch/o Humphrey SHEPHERD) on NW fork of Goose Creek adj David SMITH, Isaac NICHOLS. Wit: Presley CORDELL, Henry T. HARRISON.

4C:392   Date: 21 Feb 1835   RtCt: 21 Feb 1835
John J. MATHIAS of Ldn to Bazil NEWMAN. Release of trust of Jan 1831 for debt to William AULT using 47a on Goose Creek.

4C:393 Date: 1 Jan 1835 RtCt: 25 Feb 1835
Thomas BIRKBY of Ldn to William CARR of Ldn. Bond for CARR to
extend trust for 13 years.

4C:395 Date: 1 Jan 1835 RtCt: 25 Feb 1835
Thomas BIRKBY & wife Sally to David CARR & Saml. M. BOSS.
Trust for debt to William CARR using lot as Liberty & Royal Sts in
Lsbg adj John A. BINNS (see DBk PPP:338). Wit: John J.
MATHIAS, Saml. HOUGH. Delv. to BOSS 29 Jan 1836.

4C:398 Date: 23 Feb 1835 RtCt: 26 Feb 1835
Robert J. TAYLOR, Richard H. HENDERSON & Charles BENNETT
to Daniel G. SMITH. Release of trust of Jun 1828 from Eleanor (now
dec'd) & dau. Ann H. PEERS (now dec'd) for debt to Charles
BENNETT of AlexDC using house & lot on Market St. in Lsbg now
sold to SMITH (see DBk QQQ:333 and RRR:324).

4C:400 Date: 27 Feb 1835 RtCt: 2 Mar 1835
Mahlon TAVENER & wife Mary Ann to Jonathan TAVENER. Trust
for debt to Joseph P. McGEATH, James BROWN & Isaac G.
BOWLES using 5a (prch/o James BROWN), farm animals,
household items. Delv. to Jonathan TAVENER 11 Dec 1835.

4C:402 Date: 25 Feb 1835 RtCt: 2 Mar 1835
Lewis METCALF of Ldn to Wm. H. ROGERS of Ldn. Trust for debt
to Asa ROGERS using farm animals, timber, farm and household
items. Delv. to ROGERS 8 Jan 1838.

4C:404 Date: 3 Mar 1835 RtCt: 3 Mar 1835
Levi WINEGARNER of Ldn to John S. EDWARDS of Ldn. Trust for
debt to George RICKARD of Ldn using horse and wagon. Delv. to
Michael VERTS pr order 10 Oct 1836.

4C:405 Date: 28 Jan 1835 RtCt: 6 Mar 1835
Elizabeth JACKSON wd/o of Stiles JACKSON dec'd and son John
JACKSON of Ffx to Priscilla SHOEMAKER of Ldn. B/S of 22a adj
Simon SHOEMAKER, John JACKSON, Jacob EMERY, Broad run.
Wit: F. PEYTON.

4C:407 Date: 5 Mar 1835 RtCt: 5 Mar 1835
William FITZSIMMONS of Ldn to George NIXON of Ldn. B/S of int.
in 2a (descended from Mary FITZSIMMONS to children Wm.,
Samuel & James; cnvy/b George NIXON since dec'd to Mary) adj
Wm. HOLMES, heirs of James CARR.

4C:409 Date: 7 Oct 1834 RtCt: 6 Mar 1835
Thomas P. GLASCOCK & wife Catharine of Ldn to Benjamin RUST
of Ldn. B/S of int. in land of Patrick McINTYRE dec'd adj Abraham
SKILLMAN, John WRIGHT, William WILKINSON. Wit: John WHITE,
James McILHANEY. Delv. to RUST 11 Nov 1841.

4C:411 Date: 3 Jan 1835 RtCt: 9 Mar 1835
Adam SLATES dec'd. Division – 57¼a to dower; 23a Lot #1 & 8a
Lot #5 to Solomon SLATES; 31a Lot #2 to Eliza Ann SLATES; 27¾a

Lot #3 to Mary SLATES; 31½a Lot #4 to William SLATES. Divisors: Truman GORE, Joseph EVERHEART, Jacob WATERS. Gives plat. From case of Elizabeth Ann SLATES, Soloman SLATES, Wm. SLATES & Mary Ann SLATES infants <21y by Jacob SHAFFER next friend agst John SNOW & Sybilla SNOW late SLATES & Guardian of infants.

4C:414   Date: 3 Jan 1835   RtCt: 9 Mar 1835
Jacob WIRTZ & wife Catharine of Ldn to John CONARD of Ldn. B/S of 40a Lot #3 and 10a Lot #12 from div. of Jacob WIRTZ dec'd. Wit: Thomas J. MARLOW, Charles B. HAMILTON. Delv. to CONNARD 3 Dec 1836.

4C:416   Date: 9 Mar 1835   RtCt: 9 Mar 1835
Notley C. WILLIAMS, Thomas ROGERS, Elijah HOLMES, C. BINNS, Jared CHAMBLIN, Samuel ROGERS, Fielding LITTLETON, Horace LUCKETT, Robert T. LUCKETT, Wm. MERSHON, Newton KEENE, Sandford HUTCHISON, Thomas B. MERSHON, John S. EDWARDS, Saml. M. EDWARDS, Edward HAMMAT, Saml. M. BOSS, James C. WILLIAMS, Silas GARRETT, Thomas FRED & John BEAVERS. Bond on WILLIAMS as Sheriff to collect officer fees.

4C:418   Date: 9 Mar 1835   RtCt: 9 Mar 1835
Notley C. WILLIAMS, Thomas ROGERS, Elijah HOLMES, C. BINNS, Jared CHAMBLIN, Samuel ROGERS, Fielding LITTLETON, Horace LUCKETT, Robert T. LUCKETT, Wm. MERSHON, Newton KEENE, Sandford HUTCHISON, Thomas B. MERSHON, John S. EDWARDS, Saml. M. EDWARDS, Edward HAMMAT, Saml. M. BOSS, James C. WILLIAMS, Silas GARRETT, Thomas FRED & John BEAVERS. Bond on WILLIAMS as Sheriff to collect levies.

4C:419   Date: 9 Mar 1835   RtCt: 9 Mar 1835
Notley C. WILLIAMS, Thomas ROGERS, Elijah HOLMES, C. BINNS, Jared CHAMBLIN, Samuel ROGERS, Fielding LITTLETON, Horace LUCKETT, Robert T. LUCKETT, Wm. MERSHON, Newton KEENE, Sandford HUTCHISON, Thomas B. MERSHON, John S. EDWARDS, Saml. M. EDWARDS, Edward HAMMAT, Saml. M. BOSS, James C. WILLIAMS, Silas GARRETT, Thomas FRED & John BEAVERS. Bond on WILLIAMS as Sheriff to collect taxes.

4C:420   Date: 1 Dec 1834   RtCt: 10 Mar 1835
Thomas WILLIAMS & wife Lydia of Bond Co Illinois to Mortimer McILHANY of Ldn. B/S of int. in land of Elizabeth McILHANEY on E side of Blue Ridge.

4C:422   Date: 27 Jan 1835   RtCt: 10 Mar 1835
Jonathan CARTER of Ldn to Abner GIBSON. Trust for debt to William H. TRIPLETT using 166a on S side of Goose Creek cnvy/b TRIPLETT. Delv. to Abner GIBSON 1 Jun 1839.

4C:424   Date: 20 Feb 1835   RtCt: 10 Mar 1835
John BEVERIDGE & wife Keziah of Ldn to Humphrey B. POWELL
of Ldn. Trust for debt to Noble BEVERIDGE using land cnvy/b
James GUNN Nov 1817 adj Robert T. LUCKETT, Balaam OSBURN.
Wit: A. GIBSON, Hugh SMITH. Delv. pr order DBk 4M:100, 8 Jan
1841.

4C:426   Date: 3 Mar 1835   RtCt: 10 Mar 1835
James GRUBB of Ldn to Curtis GRUBB of Ldn. B/S of 26a on E
side of Short Hill adj __ BRADEN, Benjamin GRUBB, Peter WIRTZ.
Delv. to Curtis GRUBB 3 Aug 1835.

4C:428   Date: 10 Sep 1833   RtCt: 10 Mar 1835
Samuel TURNER & wife Amanda and Robert KEYS & wife Caroline
to Mortimer McILHANY. B/S of 17a allotted to Thomas P. WILLIAMS
and Amanda WILLIAMS now TURNER and Caroline WILLIAMS
now KEYS in div. Elizabeth McILHANY dec'd. Wit: John WHITE,
James McILHANY.

4C:429   Date: 10 Mar 1835   RtCt: 10 Mar 1835
Burr W. HARRISON, Thomas ROGERS & William ELLZEY of Ldn to
Jacob SHRIVER, David SHAWEN & Saml. BAKER of Ldn. Release
of trust of Oct 1831, DBk WWW:465, for debt to William ELLZEY
using 135a.

4C:430   Date: 27 Feb 1835   RtCt: 10 Mar 1835
Enoch FRANCIS of Ldn. DoE for man Daniel BERRY (promised 5y
ago). Wit: Thos. FRANCIS, Stephen W. McCARTY.

4C:431   Date: 9 Mar 1835   RtCt: __ Mar 1835
John LOVE dec'd. Division – court ordered 9 Feb 1835 – 90a Lot #1
to Richard ADAMS; 95½a Lot #2 to Thomas LOVE; 22¾a Lot #3 to
Henry & Sally LOVE; 13½a Lot #4 to Eli PIERPOINT & wife Hannah.
Gives plat. Joseph GRUBB & wife sold their int. to Richard ADAMS.
Divisors: Jno. J. MATHIAS, Wm. WILSON, Jas. McILHANEY. Case
of Richard ADAMS agst Thomas LOVE s/o James, Eli PIERPOINT
& wife Hannah, Joseph GRUB, Joseph GRUB & wife Mary, Henry
LOVE and Sally Love infants <21y by Thos. ROGERS their
Guardian ad litem.

4C:434   Date: 17 Dec 1834   RtCt: 10 Mar 1835
H. B. POWELL to Miller HOGUE. Release of trust of Aug 1825 for
debt to Joseph HOGUE, DBk RRR:378 using

4C:435   Date: 11 Mar 1835   RtCt: 11 Mar 1835
Archibald N. DOUGLAS to John S. EDWARDS. Trust for debt to
Charles LEWIS (Commr in case of Vincent LEWIS &c reps. of
James M. LEWIS dec'd agst Charles DOUGLAS & Archibald N.
DOUGLAS) using 188a.

4C:437   Date: 11 Mar 1835   RtCt: 11 Mar 1835
Mahlon BASFORD of Ldn to Joseph L. RUSSELL. Trust for debt to
Philip COONS of JeffVa using household items.

4C:438   Date: 14 Feb 1835   RtCt: 11 Mar 1835
Jacob WALTMAN & wife Mary to Michael SOUDER and Samuel SLATER. Trust for debt to John SOUDER using 109½a on Catoctin Creek adj Henry BROWN, Roaches Mill road. Wit: C. B. HAMILTON Jr., Wm. SLATER.

4C:441   Date: 1 Dec 1834   RtCt: 11 Mar 1835
William GALLEHER & wife Margery of Ldn to Thomas H. GALLEHER of Ldn. B/S of 2a (Lot #6 in div. of William GALLEHER dec'd less 3a sold to Seth SMITH, also see DBk VVV:121). Wit: E'd. HALL, Ludwell LEE. Delv. to T. WALKER Esqr. by order of GALLAHER 18 Mar 1836.

4C:442   Date: 22 Sep 1830   RtCt: 11 Mar 1835
Fanny ARMISTEAD of Ldn to John ISH of Ldn. B/S of log house & two ½a lots in Aldie subject to dower int. of Elen FULTON formerly prop. of Abraham FULTON dec'd. Delv. to ISH 21 Jun 1843.

4C:443   Date: 14 Nov 1834   RtCt: 12 Mar 1835
John CHAMBLIN & wife Lydia and Mason CHAMBLIN & wife Dewanner of Ldn to Charles J. KILGORE of MontMd. B/S of 100a in Scotland adj Abel MARKS, J. WALRAVEN, Alexander HARRISON. Wit: James McILHANEY, Timothy TAYLOR. Delv. to Jas. M. KILGORE 12 Dec 1853.

4C:445   Date: 11 Mar 1835   RtCt: 12 Mar 1835
Michael SPRING & wife Rachel of Ldn to Joshua PUSEY of Ldn. B/S of 23a Lot #4 in div. of Wm. ALT dec'd allotted to Rachel; and undivided ½ (2 shares, other prch/o Michael SPRING of heir Wm. ALT) int. in 30a Lot #3 in div. allotted to Rachel ALT wd/o Wm. dec'd. See DBk FFF:202. Wit: Thos. J. MARLOW, William SLATER.

4C:447   Date: 4 Feb 1830   RtCt: 12 Mar 1835
John CRIM & wife Margaret of Ldn to Adam CRIM of Ldn. B/S of 1/12th int. in 100a dower where widow Catharine CRIM wd/o Charles CRIM dec'd now lives adj Michael FRY, Jacob CRIM. Wit: George W. SHAWEN, Mortimer McILHANEY.

4C:449   Date: 16 Jan 1835   RtCt: 13 Mar 1835
Robert ELGIN & wife Elizabeth of Ldn to Gustavus ELGIN of Ldn. B/S of 49a Lot #5 in div. of __ ELGIN dec'd, adj Saml. T. ELGIN. Wit: Henry T. HARRISON, Hamilton ROGERS.

4C:451   Date: 19 Sep 1833   RtCt: 13 Mar 1835
David POTTS & wife Rebecca of Ldn to William POTTS and Jonas POTTS of Ldn. B/S of int. in 33a farm of John POTTS Sr. dec'd. Wit: Ebenezer GRUBB, John WHITE.

4C:454   Date: 11 Mar 1835   RtCt: 14 Mar 1835
Michael WIARD to William DERRY. Release of trust of Apr 1829 for debt to Jacob WATERS agent of George DERRY Admr. of Jacob & Catharine DERRY dec'd using 72a. Ackn. of WIARD and WATERS in JeffVa.

4C:455   Date: 27 Feb 1835   RtCt: 14 Mar 1835
William DERRY of Ldn to Christian NYSWANGER of Ldn. B/S of
32a adj __ PRINCE, NYSWANGER. Ackn. of DERRY in JeffVa.
Delv. to NISEWANGER 22 Apr 1836.

4D:001   Date: 18 Feb 1835   RtCt: 9 Mar 1835
James UNDERWOOD & wife Susannah of Ldn to Gerard B.
WAGER of JeffVa. Trust for debt to Samuel GIBSON of JeffVa using
int. in land now belonging to heirs of David NEAR dec'd and in
dower lands adj Philip COONS, Richard HURDLE, John NEER. Wit:
F. BECKHAM, Eli H. CANNELL.

4D:003   Date: 24 Dec 1833   RtCt: 20 Mar 1835
Uriel GLASSCOCK & wife Nancy to Charles L. POWELL. Trust for
debt to Mary E. POWELL using 133a from div. of Leven POWELL
Jr. Wit: William BENTON, Ludwell LUCKETT.

4D:006   Date: 2 Feb 1835   RtCt: 20 Mar 1835
Bernard TAYLOR & wife Sarah of Ldn to Jonathan TAYLOR of Ldn.
B/S of 150a on NW fork of Goose Creek adj __ DILLON, __ IDEN,
__ MILTON, Robert WHITE. Wit: James McILHANY, Timothy
TAYLOR. Delv. to TAYLOR 29 Jul 1835.

4D:008   Date: 21 Mar 1835   RtCt: 21 Mar 1835
William GLASSGOW & wife Ann of Ldn to Edward FRANCIS of Ldn.
B/S of 1/6th int. (from father Henry GLASSGOW)) in lot with brick
house in Lsbg adj widow of Thomas MORALLEE and 1/6th int. in lot
and brick house on Royal St. in Lsbg adj John SURGHNOR,
Edward FRANCIS. Wit: William ELLZEY, Francis W. LUCKETT.

4D:010   Date: 11 Mar 1835   RtCt: 26 Mar 1835
Charles LEWIS (Commr in case of Vincent LEWIS, Vincent LEWIS
2nd, Susan LEWIS, Catharine DARNE, Martha LEWIS, __ LESTER
& wife Eliza late LEWIS, Samuel HANCOCK & wife Jane late
LEWIS, James Battaile LEWIS, Fisher A. LEWIS, Charles H.
LEWIS, John H. LEWIS, Mary J. LEWIS, Margaret M. LEWIS,
Joseph E. N. LEWIS, Robert V. LEWIS, William F. LEWIS by
Charles LEWIS their next friends, Thomas B. LEWIS, Charles L.
LEWIS, James M. LEWIS, __ BRYANT & wife Sarah J. late LEWIS,
and Mary LEWIS wd/o John LEWIS vs. Archibald N. DOUGLAS) to
Archibald N. DOUGLAS of Ldn. B/S of 162a (from the late James M.
LEWIS dec'd, cnvy/b Betsey TEBBS May 1817, DBk 2W:157).

4D:012   Date: 16 Mar 1835   RtCt: 26 Mar 1835
Ludwell LUCKETT & wife Ann C. and Jane BRONAUGH (1 of 3
daus. and wd/o William BRONAUGH dec'd) of Ldn to Israel Peyton
THOMPSON of AlexDC. B/S of 334a Lot #2 (from div. of Wm.
BRONAUGH dec'd) in Mason Co Va on E side of Great Kanhawa
River. Wit: Francis W. LUCKETT. E. B. GRADY.

4D:015   Date: 13 Sep 1834   RtCt: 27 Mar 1835
William TORBERT & wife Hannah of Ldn to James JOHNSTON of
Ldn. Trust for debt to Stephen McPHERSON of Ldn using 10a adj
Thomas A. HEREFORD. Wit: N. C. WILLIAMS, Edw'd B. GRADY.
Delv. to Jno. G. HUMPHREY per order 24 Feb 1840.

4D:017   Date: 21 Mar 1835   RtCt: 27 Mar 1835
Lloyd NOLAND of Fqr to William R. SWART of Fqr. Release of trust
(from Richard COCKRAN in Sept 1819 who cnvy/t SWART) for debt
to Burr POWELL of Ldn using lot in Mdbg.

4D:020   Date: 5 Mar 1834   RtCt: 27 Mar 1835
Albert G. WATERMAN of PhilPa to William R. SWART of Fqr.
Release of trust of Aug 1828 for debt to Conrad BITZER using 3a.

4D:023   Date: 24 Feb 1834   RtCt: 27 Mar 1835
William R. SWART & wife Elizabeth of Fqr to William F. BROADDUS
of Rappahannock Co Va. B/S of 3a (prch/o Dr. Richard COCKRAN
Sep 1820) in Mdbg on Ashby's Gap Turnpike adj Sarah UPP,
Richard COCKRAN, SWART. Wit: Hugh SMITH, Asa ROGERS.
Delv. per order 3 Apr 1840.

4D:025   Date: 1 Aug 1834   RtCt: 27 Mar 1835
James B. WILSON & wife Sarah of Ldn to Ezekiel MOUNT of Ldn.
B/S of 1a (except small part condemned by Dennis & George W.
McCARTY to abut mill dam) on Goose Creek, Jonathan CARTER.
Wit: Peyton POWELL, John LUM, John SINCLAIR, Hamilton
ROGERS, Asa ROGERS.

4D:028   Date: 1 Aug 1834   RtCt: 27 Mar 1835
Ezekiel MOUNT of Ldn to James B. WILSON of Ldn. B/S of 2a on N
side of Goose Creek adj MOUNT, __ RUSE. Wit: Peyton POWELL,
John LUM, John SINCLAIR. Delv. to WILSON 11 May 1838.

4D:029   Date: 6 Oct 1826   RtCt: 14 Mar 1835
Joseph SMITH of AlexDC, Thomas SIM of WashDC, Armistead
LONG of Culpeper Co Va and John LITTLEJOHN of KY (Stephen
COOKE since dec'd) as Commrs. for sale of mortgage to Robert
WADE, Edward DORSEY, John McCORMICK and Alexander
LAWRENCE (trustee of Presbyterian Church) of Ldn. B/S of 2a
(trust of Mar 1794 by Patrick CAVAN for debt to Jesse TAYLOR
using ½ of Lot #6, ½ of Lot #23, 2a on W line of Lsbg, CAVAN and
TAYLOR died intestate). Wit: Roberdeau ANNIN, Alfred A.
ESKRIDGE, John JANNEY, William J. JONES, R. S. BRISCOE,
William WATERS. Delv. to A. J. BRADFIELD 6 Feb 1877.

4D:032   Date: 3 Feb 1835   RtCt: 31 Mar 1835
Abraham SILCOTT & wife Barsheba to Thomas HATCHER and
Joshua HATCHER. Trust for debt to Lydia PANCOAST using 80a
(dev. to Barsheba by George TAVENER). Wit: Edward B. GRADY,
Timothy TAYLOR Jr. Delv. per order 4 Feb 1843.

4D:037 Date: 31 Oct 1834 RtCt: 31 Mar 1835
John N. MARKS & George MARKS of Fqr and Stephen DULANEY
of Ldn to Stephen McPHERSON of Ldn. Release of trust of Aug
1831, DBk 3Y:066, for debt to George MARKS using 146a.

4D:039 Date: 31 Oct 1834 RtCt: 31 Mar 1835
John N. MARKS and George MARKS of Fqr and John P. DULANEY
of Ldn to Thomas FREDD. Release of trust of Aug 1831, DBk
3Y:068, for debt to George MARKS using 198a.

4D:042 Date: 31 Mar 1835 RtCt: 31 Mar 1835
Nelson HEAD and Geo. HEAD to Richard H. HENDERSON (Exor of
James SWART). Mortgage on house & lot on King St in Lsbg. Wit:
Saml. M. EDWARDS.

4D:042 Date: 31 Mar 1835 RtCt: 1 Apr 1835
Theodore C. DOWDLE to Fielding LITTLETON. Trust for debt to
John ISH using int. in estate of late John MUDD dec'd or from his
widow Martha GULICK. Wit: Burr W. HARRISON, W. A. POWELL,
Thos. W. EDWARDS.

4D:045 Date: 1 Oct 1834 RtCt: 1 Apr 1835
John B. YOUNG to Saml. MOORE. Trust for MOORE as security for
YOUNG & McCULLOUGH to Jacob JANNEY using Negroes
Wesley, Isaac & Lewis.

4D:046 Date: 30 Mar 1835 RtCt: 2 Apr 1835
Joshua HATCHER & wife Sarah Ann of Ldn to Henry S. TAYLOR of
Ldn. Trust for debt to Jacob BROWN of Ldn using 1/3rd of 176a
(originally of Richard BROWN) adj Shelburne Glebe, John
BROWN's saw mill, Andrew BIRDSALL, Alfred LOGAN. Wit: John
SIMPSON, David RUSE. Delv. to TAYLOR 13 Jun 1842.

4D:050 Date: 2 Mar 1835 RtCt: 4 Apr 1835
Joseph MILLER & wife Mary Ann of Ldn to John NICEWANNER of
Ldn. B/S of 114a adj David AXLINE, Gideon HOUSHOLDER. Wit:
Thomas J. MARLOW, William SLATER. Delv. to NICEWANGER 11
Jun 1838.

4D:053 Date: 30 Mar 1835 RtCt: 2 Apr 1835
Jacob BROWN & wife Judith of Ldn to Joshua HATCHER of Ldn.
B/S of 1/3rd of 176a adj Shelburne Glebe, John BROWN, Alfred
LOGAN, John BROWN's saw mill. Wit: John SIMPSON, David
RUSE. Delv. to HATCHER 11 Jan 1836.

4D:055 Date: 4 Apr 1835 RtCt: 4 Apr 1835
Samuel HOUGH & wife Jane to Charles G. ESKRIDGE and John
JANNEY. Trust for George RUST Jr., David SHAWEN and Charles
G. EDWARDS as security of George S. LACKLAND and HOUGH as
Admr. of Silas WHERRY dec'd using 436a "Goshen" or "Edwards
Ferry Farm" (prch/o Charles G. EDWARDS Oct 1832, DBk 4A:350).
Delv. to JANNY 7 Apr 1836.

4D:058   Date: 1 Apr 1835   RtCt: 4 Apr 1835
Joseph HILLIARD of Ldn to Archibald M. KITZMILLER of Ldn. B/S of ½a in Lsbg between John GRAY's lot on Back St and __ MORRALLEE. Wit: John THOMAS.

4D:060   Date: 1 Apr 1835   RtCt: 4 Apr 1835
Archibald M. KITZMILLER to Joseph HILLIARD. Mortgage for the above land. Wit: John THOMAS.

4D:060   Date: 25 Mar 1833   RtCt: 4 Apr 1835
Rebecca REECE of Newtown township, Delaware Co Pa (payment made to James TORBERT of Ldn) to John TORBERT. Release of trust for debt to Rebecca REESE.

4D:061   Date: 6 Apr 1835   RtCt: 6 Apr 1835
Charles SCHISLER of Ldn to James LEWIS of Ldn. Trust for benefit of Lewis Charles SCHISTER of Ldn using farm animals, household items, tools. Wit: A. M. KITZMILLER.

4D:062   Date: 28 Mar 1835   RtCt: 7 Apr 1835
Amos SKINNER & wife Peggy of Ldn to Nathan SKINNER Sr. of Ldn. B/S of 243a (where Amos resides, reserving 1/8[th]a for graveyard and area for schoolhouse adj John SKILLMAN, Dean JAMES, __ ROZEL, Richard McGRAW. Wit: Robert BAYLY, Charles LEWIS. Delv. to Nathan SKINNER 27 Sep 1839.

4D:065   Date: 7 Apr 1835   RtCt: 7 Apr 1835
John THOMAS of Lsbg to Henry W. THOMAS of Ffx. Gift of house & lot on N corner of Church & __ Sts in Lsbg (lower part of lot prch/o Charles DRISH). Wit: A. M. KITZMILLER, Robt. McINTYRE, Thos. W. EDWARDS. Delv. to H. W. THOMAS 24 Sep 1835.

4D:066   Date: 8 Apr 1835   RtCt: 8 Apr 1835
William JOHNSON & wife Margaret of Ldn to Alexander JOHNSON of Ldn. B/S of lot on E side of King St in Lsbg adj store house occ. by Alexander. Wit: William ELLZEY, Presley CORDELL. Delv. to Alx. JOHNSON 18 Jun 1835.

4D:068   Date: 8 Apr 1835   RtCt: 9 Apr 1835
James STEADMAN & wife Alice of Ldn to David STEADMAN of Ldn. B/S of 1/8a in Lsbg (cnvy/b John H. McCABE Jan 1832, DBk 3X:133) on King St. Wit: William ELLZEY, Francis W. LUCKETT. Delv. to STEADMAN 22 Jan 1840.

4D:071   Date: 20 Mar 1835   RtCt: 10 Apr 1835
Joshua PUSEY of Ldn and John COMPHER & wife Elizabeth of Ldn. Partition – Joshua owns 2 shares or ½ of undivided tract (allotted as dower to Rachel ALT wd/o William ALT dec'd, prch/b PUSEY of Michael SPRING) adj COMPHER, Wm. GRAHAM; COMPHER also owns 2 shares of this tract (1 share prch/o heir John ALT and the other dev. to wife Elizabeth an heir). They agree to div. land equally – PUSEY selling 31a dower interest. Wit: Wm.

SLATER, C. B. HAMILTON Jr. Delv. to COMPHER and PUSEY 9 Jan 1836.

4D:074 Date: 11 Mar 1835 RtCt: 13 Apr 1835
Charles DOUGLAS of Ldn to John S. EDWARDS of Ldn. Trust for debt to Commr of Charles LEWIS (Commr. in case of Vincent LEWIS & other reps. of James M. LEWIS dec'd agst Chas. DOUGLAS & Arch'd N. DOUGLAS) using 162a.

4D:076 Date: 23 Mar 1835 RtCt: 13 Apr 1835
Joel OSBURN Jr. to Timothy TAYLOR. Release of trust of Jul 1824 for debt to Morris OSBURN using 200a

4D:078 Date: 14 Apr 1835 RtCt: 14 Apr 1835
Philip BOGAR (Commr. in James BOOTH & wife agst Mary ARNOLD) to Samuel POTTERFIELD. B/S of 92a (formerly of father Michael BOGAR dec'd and Catharine ARNOLD dec'd m/o Sarah ARNOLD) adj POTTERFIELD, Robert JOHNSON, John VINCELL dec'd. Delv. to POTTERFIELD 24 Mar 1837.

4D:079 Date: 13 Apr 1835 RtCt: 14 Apr 1835
Isaac VANDEVANTER dec'd. Renunciation of will by widow Mary VANDEVANTER. Wit: Geo. K. FOX, Presley CORDELL.

4D:079 Date: 13 Apr 1835 RtCt: 14 Apr 1835
Lewis TORRISON. Oath as 1st Lt. in Va Militia.

4D:080 Date: 14 Mar 1835 RtCt: 13 Apr 1835
Robert RUSSELL of Ldn to Israel WILLIAMS of Ldn. B/S of 3/7th of "Taylor Town Tract" (cnvy/b James McILHANY and Conrad R. DOWELL). Delv. to WILLIAMS 26 May 1835.

4D:081 Date: 11 Oct 1834 RtCt: 13 Apr 1835
Enos NICHOLS & wife Edna, Jonah HATCHER & wife Adaline and William HATCHER & wife Elizabeth of Ldn to John CHAMBLIN of Ldn. B/S of 125a on NW fork of Goose Creek (formerly owned by Mahlon GREGG) adj Burr P. CHAMBLIN, Charles CHAMBLIN, James COCHRAN, Sarah GREGG, Issachar BROWN. Wit: Timothy TAYLOR Jr., James McILHANY, David REECE. Delv. to CHAMBLIN 27 Dec 1838.

4D:085 Date: 13 Sep 1834 RtCt: 13 Apr 1835
Joshua NICHOLS & wife Naomi of Ldn to William BOLON of Ldn. B/S of 19a on NW fork of Goose Creek adj Daniel COCKRELL, David SMITH, John SMITH. Wit: John SIMPSON, David REECE. Delv. to BOLON 10 Jun 1837.

4D:087 Date: 2 Feb 1835 RtCt: 3 Apr 1835
John REED late of Ldn now of Ohio to James C. JANNEY of Ldn. Trust for benefit of Nancy HOE w/o Howsen HOE and d/o REED using household items. Wit: John JONES, Aquilla JANNEY.

4D:088 Date: 14 Mar 1835 RtCt: 13 Apr 1835
Israel WILLIAMS of Ldn to Samuel STOUTSENBERGER of Ldn. Trust for debt to Robert RUSSELL using 3/7th of "Taylor Town

Tract". Delv. to Jacob STOUTSENBERGER Exor of Saml. STOUTSENBERGER 15 Jun 1847.

4D:091   Date: 13 Sep 1834   RtCt: 13 Apr 1835
Humphrey SHEPHERD & wife Catharine of Ldn to Joshua NICHOLS of Ldn. B/S of 166a on NW fork of Goose Creek adj John SMITH, David SMITH. Wit: John SIMPSON, David REECE. Delv. to Thomas NICHOLS Admr of Joshua NICHOLS dec'd 11 Dec 1854.

4D:093   Date: 14 Jun 1834   RtCt: 13 Apr 1835
John ROBERTSON & wife Elizabeth of Ldn to Sidney WILLIAMS and Elijah JAMES of Ldn. B/S of 8 sq. pole lot at "cross roads" on W side of Catoctin Mt. (SE part of ROBERTSON's plantation) to build a school and for occasional use as house of public worship for christian professors. Wit: Geo. W. SHAWEN, C. B. HAMILTON.

4D:095   Date: 13 Apr 1835   RtCt: 13 Apr 1835
Thomas SCHOOLEY of Ldn to Eli L. SCHOOLEY of Ldn. B/S of 65a as William SCHOOLEY, Ephraim SCHOOLEY, John SCHOOLEY.

4D:097   Date: 26 Nov 1834   RtCt: 13 Apr 1835
Thomas SWANN of WashDC but now of Ldn to George M. CHICHESTER Esqr of Ldn. B/S of 22a on Catoctin Mt. on NW side of Limestone run adj Charles P. TUTT, Mrs. SULLIVAN. Gives small plat. Delv. to CHICHESTER 7 Aug 1835.

4D:099   Date: 21 Jun 1834   RtCt: 13 Apr 1835
Seth SMITH of Union to James JOHNSON of Ldn. B/S of ¼a adj SMITH and carting [carding?] machine (from defaulted trust of Sept 1826 by Craven WALKER of Union to Jesse HOGE for debt to James HOGE now dec'd; SMITH apptd. in place of Jesse HOGE now dec'd). Wit: Jonas JANNEY, William GALLEHER, John R. HIBBS. Delv. to Jno. COOPER 25 Oct 1841.

4D:101   Date: 21 Mar 1835   RtCt: 13 Apr 1835
John TIMMS & wife Elizabeth of Ldn to John COOPER Sr. of Ldn. B/S of 51a adj Dr. BOGEN, Geo. COOPER. Wit: Newton KEENE, Presley CORDELL.

4D:103   Date: 27 Mar 1835   RtCt: 13 Apr 1835
John COOPER Sr. & wife Eve to Wm. CLENDENING Jr. Trust for debt to John TIMMS using 51a as above. Wit: William CLENDENING, Joshua PUSEY.

4D:106   Date: 10 Apr 1835   RtCt: 13 Apr 1835
Thomas SWANN now at his farm in Ldn to son Robert P. SWANN of Ldn. Gift of land on road from Big Spring thru the mt.

4D:107   Date: 18 Jul 1832   RtCt: 14 Apr 1835
Jane LOVE of Mdbg to James W. BRAWNER of Aldie. B/S of ½a Lot #5 on Mercer St in Aldie with brick house. Wit: William NOLAND, Benj'n. SMITH, Thomas J. NOLAND. Delv. to ___ 13 Jun 1836.

4D:109   Date: 5 Dec 1834   RtCt: 14 Apr 1835
Charles B. HAMILTON Jr. & wife Sarah C. of Ldn to George
COOPER of Ldn. B/S of 105a "Ogden farm" (cnvy/b trustee James
McILHANY to John HAMILTON now dec'd). Wit: George MARLOW,
Wm. SLATER.

4D:111   Date: 1 Jan 1835   RtCt: 14 Apr 1835
William G. FURR of Ldn to John K. LITTLETON of Ldn. B/S of 20a
(called in title bond of Maaziah THOMAS the Tan Yard Lot) adj
Enoch FURR Sr., "Fred's meadow", LITTLETON. Delv. to
LITTLETON 19 Mar 1836.

4D:112   Date: 20 Mar 1835   RtCt: 14 Apr 1835
Maaziah THOMAS & wife Elizabeth of Fqr to William G. FURR of
Ldn. B/S of 20a as above. Wit: Abner GIBSON, Hugh SMITH. Delv.
to __.

4D:114   Date: 13 Apr 1835   RtCt: 15 Apr 1835
John ABRAHAM & wife Mary of Ldn to William, Jacob and Emanuel
WENNER of Ldn. B/S of 10a and 1½a on Short Hill and right in the
dower lot (allotted Mary WENNER now Mary ABRAHAM). Wit: C. B.
HAMILTON Jr., Wm. SLATER. Delv. to William W. WENNER 1 Sep
1851.

4D:117   Date: 14 Feb 1835   RtCt: 13 Apr 1835
Ignatius TILLETT & wife Mary Ann and Margaret HUMPHREY of
Bellmont Co Ohio to James THOMPSON of Ldn. B/S of ½ int. in
136a (former prop. of Charles HUMPHREY dec'd) between Blue
Ridge and Short hill on headwaters of little Kitoctin and John
CONARD, James WHITE's heirs, Andrew COPELAND, Thomas
HOUGH and 14a (cnvy/b James COPELAND to Will HUMPHREY
and Mary Ann Humphrey then infant ch/o Charles dec'd) on NW side
of Short Hill adj Andrew COPELAND, William and James
THOMPSON, heirs of Josiah WHITE dec'd. Wit: Mead JARVIS,
James TILLET. Delv. to THOMPSON 26 Apr 1836.

4D:119   Date: 25 Oct 1835   RtCt: 16 Apr 1835
Edmund J. LEE & wife Sally and Everit SAUNDERS of Lsbg.
Exchange of adj 1a and 7a on N side of Lsbg turnpike road. Wit:
Jno. J. MATHIAS, Wilson C. SELDEN.

4D:122   Date: 17 Apr 1835   RtCt: 17 Apr 1835
John BEST of Ldn to George H. ALDER of Ldn. Trust for debt to
Lydia HEATON (Guardian of Jane C. HEATON) and William C.
PALMER of Ldn using farm animals.

4D:123   Date: 17 Apr 1835   RtCt: 17 Apr 1835
William K. ISH & wife __ of Ldn to R. H. HENDERSON of Ldn. Trust
for debt to A. G. WATERMAN, Saml. CAMPBELL, Burr WEEKS &
Horace LUCKETT using 3/5th of 435a where ISH now lives. Delv. to
WEEKS 15 Dec 1835.

4D:125   Date: 15 Apr 1835   RtCt: 17 Apr 1835
William S. EACHES & wife Ann R. to Gourley REEDER. Trust for debt to Henry S. TAYLOR, Aquila MEAD, Thomas EACHES, heirs of Charles BENNETT Jr. dec'd, Arch'd MAINS, Henry TAYLOR and Chas. B. HAMILTON and as endorsers on bank note using 61¼a (cnvy/b Exors of Israel JANNEY), farm animals, farm and household items. Wit: John SIMPSON, Timothy TAYLOR Jr.

4D:128   Date: 17 Apr 1835   RtCt: 17 Apr 1835
Judson EMBERSON of Ldn to A. M. KITZMILLER. Trust for debt to George FOSTER using wagon. Delv. to FOSTER 12 Aug 1835.

4D:129   Date: 17 Apr 1835   RtCt: 17 Apr 1835
Michael MORALLEE & wife Emily P. of Ldn to Conrad P. DOWELL and James McILHANY of Ldn. Trust for debt to Conrad BITZER of Ldn using house & lot on N side of Market St in Lsbg occ. by Samuel HARPER as a tavern; house & lot on No side of Loudoun St occ. by MORRALLEE; house and lot on S side of Loudoun St. occ. by William MERCHANT. Wit: Wilson C. SELDEN, John J. MATHIAS. Delv. to Conrad DOWELL 26 Oct 1837.

4D:131   Date: 17 Nov 1834   RtCt: 18 Apr 1835
Mahlon JANNEY of Ldn to Josiah J. JANNEY of Ldn. B/S of 71a (cnvy/b Arch'd McDANIEL Mar 1830) adj Edward McDANIEL, Rich'd BROWN, Wm. SMITH. Delv. to Josiah J. JANNEY 26 Jun 1837.

4D:132   Date: 7 Jan 1834   RtCt: 18 Apr 1835
Henry CLAGETT of Ldn to Benjamin SHREVE Jr. of Ldn. B/S of 78a on Tuscarora adj Benj. SHREVE Sr., Carolina rd., Mary FOSTER patent. Wit: Chas. SHREVE, Robert TAYLOR, Wm. H. SIMPSON. Delv. to SHREVE 9 Jun 1838.

4D:133   Date: 7 Apr 1835   RtCt: 18 Apr 1835
Garret WINECOOP/WYNKOOP of Ldn to Lewis CROSS. BoS for farm animals and items, crops. Wit: David WEATHERBY.

4D:134   Date: 30 Mar 1833   RtCt: 20 Apr 1835
David LOVETT and Craven OSBURN of Ldn to Henry M. DOWLING of Ldn. B/S of ½a in Hllb (prch/o __ GLASSCOCK) adj Josiah WHITE dec'd. Wit: J. H. BENNETT, Wm. DIVINE, Joshua WHITE.

4D:135   Date: 23 Mar 1835   RtCt: 20 Apr 1835
Peter WIRTZ & wife Leah of Ldn to Thomas J. MARLOW of Ldn. B/S of 59a (Lot #7 allotted in div. of Jacob WIRTZ dec'd). Wit: Joshua PUSEY, William CLENDENING. Delv. per order filed 4M:178, 3 Jun 1847.

4D:137   Date: 14 Feb 1835   RtCt: 20 Apr 1835
Thomas J. HARPER & wife Margaret of Warren Co Ohio to Robert MOFFETT of Ldn. B/S of int. in land of Andrew HIXON, half brother of Margaret who died intestate entitled to part of estate of father Timothy HIXON dec'd. Andrew's 2 infant children died in infancy. Ackn. in Montgomery Co Ohio. Delv. to MOFFETT 11 Nov 1835.

4D:139   Date: 14 Apr 1835   RtCt: 14 Apr 1835
John SMALE – native of England, admitted as citizen of US. He was <21y at time father Simon SMALE was naturalized, has been in US at least 5y and in Va at least 1y. Renounces king of Great Britain and Ireland.

4D:140   Date: __ 1835   RtCt: 20 Apr 1835
Isaac HOLMES & wife Hannah S. of Ldn to Robt. L. WRIGHT of Ldn. Trust for debt to John WRIGHT of Ldn and as security on bond to William PIGGOTT using 44a. Delv. to Jno. WRIGHT 9 Oct 1835.

4D:142   Date: 14 Feb 1835   RtCt: 20 Apr 1835
John P. TICE & wife Ruth (late GREGG d/o Aaron GREGG dec'd & gr-dau/o William GREGG dec'd of Ldn) of Warren Co Ohio to Robert MOFFETT of Ldn. B/S of ¼th int. in land of Ruth's grandfather and of 8a of her father and ¼ of estate of brother Rezin GREGG dec'd and ¼th of his share in the 8a. Wit: Jno. S. McDONALD, Wm. J. McKINNEY. Delv. to MOFFETT 11 Nov 1835.

4D:144   Date: 20 Apr 1835   RtCt: 20 Apr 1835
William COOPER & wife Elizabeth of Ldn to Ann SAUNDERS of Ldn. B/S of 16a on E side of Catocton Mt. adj 20a lot formerly prch/o COOPER. Wit: Francis W. LUCKETT, Saml. M. EDWARDS. Delv. to B. SAUNDERS & wife 27 May 1837.

4D:146   Date: 27 Apr 1835   RtCt: 27 Apr 1835
Edward CARTER of Ldn to grandchildren Emily J. GIBSON, Eliza H. GIBSON and Julia A. GIBSON and Carter H. GIBSON, Albert L. GIBSON and Landon C. GIBSON (ch/o Israel & Alice GIBSON). Gift of household items, cows. Wit: Landon L. CARTER, Geo. W. B. CURNS.

4D:148   Date: 1 Sep 1834   RtCt: 22 Apr 1835
James BROWN & wife Ruth of Ldn to Mahlon TAVENER of Ldn. B/S of 5a on W edge of Turnpike adj S. J. TAVENER, Gabriel MEGEATH. Wit: Edward HALL, Ludwell LUCKETT. Delv. to Jos. P. McGEATH per order 21 Mar 1836.

4D:150   Date: 4 Feb 1834   RtCt: 22 Apr 1835
James MERCHANT & wife Mary of Ldn to William KEYS of Ldn. B/S of 3a adj Mr. WIGGINTON, Church lot, __ GRUBB, __ COOPER. Wit: John WHITE, Mortimer McILHANEY. Delv. to KEYS 8 Jun 1836.

4D:152   Date: 22 Apr 1835   RtCt: 23 Apr 1835
Samuel M. EDWARDS of Lsbg to Edmond J. LEE of AlexDC. Release of trust of Aug 1832 for bonds to Samuel M. EDWARDS as Commr. Delv. pr order in 3Y:327 on __.

4D:154   Date: 15 Mar 1835   RtCt: 23 Apr 1835
Mary THATCHER (wd/o William dec'd) and Calvin THATCHER to Thos. ROGERS Dpty Shff for Johnston CLEVELAND late Shff of

Ldn Committee Admr dbn of William THATCHER dec'd. Bond to refund payments to cover any debts. Wit: Thomas W. EDWARDS.

4D:154 Date: 26 Mar 1835 RtCt: 23 Apr 1835
Emeline THATCHER (ch/o William dec'd) and William LODGE to Thos. ROGERS Dpty Shff for Johnston CLEVELAND late Shff of Ldn Committee Admr dbn of William THATCHER dec'd. Bond to refund payments to cover any debts. Wit: Calvin THATCHER.

4D:155 Date: 27 Mar 1835 RtCt: 23 Apr 1835
Elvira THATCHER (ch/o William dec'd) and Calvin THATCHER to Thos. ROGERS Dpty Shff for Johnston CLEVELAND late Shff of Ldn Committee Admr dbn of William THATCHER dec'd. Bond to refund payments to cover any debts. Wit: Jas. L. HAMILTON.

4D:156 Date: 23 Dec 1834 RtCt: 24 Apr 1835
George KEEN of Ldn to Thomas ROGERS. Trust for debt to Fielding LITTLETON (Commr. in case of Elijah HATCHER agst Mahlon TAVENER) using of __a (cnvy/b ROGERS, formerly owned by John HATCHER now dec'd) adj William C. PALMER. Delv. to ROGERS 14 Jun 1837.

4D:159 Date: 13 Mar 1835 RtCt: 24 Apr 1835
Washington G. SINGLETON of Winchester, FredVa to Theo'd. LEITH of Ldn. B/S of house & lot in Union (from trust of Oct 1833 from John M. ANDERSON).

4D:161 Date: 13 Apr 1835 RtCt: 25 Apr 1835
Garrett WALKER of Ldn to Joseph GORE of Ldn. Trust for Enos NICHOLS, Guilford GREGG dec'd and Samuel BROWN as security on loan from Thomas JAMES of Ldn using 1/7th of 50a dower lot of mother Sophia WALKER from Benjamin WALKER dec'd. adj James WELSH, Samuel BEAVERS, Benjamin WALKER, Gabriel McGEATH.

4D:162 Date: 21 Apr 1835 RtCt: 25 Apr 1835
Samuel CHINN (Commr. in Mar 1835 suit of CREBBS & THOMPSON agst WILSON) to Israel B. THOMPSON. B/S of 66a (beq. by Rawleigh CHINN dec'd to dau the late Elizabeth WILSON during her life). Delv pr order 9 Jan 1836.

4D:164 Date: 21 Apr 1835 RtCt: 25 Apr 1835
Israel B. THOMPSON of Fqr to Samuel CHINN. Trust for debt to Samuel CHINN (as Commr.) using above land. Delv. pr order 9 Jan 1836.

4D:166 Date: 4 Sep 1834 RtCt: 26 Apr 1835
John KILE & wife Winnefred of Ldn to Marcus DISHMAN of Ldn. B/S of ½a (part of lot where KILE now resides) at pot house at junction of road from Mount's Mill to Mdbg, adj BRONAUGH's heirs, William BENTON. Wit: Abner GIBSON, Ludwell LUCKETT. Delv. to DISHMAN 8 Apr 1836.

4D:168   Date: 21 Apr 1835   RtCt: 27 Apr 1835
John THOMAS to Henry W. THOMAS. B/S of 23a with merchant mill (Henry W. was trustee in deed of Jan 1833 from George RICKARD, John bought defaulted trust but sale pronounced invalid) adj Peter COMPHER.

4D:170   Date: 27 Apr 1835   RtCt: 28 Apr 1835
William W. KITZMILLER to John THOMAS. Trust for debt to James GARRISON using int. in house & lot where he resides on S side of Loudoun St in Lsbg. Delv. to THOMAS 20 Nov 1835.

4D:171   Date: 16 Dec 1834   RtCt: 29 Apr 1835
Peter O'BRIEN of Ldn to Robert BARRETT of Ldn. B/S of 11a (Lot #4 allotted Elizabeth JACOBS in div. of Hugh FULTON dec'd, less 1½a deeded by Elizabeth now dec'd to John VARNES).

4D:173   Date: 30 Mar 1835   RtCt: 29 Apr 1835
Thomas B. LOVE of Ldn to James D. LOVE, Fenton M. LOVE and Mary R. LOVE of Ldn. B/S of int. in 361a farm where father James LOVE dec'd resided except dower right of widow Susannah (James D., Fenton M. and Mary R. convey their 3/4ᵗʰ undivided int. in 12a of father James LOVE dec'd).

4D:175   Date: 13 Sep 1834   RtCt: 30 Apr 1835
John W. DAVIS & wife Jane D. of Ldn to Edward JENKINS. B/S of 75a (prch/o Wm. WARFORD) adj WARFORD, Stephen BEARD, Abraham WARFORD, Wm. ALLEN; and 100a (prch/o Burr W. HARRISON May 1834) adj __ DAVIS, __ FURGUSON, Thos. MOSS. Wit: Charles LEWIS, John MOORE. Delv. to JENKINS 7 Sep 1835.

4D:177   Date: 5 May 1835   RtCt: 5 May/11 May 1835
Uriel GLASSCOCK & wife Nancy of Ldn to Richard H. HENDERSON, Jesse TIMMS & William A. POWELL. Trust for debt to George CARTER of Oatlands using 98a (cnvy/b James VERNON Apr 1827); and 102a (cnvy/b John VERNON Nov 1827); and 195a (cnvy/b Francis W. LUCKETT Exor of William BRONAUGH and his widow Jane); and 133a (cnvy/b Mary Emily POWELL, William A. POWELL, Lucy P. POWELL, John L. POWELL, Maria L. POWELL, A. GIBSON, S. Elizabeth GIBSON and A. H. POWELL Dec 1833). Wit: James RUST, Ludwell LUCKETT. Delv. to CARTER 14 Aug 1840.

4D:183   Date: 10 Sep 1834   RtCt: 4 Sep 1834/5 May 1835
Presley CORDELL of Ldn to John HAWLING of Ldn. Release of trust of May 1819 for debt to Henry CLAGETT of Ldn using 73a.

4D:184   Date: 4 May 1835   RtCt: 6 May 1835
Bailey BARTON of Ldn to Marcus DISHMAN of Ldn. Trust for debt to Ludwell LUCKETT using int. in thrashing machine.

4D:186 Date: 7 Jan 1835 RtCt: 10 Mar/7 May 1835
Stephen McPHERSON & wife Cecelia of Ldn to John Leven
POWELL of Ldn. B/S of 322a on Beaverdam (where McPHERSON
now lives under deeds from John MARKS and George MARKS) adj
Joshua GREGG. Wit: Notley C. WILLIAMS, Edw'd. B. GRADY. Delv.
to POWELL 31 May 1839.

4D:190 Date: 31 Jan 1835 RtCt: 8 May 1835
Hamilton ROGERS & wife Mary of Ldn to H. B. POWELL of Ldn.
Trust for debt to Townsend D. PEYTON using land and slaves
Charlotte and 3 children Caroline, Elizabeth & Shadrack and his 2
children Dade and Mary prch/o PEYTON. Delv. to Asa ROGERS per
order 9 Jun 1857.

4D:192 Date: 8 Aug 1833 RtCt: 8 May 1835
Kemp COCK & wife Amanda of Fqr to Samuel RECTOR of Ldn. B/S
of int. in land of Amanda's father Joseph HATCHER dec'd, adj
Gourley REEDER, Price JACOBS, Jonas LOVETT. Wit: Hugh
SMITH, Asa ROGERS. Same deed as 4B:101 – relinq. of dower
now returned.

4D:194 Date: 10 May 1835 RtCt: 9 [10?] May 1835
John McINTYRE of Lsbg to Edward FRANCIS of Lsbg. B/S of
undivided 1/8th int. in 296a of father Patrick McINTYRE dec'd subject
to dower of his mother adj Abraham SKILLMAN, William
WILKINSON. Delv. to FRANCIS 5 Sep 1838.

4D:195 Date: 1 Apr 1835 RtCt: 11 May 1835
John SPRING of Ldn to Samuel S. STONE of Ldn. Trust for debt to
Jonas P. SCHOOLEY & Samuel C. LUCKETT using farm animals,
household items. Delv. to STONE 16 Aug 1837.

4D:197 Date: 11 May 1835 RtCt: 11 May 1835
Francis DONOHOE of Ldn to Edward HAMMAT of Ldn. B/S of
undivided 1/8th of 151a of father Francis DONOHOE dec'd adj __
HAWLING, __ SHREVE, __ WILDMAN. Delv. to HAMMAT 11 Nov
1836.

4D:199 Date: 7 Feb 1832 RtCt: 29 May 1835
Johnston CLEVELAND, William MERSHON, Wilson C. SELDON Jr.
& wife Eliza of Ldn and James L. McKENNA & wife Ann C. of Ffx to
Alfred DULIN of Ldn. B/S of 13a. Wit: William B. HARRISON,
Thomas SAUNDERS, Thomas MOSS, Albert FAIRFAX.

4D:202 Date: 25 Apr 1835 RtCt: 11 May 1835
Reuben COCKERELL & wife Mary Ellen (late COE) of Ldn to
William WILKINSON of Ldn. Trust for debt to William & A. WRIGHT
of Ldn using land allotted Mary Ellen in div. of father Edward M.
COE dec'd, DBk 4B:213; and int. in dower of widow Mary COE; farm
animals, farm and household items, crops. Wit: John SIMPSON,
Timothy TAYLOR.

4D:205   Date: 23 Sep 1834   RtCt: 11 May 1835
Betsey TEBBS of PrWm to Charles DOUGLAS and Archibald N.
DOUGLAS of Ldn. B/S of int. in 22a Lot #4, 57-1/10a Lot #9 and 15a
Lot #10 from estate of Hugh DOUGLAS dec'd f/o Charles &
Archibald in which the two have a lease interest.

4D:207   Date: 16 Apr 1835   RtCt: 11 May 1835
William COE Jr. and George BARR of Ldn to William COE Sr. of
Ldn. Trust for debt to Benjamin RUST using int. in farm left by
Edw'd. COE dec'd, farm animals, household items. Delv. to F. W.
EDWARDS trustee appt'd by ct Aug 1839 in place of Wm. COE Sr.
21 Aug 1830.

4D:210   Date: 26 Dec 1834   RtCt: 11 May 1835
Amos JANNEY of Ldn to Samuel KALB of Ldn. B/S of 51a (Lot #1 in
div. of Edmond JENNINGS dec'd) adj __ BRADEN, David AXLINE.
Wit: Harvey COGSIL, Joseph MORRISON, Susannah C. ROWLES,
John GRUBB.

4D:212   Date: 10 Sep 1834   RtCt: 12 May 1835
John GIBSON & wife Rachel of Ldn to George GIBSON of Ldn. B/S
of 2¼a "Tan Yard Lot" where John now lives on Panther Skin Creek
on E side of road thru Upperville by the Baptist Meeting house to
Triplett's Mill. Wit: Wm. O. CHILTON, And'w SALE, Ralls CALVERT,
Edward HALL, Cuthbert POWELL. Delv. to Geo. GIBSON 4 Oct
1842.

4D:214   Date: 13 May 1834   RtCt: 16 May 1835
Burr W. HARRISON & wife Sally H. of Ldn to John W. DAVIS of Ldn.
B/S of 100a (part of div. of estate of Matthew HARRISON dec'd, for
many yrs occ. by Hezekiah W. ATHEY as tenant) adj Stephen
BEARD, James ALLEN of Agnes, DAVIS. Wit: Saml. M. EDWARDS,
Henry T. HARRISON.

4D:216   Date: 14 May 1835   RtCt: 16 May 1835
William LITTLETON of Ldn to sons Eli LITTLETON and William
Dickens LITTLETON. Gift of land where Wm. resides. Wit: Minor
FURR. Delv. to Eli & Wm. D. LITTLETON 16 May 1837.

4D:218   Date: 1 Apr 1835   RtCt: 16 May 1835
Philip HEATER & wife Magdalen of Ldn to son John HEATER of
Ldn. Gift of 93½a (cnvy/b Israel WILLIAMS) adj __ HIXON, __
CLAPHAM, __ POTTERFIELD; and 89a on W side of Catocton Mt.
adj other land. Wit: C. B. HAMILTON Jr., Wm. SLATER. Delv. to
John HEATER 3 Jul 1835.

4D:221   Date: 28 Oct 1834   RtCt: 16 May 1835
John BRAGG & wife Rebekah of Guersea Co Ohio to Silas
HUTCHISON of Ldn. B/S of 68a adj James WHALEY. Wit: T. A.
BEATTY, J. BLACK.

4D:223   Date: 11 Oct 1834   RtCt: 11 May 1835
Jacob WATERS of Ldn to Michael DERRY and John JANNEY of
Amos of Ldn. Trust for debt to Peter DERRY of Ldn using 115a
(prch/o David WALTMAN, Samuel & Maria WALTMAN) and int. in
lands of John WALTMAN dec'd. Wit: C. B. HAMILTON Jr., Wm.
SLATER.

4D:227   Date: 12 May 1835   RtCt: 20 May 1835
Asa B. CORDELL of Lsbg to Presley CORDELL of Lsbg. Trust for
benefit of numerous creditors using entire stock of goods, book
accts. horse.

4D:229   Date: 4 Feb 1835   RtCt: 22 May 1835
Andrew TORBERT & wife Jane of Montgomery Co Pa to James
TORBERT of Morgan Co Ohio. B/S of 1/9th int. in 184a adj Peter
ROMINE, Benjamin OVERFIELD (see bond by Jenkin PHILLIPS
and Thomas BOTTS Oct 1793). Wit: Wm. P. HIBBERD, B. F.
HANCOCK, J. W. EVANS.

4D:233   Date: 12 Feb 1835   RtCt: 22 May 1835
James TORBERT & wife Hannah Mariah of Morgan Co Ohio to
William SETTLE of Ldn. B/S of 1/9th int. in 184a (less 14a) as above.
Wit: Benjamin GRAYSON, Notley C. WILLIAMS.

4D:236   Date: 26 Mar 1835   RtCt: 22 May 1835
William SETTLE & wife Margaret of Ldn to Balaam OSBURN of Ldn.
B/S of int. in 184a (less 14a). Wit: Ludwell LUCKETT, Edw'd. B.
GRADY. Delv. to OSBURN 2 Dec 1835.

4D:238   Date: 31 Jan 1835   RtCt: 22 May 1835
Joseph FREDD & wife Hannah of Ldn to Balaam OSBURN of Ldn.
B/S of 5/9th and 1/6th of the sixth share of 184a (less 14a) where
Samuel TORBERT dec'd formerly resided as above. Wit: Ludwell
LUCKETT, Roger CHEW. Delv. to OSBURN 2 Dec 1835.

4D:241   Date: 27 Feb 1835   RtCt: 22 May 1835
Hugh ROGERS & wife Mary of Belmont Co Ohio to Balaam
OSBURN of Ldn. B/S of int. (3 shares purchased Feb 1835, see
below) in "Torbert Tract" prch/o Jenkin PHILLIPS by Samuel
TORBERT now dec'd and left to his parents Thomas & Elizabeth
TORBERT then div. between brothers and sisters. Wit: John T.
SIMPSON, Saml. WILSON. Delv. to OSBURN 2 Dec 1835.

4D:242   Date: 23 Feb 1835   RtCt: 22 May 1835
Thomas TORBERT, John FRED & wife Mary and William
LIVINGSTON & wife Daidasy of Belmont Co Va to Hugh ROGERS.
B/S of int. in land as above. Wit: Asa HOGE, Saml. TORBERT.

4D:244   Date: 7 Apr 1835   RtCt: 22 May 1835
James B. WILSON of Ldn to George BITZER of Ldn. Trust for debt
to Dorothy BITZER using 120a on S side of Goose Creek where
WILSON resides including where father Moses WILSON now lives.
Delv. to Jno. A. WILSON per order 8 Jun 1835.

4D:246 Date: 2 Apr 1835 RtCt: 24 Apr/22 May 1835
William MERSHON, John J. COLEMAN and Jas. L. McKENNA of Ldn to Wilson C. SELDEN and Ludwell LUCKETT of Ldn. B/S of ¼a (part of Belmont tract) on NW corner of garden – usual place of interment of deceased members of Ludwell's family. Delv. to SELDEN 1 Aug 1840.

4D:248 Date: 21 May 1835 RtCt: 22 May 1835
Mary HOUGH of Lsbg to Richard H. HENDERSON of Lsbg. B/S of lot in Lsbg (cnvy/b sister Fanny SHEPHERD) adj HENDERSON. Wit: Saml. M. EDWARDS.

4D:249 Date: 12 May 1835 RtCt: 26 May 1835
William TORBERT & wife Hannah of Ldn to Samuel TORBERT of Fqr. B/S of 10a (part of land cnvy/b Thomas DRAKE to Stephen McPHERSON Feb 1830, DBk 3Y:088) adj __ HEREFORD. Wit: Edward B. GRADY, Roger CHEW. Delv. to TORBERT 1 Aug 1838.

4D:250 Date: 30 May 1834 RtCt: 26 May 1835
Yeoman Stephen McPHERSON & wife Cecilia of Ldn to William TORBERT of Ldn. B/S of 10a as above. Wit: Notley C. WILLIAMS, Edward B. GRADY.

4D:252 Date: 28 Apr 1835 RtCt: 26 May 1835
Daniel EVERHART & wife Catharine of Ldn to Ishmael VANHORN of Ldn. B/S of ¼a in Lovettsville on E end of Lovetts farm. Wit: William SLATER, Thomas J. MARLOW. Delv. to Saml. MILLER per order 29 Jun 1839.

4D:254 Date: 27 Mar 1835 RtCt: 27 May 1835
John MULL of Ldn to John LONG of Ldn. B/S of 10a Lot #2 from div. of father David MULL dec'd and 1/7th int. in 36a dower Lot #8 of widow Mary MULL. Delv. to Solomon VINCELL per order 19 Mar 1849.

4D:256 Date: 21 Apr 1835 RtCt: 27 May 1835
Polly MULL and John BOOTHE (attorney of John BOOTHE of Indiana) of Ldn to John JANNEY of Ldn. B/S of 10a (part of Lot #4 in division of David MULL dec'd allotted Polly) and int. in 36a dower lot of widow. Delv. per order 27 Apr 1842.

4D:258 Date: 9 Jan 1835 RtCt: 28 May 1835
George W. BRONAUGH of Ldn to Ludwell LUCKETTS of Ldn. B/S of 2 roods strip on road from pot house to Union at corner of both parties. Delv. to LUCKETT 6 Jun 1867.

4D:259 Date: 18 Feb 1835 RtCt: 28 May 1835
Charles Taylor & wife Nancy to Thomas NICHOLS. Trust for debt to Thomas JAMES using 50a adj Timothy TAYLOR, David JAMES, Rufus UPDIKE. Wit: David REECE, Timothy TAYLOR Jr. Delv. to JAMES 11 Jan 1836.

4D:262 Date: 2 May 1835 RtCt: 28 May 1835
Samuel M. EDWARDS of Ldn to William LODGE of Ldn. B/S of 85a reserving crop of tenant Robert WHITACRE (from defaulted trust of Dec 1829 from Joshua B. OVERFIELD, DBk 3T:072 using 85a and 200a for debt to John PANCOAST Sr., also see 3O:230)

4D:264 Date: 27 May 1835 RtCt: 29 May 1835
Adam CRIM of Ldn to Thomas WHITE of Ldn. Trust for debt to Cunrod BITZER using 30a (allotted in div. of Charles CRIM dec'd) adj Benjamin SHREVE, Mrs. SHOEMAKER. Delv. to S. D. LESLIE 8 Jan 1838.

4D:266 Date: 17 Apr 1835 RtCt: 30 May 1835
John KILE & wife Winifred of Ldn to Marcus DISHMAN of Ldn. Trust for debt to Catherine BOWMAN of Ldn using 30¼a (prch/o brother George KILE, bequeathed from father John KILE Sr. dec'd) at junction of road from pot house to Mdbg and to Millsville. Delv. to Jno. M. HARRISON per order 16 Mar 1836. Wit: Ludwell LUCKETT, A. GIBSON.

4D:269 Date: 1 Jun 1835 RtCt: 1 Jun 1835
Sheriff Ariss BUCKNER to Sarah LACEY. B/S of int. in 110a (from insolvent William HEATH, Jul 1834, his int. in estate of David LACEY dec'd) adj late Isaac VANDEVENTER, Mrs. MANNING, William HOLMES, Joshua PUSEY.

4D:270 Date: 12 May 1835 RtCt: 1 Jun 1835
John JANNEY of Lsbg to David REECE and Charles B. HAMILTON (Exors of Nathan GREGG dec'd) of Ldn. Release of trust of Apr 1831 for debt to Abijah JANNEY (trustee for Ann HARPER w/o Washington T. HARPER late ELLIOTT of AlexVa, DBk 3W:007).

4D:272 Date: 7 Jun 1834 RtCt: 1 Jun 1835
John COOPER & wife Magdalane of Ldn to Sarah BINNS of Ldn. B/S of ½a. Wit: Charles B. HAMILTON Jr., Wm. SLATER. Delv. to BINNS 26 Feb 1851.

4D:274 Date: 12 May 1835 RtCt: 2 Jun 1835
John BOYD of Mdbg to Hugh SMITH of Ldn. Trust of house and lot in Mdbg now occ. by John BOYD as a tavern keeper and household items (for debts of John BOYD & his wife Elizabeth).

4D:276 Date: 23 May 1835 RtCt: 3 Jun 1835
Jonathan BUTCHER of AlexDC and Richard H. HENDERSON of Lsbg to Thomas R. SAUNDERS, Aaron R. SAUNDERS, Curtis R. SAUNDERS, Susan R. SAUNDERS, Catharine A. R. SAUNDERS, the children of Fanny WHITE dec'd late SAUNDERS (heirs of Aaron SAUNDERS dec'd). Release of trust of Nov 1823 for debt to Phineas JANNEY and Joseph JANNEY Jr. (Exors of John JANNEY dec'd) on Limestone Mill.

4D:277   Date: 17 Sep 1834   RtCt: 22 Jan/6 Jun 1835
Agnes POULSON Jr. of Ldn to Maria GOODIN of Ldn. B/S of 12a
Lot #3 allotted Agnes from estate of Jasper POULSON dec'd; and
12a Lot #3 allotted John TRIBBY & wife Lydia that was cnvy/t
Agnes. Wit: Stacy TAYLOR, Wm. STREAM, Jas. McILHANY, Saml.
BEANS.

4D:279   Date: 4 Jun 1835   RtCt: 6 Jun 1835
William Vandyke NEILLE & wife Catharine of Ldn to Thos. H.
LUCKETT of Fqr. Trust for debt to H. & J. H. McVEIGH using
undivided 1/14th of estate of Willoughby W. TEBBS dec'd in PrWm.
Wit: A. GIBSON, Hugh SMITH. Delv. to McVEIGH 10 Aug 1835.

4D:281   Date: 1 Jul 1834   RtCt: 8 Jun 1835
Sarah UPP of Ldn to Samuel CHINN of Ldn. B/S of Lots #30 and
#36 in Mdbg (from div. of Sarah and Thomas J. NOLAND, who m.
Sarah C. MYERS an heir of Thomas CHINN dec'd f/o Sarah UPP).
Delv. to Saml. CHINN 11 Jan 1841.

4D:283   Date: __ 1835   RtCt: 8 Jun 1835
Yeoman David YOUNG of Ldn to Stephen McPHERSON (of
William) of Ldn. Release of trust of Jun 1831 for debt to Joshua
PANCOAST on 148a.

4D:285   Date: 1 Apr 1835   RtCt: 8 Jun 1835
George SAUNDERS & wife Elizabeth of Ldn to Robert L. WRIGHT
of Ldn. Trust for debt to John WRIGHT (Admr wwa of Michael
COOPER dec'd) using 181a adj Andrew GRAHAM, James
WILKINSON, Reubin HIXON, George MULL. Delv. to Saml. M.
EDWARDS 9 Aug 1841.

4D:287   Date: 5 Apr 1835   RtCt: 8 Apr [Jun?] 1835
Edward CARTER & wife Martha of Ldn to Michael PLASTER of Ldn.
B/S of 12a adj Henry PLASTER, Gourley REEDER, house of
Samuel DUNKIN. Wit: Ludwell LUCKETT, Asa ROGERS. Delv. per
order 14 Apr 1836.

4D:289   Date: 1 Jun 1835   RtCt: 8 Jun 1835
Isaac TAVENER to Thomas HATCHER and Joshua HATCHER.
Trust for debt to Lydia PANCOAST using land where he now resides
left by will of father.

4D:292   Date: 11 Apr 1835   RtCt: 8 Jun 1835
Samuel SHRIGLEY & wife Louisa of Ldn to John BOGAR (s/o
Michael BOGAR dec'd) of Ldn. B/S of int. in 37a allotted wife of
Samuel AMICK dec'd from div. of Michael BOGER dec'd; and 1/10th
int. in dower lands of widow of Michael dec'd. Wit: C. B. HAMILTON
Jr., Wm. SLATER. Delv. to John BOGAR 15 Sep 1838.

4D:294   Date: 19 Mar 1835   RtCt: 8 Jun 1835
John COOPER & wife Magdalane of Ldn to Henry RUSSELL of Ldn.
B/S of 48a on Catocton Mt. (Lot #4 in div. of father Frederick

COOPER dec'd). Wit: C. B. HAMILTON Jr., Wm. SLATER. Delv. to RUSSELL 27 Aug 1846.

4D:296 Date: 18 Apr 1835 RtCt: 8 Jun 1835
Thadeus RUSSELL of Ldn to George BITZER of Ldn. Trust for debt to James B. WILSON using undivided 1/9th int. to estate of mother Sarah E. RUSSELL dev. in trust to Dennis McCARTY dec'd for use of her and her children according to will of Thadeus MCCARTY dec'd. Delv. to WILSON 11 May 1838.

4D:298 Date: __ 1835 RtCt: 8 Jun 1835
Edward M. BAKER of Ldn to Gabriel SKINNER of Ldn. Trust for Silas BEATY as security on debt to Henry F. LUCKETT using cow, household items.

4D:300 Date: 29 Nov 1834 RtCt: 8 Jun 1835
John S. HARNED of Washington Co Indiana, Thomas B. HARNED and Samuel HARNED of Orange Co Indiana and William FAULKNER of Green Co Ky in right of his wife Ann late HARNED (ch/o Rosanna HARNED late SRYOCK dec'd of Ldn) to uncle Samuel SRYOCK of WashDC. PoA for moneys from estate of Michael SRYOCK dec'd late of Ldn. Wit: Wm. H. CARTER, Isaac THOMAS.

4D:303 Date: 5 Jun 1835 RtCt: 8 Jun 1835
Sheriff Burr POWELL to Noble BEVERIDGE. B/S of int. in houses & lots in Mdbg (from trust of Nov 1820 from John HARRIS, prch/o Jesse McVEIGH and Burr POWELL).

4D:305 Date: 3 Jun 1835 RtCt: 8 Jun 1835
Sarah UPP of Mdbg to Asa ROGERS of Mdbg. Trust for debt to Robert Y. CONRAD of Winchester using 84a in Ldn and Fqr (allotted from div. of father Thomas CHINN dec'd) adj Wm. R. SWART, heirs of Elizabeth NOLAND, nr Mdbg.

4D:307 Date: 30 Apr 1835 RtCt: 8 Jun 1835
Sampson HUTCHISON & wife Elizabeth of Ldn to Stephen BEARD of Ldn. B/S of Elizabeth's int. in land of father John CRAIN due her before and after death of her mother. Wit: Robert BAYLY, John MOORE.

4D:309 Date: 30 Apr 1835 RtCt: 8 Jun 1835
Stephen BEARD of Ldn to Sampson HUTCHISON of Ldn. B/S of int. of Elizabeth HUTCHISON in land of father John CRANE dec'd before and after death of her mother, as above.

4D:310 Date: 8 Jun 1835 RtCt: 8 Jun 1835
Abraham SKILLMAN (Exor of Henry BROWN dec'd) of Ldn to John HOLMES of Ldn. B/S of 40½a adj Andrew BIRDSALL.

4D:312 Date: 8 Jun 1835 RtCt: 8 Jun 1835
Wm. CLENDENING Jr., William CLENDENING and Emanuel WALTMAN. Bond on Wm. CLENDENING Jr. as constable.

4D:313   Date: 8 Jun 1835   RtCt: 8 Jun 1835
James GARRETT, Stephen GARRETT and Enoch GARRETT. Bond on James GARRETT as constable.

4D:314   Date: 8 Jun 1835   RtCt: 8 Jun 1835
Benjamin JACKSON, John G. HUMPHREY and Jonathan TAVENER. Bond on JACKSON as constable.

4D:315   Date: 11 Jun 1835   RtCt: 11 Jun 1835
Albert G. CHAMBLIN, Samuel COX and Herod GLASCOCK. Bond on CHAMBLIN as constable.

4D:316   Date: 11 Jun 1835   RtCt: 11 Jun 1835
John MARTIN, Samuel M. BOSS and Charles B. HAWKE. Bond on MARTIN as constable.

4D:316   Date: 8 Jun 1835   RtCt: 8 Jun 1835
John L. HATCHER and Thomas E. HATCHER of Ldn to Thomas ROGERS Admr wwa of John HATCHER dec'd. Bond that John L. HATCHER (ch/o Noah HATCHER and legatee of John HATCHER dec'd) will refund payment to cover any debts.

4D:317   Date: 13 Dec 1834   RtCt: 9 Jun 1835
Michael COOPER, Joseph COOPER and Margaret COOPER of Ldn to Jonas P. SCHOOLEY of Ldn. B/S of 24a and 8a (dev. by Margaret SAUNDERS dec'd). Delv. to grantee 21 Mar 1856.

4D:320   Date: 10 Jun 1835   RtCt: 10 Jun 1835
Isaac HOLMES & wife Hannah to John JANNEY. Trust for debt to William GEORGE, Henry TIFFANY and Chancy BROOKS using lot cnvy/b John WHITE, Ebenezer GRUBB and John WHITE as trustees of Nathaniel MANNING, DBk 3X:354.

4D:322   Date: 6 Dec 1834   RtCt: 11 Jun 1835
Mahlon WHITE & wife Margaret of Ldn to Alfred LOGAN of Ldn. B/S of 13a on NW fork of Goose Creek adj Widow CRAIG, L. G. EWERS, Jacob BROWN; and 13a adj Stephen C. ROZELL dec'd, John ALDRIDGE, Richard BROWN's patent, Philip VANSICKLER. Wit: Edward B. GRADY, Timothy TAYLOR.

4D:324   Date: 10 Jun 1835   RtCt: 12 Jun 1835
Isaac HOLMES & wife Hannah of Ldn to Richard H. HENDERSON. Trust for debt to Chauncey BROOKS, William GEORGE, Henry TIFFANY using land cnvy/b trustees of Nathaniel MANNING, DBk 3X:354 and land cnvy/b Thomas WHITE, DBk 3Z:417.

4D:327   Date: 4 Jun 1835   RtCt: 12 Jun 1835
Rich'd. H. HENDERSON of Ldn to Phebe HUFFMAN w/o John HUFFMAN and d/o William CLAYTON the elder dec'd of Ldn. B/S of 10a willed to Phebe (HENDERSON took letters of Admr wwa to PhilPa and had deed made to him by __ WHALEN since CLAYTON had no deed).

4D:328 Date: 13 Jun 1835 RtCt: 13 Jun 1835
John McKEMMIE of Ldn to John LESLIE of Ldn. B/S of 11a (Lot #2 in div. of Francis McKEMMIE dec'd) and int. in widow's dower and 4a Lot #7 on Short Hill.

4D:330 Date: 31 Jan 1835 RtCt: 19 Jun 1835
Townsend. D. PEYTON & wife Sarah M. of Ldn to Hamilton ROGERS of Ldn. B/S of int. in 169a (less 1/8a of family burying ground) held by Nancy PEYTON as tenant for life from late Col. Francis PEYTON, adj __ McCARTY, Jesse McVEIGH, Little River. Wit: A. GIBSON, H. SMITH. Delv. to Gen. ROGERS for Hamilton ROGERS 20 Aug 1841.

4D:333 Date: 19 Jun 1835 RtCt: 19 Jun 1835
Thomas ROGERS (Commr. in Richard H. HENDERSON Admr. of Alexander SUTHERLAND dec'd agst John JOLLEFFE late Shff of Frederick as Admr of Thomas N. BINNS dec'd and his heirs) to William LEFEVER of Ldn. B/S of ½ int. of 136a (dev. to son Henry LAFEVER by Henry LAFEVER dec'd subject to life estate of Honorea LAFEVER, other half willed to William LAFEVER). Delv. to W. LAFEVER 22 Aug 1836.

4D:334 Date: 31 Jan 1835 RtCt: 19 Jun 1835
Townsend D. PEYTON & wife Sarah M. of Ldn to Hamilton ROGERS of Ldn. B/S of 519a where PEYTON now resides adj James ROGERS, Nancy PEYTON, road from Mdbg to Lsbg, Snickers Gap Turnpike road, Ashby's Gap Turnpike. Wit: A. GIBSON, Hugh SMITH. Delv. to Gen. ROGERS for Hamilton ROGERS 21 Aug 1841.

4D:337 Date: 1 Jan 1835 RtCt: 22 Jun 1835
Stephen GARRETT & wife Euphamia of Ldn to Fielder HOOPER of Ldn. B/S of Lot #82 & #83 on Mercer St. in Aldie. Wit: Hamilton ROGERS, John MOORE.

4D:339 Date: 26 Jan 1835 RtCt: 22 Jun 1835
Fielder HOOPER & wife Ann of Ldn to Edmund TYLER of Ldn. Trust for debt to Stephen GARRETT of Ldn using above land. Wit: Robert ROSE, Hamilton ROGERS, John MOORE. Delv. to S. GARRETT 28 Mar 1837.

4D:341 Date: 6 Dec 1834 RtCt: 25 Jun 1835
Alfred LOGAN to Levi WHITE. Trust for debt to Mahlon WHITE using 13¾a adj Widow CRAIG, Levi G. EWERS, Jacob BROWN; and 13a adj Stephen C. ROZLE, Glebe (now John ALLRIDGE), Richard BROWN, Philip VANSICKLER. Delv. to Mahlon WHITE 10 Jan 1839.

4D:345 Date: 16 Mar 1835 RtCt: 25 Jun 1835
Jacob COOPER & wife Mary of Ldn to Benjamin JACKSON of Ldn. B/S of 42a on E side of Catocton Mt. Gives small plat. Wit: Charles

B. HAMILTON Jr., Geo. MARLOW. Delv. to JACKSON 14 Dec 1835.

4D:347   Date: 26 Jun 1835   RtCt: 26 Jun 1835
Samuel M. EDWARDS to William JOHNSON. Release of trust May 1831 for debt to Joseph MEAD (Admr wwa of John WORSLEY dec'd) using lot on King St in Lsbg.

4D:349   Date: 7 Apr 1834   RtCt: 27 Jun 1835
Levi COOKSEY & wife Elizabeth of Ldn to Lot TAVENER of Ldn. B/S of 3a (formerly owned by Walter KERRICK) adj Bernard TAYLOR, TAVENER, Amos WHITACRE, Stephen WILSON. Wit: Timothy TAYLOR Jr., David REECE. Delv. to TAVENNER 14 Feb 1837.

4D:351   Date: 3 Dec 1834   RtCt: 29 Jun 1835
Joshua COOPER & wife Catharine of Ldn to William COLE of Ldn. B/S of 2a adj __ NETTLES, __ UMBAUGH, __ THOMPSON. Wit: Geo. MARLOW, C. B. HAMILTON Jr.

4D:353   Date: 12 May 1835   RtCt: 29 Jun 1835
John JANNEY of Lsbg to George WARNER of Ldn. Release of trust of Apr 1831 for debt to Abijah JANNEY (trustee of Ann HARPER w/o Washington T. HARPER late ELLICOTT) of AlexVa, DBk 3W:148). Delv. to WARNER 5 May 1837.

4D:354   Date: 7 Jan 1835   RtCt: 1 Jul 1835
Stephen McPHERSON & wife Cecelia of Ldn to Francis T. GRADY of Ldn. B/S of 59a (cnvy/b Samuel DUNKIN) on Beaverdam adj __ MARKS, GRADY; and 15a on N side of Creek adj Ury GRADY. Wit: Notley C. WILLIAMS, Edw'd. B. GRADY.

4D:356   Date: 15 Jun 1835   RtCt: 2 Jul 1835
Harvey HAMILTON & wife Lucina of Ldn to William LODGE of Ldn. B/S of 45a on Rock(y) run adj Stephen JANNEY, LODGE, Joshua B. OVERFIELD, __ EWERS. Wit: Edw'd B. GRADY, Roger CHEW. Delv. to LODGE 16 Aug 1837.

4D:358   Date: 22 Jun 1835   RtCt: 4 Jul 1835
Thomas SWANN of WashDC to Richard SMITH Cashier of Bank at WashDC. Trust for debt to Bank of the U.S. using 469a "Black Walnut Island" in Potomac River and MontMd. Delv. – see 398 rec'd again.

4D:363   Date: 30 Jun 1835   RtCt: 4 Jul 1835
Samuel PALMER Sr. to Mary PORTER. Marriage Contract – trust of Samuel's Negro man Aaron, 150a, farm and household items to Mason CHAMBLIN. Mary to have no claim after Samuel dies.

4D:365   Date: 14 Mar 1835   RtCt: 9 Jul 1835
Eli C. GALLEHER & wife Susan of Fqr to Seth SMITH of Union. B/S of ½a lot on E side of SMITH's lot in Union on Main rd. Wit: Ludwell LUCKETT, Abner GIBSON. Delv. to SMITH 9 May 1836.

4D:367   Date: 29 Jun 1835   RtCt: 11 Jul 1835
Jacob HIGER & wife Mary, John LOOSE and Catharine LOOSE, Adam HIGER, Daniel HIGER & Ruth HIGER and Rebecca HIGER of Cashocton Co Ohio to Jacob CRIM of Ldn. B/S of 1/12th int. in dower land of Catharine CRIM, since dec'd, wd/o Charles CRIM dec'd. Wit: Jos. D. WORKMAN, Thomas DEANE.

4D:369   Date: 1 Jul 1835   RtCt: 11 Jul 1835
Mary SHOYER of Harrison Co Ohio to Jacob CRIM of Ldn. B/S of 1/12th int. in dower land of Catharine CRIM, since dec'd, wd/o Charles CRIM dec'd. Wit: Christina LOUDIG, Wm. T. CULLEN. Delv. to CRIMM pr order 11 Mar 1836.

4D:370   Date: 13 Jun 1835   RtCt: 11 Jul 1835
John WITTEMAN & wife Catharine of Warren Co Ohio to Jacob CRIM of Ldn. B/S of 1/12th int. in dower land of Catharine CRIM, since dec'd, wd/o Charles CRIM dec'd. Wit: Wm. EULASS, Geo. HARLAN, Moses HARLAN. Delv. to CRIM per order 11 Mar 1836.

4D:373   Date: 27 Jun 1835   RtCt: 11 Jul 1835
Simon SHOEMAKER Sr. & wife Charlotte of Ldn to Jacob CRIM of Ldn. B/S of 7a (cnvy/b Aaron MILLER) on E side of Short Hill adj CRIM, __ HARDACRE, __ MORRISON. Wit: William CLENDENING, Mortimer McILHANEY. Delv. to CRIM pr order 11 Mar 1836.

4D:375   Date: 6 Jun 1835   RtCt: 11 Jul 1835
Joseph D. TAYLOR of Ldn to Townshend McVEIGH of Ldn. Trust for debt to H. & J. H. McVEIGH using farm animals, household items.

4D:376   Date: 1 Jun 1835   RtCt: 13 Jul 1835
Charles A. ALEXANDER of Ldn to Wilson C. SELDON of Ldn. B/S of 16½a (cnvy/b Dr. Wilson C. SELDEN Aug 1832) nr Turnpike road to AlexDC, SELDEN.

4D:378   Date: 1 Jun 1835   RtCt: 15 Jul 1835
Joshua GREGG to William CHAMBLIN. Release of trust of Jun 1829 for debt to John HESSER using 40a.

4D:380   Date: 17 Jul 1835   RtCt: 18 Jul 1835
John W. COE of Ldn to Robert BENTLEY of Ldn. B/S of 168a - lot (dev. by father Edward COE dec'd) on Goose Creek now occ. as tenant by Bernard PURCELL adj Ann SMITH, Mary COE, heirs of Presley SAUNDERS dec'd; int. in estate of Menan COE; lot prch/o David J. COE; also crops and farm animals on farm. Delv. to Bob BENTLEY 16 Dec 1835.

4D:382   Date: 6 Jul 1835   RtCt: 21 Jul 1835
Joel CRAVEN to Thomas NICHOLS. Trust for debt to Charles TAYLOR and Timothy TAYLOR Jr. using 79½a adj __ BIRDSALL, Thos. NICHOLS, __ HATCHER, __ HOGUE.

4D:385   Date: 26 Jun 1835   RtCt: 23 Jul 1835
Hamilton STEWART & wife Jane Ann of Clinton, Allegany Co Pa to
Charles A. JOHNSTON of Lsbg. B/S of lot on S side of Market St in
Lsbg (from div. of William WRIGHT dec'd grandfather of Jane Ann)
adj heirs of James WOOD dec'd (also see DBk 3X:381). Delv. to
JOHNSON 13 Aug 1841.

4D:387   Date: 26 Jun 1835   RtCt: 23 Jul 1835
Charles A. JOHNSTON of Ldn to Saml. M. BOSS. Trust for debt to
Hamilton STEWART using above land.

4D:389   Date: 10 May 1835   RtCt: 23 Jul 1835
Richard H. HENDERSON (Admr wwa of William CLAYTON dec'd) of
Ldn to Sarah LUKE w/o Jacob LUKE of FredVa. B/S of 44a (legal
title to Sarah as heir of CLAYTON); and 66 sq. perch Lot #11 and
51a Lot #17 and 15a Lot #7.

4D:390   Date: 23 Jul 1835   RtCt: 25 Jul 1835
Richard H. HENDERSON of Ldn to John P. SMART of Ldn. Release
of trust of Dec 1834 for debt to George PRICE using "Elizabeth
Mills" water grist mill.

4D:391   Date: __ 1835   RtCt: 27 Jul 1835
Henry CLAGETT Sr. of Ldn to Henry CLAGETT Jr. of Ldn. B/S of
house & lot at Markett & Back Sts in Lsbg now occ. by John
EDWARDS. Delv. to Henry CLAGETT Jr. 29 Oct 1838.

4D:392   Date: 30 Jul 1835   RtCt: 30 Jul 1835
Ignatius ELGIN of Ldn to Francis ELGIN (of Gustavus ELGIN dec'd)
of Ldn. B/S of undivided share of William ELGIN (br/o Francis) in
land dev. by Gustavus dec'd to sons William and Francis (cnvy/t
Ignatius Mar 1834, DBk 4B:391). Delv. to Francis ELGIN 26 Oct
1838.

4D:394   Date: 1 Apr 1835   RtCt: 1 Aug 1835
Joshua OSBURN (Commr. in case of John NICHOLS agst Charity
NICHOLS) and David NICHOLS of Ldn to Thomas S. STONE of
Ldn. B/S of 4a (from div. of land of James NICHOLS the elder
dec'd) on Lsbg and Snickersville Turnpike road nr Blue ridge mt. adj
heirs of Joseph THOMAS, Benjamin JACKSON. Delv. to STONE 19
Mar 1836.

4D:395   Date: 31 Jul 1835   RtCt: 4 Aug 1835
John C. SHELTON and Bazil GORDON of StafVa to George PRICE
& wife Elizabeth late CLAPHAM of Ldn. Release of trust of Feb 1828
for debt to Bazil GORDON.

4D:397   Date: 4 Aug 1835   RtCt: 4 Aug 1835
Mahlon TAVENER (insolvent debtor) of Ldn to Sheriff Notley C.
WILLIAMS of Ldn. B/S of int. in lot prch/o James BROWN.

4D:398   Date: 22 Jun 1835   RtCt: 5 Aug 1835
Thomas SWANN of WashDC to Richard SMITH Cashier of Bank of
the U.S. Trust for debt to Bank of the U.S. using 469a "Black Walnut

Island" in Potomac and MontMd, all slaves, livestock and farming utensils. Delv. to J. A. BINNS pr order 12 Aug 1836.

4D:403 Date: 24 Jul 1835 RtCt: 24 Jul 1835
Jacob STREAM (insolvent debtor) to Sheriff N. C. WILLIAMS. B/S of int. in land prch/o William ELLZEY (formerly prop. of Michael STREAM dec'd)

4D:404 Date: 7 Aug 1835 RtCt: 7 Aug 1835
Charles Fenton MERCER of Aldie to Capt. John MOORE of Aldie. B/S of 50a abt 2m from Aldie adj Usher SKINNER, Samuel SIMPSON; and 4a Aldie Mill on Ashby's Gap Turnpike. Gives plat and description of Aldie Mill lot. Delv. to MOORE 5 Mar 1845.

4D:409 Date: 7 Aug 1835 RtCt: 7 Aug 1835
John MOORE & wife Matilda L. of Aldie to Richard H. HENDERSON and Jesse TIMMS. Trust for debt to George CARTER of Oatlands using Aldie Mill as above. Delv. to CARTER 3 May 1839.

4D:413 Date: 7 Aug 1835 RtCt: 7 Aug 1835
James NORTH of Aldie to Noble H. MOONEY of Aldie. Trust for debt to MOONEY using household items. Wit: Geo. RICHARDS.

4D:414 Date: 7 Oct 1834 RtCt: 10 Aug 1835
James CARTER & wife Jemima of Ldn to Jacob F. GILLIPSY of Ldn. B/S of house and lot in Union (prch/o A. G. TIBBETT) now occ. by Abner CARTER. Wit: Edw'd HALL, Ludwell LUCKETT.

4D:416 Date: 15 Jul 1835 RtCt: 10 Aug 1835
Ct. of 11 May 1835 – application of James KETTLE to have road opened from W end of Franklin St in Mt. Gilead to intersect with road leading to North fork near Charles MERCHANT's house. Report by Isaac EATON, John COCKERILL and John VANSICKLER that road should extend thru land of Miss Ann SMITH, less than ¼ mile in length. Starting on E end of Franklin St to intersect on Lsbg road between KETTLE and Mrs. Mary BRABHAM. Jury: Joshua HATCHER, Joseph GORE, Thomas P. MATHEWS, David YOUNG, Samuel BROWN, George W. SAGAR, James MOUNT, James WELCH, Even WILKINSON, Geo. TAVENER, Ezra BOLON and Jesse ATWELL find damages to Charles MERCHANT of $5.

4D:418 Date: 15 Jul 1835 RtCt: 10 Aug 1835
Ct. of 11 May 1835 – same road case as above. Cost to Ann SMITH to be determined. Same jury finds damages of $31.91.

INDEX

ABEL
George, 157
ABLE
George, 42
ABRAHAM
John, 223
Mary, 223
ADAM
John M., 49
Martha L., 49
Mathew, 140
Matthew, 49
Susan L., 49
William F., 49
ADAMS
___, 126
Abigail, 199
Ann J. M., 180
Daniel, 199
Henry, 58, 64
James, 199
John, 100
Juliet A., 64
Mathew, 164, 187
Peter, 154, 199
Richard, 51, 67,
79, 105, 163,
215
Samuel R., 190
Susan, 199
William, 152
ADDISON
A., 131
Anthoney, 38
Anthony, 81, 153,
200
ADIE
George, 68
ADISON
A., 111
AISQUITH
Sally L., 131
AKE
Joseph B., 20
AKERS
Ann, 148

ALBAN
George, 15, 46
ALDER
George D., 146
George H., 51,
87, 200, 223
James, 8
John, 129, 132
Mary, 129
ALDRIDGE
John, 103, 114,
165, 235
ALEXANDER
Charles A., 74,
238
Charles B., 116,
138, 165, 180
David, 57
Eliza, 116, 180
James, 72, 151
Jane, 151
Peter, 44
ALLBRITAIN
Mary, 188
ALLBRITTON
Mary, 56
William, 56
ALLDER
John, 97
ALLEN
Agnes, 229
Edmund, 87, 194
Elizabeth, 56
James, 3, 77, 229
William, 56, 204,
227
ALLISON
Henry, 53
ALLNUTT
James L., 203
John H., 203
Thomas D., 202
ALLRIDGE
John, 236
ALT
John, 220

Rachel, 216, 220
William, 216, 220
AMBLE
William, 166
AMBLER
Lewis, 152
Sarah, 152
William, 85, 148
AMICH
Henry, 46
AMICK
George, 211
Henry, 46, 82
Mary, 211
Samuel, 211, 233
AMMEN
Jac., 180
AMOND
Anthony, 172
ANDERSON
A. S., 38, 50
Abbe, 112
Alexander, 145
Andrew S., 38,
69, 76, 177
Eleanor, 88, 177
Elijah, 44, 65, 88,
92, 208
John, 26
John M., 157, 226
Malinda, 157
S., 112
W. & S. B. Co.,
190
William, 190
ANNIN
Roberdeau, 31,
55, 72, 218
ANSELL
Leonard, 162
Susanna, 36, 185
APSEY
Jacob, 71

Lott, 1, 90
William, 171
BARRETT
Caroline M. E., 49
John, 12
John F., 49, 113, 168
John T., 52
Robert, 227
BARROTT
Elizabeth, 55
BARRY
Eliza A., 5, 96
BARTON
Bailey, 227
John, 45
Levi, 196
BASFORD
Mahlon, 215
BATEMAN
Jesse, 152
BATEY
Elizabeth, 30
BATTAILE
Laurence, 6
Lawrence, 173
BATTAILLES
Laurence, 117
BATTSON
Hannah, 100
BAUGHMAN
Andrew, 33
BAYLY
George, 7, 102
John, 34, 48, 98, 102, 174, 210
Mary A., 7
Mountjoy, 102
Peirce, 102
Robert, 49, 77, 80, 87, 100, 148, 204, 220, 234
BAZIL
John, 15
BAZILL
John, 31
BEALE

Amos, 102, 112, 156
David, 102, 112, 156
Elizabeth, 102
BEALES
Amos, 17, 31
David, 31
Elizabeth, 31
BEALL
___, 39
David F., 39, 124, 135, 148, 159
David L., 135
Mary C. E., 135
Robert E., 124, 135
BEAMER
___, 22, 23
George, 19, 22, 92, 101
BEANS
Absalom, 65, 175
Absolom, 51
Amos, 110
Elizabeth, 18, 158
Isaiah B., 18, 158
James, 159
Matthew, 13
Pleasant, 18
Samuel, 18, 233
William, 173
BEARD
Jonathan, 34, 85, 86, 178
Joseph, 34, 188
Joshua, 188
Lewis, 86
Stephen, 77, 204, 227, 229, 234
BEATTY
David, 52
John, 52, 81
John H., 33
Josias W., 42
Mary E., 52
Otho R., 208
Polly, 27

Robert, 52
S. Catharine, 52
Sally, 27
Sarah, 27
Silas, 1, 169
T. A., 229
Thomas B., 27
William, 27, 52, 114
BEATY
Elizabeth, 16
Martha, 188
Mary, 160
Polly, 16
Silas, 198, 234
BEAVERS
___, 77
John, 74, 214
Mahala, 52
Samuel, 14, 37, 226
Thomas, 37
William, 33
BECK
L. S., 180
Samuel, 134
BECKHAM
F., 217
BELL
Henry, 6, 107
Ruth, 6
BELT
A., 62
Alfred, 53, 62, 104
BELTZ
___, 51
Mary, 165
BENEDUM
___, 128
Henry, 106
John, 7
Peter, 28, 43, 95, 162
BENNEDUM
Peter, 118
BENNET
Charles, 150

James H., 102
Mary A., 102
BENNETT
___, 13
Charles, 9, 35,
  56, 91, 102,
  154, 169, 213,
  224
J. H., 224
James, 35
James H., 56, 79,
  85, 154, 195
John, 9
John H., 28
Joseph, 164
Josiah, 208
M. Winefred, 35
Mary, 9, 56
Mary A., 56, 195
Sydney, 35
Thomas J., 1, 137
Thompson, 9
BENTLEY
Kitty L., 150
Robert, 3, 40, 44,
  134, 150, 153,
  181, 185, 238
BENTLY
Robert, 208
BENTON
Sarah, 92
William, 63, 73,
  76, 92, 99, 102,
  119, 120, 135,
  146, 147, 150,
  158, 159, 160,
  161, 162, 165,
  169, 170, 172,
  176, 177, 189,
  195, 217, 226
BERKLEY
___, 126
Ann, 209
Catherine, 150
John L., 209, 210
Lewis, 72, 75, 95,
  133, 212
Mrs., 2

Rufus, 209
Thomas, 1
William, 1, 2, 197
BERRY
Daniel, 215
BESICKS
Henly, 128
Jesse, 128
Priscilla, 128
BESIX
Hendley, 165
BESSIX
Prescilla, 165
BEST
Alfred, 210
Enos, 77, 182
James, 3, 68,
  164, 191
John, 223
BEVERIDGE
Andrew, 30, 83
John, 5, 215
Keziah, 215
Mary, 52
Noble, 15, 73, 91,
  100, 123, 124,
  129, 134, 136,
  142, 169, 200,
  211, 215, 234
William, 16, 75,
  104, 128, 198,
  211
BEVERIDGE &
  SMITH, 189
BICHARD
Daniel, 152
BINCKLEY
Samuel, 123
BINNS
Alexander, 83
Ann A., 139
Anna R., 164, 167
C., 65, 194, 214
C. W., 178
C. W. D., 55, 167
Charles, 3, 13,
  17, 36, 38, 57,
  59, 61, 67, 75,

77, 79, 83, 85,
  95, 110, 118,
  119, 128, 134,
  138, 139, 141,
  144, 150, 155,
  158, 161, 162,
  164, 167, 178,
  188, 193, 206,
  212
Charles W. D.,
  42, 84, 134,
  141, 144, 167,
  193
Dewanner, 67
Elizabeth, 71
Elizabeth D., 83,
  139
Hannah, 57, 95,
  134, 138, 139,
  150, 155, 167,
  206
J. A., 240
John, 118, 153
John A., 3, 13,
  40, 48, 57, 61,
  67, 69, 70, 71,
  73, 77, 81, 96,
  104, 105, 111,
  144, 154, 163,
  164, 165, 167,
  170, 175, 177,
  178, 188, 211,
  213
Mary Ann A., 67
Mary M., 154,
  164, 165
Mathy, 67
Nancy, 111
Sarah, 67, 211,
  232
Simon A., 67
Thomas N., 236
William A., 110,
  111, 134, 165
BIRDSALL
___, 70, 111, 124,
  150, 238

Andrew, 124,
165, 219, 234
Anna, 186
Benjamin, 42,
112, 150
Elizabeth, 150,
186
Hannah, 150
Mary, 186
Rachel, 186
Whitson, 186
BIRK
Enoch, 1
BIRKBY
__, 166, 167
Sally, 213
Thomas, 45, 149,
213
BIRKLEY
Thomas, 106
BISCOE
James B., 1, 169
Thomas, 107
BISHOP
Jememia, 135
BITZER
Catharine, 57,
113
Conard, 65
Conrad, 30, 38,
55, 57, 113,
164, 173, 183,
218, 224
Conrod, 116
Coonrad, 16
Cunrod, 232
Dorothy, 230
G. L., 7
George, 230, 234
Harmon, 7
John, 16
Polly, 16
BLACK
J., 229
BLAIR
John, 19
BLAKER
John, 102

BLEAKLEY
William, 108
BLINCO
Sampson, 134
Sarah A. E., 134
BLINCOE
Martha, 106
Mrs., 79, 106,
166, 167
BLINSTON
Elizabeth, 45
Thomas, 45
William, 45
BLUE
Cupid, 76
BLUNDREN
Elisha, 134
John, 134
Sarah, 134
William, 134
Winefred, 134
BODINE
Henry, 131
BOGAN
__, 206
BOGAN
John H., 108
BOGAR
John, 233
Michael, 211,
221, 233
Philip, 186, 196,
221
BOGEN
Dr., 222
John H., 78
BOGER
John, 126, 156,
180
Mary, 196
Michael, 113,
126, 196
Samuel, 126
BOGGESS
__, 59
Peter H., 42
BOGUE
Francis S., 111

BOLAN
Eli, 186
Lydia, 186
William, 203
BOLAND
Daniel, 43, 85,
93, 172
BOLEN
Edward, 140
Elizabeth, 57
Ellen, 10, 162
Israel, 162
BOLON
__, 124, 149, 150
Elizabeth, 122
Ezra, 124, 240
Ferdinando, 137
William, 111, 113,
221
BOMCROTS
John, 22, 64
BOND
Asa M., 143
Edward, 73, 185
Joseph, 143, 166
BONTZ
Mary, 178
BOOTH
__, 125
Betsy, 172
James, 221
Jane, 172
John, 82, 153
Philip, 172
BOOTHE
__, 111
John, 231
BOOTHE &
BROOKS, 1
BOSS
Elizabeth F., 181
Samuel M., 3, 25,
29, 35, 36, 43,
44, 48, 53, 54,
58, 67, 80, 98,
105, 107, 124,
126, 129, 164,
178, 181, 182,

William O., 150,
229
CHINN
Catharine M., 1,
90
Martha R., 90
Rawleigh, 226
Samuel, 104,
226, 233
Thomas, 148,
233, 234
CHRISTIAN
Edmund, 74
CLAGETT
Henry, 13, 17, 44,
57, 76, 84, 142,
151, 224, 227,
239
CLAGGETT
Dr., 133
Henry, 17
Julia, 15
CLAPHAM
__, 35, 81, 229
Elizabeth, 99,
155, 239
Samuel, 19, 66,
117, 208, 211
CLARK
Richard, 114
Samuel C., 15, 28
CLARKE
Addison H., 22,
103
Nancy, 196
William F., 84
CLAYCOMB
Elizabeth, 4
CLAYCOME
Dolly, 19, 20
Henry, 19
CLAYTON
Amos, 48, 61, 70,
78, 116, 187,
193, 211
Catharine, 116
Charles F., 116
Eliza, 116

Elizabeth, 61, 193
Israel, 116
Jacob, 116
Martha, 70, 116,
130, 191
Nancy, 196
Patty, 191
Sarah, 116
Susan, 116
Thompson, 116
Townsend, 116
Washington, 116
William, 16, 70,
116, 130, 187,
191, 196, 235,
239
CLENDENING
__, 26
John, 62
Samuel, 62, 99
William, 5, 62,
118, 130, 139,
151, 153, 155,
157, 162, 163,
169, 178, 179,
197, 201, 205,
206, 209, 222,
224, 234, 238
CLENDENNING
William, 62, 182,
205
CLEVELAND
__, 2, 29
J., 66, 85, 92, 166
Johnston, 27, 47,
61, 65, 77, 90,
93, 98, 104,
107, 108, 109,
141, 170, 225,
226, 228
William, 83
CLICE
Henry, 100
Sally, 100
CLICE
__, 123
CLINE
__, 161

Alfred, 83
Margaret, 187
William, 2, 3, 16,
74, 128, 155,
177, 187
William C., 79
CLOVES
Charles S., 195
Thomas, 195
CLOWES
C. L., 137
Charles L., 26, 62
Edith P., 62
CLOWS
Joseph, 192
COATS
Daniel, 44
COCHRAN
Edwrd, 127
James, 10, 221
Mary P., 128
Nathan, 128
Richard, 169,
189, 190
Tholemiah, 10
COCK
Amanda, 228
Kemp, 228
COCKE
__, 199
Amanda M., 145,
197
Kemp, 197
Kemp F., 145
COCKERELL
Daniel, 20
Esther, 20
Mary E., 228
Reuben, 228
COCKERILL
__, 42, 114
Daniel, 114, 152,
194, 203
Esther, 194
John, 199, 240
Joseph R., 190
Mary E., 156, 199
Reuben, 199

Reubin, 156
Richard H., 122
Robert, 63, 122,
 163
Sandford, 58
Thomas, 34
COCKRAN
Fanny, 65
J. H., 190
James, 12, 77
Richard, 99, 218
Robert H., 65
COCKRELL
Daniel, 221
Robert, 19
COCKRILL
Daniel, 77, 114,
 182
John G., 34
Robert, 197
COE
Catharine, 167
David J., 238
Edward, 229, 238
Edward M., 156,
 199, 228
Elizabeth, 190
Elizabeth A., 156
Elizabeth C., 55,
 171
Emily J., 156
Horatio, 152
John W., 238
Mary, 156, 199,
 228, 238
Mary E., 228
Menan, 168, 238
Robert, 171, 184
William, 167, 171,
 190, 229
COGHLIN
Edward, 85
COGILL
__, 74
COGSIL
Harvey, 229
COGSILL
Harvey, 56

COLE
__, 202
William, 237
COLEMAN
__, 157
Edmund, 200
Edmund W., 12
George, 131
James, 122
James R., 98,
 122
Jane M., 122
John, 118
John J., 32, 184,
 200, 231
Johnston, 59
Johnston J., 122,
 166
Julia E., 12
Lydia, 12, 200
Thomas P., 131
William, 12
COLESON
__, 6
COLLINS
John, 92
Levi, 2
Nancy, 92
COLSON
Thomas, 117
COLSTON
__, 173
Thomas M., 151,
 171, 176, 184,
 192, 194, 197,
 199
COMBS
Abigail, 69
Andrew, 69
Edward, 69
Israel, 69
John F., 20
Joseph, 69
Lucinda, 69
Mahlon, 69
Mary, 69
Patty, 69
Presley, 22

Viena, 69
William, 69
COMPHER
__, 79, 212
Abigail, 199
Catharine, 187
Elizabeth, 45, 220
John, 18, 22, 32,
 45, 86, 220
Peter, 46, 47, 50,
 53, 69, 101,
 172, 186, 199,
 202, 212, 227
CONARD
__, 199, 209
Abner, 50
Adah, 86
Anthony, 185
David, 93, 185
Edward, 84, 86,
 94
John, 10, 18, 50,
 104, 117, 123,
 152, 155, 159,
 201, 205, 214,
 223
Luther, 86
Stephen, 86
Stephen T., 1, 2,
 94, 166, 184,
 197, 200
Vashti, 184, 197
CONDEN
Mary, 156
Susan, 156
CONNARD
John, 51
CONNELLY
Edward, 185
CONNER
Ann, 111
John, 140
Timothy, 16
CONRAD
Anthony, 42
D., 38, 131
Daniel P., 42, 49
Robert Y., 234

CONROD
  Stephen, 83
CONWELL
  Ann, 162
  Elizabeth, 10, 30,
    77, 162
  Isaac, 10, 71, 76,
    98, 124, 162,
    178
  Jacob, 162
  Jonathan, 10, 76,
    162
  Josiah, 10, 162
  Lovelace, 77
  Loveless, 10,
    106, 162
  Margaret, 76, 98,
    162
  Mary, 10, 162
  Sarah, 162
COOK
  Edward E., 129
  William J., 75
COOK
  Charles, 180
  Joe, 180
COOKE
  Edward E., 17,
    78, 129
  Henry S., 208
  John R., 40, 131,
    208
  Maria P., 40
  Stephen, 218
  William, 21, 157
COOKSEY
  __, 111, 124, 149,
    150
  Elizabeth, 131,
    166, 237
  Levi, 8, 97, 131,
    166, 237
  Obed, 97
  Obediah, 8
  Susan, 97
COONS
  Philip, 152, 215,
    217

COOPER
  George, 186
COOPER
  __, 68, 72, 86,
    108, 225
  Aaron, 14
  Catharine, 201,
    202, 203, 237
  Daniel, 24, 68,
    69, 123, 151,
    154, 173, 212
  Elizabeth, 69, 79,
    123, 151, 154,
    197, 225
  Elizabeth M., 197
  Eve, 222
  Frederick, 18, 46,
    79, 86, 211,
    234
  George, 22, 23,
    47, 71, 87, 95,
    96, 129, 222,
    223
  Jacob, 47, 236
  John, 45, 46, 222,
    232, 233
  Joseph, 123, 154,
    235
  Joshua, 201, 202,
    203, 237
  Magdalane, 232,
    233
  Margaret, 119,
    123, 154, 235
  Mary, 236
  Michael, 28, 123,
    151, 154, 233,
    235
  Nancy, 123, 154
  Peter, 123, 154
  Susannah, 14
  William, 47, 79,
    197, 225
COPELAND
  Andrew, 190,
    191, 223
  Bennet, 191
  Bennett, 190

  David, 190
  Eliza, 191
  Elizabeth, 190
  James, 25, 69,
    110, 164, 223
  Maria, 191
  Mary, 191
  Nancy, 191
  Richard, 7, 164
  Sarah, 110
CORDELL
  __, 130, 172
  Adam, 5, 154
  Alexander, 138,
    179
  Amelia, 82
  Asa B., 230
  Catherine, 154
  Diana, 179
  Enos B., 53, 102,
    209
  Presley, 3, 5, 6, 7,
    9, 10, 11, 14,
    18, 26, 30, 31,
    35, 51, 55, 56,
    61, 68, 69, 71,
    74, 76, 77, 78,
    79, 80, 82, 86,
    89, 90, 91, 93,
    95, 96, 97, 101,
    102, 103, 105,
    106, 107, 108,
    109, 110, 111,
    112, 113, 115,
    120, 122, 123,
    130, 132, 137,
    143, 147, 150,
    152, 155, 157,
    158, 160, 166,
    169, 177, 180,
    181, 182, 184,
    185, 186, 187,
    188, 193, 194,
    195, 196, 198,
    201, 203, 204,
    205, 207, 209,
    212, 220, 221,
    222, 227, 230

George W. B.,
225
CURRELL
___, 168
John J., 50
Margaret, 50
Mary F., 50
Nancy, 50
Pamelia, 50
CURREY
P. M., 168
CURRY
John, 138
Robert, 171

DAGG
John L., 48, 190
DAGGER
John, 46
DAILEY
Aaron, 40, 118
Fanny, 43, 78
Samuel, 40, 43,
78, 203
DANIEL
Benjamin, 25, 78,
137, 190
David, 128
Eliza B., 104
Esther, 25
Hannah, 51, 137
Hannah L., 25
Hester, 51
Humphrey, 188
James, 25, 51,
137
Jane, 25, 190
Joseph, 29, 104,
189
Mary, 25
Tacey, 29
Tacy, 189
Wallace, 188
Wallace W., 104
William D., 188
DANIELS
Joseph, 56, 133
Stephen, 91

DARLENTON
M., 3
DARN
Robert, 58
DARNE
Catharine, 210,
217
Corbin, 147
Elizabeth, 147
Frances, 80, 108
Gunnell, 11, 147
Hannah, 147
James, 118
John, 147
Robert, 16, 58,
80, 108, 147
DARNES
Thomas, 5, 122
DAVIS
___, 50, 85, 204,
227, 229
Benjamin, 61, 64,
129, 136
Elisa, 101
Elizabeth, 131
Henry M., 105
Howell, 61, 64,
136
James, 165
Jane D., 227
John, 10, 85, 96,
175, 206
John W., 204,
227, 229
Joseph, 173
Lewis, 80
Mary, 206
Sarah, 61, 96
Thomas, 129
Thomas M., 27
DAVISON
F. A., 61
Frederick A., 10,
28, 62, 162
DAVISSON
___, 142, 163
Frederick A., 24,
41, 98, 159

Josiah, 106
Margaret, 41
Sally, 98
Theodore N., 98
DAVY
___, 94
DAWSON
Samuel, 2, 14,
18, 22, 24, 30,
32, 45, 48, 50,
53, 56, 66, 72,
95, 99, 101,
108, 127, 155,
160, 164, 176,
202
DAY
Enoch G., 84,
124, 174, 183
George, 83
John W., 174
D'BELL
William, 61
DEANE
Thomas, 238
DEButts
Samuel W., 56
DECamp
Samuel G. J., 180
DECK
Frederick D., 133
DEMORY
___, 205
John, 78
DENHAM
Amey, 208
Amos, 105, 208
Charles T., 208
David B., 208
Oliver, 60, 123
DENNIS
___, 96
Thomas A., 1
DERRY
___, 159
Catharine, 216
Christian, 89
David, 139
Eliza, 196

Michael, 95, 96, 186
Peter, 88
FULKERSON
William C., 26
FULTON
___, 202
Abraham, 216
Abraham M., 9
David, 171
David P., 44, 198
Elen, 216
Hugh, 50, 227
Jane S., 194
John, 113, 161
Mahlon, 105, 146, 194
Phebe, 171
Robert, 27, 146, 171
Robert S., 146, 171, 194
Sarah, 194
William, 44, 92, 113, 198
FUNK
Michael, 45
FURGUSON
___, 227
J., 52
FURR
Enoch, 36, 74, 223
F., 32
Jeremiah, 74
Minor, 229
Sarah, 74
William G., 223

GALAWAY
Sarah, 125
GALIHERE
William, 54
GALLAHER
___, 16
Caleb N., 33
Mary, 119

William, 103, 115, 119
GALLAWAY
Madison, 130
GALLEHER
___, 107, 158
C. N., 4
Caleb N., 25, 57, 123, 163
David, 122, 123
Eli C., 237
John, 119
Lucinda, 57, 163
Margery, 216
Mary, 119
Samuel, 119
Samuel N., 114
Susan, 237
Thomas, 146
Thomas H., 216
William, 22, 55, 103, 134, 146, 147, 216, 222
GALLIHER
C. N., 31
Caleb N., 94
GALLOWAY
Sarah, 125
GARDENER
Joseph, 54
GARDNER
Jim, 34
Joseph, 55, 126
GARNER
J., 118
James, 35, 54, 70, 174, 181, 191, 196, 203, 204
William, 144
GARRET
Stephen, 122
GARRETT
___, 90, 150
Alfred, 67
Elizabeth, 57
Enoch, 235
Euphamia, 236

James, 235
Jemima, 28
Marthey, 139
Matha, 151
Nicholas, 139
Silas, 28, 32, 49, 174, 214
Stephen, 42, 55, 95, 114, 235, 236
GARRISON
___, 74
Elizabeth, 110, 142, 155, 158, 185, 209
James, 11, 17, 50, 72, 110, 130, 133, 142, 155, 158, 181, 185, 187, 203, 209, 227
GASSAWAY
Charles, 56, 164
Thomas, 193
GATCH
Benjamin W., 90
Martha R., 90
GAVER
C. C., 53
GEATH
Charles W., 199
GEESLING
George A., 202
GEORGE
John, 10, 33, 34, 60, 68, 111, 140, 141, 142, 153, 160, 186, 193
William, 235
GETTYS
James, 32, 178
GHEEN
Catharine, 156
James, 12
Marcissa, 198
Margaret F., 87

Narcissa, 2, 12, 140
Narsisa, 184
Thomas, 2, 156
William, 2, 12
GIBBS
Edward A., 13, 15, 17
Elizabeth, 13
GIBSON
A., 8, 9, 19, 65, 73, 84, 88, 92, 95, 100, 104, 117, 121, 126, 127, 128, 168, 192, 195, 197, 198, 202, 208, 212, 215, 227, 232, 233, 236
Abner, 1, 16, 21, 25, 47, 51, 60, 65, 73, 75, 84, 85, 91, 103, 132, 133, 134, 148, 164, 182, 189, 211, 214, 223, 226, 237
Albert L., 225
Alice, 37, 225
Alpheus, 132
Amos, 71, 136
Betsey W., 25
Carter H., 225
David, 84, 98, 132
David, 103
Elenora, 86, 167
Eli, 84, 132
Eliza H., 225
Elizabeth, 11, 36, 86, 148, 166
Emily J., 225
Emsey, 121
Emsey F., 55, 121
Emzey, 197
Eve, 1

George, 149, 179, 229
Hannah, 136
Isaac, 25, 89, 97, 101
Israel, 225
John, 11, 16, 36, 86, 136, 166, 229
Joseph, 25
Julia A., 225
Landon C., 225
Levi, 84, 132
Mahlon, 37, 86, 117, 136, 166, 167
Moses, 25
Nancy, 98
Nelson, 55, 121, 197
Rachel, 229
S. Elizabeth, 227
Samuel, 217
Sarah S., 25
Susan E., 211
Susanna, 84
Susanna E., 132
William, 25
GILL
Charles, 15, 64
Dolly, 64
Jeremiah, 77
John L., 19, 74, 91, 114, 200
GILLIPSY
Jacob F., 240
GILLMORE
William, 170
GILMORE
__, 151, 202
James, 30, 43
William, 48, 66, 151
GLASCOCK
Abriel, 63
Alfred, 91
Bailey R., 161
Catharine, 213

Elisha, 118
Enoch, 100
Herod, 235
John, 150
Thomas P., 213
Uriel, 38, 76, 98
GLASCOW
Henry, 110
GLASGOW
Ann, 30, 43
Eliza, 191
Henry, 30, 43, 102, 191
William H., 30, 43
GLASSCOCK
__, 66, 224
Aquila, 146
Enoch, 121
Nancy, 159, 217, 227
Uriel, 159, 211, 217, 227
GLASSGOW
Ann, 217
Henry, 217
William, 217
GOCHENOUR
Isaac, 127
GOCHNAUER
__, 98, 197, 202
GOODHEART
__, 154
Henry, 19
Jacob, 151
GOODIN
Anna, 50, 65, 186
Catharine A., 51
David, 50, 65
Elizabeth, 50
John, 50
Jonathan C., 51
Maria, 50, 233
Martha, 50
Rachel, 50
GOODING
Anna, 51
David, 51

GOOSE CREEK
MEETING
HOUSE, 81
GORDON
Bazil, 155, 239
GORE
Jane, 53
Joseph, 4, 31, 53,
99, 114, 118,
136, 207, 226,
240
Joshua, 53
Rowena, 210
Sarah, 53
Thomas, 4, 53,
114, 118
Tilghman, 210,
212
Truman, 56, 176,
214
GOUCHENOUR
__, 160
GOURLEY
Joseph, 115
GOVAN
James, 74
GOVER
Ann, 144
Edwin, 144
Jesse, 39, 42,
176
Miriam G., 176
Robert, 118
Samuel, 144
GOWER
Adam, 63, 64
Daniel, 64
Elizabeth, 63
Henry, 63, 64
Jacob, 63, 64
John, 63, 64
Mary, 63
Nicholas, 63, 64
Peter, 63, 64
Sarah, 63
GOZZLER
Thomas D., 178
GRADY

E. B., 132, 217
Edward B., 21,
151, 166, 174,
218, 228, 230,
231, 235, 237
Francis T., 146,
237
Ury, 237
GRAHAM
__, 193
Andrew, 28, 86,
125, 127, 133,
233
James, 99
John, 77, 84
Mary, 133
Tamer, 5
William, 5, 7, 54,
55, 88, 115,
220
GRANT
Esther, 120
GRAY
Agnes, 38
John, 3, 38, 60,
74, 97, 118,
125, 134, 150,
153, 184, 189,
208, 220
S., 180
GRAY CAMPBELL
& CO, 153
GRAYSON
__, 88
Benjamin, 5, 16,
19, 22, 33, 34,
36, 37, 46, 50,
51, 55, 56, 57,
64, 70, 74, 89,
98, 102, 103,
108, 114, 115,
146, 159, 160,
162, 177, 194,
199, 230
George M., 6
John W., 5, 6, 33
Mary D., 6
Nancy, 5, 199

Richard O., 5, 6,
34, 157, 177,
199
Robert H., 52
William, 5
GRAYSON
Benjamin, 6
GREEN
Albert, 198
Dudley D., 100
John C., 15, 54,
55, 126, 154,
176
N., 76
Triplett C., 176
William M. C. G.,
69
GREENLEASE
Catharine, 157
James, 31, 42,
102, 157
GREENLEES
James, 136
GREENLEESE
__, 136
GREENUP
__, 116, 180
Christopher, 188
GREENWOOD
Henry, 24
Margaret, 24
GREGG
Aaron, 80, 123,
174, 225
Aaron S., 65
Asenith, 174
Elisha, 152
Elizabeth, 65, 174
Emily, 65, 174
George, 63, 118,
152
Guilford, 226
Henry, 58
John, 54, 89, 103
Joseph, 65, 174
Joshua, 28, 32,
49, 65, 228,
238

Josiah, 1, 176
Lydia, 32, 168
Mahlon, 10, 174,
221
Mahlon S., 65
Margaret, 80
Martha L., 152
Mary, 174
Nathan, 1, 7, 16,
75, 129, 168,
175, 186, 189,
205, 232
Peter, 37, 95,
134, 150, 177,
197, 202
Phebe, 174
Rebecca, 123
Rezin, 63, 80,
123, 225
Ruth, 63, 225
Samuel, 75, 175
Sarah, 221
Smith, 186, 205
Stephen, 186,
194, 205
Susan R., 175
Thomas, 164,
186, 205
William, 59, 63,
80, 123, 174,
225
GRIFFITH
G. W., 186
Israel T., 128,
130, 201
Js. T., 38
Rebecca, 83
Samuel G., 27
GRIGBSY
John, 20
Sarah, 20
GRIGGS
Thomas, 28
GRIGSBY
John, 194
Lewis, 174
Malinda, 174
Sarah, 194

GRIMES
__, 181
Andrew, 138
Elizabeth, 109
George, 49, 143,
175, 181
Thomas, 109
GRUBB
__, 26, 42, 50, 54,
72, 117, 139,
209, 225
B., 83, 90
Benjamin, 41, 58,
71, 175, 186,
206, 215
Curtis, 37, 39,
129, 132, 142,
173, 184, 215
E., 62, 100, 152
Ebeneser, 115
Ebenezer, 10, 13,
17, 18, 19, 20,
26, 33, 37, 40,
41, 42, 50, 58,
69, 82, 88, 98,
103, 115, 116,
117, 122, 129,
142, 155, 157,
160, 163, 181,
194, 201, 205,
216, 235
Harriet, 39, 132,
142
J., 34
James, 21, 39,
41, 122, 215
John, 10, 31, 68,
155, 229
Joseph, 137, 159,
215
Joseph P., 51, 75
Mary, 51, 137
R., 62
Richard, 69, 155,
194
GUIDER
Peter, 132
GULATT

Charles, 119
GULICK
__, 126
Alfered, 128
Alfred, 78, 86,
100, 124, 158,
192
Amos, 64, 109,
124, 128, 129,
136
Elizabeth, 85
George, 122, 124,
192
John, 49
Leana, 100
Levi, 36
Ludwell, 85
Martha, 219
Matilda, 192
Moses, 64, 78,
85, 86, 124,
129, 158, 192
Nancy, 100
Sarah M., 124
William, 42, 55,
95, 100
GULLAT
Charles, 107
GULLATT
Charles, 144
GUNN
James, 215
GUNNELL
George, 152
George W., 44
Henry, 152
Robert, 44, 152
Thomas, 152
William, 122, 152
GUY
Sampson, 92

HACKLEROAD
John, 24
HAGER
Nicholas, 63
HAGERMAN
Benjamin, 49

Fleming, 33, 138,
142, 159, 177
Fleming W. P., 89
James, 36, 56,
133, 134
Mary, 133, 134
Nancy, 84, 132
Rebecca, 117,
132
Reuben, 129
Samuel, 38
Stephen, 138
Tacy, 133
Timothy, 38
HOCKINGS
Joseph, 95, 167,
170
HODGSON
Portia, 68, 180
William L., 79, 85
HODSON
__, 94
HOE
Howsen, 221
Nancy, 221
HOEY
James, 97, 181
William, 97, 181
HOFFMAN
George, 13
John, 13, 196
Peter, 13
Samuel, 13
HOGE
__, 150
Asa, 230
Asenath A., 199
Isaac, 39, 203
James, 222
Jesse, 104, 222
Mary, 191
Samuel, 191
William, 29, 76,
104, 114, 136,
165, 176
HOGESON
Mrs., 116
HOGUE

__, 194, 238
Betsey, 103
Isaac, 20
James, 36, 69,
120
Jesse, 93
Joseph, 93, 215
Joshua, 121
Miller, 215
William, 42, 49,
121, 165
HOLE
Abeleno, 161
Ann, 75, 97
Levi, 75, 97, 178
Miriam, 2, 75, 178
HOLLINGSWORTH
Elizabeth, 199
Jehu, 69
John, 199
HOLMES
__, 13
Catharine, 183
Edward C., 183
Elijah, 31, 136,
174, 181, 191,
214
Eliza T., 11
Elizabeth, 136,
181, 191
Elizabeth E., 183
Hannah, 191, 235
Hannah S., 225
Henry N., 183
Isaac, 50, 110,
191, 225, 235
Jacob F., 183
James A., 183
Jesse, 191, 192
John, 17, 22, 39,
136, 234
John W., 183
Joseph, 192
Joseph D., 183
Lot, 191
Mary, 136
Peter, 207

William, 9, 11, 30,
35, 60, 128,
136, 147, 154,
183, 188, 191,
192, 213, 232
HOLTZMAY
J., 32
HOOD
Jonah, 89
HOOE
__, 132
HOOF
John, 102, 154
HOOFF
John, 79
HOOK
Daniel, 63
HOOPER
Ann, 236
Fielder, 236
James, 164
HOPE
Joshua T., 161
HOPKINS
Cornelia, 201
Joel, 173
John, 201
Johns, 28
Lucy L., 202
HOPSON
James, 185
HORREL
Joseph, 99
HORTON
Malcom, 208
Margaret A., 208
HOSKINSON
__, 206
Andrew J., 176
Andrew S., 45
Robert J., 176
Thomas W., 176
HOUGH
__, 116, 138, 141,
202
Amasa, 39, 73
Ann E., 39
B., 34

Eli, 75, 97, 204
Gerard L. W., 33
Jane, 33
John, 75, 97, 130, 204
Lewis, 26, 62
Major, 2, 75, 204
Mary, 20, 194
Philip, 20, 194
Unah, 204
HUNTER
George, 44
George W., 5
Gerard L. W., 127
James, 122
John, 92
Joseph, 13
Robert, 16, 58, 80, 108
William, 204
HURDLE
Nancy, 159
Richard, 217
HUTCHISON
Andrew, 152, 167
Elizabeth, 234
Henry, 16
Henry H., 49, 81, 103, 146
John, 91
John T., 167
Lewis, 145, 148
Martha L., 167
Melville B., 209
Redding, 148
Reuben, 77
Sampson, 92, 234
Sandford, 214
Silas, 229
Susan, 103
Thomas, 91
Wesley, 91
William, 167
HYLER
__, 145

IDEN

__, 217
James, 127, 197, 202
John, 98, 127
Jonah, 132
Margarett, 202
Mary, 132
Samuel, 8, 58, 66, 97, 127, 166
INGRAM
John, 46, 82, 86
Tamer, 82
Thamer, 46
Thomas, 3
INSKEEP
John, 46
INSOR
John, 35, 69, 72
Mary J., 35, 69, 72
IREY
John, 49, 174
William, 103
IRVINE
Thomas, 203
ISH
John, 9, 16, 86, 88, 216, 219
Robert A., 86
Sophonia, 75
W. K., 118
William, 75
William K., 8, 15, 67, 72, 74, 75, 120, 223

JACKMAN
William, 179
JACKSON
__, 85
Asa, 36, 123
Benjamin, 25, 31, 35, 53, 65, 79, 99, 120, 146, 151, 179, 196, 210, 235, 236, 239

David, 70
Ebenezer, 151
Elizabeth, 213
John, 17, 213
Lewis, 144
Margaret, 52
Mary, 17
Samuel, 93
Stiles, 213
Thomas, 52
William, 52
JACOB
William, 179
JACOBS
Adam, 41, 123, 166
Catharine, 16, 51, 55, 70, 208
Catherine, 54
Christian, 209
Christina, 100
Elizabeth, 17, 42, 50, 227
George, 17, 100
Harriet, 20
John, 41, 42
John P., 119, 134
Peter, 20, 41, 118, 209
Price, 16, 50, 51, 55, 56, 120, 145, 197, 204, 208, 228
Rachel, 41
Rozzell, 1
Thomas, 25
Valentine, 17, 20
Vallentine, 157, 202, 209
William H., 54, 55, 70, 72, 175
JAMES
__, 45, 51
Aaron, 91
Abigail, 92
Benjamin, 91, 117, 145, 174, 200

Malinda, 138
Margaret, 196, 220
Melinda, 4
Moses, 183
P. B., 100
Robert, 109, 138, 139, 221
Thomas J., 99
William, 7, 131, 196, 220, 237
JOHNSON, WATERMAN & CO, 153
JOHNSTON
Alexander M., 27
Charles A., 185, 239
Charles P., 27
Dennis M., 27
James, 109, 176, 177, 218
John D., 27
Levi, 4
R., 83
Sarah M., 27
Thomas, 76
JOICE
Thomas, 31
JOLLEFFE
John, 236
JONES
Jesse, 90, 92
John, 20, 62, 90, 195, 221
Joseph, 195
Rachel, 90, 92
Thomas M., 29
Thomas N., 87, 134
William J., 31, 55, 218
William M., 85
JORDON
Joshua, 92
Susanna, 92
JUDY
John, 184

JUREY
David, 8
Lewis, 8
JURY
Mary A., 157
Townsend J., 157, 167

KABRICK
George, 186
KALB
__, 193
Absalom, 163
Absolam, 159
John, 163
Samuel, 64, 96, 130, 163, 229
Susanna, 163
KARN
Adam, 10, 33
KARNE
Adam, 145
KAYLOR
John W., 161
KEEN
George, 134, 158, 179, 226
KEENAN
James, 157
KEENE
__, 18, 51
Elizabeth, 59
George, 22, 70, 95, 194, 206
N., 89
Nancy, 95
Newton, 12, 27, 59, 145, 194, 214, 222
Richard, 150
KENDAH
Charles, 99
KENNERLY
Ann A., 41
Samuel, 41
KENT
Daniel, 54
Elijah, 27, 138

KENWORTHY
Rebecca, 7, 144
KERFORT
Daniel S., 150
KERN
Adam, 125
Jacob, 22
KERR
James D., 53
Kerr & Fitzhugh, 81
KERRICK
Walter, 8, 237
KETTLE
James, 240
KEYES
Jane, 55, 71
William, 55, 71
KEYS
Caroline, 215
Robert, 215
William, 72, 173, 175, 206, 225
KIDWELL
Thomas, 94, 157
Zedekiah, 42
KILE
Christiana, 73
George, 73, 134, 232
John, 65, 73, 90, 91, 92, 170, 226, 232
Mary, 65
Sally, 73
Winefred, 65, 170
Winifred, 232
Winnefred, 226
KILGORE
Charles, 199
Charles J., 2, 216
James M., 216
Louisa, 2
KILGOURE
Charles J., 194
KIMBER
Daniel, 117
KIMBLER
David, 92

KING
Francis F., 146
G. W., 4
Susan, 5, 38, 44
William, 5, 29, 38,
44, 54, 121,
181
KINSEL
George, 84
KIRK
Malcolm C., 199
Mary A., 199
KIRKPATRICK
Thomas, 2, 197
KIST
Ann, 82
Philip, 82
KITCHEN
Elisha, 61, 108
KITTLE
James, 124
KITZMILLER
A., 178
A. M., 159, 185,
220, 224
Arch M., 169
Archibald M., 130,
167, 170, 178,
185, 191, 220
Elizabeth, 16
Martin, 16, 130,
177
William W., 11,
16, 43, 54, 70,
164, 177, 181,
191, 203, 227
KIZER
Barbara, 56
Martin, 56
KLEIN
Maddison C., 70
KLINE
John N., 191
KNOX
Janet, 71
Joseph, 71, 98
KOENER
Catharine, 88

John G., 88
KOONCE
George, 157
KOONSE
widow, 202
KRAMER
Allen, 179
KUNTS
Augustus, 64
Sarah, 64
KUNTZ
Augustus, 63
KURTZ
Daniel, 99

LACEY
Benjamin R., 168
David, 35, 64,
183, 188, 232
Diadama, 183
Elias, 117
Huldah, 58
Israel, 21
Mahala, 22
Neomi, 58
Ruth, 58
Sarah, 64, 232
Stacey, 22
LACKLAND
Eliza, 130
George L., 130
George S., 219
LACY
Benjamin R., 35,
49, 88
Catharine E., 36,
58
Elias, 49
Israel, 36
John, 109
Robert A., 36
Tacy, 58
LADD
John H., 61
LAFEVER
Henry, 236
Honorea, 236
William, 236

LAKE
Agnes, 49, 168
Ludwell, 35, 49,
168
LAMBAUGH
Anthony, 79
LAMBON
James, 208
LAMPHIER
John, 49
LANE
Catharine, 37, 63
DeWitt, 95
Joseph, 37, 63,
98, 160
Lydia, 16
Lyman, 139
Ralph, 65
William, 16
LANGLEY
Walter, 132
LANHAM
Zadock, 59
LANNING
Isaac M., 132
LARMOUR
Samuel B., 174
LAROWE
Isaac, 124
LATIMER
James B., 180
LATIMORE
Thomas, 89
LAURENS
Augustus P. F.,
144
LAWRENCE
Alexander, 218
LAYCOCK
Joseph, 7, 106
Samuel, 126
LEADHAM
Isaac, 145
LEE
__, 82, 145
A., 5
Alexander D., 11,
38, 210

LUCK
  Jordon B., 36
LUCKETT
  Alfred, 25
  Ann C., 176, 217
  Craven P., 188
  F. W., 111, 193
  Francis, 38
  Francis W., 8, 16,
    19, 21, 22, 26,
    34, 35, 37, 44,
    48, 51, 55, 57,
    65, 70, 74, 77,
    88, 92, 96, 98,
    102, 105, 107,
    112, 113, 120,
    128, 134, 136,
    138, 143, 146,
    150, 153, 169,
    178, 181, 187,
    204, 208, 211,
    217,220, 225,
    227
  Henry F., 65, 128,
    171, 174, 183,
    234
  Horace, 9, 10, 15,
    25, 36, 94, 108,
    109, 127, 152,
    163, 170, 171,
    192, 214, 223
  Josiah C., 82
  L., 147
  Leven, 41, 91
  Louisa A., 9, 25
  Ludwell, 113,
    135, 146, 147,
    150, 157, 158,
    160, 169, 170,
    176, 178, 187,
    189, 192, 193,
    195, 208, 217,
    225, 226, 227,
    230, 231, 232,
    233, 237, 240
  Luther C., 82
  Maria A., 65
  Mary B., 144

Matilda, 50
Robert C., 82
Robert T., 183,
  214, 215
Samuel, 82, 85,
  99
Samuel C., 85,
  144, 228
Sarah C., 82
Sarah S., 113
Thomas H., 233
William C., 50,
  82, 85
LUCKETTS
  Ludwell, 231
LUFBOROUGH
  Hamilton, 46, 103
  Nathan, 46
LUKE
  Catharine, 130
  Jacob, 239
  Sarah, 239
LUM
  John, 218
LUPTON
  Amos, 40, 60
  Hannah, 40, 60
LYDER
  __, 195
  Landon, 92
  Lewis, 92, 194
  Mary, 77, 194
LYLE
  __, 158
  Robert, 65
  William, 65
LYLES
  Archibald M., 43,
    107
  Harriet T., 43
LYNN
  Adam, 83, 89
  Fielding, 118
  Michael, 212
LYON
  John C., 29
LYONS
  Joseph, 40

William, 66

MACHEN
  Rebecca, 211
  Thomas, 211
MACKELFRESH
  Philemon S., 139
MACRAE
  Amanda M., 16
  James W., 89,
    101, 102
  James W. F., 16
MACrae
  James, 103
MAGILL
  Archibald, 169
  Charles, 175
  Charles T., 48,
    113, 169, 175,
    187
  John S., 27, 69,
    165, 169
  Mary D., 113,
    175, 187
MAGILL
  Archibald, 175
MAGINNIS
  Daniel, 64
MAGOWAN
  Johnston, 13
MAGUIRE
  J. L., 71
MAINES
  Archibald, 116
  William, 116
MAINS
  Anne, 94
  Archibald, 38, 50,
    67, 158, 159,
    177, 224
  William, 67, 94,
    105, 159
MALIN
  Ann, 200
  Joseph, 200
MALONE
  G. W., 83
  Rudolph, 83

MANDEVILLE
Joseph, 174
MANKIN
Lewis F., 66, 85,
92, 166, 206
MANN
Jacob, 93, 112
MANNING
Euphemia, 26,
183
Mrs., 188, 232
Nathaniel, 50,
110, 235
Sally L., 11, 26
Sarah, 11
MARKLEY
Ph. S., 153
MARKS
___, 237
Abel, 2, 5, 9, 21,
61, 216
David D., 73
Elisha S., 8, 14,
73, 79
Elizabeth, 2, 8, 73
George, 25, 31,
64, 65, 66, 79,
107, 108, 109,
114, 219, 228
George S., 86
Hannah, 188
Isaiah, 8, 14, 73,
79
John, 79, 228
John D., 73
John N., 64, 65,
219
Lucinda D., 8, 73
Lydia, 9, 61
Mahala, 25, 31,
66, 107
Nancy, 86
Samuel, 2
Thomas, 161
MARLATT
Hannah, 163
John, 163
MARLOW

___, 50, 85, 101,
125
Edward, 19, 22,
23
George, 82, 142,
155, 162, 177,
201, 202, 203,
210, 223, 237
Henson, 19, 172
Mary, 35
Thomas J., 10,
35, 53, 66, 85,
90, 113, 115,
116, 125, 140,
141, 142, 145,
152, 153, 159,
163, 171, 172,
173, 175, 183,
190, 197, 199,
206, 214, 216,
219, 224, 231
MARLOWE
George, 99
MARMADUKE
J. A., 99
Silas, 99
MARSHALL
Betsey, 34
MARTAIN
James, 151
MARTIN
___, 142
Frances A., 121
James L., 11, 41,
48, 54, 60, 118,
126, 143, 167
John, 2, 3, 43, 48,
54, 61, 96, 105,
118, 121, 126,
132, 133, 143,
149, 164, 181,
186, 235
Mary, 105
Robert, 88
MASH
James, 76
MASON
___, 35, 55, 134

Ann, 118
Armistead, 13
Armstead T., 13
Betsey C., 83,
101
Charlotte E., 13
John T., 13
T., 180
Thompson, 199
Thompson F., 66,
83, 118
Thomson, 13
Thomson F., 101,
122
Thomson T., 101
Westwood T., 199
William T. T., 13,
88, 202
MASSEY
___, 45
MASSIE
Catharine, 1, 2
Samuel, 1, 2
MATHEWS
___, 122
Thomas P., 39,
240
MATHIAS
D. T., 118
Daniel T., 51, 53,
54, 59, 95, 119
H. R., 28
Hamilton R., 34,
53, 59, 119
Harriot H., 119
J. J., 93
Jane, 119
John J., 14, 35,
38, 41, 48, 51,
52, 53, 54, 55,
56, 57, 59, 66,
71, 74, 75, 79,
85, 88, 92, 93,
95, 97, 98, 101,
102, 105, 110,
111, 113, 115,
118, 119, 120,
123, 134, 138,

William, 169
NEAR
Amos, 104, 152,
153, 190
Ann, 104
David, 104, 152,
153, 169, 217
Eliza, 152, 153
Elizabeth, 104
Hannah, 104
James, 152
Jesse, 24, 29,
163, 202
John, 153
Nathan, 75, 135
Samuel, 155, 157
Sarah, 157
Susannah, 153,
169
NEER
Ann, 26, 115, 117
Conard, 26
Connard, 33
Conrad, 115, 117
David, 104
Eliza, 6, 78, 115,
117
Jesse, 26, 115,
117, 206
John, 217
Joseph, 26, 115,
117
Martha, 115, 117
Matilda, 26
Nathan, 6, 78,
115, 117
Samuel, 17, 32,
42, 115, 117
Sarah, 32, 117
Susannah, 104
Susannah G., 104
NEGRO
Aaron, 237
Abner, 180
Adalaide, 110
Adam, 34, 139
Adeline,, 155
Admiral, 8

Agnes, 203
Alfred, 79, 151,
155
Alice, 79
Amanda, 62
Amelia, 3
Amey, 155
Amos, 156
Ampsey, 79
Andrew, 53, 59
Ann, 62, 71, 91,
99, 138, 178
Anna, 180
Anthony, 79, 202
Armistead, 65
Barbara, 3, 42
Ben, 155
Benjamin, 30
Betsey, 79, 154,
155, 172
Betsey Marshall,
34
Betsy, 79, 151
Betty, 96, 106
Betty Patty, 34
Bill, 34, 155, 203
Bill Shaver, 155
Billy, 34, 79
Bronssais, 122
Burr, 65
Caroline, 211,
228
Cassius, 79
Catharine, 156
Catherine, 151
Caty, 65, 79
Ceasar, 106
Charity, 29, 202
Charles, 79, 83,
106, 109, 180,
203
Charles Cook,
180
Charles Fenton,
210
Charlotte, 109,
154, 167, 180,
228

Cintha, 53
Cregar, 79
Cynthia, 29
Dade, 228
Daniel, 155
Daniel Berry, 215
Davy, 34
Delila, 3
Dick, 79
Dilsa, 79
Dinah, 79, 83
Dolly, 106
Easter, 155
Easther, 99
Edie, 155
Edmund, 106
Elias, 155
Eliza, 116, 151,
180, 203
Elizabeth, 79, 228
Ellen, 106
Ellias, 79
Ellzey, 91
Emily, 42, 91, 99,
155, 210
Emma, 134
Fanny, 29, 122
Fanny Smith, 122
Fenton, 151
Flora, 155
Frances, 91, 122
Frederick, 155
George, 52, 63,
84, 106, 167,
178, 180, 203,
210
Georgiana, 155
Hagar, 202
Hannah, 63, 91,
99
Harriet, 3, 155,
210
Harrison, 211
Harry, 109, 202
Henna, 106
Hennery, 116
Henry, 42, 155,
180

Phillip, 105
NETTLE
William, 26, 177
NETTLES
___, 237
NEWCOMER
Emanuel, 103
NEWKIRK
Absalom, 156
Elizabeth, 156
NEWMAN
Basil, 211
Bazil, 211, 212
Robert M., 47
William G., 171
NEWTON
Ann, 188
Charles C., 111, 196
Elizabeth L., 188
J. T., 118
James, 27, 211
James F., 67, 125, 158
Jane H., 115
John, 45
John C., 188
John T., 165
Joseph, 17
Joseph T., 40, 125, 158
Margaret, 188
Mary A., 177
Robert, 188
Robert C., 188
Widow, 106
NICEWANNER
John, 219
NICHOLS
___, 92, 159
Abraham, 70
Amer, 69
Ann, 199
Cassandra, 143, 181
Catherine, 169
Charity, 94, 131, 239

David, 239
Dolphin, 45
Edna, 221
Emily, 191
Enos, 10, 77, 94, 102, 156, 221, 226
Fanny, 174
George, 15, 45, 199
Hannah, 206
Hannah F., 119
Harman, 45
Henry, 168
Isaac, 29, 36, 54, 56, 69, 104, 120, 132, 136, 148, 150, 165, 176, 206, 207, 212
Isaiah, 84
James, 1, 15, 24, 45, 46, 84, 94, 131, 184, 239
James H., 78
Joel, 45
John, 15, 94, 131, 239
Jonah, 78, 174, 175, 181
Joseph, 81
Joshua, 140, 203, 212, 221, 222
Letitia, 119
Lydia, 9, 165, 168, 195
Maria, 69
Naomi, 203, 212, 221
Nathan, 61, 84, 87, 158, 200
Nathaniel, 5, 44, 46, 131
Samuel, 36, 81, 120, 149, 169, 170, 179
Sarah, 5, 45, 46, 61

Swithen, 9, 139, 191
Swithin, 2, 153
Thomas, 1, 4, 7, 9, 20, 24, 25, 27, 28, 32, 35, 39, 40, 47, 57, 58, 60, 65, 77, 78, 80, 81, 88, 113, 119, 124, 125, 135, 139, 150, 161, 191, 194, 212, 222, 231, 238
William, 9, 57, 119, 143, 166, 169, 174, 181, 191
NICKOLS
James, 68
Nathan, 68
Thomas, 14
NISEWANGER
Catherine, 183
Christian, 139
Henry, 183
John, 139
NIXON
Cassandra, 207
George, 6, 70, 87, 89, 107, 108, 121, 160, 207, 213
James, 22, 33, 51, 89, 96, 129
James W., 69
Joel, 30, 79, 156, 160
John, 160, 207
Samuel, 57, 83
Sarah, 27, 61, 69, 86, 110, 144
Susan A., 89
NIXSON
John, 116
NOAH
Mordecai M., 180
NOBLE

Bailey, 148
Benedict, 26
Eleanor, 26
Elizabeth, 148
Francis, 148
Harriet T., 148
PADGETT
Benedict, 135
Eleanor, 135
Timothy, 178
PAGE
Carter B., 29
Jane M., 122
Rebecca, 29
PAINTER
Delilah, 100
Edward, 17
Guliema, 17
Jonathan, 20,
100, 197
PALMER
John, 74
Lucinda, 108
Samuel, 35, 44,
237
Sarah H., 35
Thomas, 74
William C., 107,
108, 134, 171,
223, 226
Palmer & Chamblin,
51
PANCOAST
__, 111, 134, 149,
195
John, 2, 73, 89,
103, 112, 118,
175, 179, 232
Joshua, 8, 14, 49,
89, 114, 118,
139, 233
Lydia, 9, 165,
218, 233
Sarah, 89
PARKER
Hannah, 46, 62
PARRETT
__, 130

PARSON
John L., 161
PARSONS
Anne, 19
Israel, 19
John L., 207
PATERSON
Margaret, 200
PATTERSON
Janet, 71
Lydia, 176
Robert, 22, 176
PATTON
__, 122
PAXON
Diadema, 64
J. G., 22
Jane, 71
William, 13, 71
PAXSON
__, 108
Ann, 146
Diadama, 183
Diadema, 11
J. G., 7, 33
Jacob G., 13,
101, 115, 116,
138, 141, 142,
145
John, 39, 146
Mahala, 13, 115,
116, 138
Mahala J., 141
Martha, 127
Samuel, 108,
115, 116, 127,
138, 141, 142,
166, 207
William, 30, 115,
138, 141, 177,
183, 207
PAXTON
Samuel, 207
PAYNE
John, 1
PAYTEN
__, 158
PAYTON

Richard F., 142
Sarah M., 142
T. D., 144
Townshend D.,
142
Virlinda, 142
PEACHER
John, 13
PEACOCK
__, 86, 154
Ann, 30, 133, 151
Elijah, 24, 28, 30,
112, 123, 127,
133, 142, 146,
151, 153, 212
Nancy, 24
William, 201, 202
PEAKE
Humphrey, 27,
40, 67, 125,
158
PEARCE
Hector, 70
PEARPOINT
__, 15
PECK
Asa, 34, 83
PEERS
Ann H., 213
Eleanor, 28, 169,
208, 213
PEIRPOINT
Samuel, 120
PENQUITE
__, 180
Keziah, 125
William, 44, 125
PERFECT
Robert, 188
PERL
William, 200
PERRY
Belinda, 169
Benjamin W., 167
John, 136
PETTETT
George, 134
PEUGH

111, 114, 131,
134, 135, 151,
154, 164, 167,
178, 193, 198
Mary, 87
Robert, 114, 236
William, 47, 87,
152, 170, 183
ROSS
David, 202
John, 40
Richard, 103
ROSSEL
Stephen C., 114
ROSZEL
Nancy, 32
Phebe, 32
Sarah, 32
Stephen C., 32
Stephen G., 32
Stephen W., 32,
109
ROSZELL
__, 90
Anna, 67
Nancy, 109
Peter, 155
Phebe, 109
Stephen, 32
Stephen C., 109
Stephen G., 109
Stephen W., 32
ROWAN
George, 144
ROWLES
Candall, 173
Candas, 180
Candy, 130
Caroline, 180
Edy, 173
Harriet, 180
Harriot, 130
Joshua J., 130
Nehemiah M.,
129
Sarah, 129
Susannah C.,
173, 229

Thomas J., 173
ROZEL
__, 220
ROZELL
Stephen, 145
Stephen C., 23,
235
Stephen W., 23
ROZLE
Stephen C., 236
RUCE
Henry, 23
RUS
James, 118
RUSE
__, 218
David, 186, 189,
194, 219
Henry, 23
John, 74, 89, 108,
120, 193
Lewis, 164
Mary, 33
Sarah, 74, 120
Soloman, 181,
191
Solomon, 70, 174
Tabitha, 70, 174
RUSK
James, 124
RUSSELL
__, 145, 152, 197
Aaron, 46, 53, 62
Ann, 115, 117
C. A. E. Jane, 2
Charley A. E. J., 2
Edith, 46, 62
Eliza, 2
Elizabeth, 10, 21,
77
Emily J., 62
Harrison, 183
Henry, 13, 57, 61,
140, 166, 184,
233
James, 123
Jane, 14

Joseph, 46, 115,
117
Joseph L., 169,
215
Mahlon, 46, 82
Mary A., 46, 62
Nancy, 46
Robert, 22, 23,
48, 172, 221
Sally A., 2
Samuel, 163
Sarah, 14
Sarah E., 14, 234
Tamson, 62
Thadeus, 234
Thomas, 48, 118,
204
William, 5, 21, 25,
46, 62, 138,
143, 166, 184
RUST
__, 34, 44
Benjamin, 76,
121, 144, 154,
165, 189, 213,
229
Frances, 165
George, 1, 61, 72,
88, 89, 95, 115,
116, 141, 177,
180, 185, 199,
206, 219
James, 13, 15,
18, 35, 36, 38,
55, 79, 81, 82,
95, 102, 116,
159, 180, 185,
197, 201, 227
James T., 72
Mandly T., 72, 74
Maria C., 89, 180
Martha, 67
Mathew, 67, 72,
74, 75, 196
Matthew, 67
Sally, 74, 197
Sarah, 35, 72,
201

Humphrey, 161,
195, 212, 222
James, 157
Leven W., 210
SHEPPARD
Jim, 34
T., 71
SHERARD
__, 5
SHIELDS
William R., 136
SHILLABER
Jonathan, 27
SHIPMAN
Samuel, 83
SHOBER
Jacob J., 63, 64
SHOEMAKER
__, 93
Abraham, 103,
139
Charlotte, 238
Daniel, 33
Jacob, 161
John, 212
Mrs., 232
Naylor, 90
Pricilla, 161
Priscilla, 213
Simon, 45, 50,
71, 93, 172,
178, 186, 212,
213, 238
SHORT
Henry, 129
SHORTS
Charlotte, 91
John, 91
SHOVER
Adam, 90, 91,
160
George, 33, 90,
91, 160
Jacob J., 63, 64
John, 64
Magdalena, 10,
33
Magdalina, 145

Simon, 160
SHOYER
Mary, 238
SHREAVE
Charles, 111
SHREVE
__, 48, 75, 228
B., 43, 138
Benjamin, 7, 41,
71, 75, 80, 84,
93, 102, 111,
113, 118, 157,
165, 183, 184,
224, 232
Charles, 17, 80,
181, 224
Francis, 126
Francis E., 59
SHRIGLEY
Louisa, 233
Samuel, 233
SHRIVER
__, 94
David, 26, 71,
184
Jacob, 26, 30,
123, 184, 215
John, 46
Nancy, 46
SHRY
Powell, 187
SHRYOCK
__, 206
Michael, 33, 193,
196
SHRYVER
David, 29
Jacob, 29
SHUMATE
M. C., 37
Margaret, 37
Murphey C., 37,
67, 172
SHUTT
Caroline, 41
Caroline F., 205
Jacob, 19, 41, 63,
158, 163, 205

SILCOTT
Abraham, 4, 218
Barsheba, 218
Craven, 115, 146
Elizabeth, 115,
146
J., 204
Jacob, 18, 115,
134, 146, 183
Jesse, 183
John, 57, 58
Norval, 212
Peyton, 1
Tamer, 115, 146
SILVER
William, 127
SIM
Thomas, 218
SIMMS
Isaiah, 147
SIMPSON
Deborah, 130
Edward W., 33
Elizabeth, 49
Francis, 97, 130,
204
French, 156
James, 49
John, 31, 37, 47,
48, 55, 57, 61,
62, 83, 85, 89,
90, 111, 114,
118, 123, 124,
127, 132, 149,
150, 156, 169,
170, 184, 195,
203, 219, 221,
222, 224, 228
John T., 183, 230
Mary A., 115
Richard F., 57
Samuel, 49, 67,
105, 168, 240
William, 207
William H., 224
SINCLAIR
Amos, 52, 81
George, 52, 205

George H., 104
James, 28, 54,
    62, 67, 94, 143,
    153, 175
John, 218
Leanna, 94
Leanner, 67
Samuel, 37, 52,
    104
Samuel C., 62,
    81, 118
Sarah, 104
Thomas M., 104
SINGLETON
Agnes, 22
Agness, 18
Allen, 18
Ellen, 18
Elon, 22
Jane, 18, 66
John, 37
Joshua, 18, 37
Mary A., 175
Robert, 18, 22,
    33, 37, 66
Samuel, 18, 22,
    38, 66
Washington G.,
    157, 226
William, 38
SKILLMAN
Abraham, 31, 40,
    48, 49, 87, 121,
    140, 155, 184,
    198, 203, 213,
    228, 234
Delilah H., 203
John, 220
Lucinda, 155
SKILMAN
Abraham, 12, 189
SKINNER
__, 36, 168
Alexander, 59,
    198
Amos, 220
Betsey, 198
Cornelius, 156

Eliza, 156
Elizabeth, 198
Emily, 156
Fanny, 198
Gabriel, 31, 76,
    198, 234
Harriet, 156
Jane, 198
Mary, 156, 198
Nancy, 198
Nathan, 30, 83,
    114, 156, 220
Peggy, 220
Peter, 9, 10, 156,
    167
Phebe, 198
Richard A., 156
Robert, 198
Samuel, 198
Sarah, 198
Susan, 156
Usher, 167, 240
SLACK
Abraham, 147,
    148
SLATER
Anthony, 32
George, 32, 186
John, 32, 45
John M., 45
Mary, 45
Michael, 45
Samuel, 216
Sarah, 32
William, 21, 32,
    45, 128, 144,
    154, 156, 159,
    160, 172, 179,
    187, 196, 197,
    201, 216, 219,
    221, 223, 229,
    230, 231, 232,
    233, 234
SLATES
Adam, 213
Eliza A., 213
Elizabeth A., 214
Mary, 214

Mary A., 214
Scivilla, 107
Solomon, 213
Sybilla, 214
William, 96, 214
Slates & Everheart,
    173
SMALE
John, 225
Simon, 184, 225
SMALLEY
Cynthia, 93
SMALLWOOD
__, 177
Amanda, 53, 137
Eleanor, 137
Emeline, 137
Leven, 137
Levin, 53
Sarah, 137
Sarah A., 137
SMARR
John, 31
SMART
John P., 21, 151,
    172, 202, 208,
    209, 211, 239
SMITH
__, 55, 107, 149,
    181
Ann, 238, 240
Anne, 207
Asa, 142
Benjamin, 134,
    222
Benjamin P., 99
D. G., 67
Daniel G., 43,
    105, 134, 135,
    153, 208, 213
David, 111, 150,
    159, 203, 212,
    221, 222
Eliza., 135
Elizabeth, 136
Fleet, 208
George, 4, 20, 50,
    129, 162, 201

William, 30, 43,
98, 184, 212
William B., 76,
144, 184
STEPHEN
Enos, 118
STEPHENS
Banister, 134
STEPHENSON
George B., 190
James, 12, 91,
187
John, 54, 72, 93,
131
William A., 157
STERETT
Samuel, 118
STERRET
Samuel, 181
STERRETT
Lydia, 191, 203
Samuel, 53, 126,
161, 191
STETMAN
Catharine, 90
John, 91
STEVENS
Banister P., 146
John B., 7
Thomas D., 7
STEWART
Hamilton, 52,
179, 239
Hester, 204
James W., 52,
179
Jane A., 179, 239
John T., 61
Paulina, 52, 179
Rebecca, 52
STICKLE
Henry, 175
STIFF
James M., 145
Robert, 145
STINGER
Livi, 133
STOCK

William, 114
STOCKS
William, 14
STONE
Daniel, 23, 26,
101, 156
Edward, 53
J., 84
James, 82, 83
John, 44
Ruth, 82
Samuel S., 228
Sarah, 86
Thomas, 82, 86,
184
Thomas S., 131,
184, 239
STONEBURNER
__, 2, 45, 153
Barbara, 62
Daniel, 24, 113
Henry, 19
Jacob, 62, 75
Margaret, 52
STONESTREET
Eleanor, 193, 194
Richard W., 193,
194
STOUSBERGER
Jacob, 19
John, 19
STOUTSEBERGER
Jacob, 45
Mary, 45
Samuel, 45
STOUTSEN-
BERGER
__, 2
Jacob, 45, 222
John, 199
Samuel, 221
STOVEN
Charles, 100
Charles J., 38,
100
Mary, 38, 100
STREAM
__, 108

Jacob, 139, 240
Michael, 240
Pleasant, 159
William, 159, 233
STRIBLING
__, 113, 150
Francis, 41, 124,
150
Taliaferro, 176
STRINGFELLOW
Benjamin, 14, 25,
32, 79
STROTHER
James, 133
STUBBLEFIELD
__, 94
STUCK
Peter, 21, 156
STUMP
Benjamin, 1
John, 165
SUDDITH
William, 2, 12
SUFFRON
Samuel, 2
SULLIVAN
Abram, 124
Arthur, 84
Elizabeth, 131,
207
George, 67, 75,
84
George B., 50
John L., 207
M., 103
Mortho, 124
Mrs., 222
Murtho, 207
Owen, 50
Samuel, 207
SUMMERS
Capt., 51
Edward, 8
Elizabeth, 127
Emily E., 133
Jacob, 65, 108,
109, 127, 156
Mary E., 133

Samuel, 133
William, 144
SURGHNER
Harriet P., 127
SURGHNOR
Harriet P., 89
James, 89, 127
John, 34, 43, 80,
    89, 127, 132,
    133, 217
John H., 133
Mary E., 133
Sally E., 133
SUTHERLAND
__, 41
Alexander, 188,
    236
C. C., 44, 67
Caleb C., 43, 81,
    129
SWANK
__, 113
Mary, 115, 156
Philip, 113, 115,
    116, 156
SWANN
__, 161
Robert P., 222
Thomas, 34, 105,
    107, 118, 145,
    151, 195, 202,
    222, 237, 239
SWART
__, 36, 145, 168
Elizabeth, 100,
    152, 153, 155,
    171, 218
James, 38, 47,
    58, 88, 107,
    117, 122, 126,
    127, 152, 153,
    155, 171, 195,
    204, 219
Manly, 154
Mary A., 153
William R., 100,
    218, 234
SWEARINGEN

Franklin A., 34
SWICK
__, 14
SWIFT
Jonathan, 53
SYPHERD
__, 10
Sarah, 145

TAGGERT
Daniel, 18
TAILOR
Elizabeth, 156
TALBOTT
Henry W., 84
Joseph, 39, 103
TALIAFERRO
Frances, 117
Frances B., 6
William T. W., 6,
    117, 167
TALLY
Elizabeth, 197
Isaac, 103, 197
TASSEY
__, 103
TATE
__, 90
TAVENER
Eli, 70, 90, 195,
    207
Feilding, 47
Fielding, 212
George, 107, 157,
    177, 218, 240
Hannah, 47
Isaac, 233
James, 124
Jesse, 47, 149,
    170
John, 157
Jonah, 47, 89, 90,
    149, 169, 192,
    195
Jonathan, 47, 90,
    169, 179, 192,
    212, 213, 235
Joseph, 181

Lot, 149, 237
Lott, 47, 149, 179
Mahlon, 47, 213,
    225, 226, 239
Mariam, 90
Martha, 70
Mary A., 213
Patty, 107
Phebe, 149, 179
Pleasant, 90, 195
Richard, 158, 181
S. J., 225
Sarah, 70
Stacey, 112
Stacey J., 83
Stacy J., 90, 195
Urah, 157
TAVENNER
Eli, 120
George, 137
James, 159
Mahlon, 192
Mary A., 192
Nancy, 120, 159
Richard, 136, 159
Sarah, 137
TAVERNER
Jonah, 152
TAYLOR
__, 92, 149
Amey, 143
Ann, 134
Ann E., 44, 185
Benjamin F., 114,
    206
Benjamin S., 42
Bernard, 8, 77,
    80, 81, 97, 165,
    166, 189, 217,
    237
Betsy, 123
Charles, 4, 20,
    112, 113, 123,
    140, 145, 194,
    231, 238
George W., 44,
    185
Henry, 123, 224

Henry S., 36, 49,
58, 81, 136,
219, 224
Jesse, 21, 218
John, 21, 124
Jonathan, 41, 81,
134, 217
Joseph, 70, 148,
163, 170, 186
Joseph D., 238
Lydia, 70, 170
Mahlon, 81
Mahlon K., 174
Martha P., 185
Mary, 26
Molly E., 74, 82
Nancy, 112, 231
Peyton, 148
R. J., 145
Richard, 156
Robert, 224
Robert J., 34, 35,
39, 74, 82, 122,
153, 213
Ruth B., 70
Sarah, 80, 217
Stacey, 70
Stacy, 233
Susannah, 21
Timothy, 2, 4, 17,
20, 35, 47, 111,
112, 113, 114,
121, 123, 136,
140, 145, 149,
150, 165, 166,
169, 170, 174,
175, 179, 186,
194, 216, 217,
218, 221, 224,
228, 231, 235,
237, 238
William, 34
Yardley, 8, 33,
80, 81, 112,
124, 125, 136,
165, 174
Yardly, 139, 179
TEBBETTS

A. G., 108
TEBBS
___, 33
Betsey, 174, 210,
217, 229
Foushe, 174
James, 148
Margaret, 174
Mary, 148
Samuel J., 185
Willoughby W.,
233
TEMORY
___, 152
TEMPLER
James, 50
John, 31, 102
Thomas, 57
William, 198
THARP
John, 204
THATCHER
Calvin, 24, 46, 52,
82, 86, 131,
225, 226
Elvira, 226
Emeline, 226
Mary, 225
Richard, 1, 197
William, 225, 226
THAYER
John, 14
John W., 211
Sarah, 14, 89
THEYR
Sarah, 89
THOGMORTON
Mortica, 134
THOMAS
___, 40, 87
Ann, 25
Daniel, 117
Elizabeth, 43, 223
Elizabeth U., 86
Evan, 146
George, 2, 66, 85,
92, 166

Henry W., 101,
202, 220, 227
Herod, 72, 171
Hester, 68
Isaac, 234
James, 3, 25, 64,
107, 119
Jefferson C., 86,
94, 184
Jesse, 68
John, 13, 44, 91,
101, 137, 149,
192, 196, 202,
203, 220, 227
Jonah, 68
Joseph, 1, 24, 27,
61, 68, 69, 94,
197, 239
Leonard, 97
Maaziah, 36, 223
Mahlon, 23, 68
Margaret, 101
Martha, 27, 68
Nancy, 60, 68,
77, 158
Owen, 24, 27, 68
Philip, 23, 24, 27,
61
Phineas, 146
Ruth, 68
Sarah, 23, 27, 97
THOMPSON
___, 13, 226, 237
Amelia, 175
Andrew, 46, 77
Daniel, 118
Edward, 20, 123,
124, 183, 202
Elizabeth, 64
French, 175
Greenbarry, 175
Hugh, 6
Israel, 226
Israel B., 226
Israel P., 200,
217
James, 7, 60, 78,
223

William, 51, 212
WIRTZ
Catharine, 214
Conrad, 78
Jacob, 193, 214,
224
John, 193
Leah, 224
Peter, 215, 224
WISE
George, 27, 40,
67, 125, 158
WITTEMAN
Catharine, 238
John, 238
WOLFORD
John, 30, 142,
163
WOLFORDE
George W., 155
WOOD
Alexander H., 45
Ann, 111
James, 239
John H., 145
John W., 111,
198
Joseph, 42, 103,
104, 136, 208
Josiah, 93
Lydia, 103, 136
Mack, 198
Mary, 111, 198
WOODDY
Elizabeth, 35, 69,
72
James, 72
Mary J., 69, 72
WOODFORD
Elizabeth, 44,
125, 126, 148
James, 126
William, 12, 44,
125, 126, 148
WOODLEY
Benjamin, 167
WOODY
James, 69

WORKMAN
__, 62, 193, 206
Isaac, 206
Joseph D., 238
Sarah J., 206
WORNAL
James, 88
WORNALD
__, 160, 161
WORNALL
__, 19
WORNELL
James, 43
WORSLEY
Elizabeth, 56, 103
John, 35, 56, 103,
186, 237
L. D., 69
WORTHINGTON
Joseph, 46, 82
Landon, 193
WOSS
John, 60
WRENN
Thomas M., 86
WRIGHT
__, 118, 155
A., 184, 203, 228
Alfred, 103, 132,
135
Ann, 52
Anthony, 78, 159
Benjamin G., 92
Charles, 31, 105,
135, 184, 203
Charlotte, 78
Chistiana, 159
Isaac, 40, 52, 119
Jerome B., 173
John, 28, 49, 50,
103, 110, 140,
159, 181, 213,
225, 233
Joseph H., 71
Lewis, 159
Nancy, 71
Patterson, 71,
207

Rebecca, 52, 179
Robert L., 225,
233
Samuel, 60, 159
Sarah, 159
Susannah, 119
Thomas, 149, 210
W., 184, 203
W. G., 135
William, 36, 52,
60, 71, 103,
124, 140, 172,
179, 207, 228,
239
William G., 170
WUNDER
Henry S., 187
WYNKOOP
Garret, 224
WYNN
Elisha, 51
Robert, 51
YANTES
Sarah, 28
YEAKEY
Simon, 88
YOUNG
__, 90
Abraham, 82
Abram, 4, 46
Alfred, 46, 82
David, 2, 89, 125,
140, 179, 233,
240
Elizabeth, 38, 125
George, 125, 165
Hannah, 103, 139
J. B., 132
John, 103, 125,
139
John B., 48, 146,
191, 219
John M., 29
Lowis, 125
Sally, 38
William, 103, 125,
132, 139, 165

ZIMMERMAN

___, 149, 195
Samuel, 6

Other Books by Patricia B. Duncan:

1850 Fairfax County and Loudoun County, Virginia Slave Schedule

1850 Fauquier County, Virginia Slave Schedule

1860 Loudoun County, Virginia Slave Schedule

Clarke County, Virginia Will Book Abstracts:
Books A-1 (1836-1904) and 1A-3C (1841-1913)

Fauquier County, Virginia Death Register, 1853-1896

Hunterdon County, New Jersey 1895 State Census, Part I: Alexandria-Junction

Hunterdon County, New Jersey 1895 State Census, Part II: Kingwood-West Amwell

Genealogical Abstracts from The Lambertville Press, *Lambertville, New Jersey:*
4 November 1858 (Vol. 1, Number 1) to 30 October 1861 (Vol. 3, Number 155)

Jefferson County, Virginia/West Virginia Death Records, 1853-1880

Jefferson County, West Virginia Death Records, 1881-1903

Jefferson County, Virginia 1802-1813 Personal Property Tax Lists

Jefferson County, Virginia 1814-1824 Personal Property Tax Lists

Jefferson County, Virginia 1825-1841 Personal Property Tax Lists

1810-1840 Loudoun County, Virginia Federal Population Census Index

1860 Loudoun County, Virginia Federal Population Census Index

1870 Loudoun County, Virginia Federal Population Census Index

Abstracts from Loudoun County, Virginia Guardian Accounts: Books A-H, 1759-1904

Abstracts of Loudoun County, Virginia Register of Free Negroes, 1844-1861

Index to Loudoun County, Virginia Land Deed Books A-Z, 1757-1800

Index to Loudoun County, Virginia Land Deed Books 2A-2M, 1800-1810

Index to Loudoun County, Virginia Land Deed Books 2N-2U, 1811-1817

Index to Loudoun County, Virginia Land Deed Books 2V-3D, 1817-1822

Index to Loudoun County, Virginia Land Deed Books 3E-3M, 1822-1826

Index to Loudoun County, Virginia Land Deed Books 3N-3V, 1826-1831

Index to Loudoun County, Virginia Land Deed Books 3W-4D, 1831-1835

Index to Loudoun County, Virginia Land Deed Books 4E-4N, 1835-1840

Index to Loudoun County, Virginia Land Deed Books 4O-4V, 1840-1846

Loudoun County, Virginia Birth Register, 1853-1879

Loudoun County, Virginia Birth Register, 1880-1896

Loudoun County, Virginia Clerks Probate Records
Book 1 (1904-1921) and Book 2 (1922-1938)

(With Elizabeth R. Frain) *Loudoun County, Virginia Marriages after 1850,*
Volume 1, 1851-1880

Loudoun County, Virginia 1800-1810 Personal Property Taxes

Loudoun County, Virginia 1826-1834 Personal Property Taxes

Loudoun County, Virginia Will Book Abstracts, Books A-Z, Dec. 1757-Jun. 1841

Loudoun County, Virginia Will Book Abstracts, Books 2A-3C, Jun. 1841-Dec. 1879
and Superior Court Books A and B, 1810-1888

Loudoun County, Virginia Will Book Index, 1757-1946

Genealogical Abstracts from The Brunswick Herald, *Brunswick, Maryland:*
Mar. 6 1891-Dec. 28 1894

Genealogical Abstracts from The Brunswick Herald, *Brunswick, Maryland:*
Jan. 4 1895-Dec. 30 1898

Genealogical Abstracts from The Brunswick Herald, *Brunswick, Maryland:*
Jan. 6 1899-Dec. 26 1902

Genealogical Abstracts from The Brunswick Herald, *Brunswick, Maryland:*
Jan. 2 1903-June 29 1906

Genealogical Abstracts from The Brunswick Herald, *Brunswick, Maryland:*
July 6 1906-Feb. 25 1910

CD: *Loudoun County, Virginia Personal Property Tax List, 1782-1850*

314856

Made in the USA